God
Catholic Audacity

The origin of the Catholic Church and
the loss of the gospel message

D1605369

Alan P. Gill

ISBN: 9798785317994 (Paperback)
Imprint: Independently published

Copyright Certificate of Registration: TXu 2-282-770

Authors relevant websites
www.heavencoach.com
www.catholicsquestion.com

All author books are associated with the following LLC:

SITDN Books LLC

Table of Contents

Chapter 1
Introduction, about the author and defining audacity

1.1 Introduction

The book's title might seem to indicate it is for Catholics, but it is for all people of religion, and really for all people. Its purpose is to help every person to eternal success. Catholicism is at the center of what many believe to be Christianity. However, Christianity precedes Catholicism, and Catholicism is NOTHING like the church Jesus says He would build, did build, and continues to build. Catholic doctrine evolves gradually through the first six centuries, finally appearing in the early seventh century with the recognition as the Roman Catholic Church with their pope. The church of the scriptures was slowly fading away as the doctrine of Christ was changing even as early as it was being recorded. It was sufficiently different by the fourth century that God's purpose was rarely achieved. How was God's message corrupted? How are the errors being sustained? Today, what is the state of the church that Jesus started? It is relatively easy to demonstrate what happened and why, and more importantly, how to succeed in life. Audacity is an excellent word to describe how God's word was treated disrespectfully, resulting in something very different from God's inspired message.

This book explains Christianity as God defined it in the first century. You will notice the perfection and simplicity of God's message, while in Catholicism, there is tremendous confusion, man devised innovations, mysteries, and something very random that does not hold together. The truth from God fits everything perfectly together. You will understand God because He reveals Himself for humankind's benefit. You will make distinctions that will amaze you and excite you because you are involved with the truth, and it is different from what is taught by religion. You will have the truth, not as a result of someone telling you it is the truth but because you will understand what you believe.

When we think of pointing out something **wrong** in religion, it might be considered some technicality but certainly not something "soul threatening." Yet, **wrong religiously** equates to danger for the soul, and as you understand God and His purpose, that will become clear. There is a seriousness about God and life that is emphasized in the scriptures, but the "religions of the world" can be very casual. Both Catholicism and Protestantism paint a picture of God and life much different than God carefully revealed by inspiration. Do you understand what you believe? We are talking about the most crucial thing in your existence. In some way, every person will determine with whom to align. This book is designed to help you align with God. It must seem wrong to claim religion is the problem especially such "well-established" religions. Yet, it would be hard to design beliefs further from God, from the truth than these two "Christian" religions. We will show that neither has an association with God.

This book makes understanding God and His purpose very simple and absolutely critical to each person's success. Let me give an example of godly teaching that demonstrates God's seriousness and establishes a powerful principle. It is so fundamental that it ought to be on your mind and be an everyday consideration in how you live. The "religions of the world" provide comfort and largely accomplish that by delivering what people want to hear. Thus many can be perfectly happy in their religion, their faith, their beliefs. All is well, but life has a due date, a lifetime, and did you get life right? You hope so! God provides an interesting thought in 1 Corinthians 15 concerning the hope people have regarding success in life. It would be a reasonable assumption that most people with some knowledge of the Bible **hope** to succeed in life by having some association with Jesus. The truth from God is a potent warning.

1 Corinthians 15:19
*19 If in this life only we have **hope** in Christ, we are of all men the most pitiable.*

God is pointing out that a person with only hope in Christ will fail. God is very specific in terms of what must be done to go beyond hope to a genuine relationship with the Son of God. In other words, **knowing of Jesus** but then not doing what is required will leave a person to be pitied in their regret. You need to seek God vigorously, learn what to do, and live accordingly. The "Christian religions of the world" have people living in the hope of eternal life instead of living their lives for Christ and the gospel to ensure their hope will be realized.

The truth will have a powerful impact on how you live

It is improbable if you are Catholic that you can read this book and remain a Catholic. It is also fair to say it will be challenging to remain a Protestant. These are such brash statements but reasonable in terms of what is coming. It will NOT be the author's ability to teach/write but error exposed and, more importantly, the truth systematically, logically revealed. The author is an "uninspired" writer using inspired writing (scripture) and respecting the word of God. Remaining a Catholic will only occur if you do not "have a love of the truth," and you can convince yourself Catholicism is true despite all the problems. One of the many things you will learn to appreciate is **God's perfection in everything,** and consequently, He would not leave humankind in such a mess, with so much confusion. Then you look at the truth, and it is so different, so simple, and undeniable that you will never again see life the same. The question that is so important to your success is, "how badly do you want to achieve heaven." Is heaven more important than the pride you have in what you currently believe? Catholicism has such a broad influence over all religions that even the larger religion than Catholicism (1.3 bn) of Islam (1.8 bn) has been affected by it. The **understanding of how** the truth from God evolved to become the abhorrent religion called Catholicism has value for every person of every belief. Thus, it is quite likely that you may find it necessary to reconsider your beliefs.

Over history, there has been a tremendous amount of Catholic bashing, especially from Protestants. It is almost a rite of passage for Protestant clergy to be well-versed in attacking Catholicism. This book brings a different approach to exposing Catholicism and is equally tough on Protestantism. Although the many problems of Catholic doctrine are pointed out, it is always in the context of **replacing error with the truth**. There is only one ultimate goal interwoven into everything in this book, and repeating this focus is worthwhile. It is to **help each person have a successful eternity**. Indeed, many people, maybe most, have reached the point of not caring about the truth. They doubt there is truth and find it best to live apart from religion. It is popular to focus on getting all one can get out of life. Everyone has this option because God's test allows each person to make free-will decisions. In this free-will environment, God can easily separate good from evil in the framework of His definition of sin. Those rejecting what God has provided make His decision easy. Essentially, each person decides their eternity by their choices. It is worthwhile to point out that success in life never occurs due to luck or good fortune. Those who reject God are not in the race. Those who sit back and live a good, honest and caring life will also fail. **It is wrong to mislead people into thinking anything short of the truth, and living it will bring success.** The few that will succeed, according to the scriptures, are quite aggressive (diligent) in their pursuit of eternal life. This is one thing seldom emphasized by the "religions of the world."

Humankind's religions serve no good purpose and only distract from what people need: the truth. The Protestant attacks on Catholicism are typically poorly done because they have their own significant and similar problems. Thus Protestants never see the root problems in Catholic doctrine – neither did Luther and Calvin. It can be challenging to oppose Catholic doctrine because it is exceedingly disjointed. There is a lack of connectivity between doctrines, and thus Catholicism appears illogical. This is observed in, for instance, their Catechism, their worship, and their organization. These are complicated aspects of a confused human-devised religion and genuinely alien to the word of God. Solving this dilemma requires breaking many different links. There is also a massive problem since their errors are so fundamental, so oppositional to the scriptures that one wonders how this could happen. One of those errors is creating an earthly head of the church that Jesus started without any scriptural support. Can you imagine the fallout from that error? This error means the fall of everything Catholic. How could this happen? It is what happens when people try to make the rules for God. How can Catholics be helped when Catholicism has intimidated their members (and any opposition) using deceit and violence for over thirteen hundred years? In other words, they have a paranoia that never surrenders, never allows "escape." Due to their loss of control over nations, the last several hundred years required a change in their mode of operation. The Catholic Church now promotes itself as a compassionate supporter of goodwill while claiming to be the only link to God that leads to eternal life.

Nonetheless, with perseverance, it will be easy to demonstrate problems with Catholic teachings. We will see that **the truth from God is overwhelmingly simple** especially compared to what Catholicism has produced. Catholicism has no purpose other than propagating people's belief in Catholicism. The thing Catholicism does bring is a distraction from the truth. Dismantling Catholicism is relatively easy but may be hard to accept due to its longevity and number of devotees. However, its foundation is fragile, and thus we always see Catholicism acting in a defensive mode. Your soul is what is important. The **truth is vastly different** than portrayed by the "religions of the world," and that will astonish many. The truth you need will overwhelm you in its simplicity, in the power it can bring to your life, and in its assuredness. The most significant battle in accepting the truth will be overcoming the things a Catholic believes, the things taken for granted. There will be no problem in understanding the error in Catholicism as it will be, as they say, "crystal clear."

The author has written extensively on religion, and Catholicism has received considerable attention. My interest is to provide something that helps those Catholics (and Protestants) who have been indoctrinated from an early age. The Catholic teachings overwhelm people, not in their evidence but in how they shrewdly close the door to any other belief. Catholicism teaches they are the only way to heaven; you must be Catholic to go to heaven. I was taught this, but at different times there have been variations. The indoctrination points to the Catholic Church as the truth, and it can be overwhelming in its character, pageantry, and apparent physical presence. Over the years, many realize Catholicism is not true and leave, yet a significant number return – none the wiser. This book would be considered negative in terms of Catholic doctrine, although the author's motive is to help those within Catholicism looking for the truth. We could say helping **anyone** wanting to achieve heaven. Protestantism never had any chance of being the church Jesus started because it is only a variation of Catholicism, specifically a protest instead of restoring the inspired message from the first century.

The word of God is easily understood and all that is needed, nonetheless, Catholics always counter that they have the right to make the rules in addition to the Bible. This is due to the claim of apostolic succession that is associated with their teaching of an earthly ruler over Christianity, their pope. Catholics find some support for their teachings in the writings of the early church fathers as they are called. The writings of the early church fathers are not inspired, but they provide a history of the early church in the varied regions of the world where they lived. Catholics **combine the idea** of an ongoing revelation that is, "their right to make the rules for God," along with the scriptures. They gain support by "picking and choosing" from the writings of the early church fathers to justify their doctrines. One obvious problem with the early church fathers was that they did not write the same things. It took the wisdom of God to manage His revelation by restricting doctrine to those things inspired by the Holy Spirit and then demanding there be no changes. There is a one-to-one correlation between disrespecting God and disrespecting His word. Following the long-awaited reconciliation with God in Acts 2, and the subsequent conversions during the time the Holy Spirit was working with the apostles, various persons, such as some of the early church fathers, were **adjusting** God's word. Of course, any changes will make God's solution for sin ineffective. Catholicism will slowly appear to the world as Christianity, and the rest is history – a history of things not true.

Catholicism fails on every point of their doctrines, and Matthew 16:15-19 in no way teaches that God relinquished His rule to humankind. These verses do not even hint at such a thing. The rock spoken of is essential to complete the plan of God, as indicated in Genesis 3:15. Jesus, the Seed of woman would provide the means to allow the reconciliation. Indeed, Jesus is the Son of God, the Messiah. It is the height of carelessness to think that Peter could be what God intended since Genesis 3:15. This is easily demonstrated and will be done **undeniably** throughout this book. In particular, portions of two chapters are used to reject the Catholic teachings of Matthew 16. Those chapters are Chapter 6 (Protestants converting to Catholicism) and Chapter 8 (Scripturally, it is easy to reject Catholicism).

1.2 About the author

I define myself differently in each book, with my description being more related to why that book was written. My credentials are highly non-theological. That is always the one thing I consider essential to arriving at religious truth. After all, theologians had their chance to help people spiritually for a very long time and have provided unbelievable confusion with hundreds of different answers to the relatively simple desire from people wanting to know how to succeed in life. The God of the Bible, who is God, has a character that people with a good heart appreciate. When you understand God's motivation, really His purpose, you will see there is nothing complicated. There is no need for theologians to help you understand God and how to succeed in life. Of course, if you need to be told what to do and will accept something that sounds good, you don't need help in understanding the truth but help in something more fundamental. That is, ask yourself how you will know if something is true? It turns out you need to do some work. Start by considering the need to have a love of the truth. People seldom realize that God ties your success to having a love of the truth – this will be covered throughout the book. Can you reach the point where nothing will satisfy you unless it is the truth? Do not believe what you are told, but **understand what you believe**. Study, learn, understand, and question until you have the truth. Why? Because life is about the soul and the only thing important in your life.

A person of religious training with impressive credentials has brought you what they were taught. Lots of different answers will come from such people. This author (the non-theologian) will **emphasize understanding what you believe**. He will provide you with the simple to understand truth, and he can do this because the things of God are easily understood. The things from God are quite different than what the complex religious organizations tell you is the truth. A fair question will be if this author possesses the skills in handling the word of God as much as these theologians. I will let you decide. Read two of my websites and see if they seem to be the truth and make you wonder why your religion has not taught these things. Those two websites are www.heavencoach.com and www.catholicsquestion.com. Catholic history is at the "center stage" in this book because it indicates how Christianity was corrupted by various individuals seeking rule over the church in the early centuries.

Catholicism is a religion that can seem so right while being terribly wrong. The world's social, political, and religious problems have a common evil component, and it is lying. Lies are a way of making evil look good, and the best at this is Catholicism. Imagine believing Catholicism is an organization for good and then learning the sad final eternal outcome for those who are Catholic – almost inconceivable. We are talking about high-quality deception. As you see the pattern for this deception, you may realize it can be seen in other places like the media, universities, and politics. In the "religions of the world," the deceitful pattern is there, albeit not as sophisticated as Catholicism. Catholics are not evil people and often very much the opposite. They can feel a closeness to God due to Catholic doctrines such as the Real Presence. Catholicism is "center-stage" for this book because it emerged out of various competitors to be **recognized** as having oversight over all of Christianity. Of course, there can be no earthly head over the church started by Jesus, but Jesus is the spiritual head. It is devastating to be Catholic. Nonetheless, we point out the problems realizing it will be difficult for a Catholic to move away. Catholicism has been their life. How can you move away from the "Eucharist?" This book gives the easy answer convincingly. The author has only one motive: to help the reader achieve heaven, and he can help if everything provided on these pages is consistent with the word of God.

An author's perspective – the power of religion

The world is moving away from God and religion, and it is primarily a youth movement with contributing factors being the media, liberal education, and technology. Religion's numbers may not decrease substantially; nonetheless, it can be observed there is a very casual attitude in terms of dedication and a lack of serious participation. Religion appears confused and uncertain, and it seems reasonable to avoid the mess called religion. One frequent conclusion is to have nothing to do with religion. Despite a world moving away from God and religion, religion remains at the forefront of much of our lives. It seems unavoidable as it keeps popping up even if we have no interest. It is influential in politics, education, and all social issues, and it typically appears on both sides of every issue. Its sustainability is due to one constant, and it never goes away. That constant is the certainty of death, and thus God or the possibility of God works its way into every person's life. There is a historical perspective since religion and Catholicism, in particular, have shaped our world and been responsible for many things in our everyday existence even if we are not Catholic or know little about Catholicism. Catholicism has been impressive in creating a religion with the worst possible history yet maintaining power over more than a billion people. The history of Catholicism should deter any devotion but that has not substantially reduced its appeal. The heart of religion should be its ability to direct a person to a successful end. The truth is the one thing capable of helping people to such an end. The truth is powerful in doing that and is presented herein. However, those overwhelmed by the "religions of the world" and particularly the Catholic influence need to understand Catholicism correctly. This book provides a simple but accurate history of how Catholicism came into existence. This perspective, along with the scriptural problems, and the simple truth, will easily be sufficient to move any person who is dedicated to the truth, away from Catholicism.

Religion in its various forms continues to exert influence in social, political, economic, and personal decisions. Thus although you can ignore religion, your life will be impacted by its existence. This religious drama is attractive in figuring out what might result from the various religious interactions with people and nations, but it is not worth your time. The truth is worth your time. Seeking God is worth your time. Also, always keep in mind that life is about the soul and absolutely about nothing else. It should not be the case, but as the result of **humankind's creation of religion**, truth does not reside in religion; God does not reside there. Yet truth exists, and you can find it. Truth and God are synonymous. The bottom line is that Catholicism has no connectivity with God, but Christianity is the truth.

Why do I write about God and truth?

There is an **awareness** observed in God's message of truth that has a powerful attraction as one realizes **God's wisdom in everything**. God is even more powerful than He appears in His physical creation because that design was only a component of His purpose. Of course, humankind is rightly impressed by God's creation, yet it is only the stage where God's purpose will be achieved. God's emphasis is on each person's success in their battle with God-defined sin. God in His graciousness tells us the basics of creation, and in that message, there is nothing more important than His revelation of humankind's eternal nature. Part of the uniqueness of God's way is how life's "adventure" reveals our character in a way that allows God to divide each person for eternity correctly. This is accomplished by how we respond to God-defined sin, and thus effectively, it is our choice that determines our eternal result. There is an urgency in bringing the gospel message throughout the scriptures because, "for what is your life? It is even a vapor that appears for a little time and then vanishes away." Our life is short, and additionally, Christ's return can occur anytime. One verse that describes the seriousness of God and why I write with a passion is from 2 Corinthians 5:11, "Knowing, therefore, the terror of the Lord, we persuade men." Of course, this is one reason why Paul was so aggressive in his work, and I must say the truth of this statement is contagious.

The world thinks life is about everything except "what it is actually about." The final transition away from the physical body that each person will face is continually on my mind. Considering a world living largely in sin and "not caring," there is something to be feared. When you know the truth with certainty, it is wonderful and wonderfully frightening. Thus Paul uses the word terror. Elijah concluded that no one cared, everyone was in opposition to the truth, and the world had many gods. He went and hid in a cave. Elijah just wanted to get away from the mess and likely the danger for him. God told Elijah that he was not the only one. God was not pleased with Elijah's attitude. Elijah would go on to face Baal's priests in one of the most dramatic displays of God versus the "gods of humankind." This was much like the battle of Moses with the Pharaoh of Egypt, but "played out" in a single day. Regardless, if it is the Pharaoh, or if it is Elijah with the priests of Baal, or when Moses came down from the mountain and found the idolatry or when God rained down manna (bread) from heaven to the impatient Jews in the desert or even when Jesus fed those following Him, there are short memories of

God's goodness, of God's power. God's sovereignty is quickly forgotten. Instead of lasting gratitude and awareness of God's power, people rapidly fall back into doing and thinking about themselves and acting accordingly. This recognition makes it essential to be persistent in working with people in sustainable ways and writing about God, truth, the seriousness of life, and the need for a correct and consistent response to God's way. We might say consistency in growth, in the knowledge of God and life is essential. Life is so short, so fragile, and is the only opportunity to succeed.

This book is written to be understood by every person, no theologians are required, yet every theologian will be challenged to answer the problems with their beliefs. They will have no good answers. How can that be? Because God never intended the scriptures to be difficult as that would oppose His very purpose. Leave it to humankind with their selfish motives to create confusion and the subsequent need for all sorts of experts to direct the "common man/woman."

Note: I use notes like this throughout the book to provide added explanations and to bring clarity. The notes are as important as the text since they provide the understanding that may be missing. Also, similar topics are usually discussed differently throughout the book, as suggested by chapter titles. Although there may be some repetition, it is worthwhile to increase comprehension, especially for seeing the matter from different perspectives.

1.3 "God - Catholic Audacity," defining audacity for the book's title

Audacity defined by Oxford English and Spanish dictionary
- A willingness to take bold risks
- Rude or disrespectful behavior; impudence

The meaning of audacity for this book relates primarily to rude or disrespectful behavior and impudence to God. Also, audacity means having the boldness to disrespect God to the point of claiming His place and acting in making rules in spiritual matters. Impudence like audacity carries the meaning intended in modifying the word "Catholic." The reason for this "severity" is the cost of deceit on the souls of humankind.

<u>Synonyms for impudence:</u>

Impudence: impertinence, insolence, presumption, presumptuousness, forwardness, cheek, cheekiness, impoliteness, unmannerliness, bad manners, rudeness, effrontery, nerve, gall, brazenness, brashness, shamelessness, pertness, defiance, boldness, temerity

<u>Subtitle: "The origin of the Catholic Church and the loss of the gospel message."</u>

The origin of the Catholic Church has been quite a mystery for everyone. Catholicism implies they are the continuation of the first century-inspired church, but that is not the case. This will be clearly and overwhelmingly demonstrated in the process of revealing how Catholicism originated. The loss of the gospel message (the centerpiece of God's plan) has successfully been accepted inasmuch as it is **hardly missed**. The world thinks its absence is not of particular concern. It is the piece that, when lost, means there is no salvation, and indeed it is lost, or we might say corrupted. The significance of the gospel message and **how** it perfectly fits God's purpose and **why** it should continually be on the mind of every Christian will become clear.

Chapter 2

The historical periods of Catholicism

Further down in this chapter, we will divide Catholic history into three periods to help understand Catholicism's beginning and the evolution to the present time. Before we go to those periods, an overview of these early centuries can be helpful, especially regarding the issue of authority and the Catholic pope.

2.1 Overview of the early centuries of Christianity

One of the alluring points of Catholicism is something people look for in a church. They want to see a continual evidential timeline of the church belonging to Jesus. The Catholic Church claims to have existed since the first century. Their evidence is a continual line of popes beginning with Peter and can be referred to as apostolic succession. This sort of evidence fills the need for something physical, authentic, and having the kind of proof people can touch. Almost anyone can claim they have a connection to the church of the first century. Protestants had a historical start date in the 16th century so that they could make no such claim. **If you want to have a genuine connection to the first-century church, all you need to do is look to the scriptures and find some group that teaches the same thing today.** It would be possible that there were people always following the word of God, teaching the gospel message continually since the first century. However, it would not be necessary to have a continual line of those who were "in Christ." If one considers the mass persecution and murder of those who were Christians in the first three centuries, it would not be impossible that at some moment in time, there were very few Christians. Undoubtedly, there were many claiming to be Christians but were not. In any case, we can be confident that the word of God was there and some people were obedient. The number of Christians in these early centuries is not a provable thing, or is it essential. The gospel message was taught, and people have been reconciled to God. They are in the body of Christ. The thing that should interest one looking for truth would be to find those today who follow the pattern of the first-century church. That is, they are living consistent with the scriptures. This can easily be done, and there is considerable help in this book. The church that was built by the Lord beginning in Acts 2, will continue to be built by the Lord until the end of time.

A massive problem for Catholicism is their naming of popes back to Peter. Here is a list of those early popes – the first 70 popes. See this reference:

https://www.newadvent.org/cathen/12272b.htm

1.   St. Peter (32-67)
2.   St. Linus (67-76)
3.   St. Anacletus (Cletus) (76-88)
4.   St. Clement I (88-97)
5.   St. Evaristus (97-105)
6.   St. Alexander I (105-115)
7.   St. Sixtus I (115-125) Also called Xystus I
8.   St. Telesphorus (125-136)
9.   St. Hyginus (136-140)
10.   St. Pius I (140-155)
11.   St. Anicetus (155-166)
12.   St. Soter (166-175)
13.   St. Eleutherius (175-189)
14.   St. Victor I (189-199)
15.   St. Zephyrinus (199-217)
16.   St. Callistus I (217-222)
17.   St. Urban I (222-30)
18.   St. Pontian (230-35)
19.   St. Anterus (235-36)
20.   St. Fabian (236-50)
21.   St. Cornelius (251-53)
22.   St. Lucius I (253-54)
23.   St. Stephen I (254-257)
24.   St. Sixtus II (257-258)
25.   St. Dionysius (260-268)
26.   St. Felix I (269-274)
27.   St. Eutychian (275-283)

28. St. Caius (283-296) Also called Gaius
29. St. Marcellinus (296-304)
30. St. Marcellus I (308-309)
31. St. Eusebius (309 or 310)
32. St. Miltiades (311-14)
33. St. Sylvester I (314-35)
34. St. Marcus (336)
35. St. Julius I (337-52)
36. Liberius (352-66)
37. St. Damasus I (366-84)
38. St. Siricius (384-99)
39. St. Anastasius I (399-401)
40. St. Innocent I (401-17)
41. St. Zosimus (417-18)
42. St. Boniface I (418-22)
43. St. Celestine I (422-32)
44. St. Sixtus III (432-40)
45. St. Leo I (the Great) (440-61)
46. St. Hilarius (461-68)
47. St. Simplicius (468-83)
48. St. Felix III (II) (483-92)
49. St. Gelasius I (492-96)
50. Anastasius II (496-98)
51. St. Symmachus (498-514)
52. St. Hormisdas (514-23)
53. St. John I (523-26)
54. St. Felix IV (III) (526-30)
55. Boniface II (530-32)
56. John II (533-35)
57. St. Agapetus I (535-36) Also called Agapitus I
58. St. Silverius (536-37)
59. Vigilius (537-55)
60. Pelagius I (556-61)
61. John III (561-74)
62. Benedict I (575-79)
63. Pelagius II (579-90)

64.　St. Gregory I (the Great) (590-604)

65.　Sabinian (604-606)

66.　Boniface III (607)

67.　St. Boniface IV (608-15)

68.　St. Deusdedit (Adeodatus I) (615-18)

69.　Boniface V (619-25)

70.　Honorius I (625-38)

The most fundamental issue is that there is no such office as the pope in the scriptures. There is also a lack of documentation even within Catholicism for these early historical persons that places them in the role of the Catholic pope. It would seem many of them were bishops in the church. At some point, Catholicism determined to name their popes back to Peter, their claimed first pope. The pope is also considered the pontifex, or pontiff, a title that existed before Christianity. This title was originally a reference to the priests of the Roman religion, with the head of the college being the pontifex Maximus. This was a title held by Julian Caesar and subsequently the Roman emperors until Gratian relinquished it in the late 4th century. The Bishop of Rome started using the title in the 5th century, with the first example being "Pope" Leo I (440-461). "Bishop" Leo I convinced the Roman Emperor, Valentinian III, to issue an edict declaring the *Roman See* as the supreme court of appeal for all bishops. The fact that such a declaration was necessary indicates there was no clarity about authority in the church. That is, up to this point, there were no popes. There were discussions in the early church writings regarding a single head of the church. The desire for a leader or what might have been called a universal bishop does not mean there was one but rather indicates there was not one.

For example, early sources list Linus as the second Bishop of Rome or the first if they didn't count Peter. Irenaeus, writing not long before the year 200, said that Linus followed Peter. Yet Tertullian, writing not long after in 200, reported that the successor of Peter was Clement (i.e., Clement I), while Catholic tradition places Clement fourth.

Constantine named himself as the head of Christendom, which included both the Latin (Rome) and the Greek (Constantinople) churches. This occurred in the 312/313 timeframe. The term frequently used for Constantine was the Patron of the Christian Faith. In that terminology, it would mean the protector, the supporter, the benefactor. There is some question regarding

Constantine calling himself the head of Christendom. However, there is no question that he ruled over their bishops. That is, they did as he directed. It is also apparent that Constantine knew nothing of a singular leader for the church. That is because there was no such head of the church.

Quite a bit of disagreement within the Roman church about a universal bishop

At the 588 AD Constantinopolitan synod, John IV the Faster, **patriarch of Constantinople**, is granted the title of "ecumenical" or "universal bishop," but doesn't start using it till 595 AD. In response, the **bishop of Rome**, Gregory I, wrote: "You know it, my brother; had not the venerable council for Chalcedon conferred the honorary title of universal upon the bishop of this apostolic See, whereof I am, by God's Will, the servant, And yet none of us hath permitted this title to be given him; none has assumed this bold title, lest by assuming a special episcopate, we should seem to refuse it to all other brethren ... But far from Christians be this blasphemous name by which all honor is taken from all other priests, while it is foolishly arrogated by one."

One should find this quite astonishing that the process leading to agreeing on a single head of the church has been a constant discussion and desired by some but never decided. YET, Catholicism can name popes back to the first century following their first pope, Peter. There is only one way this could happen, and that would be to lie! That might seem ridiculous unless everything about Catholicism was a lie, AND that is the truth!

Gregory I (590-604) also wrote: "I am bold to say, that whosoever adopts or affects the title of **universal bishop** has the pride and character of anti-Christ, and is in some manner his forerunner in this haughty quality of elevating himself above the rest of his order." Gregory I is on the list of popes and yet held the idea of a universal bishop as repulsive. In 604 AD, the emperor Phocas tried to give the title to Gregory I, but he refused it. However, a successor, Boniface III, accepted the title in 607 AD. Thus for many, Boniface III is considered the first pope of Catholicism.

As mentioned, the bishop of Rome (Leo I) began to claim his supremacy over all other bishops in the fifth century, and some of the church fathers also made this claim for him. Yet until Boniface III, there was not a broad and continued agreement with the title of Pope, of Pontiff, of Universal bishop, and what would eventually be Holy Father and Vicar of Christ. Indeed, in Boniface III, the early church had finally worked its way to completing the falling away. It would officially be recognized as the Roman Catholic Church. It had been a long road, but with the help of the writings of the early church fathers, there was presumed justification for various doctrines. The writings of those early church fathers were never intended (by them) to be used as justification for doctrine. They recorded what was happening, what various persons thought should happen, and just things supposed to be good ideas. Those good ideas were typically private interpretations of scripture which changed the meanings of scripture.

2.2 Pope arrives, but where is Christianity?

Our mention of the first pope appearing in the seventh century and being Boniface III is for a reason. Namely, this is the dating typically done by secular history and the early church, which had long awaited this declaration and its acceptance. It is quite logical to realize that few "early church fathers" may have been **Christian**. The truth of the matter is that the gospel message was being perverted as Paul was recording it. That is why there is one solid thing, and in God's wisdom, it is His inspired word. When you see something different than the scriptures, you know it is not valid. Undoubtedly, in these earliest centuries in these early churches some may have been teaching a perverted gospel message and in those cases, none were added to the church by the Lord. The suggestion that some of the early church fathers may not have been Christian is supported by their careless handling, their lack of respect for the scriptures. I mention this as a possibility while Catholicism honors the early church father's writings and even honors some with "Catholic sainthood."

Peter in Rome?

The foremost reason for the **primacy of Rome** is the city's association with Peter. Tradition held that Peter visited Rome during his lifetime and was martyred there. St. Peter's

Basilica in Vatican City marks the traditional site of Peter's execution and burial. Paul was believed to have been martyred in Rome as well.

Interestingly, the Bible says nothing about Peter ever traveling to Rome. When the scriptures conclude, Peter is in Jerusalem. The last record we have of Peter is in Jerusalem, as indicated in Acts (Acts 15:7-11). The Apostle Paul, in his letters, also talks about meeting Peter in the eastern Mediterranean, namely Antioch, but there is never a mention by Paul of Peter being in Rome. This would have been a significant event and yet never mentioned. Paul describes his meetings with Peter and the other apostles beginning shortly after encountering the Lord on the road to Damascus. Then finally, they meet in Jerusalem at the "so-called" Jerusalem council, soon after Paul had confronted Peter in Antioch. It should not be overlooked that the division Paul mentions in Galatians 2:9 seemed to be agreeable to all, and, according to the inspired scriptures, it is what happened.

Galatians 2:9
9 and when James, Cephas, and John, who seemed to be pillars, perceived the grace that had been given to me, they gave me and Barnabas the right hand of fellowship, that we should go to the Gentiles and they to the circumcised.

The travels of these leaders of Christianity were indeed along the lines of Jew and Gentile in terms of the regions they visited and taught. Of course, there is overlap (Jew and Gentile), but the regions were primarily one or the other. Galatians was written between 50 and 60 AD, and there was no intention to do anything different. One must go beyond the scriptures to find a substantial change in plans that has Peter traveling to Rome.

There is no early textual evidence for Peter in Rome, so it's difficult for some people to believe he traveled there. Not only is it a very long way, but Peter was a fisherman who was not very educated and who spoke only Aramaic. He was not the type of person that might travel widely across the Roman Empire to a large city where Latin and Greek were the dominant languages. The absence of connection between Peter and Rome in the New Testament, the lack of references to him in the earliest Roman Christian literature, and what we know of Peter's background and character all combine to make it unlikely that he ever went to Rome. The verses

27

from 1 Peter 5:11-13 indicate this letter was written from Babylon. Catholics consider Babylon a code word for Rome.

In contrast, it could be a metaphor (not geographic) for Jerusalem, where **Christians** were essentially in captivity as they lived with hardships, imprisonment, torture, and death. It is also possible that Babylon was indeed the city of Babylon (in Babylonia), where there may have been a Jewish community. Finally, a good case can be made that Peter was writing from Babylon (Egypt), and the following reference is provided:

https://www.billkochman.com/Articles/AMysterySolvedPeterBabylon.html

These are reasoning indications that **Peter was never in Rome,** and there is only some weak circumstantial evidence and wishful thinking that he was there. It is not all that important except Catholicism requires Peter in Rome, dying there and heading the church there as their pope. Is it possible Peter was in Rome? Yes, it is possible, but highly unlikely. Catholicism must connect Peter and Rome no matter how improbable, no matter how oppositional Peter as "pope" would be to **God's plan**. They do not seem bothered by Peter or the other apostles ever mentioning the role of a pope. They are not bothered that Peter never assumed such a role. They do not seem bothered that the scriptures give no indication of Peter being in Rome. They do not seem bothered in naming popes back to their designated first pope, Peter. They do this even though the early church, and all the emperors including Constantine, never knew of any "universal bishop." They are not bothered by the various high bishops of Rome and Constantinople who considered such a title of the pope or universal bishop to be a terrible abuse of authority.

Clarifying the source of Catholic doctrine

There needs to be some clarity. It is not the Catholic Church doctrine that looks back to the tradition of the early church fathers **for validation**. **The writings themselves** of the early church fathers were being accepted by what was becoming the Catholic Church. The origination of Catholic doctrine is primarily from select early church fathers. It is very confusing, but the doctrines of the early church were gradually being accepted, especially by Rome. Now with an official head of all Christianity being the bishop of Rome (Boniface III, 607 AD) and being called the father of the church – the universal church, what was their doctrine. The doctrine was primarily what had been accepted by the early church. Unlike the scriptures, **some** of those early church writers supported a universal bishop. Everything was coming together as the universal physical church now had a physical head and a physical rulemaking body that accepted the non-scriptural writings of the early church fathers. One arm of that rulemaking body in those early years (and to this day) was the councils of the church.

Constantine's motive – very political

Constantine was a contributing factor that facilitated Christianity moving quickly away from the truth God had delivered. It was not his intention, but it was a coming together of a fragmented Christianity with the pagan worship of Rome. The persecutions were gone, but there was a collaboration with Rome to the point of Constantine's involvement with the church. The church would begin to look very different in terms of organization. The church, to some extent, would start to mirror the Roman hierarchy in terms of a single head and then a body of rulemaking officials. It was a far cry from the local church organization designed by God in terms of functions that emphasized serving and dedication to the scriptures (no rulemaking).

The Roman emperors going back to Constantine desired the Christian church to have a single head, and now that has happened. Constantine's Edict of Milan was not some act of kindness or some way of "righting wrongs," but the motive was related to finding some way of bringing more unity to Rome. Constantine envisioned Rome going from a polytheism environment to a monotheism (Christian) system, removing the problems with their "many-gods" society. However, Constantine learns the one God of Christianity's churches has their own in-fighting. He is frustrated by their lack of unity. He takes on a leadership role over both the "Roman and Greek" churches, calling the first church council in 325 AD at Nicaea. A vital element of the unity of the Christian church he believed would be a single head of the church similar to how Rome rules. Now centuries after his death, this aspect of Christianity was in place.

If you look at the Catholic Church's list of the first 31 popes up to the time of the Edict of Milan, you will find names of people who, if they existed, may have been bishops. **In keeping with the Catholic fable, they must be the bishop of Rome.** Neat little biographies have been created for each of these "popes." The list of the early popes is a fabrication as evidenced by no awareness of a universal head, and of course, Peter was not a pope – there were no popes. Although there is some doubt about Constantine naming himself the head of the church, he viewed himself over the various bishops. The Romans regarded the State religion to be under their control, and thus Constantine being head of state, was also head of the church in some manner. Constantine ruled over the Christian bishops as he did civil servants and required unconditional obedience. Constantine knew there was no single head of Christianity, and he never referred to one. Constantine took a leadership role since there was no head over all the churches and as mentioned called the first Christian church council in 325 AD at Nicaea. His apparent goal with Christianity was to bring unity to the Roman empire, and this monotheistic God seemed like a good answer. Unfortunately, he would learn that this "Christianity" had many doctrinal divisions. Here is the point, Constantine knew nothing of a pope, of a universal leader of Christianity. It is the fourth century.

Note: Throughout this book, I will provide references, typically links for the subject matter. They will not necessarily be favorable to the points being made in this book. Often they will be Catholic sources but may be helpful in your understanding. Here are two examples that show the diversity of thought on the papacy.

Religion facts:

https://religionfacts.com/papacy/history

Peter in Rome?

https://www.philologie.uni-bonn.de/de/personal/zwierlein/st_peter_in_rome.pdf

The church Jesus started bears zero resemblance to the Catholic Church

The church Jesus was and is building is spiritual, with a local group of those "in Christ" working together. Thus if you are looking for a continual line of Christians, you need to find those "in Christ" (Christ's spiritual body) participating in a local church. They would **not be promoting** various things in opposition to the doctrine of Christ. They would respect the only way people can be added to the body of Christ. They would **not** be baptizing babies. They would

not be supporting the idea of apostolic succession. In other words, they would be much more than referring to themselves as Christians – they would be those who the Lord added to the His spiritual church. They could be somewhat hard to find because they are not offering worldly enticements and their numbers are relatively few.

There was a gradual falling away in the early centuries following a period of growth that began in Acts 2. Their numbers were lessened by false teaching as Paul indicated the gospel message was being changed and by the various persecutions. The Lord's church is not identified by physical evidence, such as a continuous line of persons. This has never been the way to identify the Lord's church. However, you can know if a church is **not the church** by its physical character. That character might be a desire for an earthly head and include a careless and casual attitude towards the word of God. The church you should be looking for today can be identified by finding those following the doctrine of Christ and showing the greatest respect for the word of God. As it turns out, **that church is the church of the first century** that was and still is today being built by the Lord.

2.3 The Catholic validation processes

The Catholic Church cannot be justified using the scriptures, but it can be shown to be the opposite of God's intentions. To validate their authority, Catholicism claims two paths of truth, and not surprisingly, that will mean they look very different than the church of the scriptures. It is interesting to realize that during some fifty-plus years, while the Holy Spirit was working with the apostles to guide them into all truth, there remains so much missing. **There was, of course, NOTHING missing**. There were churches established by Paul throughout his missionary journeys and as long as they followed what he taught and used the available scriptures they would know nothing of a pope, of the "Real Presence," of New Testament priests, of infant baptism, of the confessional, of mortal and venial sins, of any special honor for Mary, or of hundreds of other Catholic inventions. Paul never talks/writes of such things. Peter never mentions those things in his letters.

Interestingly Peter did speak of things that were critically important such as, "If anyone speaks, let him speak as the oracles of God." Also, he would write, "knowing this first, that no prophecy of Scripture is of any private interpretation, for prophecy never came by the will of man, but holy men of God spoke as the Holy Spirit moved them." The many important things Peter delivered by inspiration are handled poorly by Catholicism, but the things important to Catholic doctrine are never mentioned by him. God's plan was coming together, and the reconciliation occurred the first time in Acts 2 as the gospel message was preached and obeyed. Those obedient persons were "in Christ," that is, in the kingdom Jesus had been preaching. This was God's way. God, in Christ, was accomplishing His purpose. Finally, the promises God made in Genesis (Genesis 3:15, Genesis 12:1-3) were fulfilled in Acts 2 and Acts 10, and therein was the reconciliation. Going forward, God continually fulfills His purpose in precisely the same manner, that is by the word of God. There is no other approved way, no other approved message but as Peter indicates in his first letter, "having been born again, not of corruptible seed but incorruptible, through the word of God which lives and abides forever."

Catholics typically have no idea how far their beliefs and practices are from the truth. We can easily show using the scriptures how **they disagree with what God has revealed on ALL issues**. However, the most critical thing is that those associated with Catholicism will not be successful in life. There is only one path to success in life, as uniquely revealed in the word of God.

Note: The second path for Catholics is a combination of accepting "apparent tradition writings" corresponding with the period of the early church fathers and the associated Catholic invention of apostolic succession, allowing them to make the rules continually. They lump all this (including the scriptures) into their Magisterium, that is, their authority in teaching.

One thing this book confronts is the abhorrent use of the early church fathers to justify the practices of the Catholic Church. Also recently complicating the landscape of truth has been the movement of various Protestants into the Catholic Church. Typically, these Protestants correctly realize the fundamental errors of Luther and Calvin while seeing Catholicism as a historical path closer to the first-century church, namely closer than the 16th century founding of Protestantism.

Discovering the apparent error in Protestant beliefs is an insufficient reason to become a Catholic. These converts often share their thought processes in leaving Protestantism and then becoming Catholics. It is easy to dismantle their analysis, and this book does that systematically.

I reluctantly use this approach because the best response to errors is to provide the truth. Nonetheless, a combination of providing the truth and pointing out errors may help some.

Note: It may not be clear why it is essential to take this approach in exposing Catholicism, that is, the approach of disputing ex-Protestants reasoning in becoming Catholics. Indeed, Catholicism is easily shown to be the opposite of the truth. However, these Protestant converts to Catholicism have taken an approach that is more appealing to non-Catholics and brings a more powerful way of emboldening Catholicism. Thus these ex-Protestant teachers are well appreciated by Catholics. There is a significant understanding of Catholicism known to older Catholics but not to "younger" Catholics. These older Catholics realize the intense historical animosity of Catholicism against Bible use by anyone except certain of their hierarchy. That might seem strange and even unbelievable to many Catholics, especially to "younger" Catholics, since Catholicism promotes Bible use today. Future generations of Catholic hierarchy will be better skilled in the scriptures, and they will have some of these Protestant converts to thank. Here is the point, in the different historical eras of Catholic persuasion (which will be discussed), there have necessarily been transitions when current "growth/maintenance" methods were failing. This latest approach (promoting Bible use) with all its seeming "goodness" needs to be identified, and its weaknesses revealed.

2.4 Catholic "historical-type" periods

I have created the concept of three historical periods of Catholicism for clarity for myself and the reader. It is a way of dividing how Catholicism came into being and has changed from its beginning (desiring leadership over Christianity) to seeking and gaining control over nations to emphasizing their right to make rules for the Christian world. No one will likely look at the history of Catholicism in the divisions that follow; nonetheless, this is the big picture for simplicity and understanding. A typical history of Catholicism would be filled with many hundreds of events, names, and dates, and there would be things like a timeline. The following reference is a timeline that favors the Catholic view.

https://en.wikipedia.org/wiki/Timeline_of_the_Catholic_Church)

This second reference is a Catholic Church version, emphasizing the middle ages, popes, and practices.

https://courses.lumenlearning.com/boundless-worldhistory/chapter/the-catholic-church/

The third reference is titled "What is the origin of the Roman Catholic Church."

https://www.gotquestions.org/origin-Catholic-church.html

This last reference (video) is a less favorable history of Catholicism. It claims there is no connection between the Catholic Church and the church Jesus has built and continues to build. The reason is that Catholicism must go beyond the scriptures to justify its practices. A large number of books, videos are strongly anti-Catholic and emphasize the violent history of Catholicism. This book highlights the doctrinal problems. Instead of "carrying on" about the cruelties and murders, I accept them as generally representing factual events. The Catholic Church agrees with those histories to a lesser degree. One of the principles of God that can be discovered in a study of the scriptures is that **God is the perfect absence of evil**. God cannot have any association with evil. Therefore, besides all the other compelling reasons, there cannot be or has there ever been any association between God and the Catholic Church; there is this fundamental barrier between God and Catholicism. God has no association with evil, and Catholicism has been and continues to be a source of evil. More importantly, that evil goes beyond their physical abuse to the ultimate terror every Catholic will face as they pass from this life.

Note: A fair criticism of this chapter would be that it is not very historical. It does not look like a history book containing dates and references and numerous names and events. This chapter is designed to show the progression of the first-century church to Catholicism (and beyond), and the flow is directionally correct, and I know of nothing that is historically inaccurate. The book's goal is not to be a history of Catholicism but to help people to the truth. Since so many readers are involved as Catholics or might be thinking about Catholicism, it is necessary to understand the truth. The truth regarding Catholic history is important because they use a very deceitful history to sell their "product." To aid the reader's understanding, I may suddenly leave the flow of history to make a point regarding the often silliness of some Catholic teaching or some deceitful practice that needs exposure. Let me give a quick example: the historical record outside the Catholic record shows no early popes (consistent with the scriptures of having no such position), but the Catholic Church requires this connection, so they back-name a list of popes following their first pope, Peter. Yes, this would be the **audacity of Catholicism** *or what some would call "malicious fabrications." History, particularly religious history, if controlled by the religion in question, cannot be trusted.*

History is like a bookmarker giving us something to measure where we are, in terms of various events. History, right or wrong, will not provide the truth about life, and thus this cannot be a history book if it is going to help. The Bible is a good history book since it provides a timeline that includes the important events related to God. If we focus on the New Testament, we see the coming of Jesus, His ministry, His suffering, death, burial, and resurrection. Then we have the beginning of the church, the revealing of all truth, and the completion of God's communication with humankind. The New Testament represents an accurate historical record because it is from God. Following this, humanity brings a history of religion that is not inspired but often prejudiced to achieve some frequently selfish goal. It might seem impossible to get the correct history past the period of inspiration. Certainly, error moves in quickly and then gradually builds something entirely different than Christianity. The truth remains and is the purpose of this book that is, to sort through the mess called religion. We begin by defining three periods of historical Catholicism and the associated events related to each period.

The three historical periods of Catholicism

First period: First century thru seventeenth century

Some might be surprised that we began in the first century since this is what Catholicism would like people to believe. Yet, it is important to realize this is possible, albeit from a drastically different perspective than Catholics would promote.

Second period: Eighteenth-century thru the mid-twentieth century

After a tumultuous ride from the creation of the papacy and the horrific years of paranoid rule, there is a slowing of cruelties, and the rule over nations has almost evaporated.

Third period: Mid-twentieth century to the end of time

The dominance of Catholicism over nations is gone, and they focus on "looking good." They continue to struggle with immorality among their clergy, and they can no longer deny it. Even their history of atrocities is accepted, and there are some apologies. They devise new techniques to maintain and grow Catholicism. Bible use is promoted, and some Protestants convert to Catholicism.

2.5 Catholicism's first historical period

(The falling away that evolves gradually to Catholicism)

How Catholicism happened – a snapshot of the how

It is suggested the first period of Catholicism began with the falling away predicted by Jesus and being experienced by Paul in the first century. It was **not Catholicism in name** but something different than the inspired message from God. It is fair to say that the falling away would be something originating amid Christianity that did not produce God's intended result. The Catholic Church became a religion that was **the opposite in every way** to the church Jesus had built and continues to build. Catholics would like to convince people that the church Jesus is building was the Catholic Church. Truly, anything different than the church defined in the scriptures would be associated with the "falling away." The doctrines of Catholicism were not yet present in the mid-late first century, but they are coming in the early churches in the writings of the early church fathers during the early centuries. As we begin looking at the history of Catholicism and try to assign blame for this travesty, it can be difficult to name the guilty parties. All we can do is generalize and mention three aspects involved in the falling away. The Catholic Church slowly evolved from the *early church father's careless handling of the scriptures,* to various persons, typically *powerful bishops seeking to gain power over all Christians,* to the *development of teachings supporting this new human devised and controlled religion*. Those teachings appeared to have credibility in the clever mixing of scripture with the writings of the

36

early church fathers. We will see that this new religion would be formalized in the early seventh century with the creation of an earthly leader in the city of Rome.

Begin the history

As we enter the period following God's **completion of His revelation** to humankind in the latter part of the first century, doctrines associated with "Christianity" were running wild. During at least the first five centuries, there were many religious names. These groups were working hard to sell their beliefs, and a few like Zoroastrianism existed long before the first century. This was a confusing period, and some of the names were Ebionites, Marcionites, Thomasines, Ascetics, Montanism, and Manicheism. In different ways, these six groups included aspects of Christian doctrine, among many other beliefs.

This first period is the most important because wolves (false prophets) are clothed by sheep's appearance. The pattern of salvation has been revealed (that form of doctrine, Romans 6.17), and people are added to the body of Christ, and if that pattern does not change, then success for individuals will be continuous. There are various locations around the world in these early years where Christians live and work, and there are local churches. Much of this diversity in location is due to Paul's missionary journeys as well as Peter, James, and John, among others. The local leadership of these churches consists of scripturally qualified elders, and the other word for elder is bishop. Already there are many different doctrines and identifiable groups, as mentioned above. One would expect that some were maintaining the truth as delivered by the Holy Spirit to the apostles.

The Catholic Church appears somewhere between the 1st century and the 7th century. I say the first century because some of the earliest church fathers were sowing the seeds of Catholicism without the name. The ones of renown came down through the centuries because their writings favored what would become Catholic doctrine. One critical awareness missing in these early church fathers was understanding the seriousness required in handling God's word. **This principle is evident within the scriptures** but clearly in all ages frequently not cherished. God allows humankind great freedom to make their life-determinations (free-will), but there are consequences associated with poor choices. God is particularly severe concerning the consequences of changing, modifying His word. This "underestimating" of the seriousness of God's word, leads to mishandling it and is something wherein God pronounces a curse. Of course, the reason is apparent: His word is critical to defining His test and the requirements for each person's success. That is, to achieve His purpose to share in the Divine Nature. Unfortunately, in disrespect, there was a significant moving away from the doctrine of Christ. This carelessness could be classified as private interpretations of scripture or changing the meaning God intended. Many of those early church father's writings would gradually become the foundation of the Catholic Church and represent teachings totally in opposition to the scriptures.

On the other hand, Catholicism has a more formal starting point in time, beginning early in the seventh century with the naming of their pope. There were in the early centuries local churches, each with elders (bishops). This was correct, and in the scriptures, we see qualified elders being selected in local churches, and Peter was an elder in the church at Jerusalem. There was no central authority over all churches. One of the early outward rejections of the scriptures came around the end of the second century when some churches changed from having multiple bishops to a single bishop. See the reference below:

https://www.michaeljkruger.com/were-early-churches-ruled-by-elders-or-a-single-bishop/

The scriptures are unambiguous regarding the requirement for multiple qualified bishops – it was God's way. God's wisdom is always perfect, and we can see how **divergence from this requirement would lead to disaster**. Some of these so-called early church fathers favored someone, some bishop to be over all churches. Eventually, we would have a single bishop in many local churches, like the bishop of Rome. It is mainly from Rome that there was a desire for preeminence, a bishop over all the Christian Churches. In third John, John wrote negatively of such a characteristic in the leadership and particularly of Diotrephes (possibly in the church at Ephesus).

3 John 1:9-11

9 I wrote to the church, but Diotrephes, who loves to have the preeminence among them, does not receive us.

10 Therefore, if I come, I will call to mind his deeds which he does, prating against us with malicious words. And not content with that, he himself does not receive the brethren, and forbids those who wish to, putting them out of the church.

11 Beloved do not imitate what is evil, but what is good. He who does good is of God, but he who does evil has not seen God.

There would be a substantial problem if any person in the Lord's church were to "lord-over" others. Unlike Catholicism and their **demanded arrogant preeminence**, we have God condemning such attitudes in the church. The move to one bishop over the church and then to that bishop seeking preeminence over all the churches is very foreign to the church of the New Testament. It is like so many before who discounted the details of God's message and were condemned – even going back to Cain. Such decisions always lead to disaster. I might say spiritual disaster. However, in the Catholic case, in addition to the ultimate spiritual catastrophe, they would eternally suffer; there would also be in this present existence excruciating torture and death for any who would dissent particularly from the time the Catholic pope came to power over all the churches.

The travesty of preeminence – nothing new

Does this power-hungry idea of having godly things the way humankind wants them sound familiar? Israel wanted a king instead of the prophets designated by God. God agrees but says they have rejected Him and warns of the consequences of an earthly king. Indeed, it was a disaster with horrible results for the nation of Israel.

1 Samuel 8:4-9

4 Then all the elders of Israel gathered together and came to Samuel at Ramah,

5 and said to him, "Look, you are old, and your sons do not walk in your ways. Now make us a king to judge us like all the nations."

6 But the thing displeased Samuel when they said, "Give us a king to judge us." So Samuel prayed to the LORD.

7 And the LORD said to Samuel, "Heed the voice of the people in all that they say to you; for they have not rejected you, but they have rejected Me, that I should not reign over them.

8 According to all the works which they have done since the day that I brought them up out of Egypt, even to this day—with which they have forsaken Me and served other gods—so they are doing to you also.

9 Now therefore, heed their voice. However, you shall solemnly forewarn them, and show them the behavior of the king who will reign over them."

The point is some of these so-called early church fathers wanted to go against God's way of independent local churches, each with their elderships. These elderships were very much servants, never "lording over" people, just helping and maintaining the single rule to be the scriptures. Some of these early church fathers desired, similar to Israel, to have a single leader, and this idea was in their writings. One count of the evil kings of Israel/Judah had thirty-three evil kings and six kings that did right. Indeed, like the kings of Israel/Judah, these popes would generally be very evil in violence, corruption, immorality, and serving other gods. The gods of Israel/Judah were Baal, Ashtoreth, Asherah, Chemosh, and Molech. In contrast, the "gods of Catholicism" would be different from the God of the Bible **because** they changed the doctrine of Christ (2 John 1:9). Thus they follow the "Catholic god," which is the Catholic Church, and frequently a Catholic will say they have faith in the Catholic Church. Do they understand what they are saying?

Early church leaders seek a universal bishop – Very human thinking

As we enter the second century, the church is very fragmented in terms of doctrine. Many groups want to have Christianity their way. There are all kinds of people wanting to step up and lead and show you what God means. There were undoubtedly some keeping true to the teachings that were properly understood and available. However, they seem to be a minority. There was no pope, that is, an earthly head of Christianity. Why would there be a pope since the "inspired" first century never had such leadership? There were bishops in different areas of the world, as this was an accomplishment of the apostles, especially Paul. The early church fathers were those associated with Christianity and might be leaders in different localities. The written things, such as the gospels and letters to the churches, continued to provide direction for the church. It was a confusing time because, in addition to available scriptures, the early church fathers also wrote but were uninspired. Uninspired should be understood as having zero authority in spiritual matters.

The one thing that these early church leaders did of great value was copying the original inspired texts or the copies of such produced in the first century. Essentially, all of the New Testament was reproduced in the early centuries. In the second century, there were persecutions, but Christianity existed and grew as long as there was commitment/respect for God's word. We will see that Christianity is only possible when the gospel message is present to allow its growth. Whenever there is a movement away from the truth Christianity is threatened. It may be promoting a universal head of the church or creating a doctrine such as original sin. Many or most of these early church fathers turn out to be villains and not heroes due to their disrespect for God's word. Of course, the consequences are paid by future generations that accept teachings different than the doctrine of Christ.

One of the **heroes of Catholicism** is Augustine of Hippo (Saint Augustine). He is typical of the more aggressive early church fathers, and by observation, his writings were often very disrespectful of God's word. The doctrine of original sin has no basis in the Bible. It began to emerge in the 3rd century. Still, it only became fully formed with the writings of **Augustine of Hippo** (354–430), who was the first author to use the phrase "original sin" (Latin: peccatum originale). Original sin is a most treacherous doctrine in terms of damage to souls. It led to various doctrines that evolved by necessary inference (necessary to sustain the error). Those doctrines would completely change the gospel message of salvation. The net outcome of these teachings would be a most inexplicable and absurd pattern for salvation.

As we approach the fourth century and Constantine's Edict of Milan, there were only bishops or a bishop of local churches. Constantine wanted Christians to have a single head, and in frustration, he began to act as the head over all Christians. He convenes the first council over which some say he presides. It is the council of Nicaea in the year 325 AD, and of course, there is no pope in attendance since there are no popes. We are headed into a period where the bishop of Rome is becoming a dominant figure in Christendom. As mentioned previously, Innocent I (402-417) was the bishop of Rome and called himself "Ruler of the church of God." In 604 AD, the emperor Phocas tried to give the title of universal bishop to Gregory I, but he refused it. However, a successor, Boniface III, accepted the title in 607 AD.

Thus the non-Catholic theologians often assign the beginning of the Catholic Church to the seventh century with the recognition of the title, pope.

Losing the doctrine of Christ, Losing the means of reconciliation

There is quite a spread regarding the "official beginning time of Catholicism and their pope." On the one hand, you have the "Catholic history, historians," and on the other, the "non-Catholic history, historians." The beginning of Catholicism is a non-critical issue and hardly worth discussing. It is hard to believe the Catholic theologians because of their undeniable prejudice. Again, it is not important! Certainly, we can establish that any meaningful existence of Catholicism occurred in the latter part of this large range (between the first and seventh centuries). However, it is easy to believe that the seeds of Catholicism were spread as soon as the doctrine of Christ was rejected (rejected means stopped practicing the doctrine of Christ and began substituting other teachings). Catholicism needs to have a continual line of their popes, and thus the church must connect back to Peter – **so they do the work to create such a scenario**. Again, it does not matter, and long before you finish reading this book, you will know why. In brief, it is because life, your life, is about the soul. That is important. You might think that believing the Catholic Church goes back to the first century is just what is needed to establish its validity. Looking at the historian's view of this timing might be interesting but not nearly as important as the message from God concerning your soul. Is that the message carried by Catholicism? We can say, No! One aspect of this dating of Catholicism has some value, namely recognizing the tragedy and viscousness of Catholicism back-naming popes to the first century, beginning with Peter. That has value in demonstrating the **willingness of Catholicism to do whatever it takes to validate their religion**. The early church fathers would undoubtedly disagree with this list of popes, as do the scriptures, as does the secular world at the time, including the emperors. The case for the things mentioned early in this book regarding Catholic doctrine will be substantiated in ways that cannot be denied.

Continuing in this first period of Catholicism

We have defined this first period of Catholicism as a time that begins unofficially in the mid-late first century. We mentioned the seeds of the Catholic Church were being planted whenever there was movement in opposition to the scriptures. Catholicism would be vastly different from the scriptures and slowly incorporate aspects of the errant early church father's writings. Some early church fathers tried to keep what they knew to be the scriptures. Nonetheless, different doctrines were appearing in various church locations. Down the road, when Catholicism was being established, the documents of early church fathers were used to justify many of the Catholic doctrines. They would claim the proximity of the early churches to the first century-inspired writings represented the **traditions intended by God**. One wonders if they ever considered that God could deliver all that was needed in the fifty-plus years the Holy Spirit worked with the apostles.

Perhaps the saddest creations of the early church father's writings were the occasional mention of the need for a universal bishop and the associated insinuation of apostolic succession. It seems that a few of the early church fathers knew some of the apostles. This enhances the Catholic story but in no way means anything in terms of doctrine. The first three centuries were difficult times for Christians, really murderous times largely at the hands of Rome. The world at that time was very pluralistic in terms of gods, and the Christian monotheistic (one God) was unacceptable. The government of Rome was the villain to Christians, and they were relentless in their pursuit, torture, and murder. Rome, by the beginning of the fourth century, was full of "Christians." Constantine was the emperor of Rome (reign from 25 July 306 – 22 May 337) and envisioned an advantage in declaring the freedom of worship for Christians. It probably had to do with all the in-fighting among Rome's many gods and the appeal of having a one-god nation.

In 313 AD, the emperor Constantine (believed to have become a Christian*) decrees the Edict of Milan, which granted Christians and all others full liberty to participate in the religion of their choice. Constantine also claimed a vision of a flaming cross with the inscription "in his sign conquer," which encouraged him to be a Christian. Additionally, Constantine favored Christians in every way, including filling chief offices with Christians. The Roman aristocracy typically continued with their multi-god beliefs. Constantine would call the first church council over which he may have presided. He would see himself in a leadership role of the church. There is the Orthodox version and the Roman version of Christianity at this time and to this day. Constantine made it clear that he recognized both groups and considered himself the leader of both. It was not a religious leadership, but he had oversight in the sense that everything in the Roman empire was under his authority.

Note: As you read about these early centuries, it is clear that the gospel message was disappearing, especially among the Roman "Christians." The critical elements of the gospel are missing, as they are seldom mentioned. Baptism is mentioned but in various ways and often confused.

*History indicates Constantine was baptized on his deathbed by Eusebius of Nicomedia in 337 AD. Thus those claiming Constantine to be a Christian just before the Edict of Milan in 313 were not correct. His death bed baptism and the likely non-existence of the truth concerning the gospel message would indicate he never became a Christian. That is, the gospel message (for one thing) would not have directed him to put off his baptism. Indeed, it is fair to consider that few were Christian at that time and especially in Rome.

About Catholic art and its pathetic portrayals

(this is a good place for a sidebar to point out the effort by Catholicism to take advantage of art to support their doctrines)

The "**Baptism** of **Constantine**" is located in the Sala di Costantino ("Hall of **Constantine**"). In this painting, Emperor **Constantine the Great** is depicted kneeling to receive the sacrament from Pope Sylvester I in the Baptistery of St John Lateran. Paintings of a religious nature from ancient times occur much later than the event. In this case, Constantine's baptism occurred in 337 AD but was not painted until the 16th century. Of course, there were no popes at this time (4th century), and in fact, Constantine was **baptized by Bishop Eusebius of Nicomedia**. Constantine's baptism occurred on his death bed, and this is correct based on the historical record. This art does support my earlier statement that the gospel message had been terribly butchered. It was not unusual that **baptism was delayed until the last possible moment of a person's life, which would indicate something very different from the first century's conversions**. The art shows Constantine being **sprinkled, not baptized** by Pope Sylvester I (no popes at this time) in the baptistry of Saint John Lateran and not on his death bed by Eusebius of Nicomedia and occurring earlier than the time of Constantine's death. This again validates the declaration that the gospel message had been corrupted and demonstrated the treachery that would not leave a stone unturned to promote Catholicism's lies.

As is so often the case, there is some truth mixed with error. Baptism was understood to be for the remission of sins – **which is true**! Somehow there was such confusion that people seeking to be Christians were concerned (likely due to their lifestyles) that sin after baptism could not be forgiven, and this should be no surprise since the truth had been butchered. We might say there were pieces of truth and elements of error, and much was missing even in the apparent truthful portions. How much evidence is required to allow humankind to realize they will never get anything right **unless it comes from outside our realm**. Truth only comes from God, and yet humanity seeks to make the rules for God. Humankind does not want to make the rules for God in some helpful way, but they seek the power that comes from the claimed association with God. Rulemaking is a necessary part of their authority, especially the rules that validate their ability to make the rules.

The fresco of Constantine's baptism was ordered by Pope Clement VII (work was interrupted during the papacy of Hadrian VI) and showed Pope Sylvester conducting the baptism. Catholic history would indicate that Sylvester I was a bishop in Rome from 314 until his death. Of course, Catholics refer to Sylvester I as a pope. This Catholic depiction of Constantine's baptism can be seen at this site.

https://en.wikipedia.org/wiki/The_Baptism_of_Constantine

Note: This is a note of convenience to make a point. The Roman Catholic Church has taken advantage of every possible opportunity, and in this case, their painters create depictions at the direction of the Roman Catholic Church. The baptism of Constantine was done by Catholic artists Raphael, Giulio Romano, Gian Francesco Penni.

*Perhaps the most pathetic painting commissioned by Rome depicts Jesus being baptized by John the Baptist. The famous **Baptism Of Christ** (c. 1472) is by **Leonardo's** master, **Andrea del Verrocchio**, and was **commissioned** by the monks of San Salvi near Florence. Of course, this picture does not represent a baptism, but water poured over the head of Jesus. This painting can be viewed at:*

https://en.wikipedia.org/wiki/The_Baptism_of_Christ_(Verrocchio_and_Leonardo)#/media/File: Verrocchio,_Leonardo_da_Vinci_-_Battesimo_di_Cristo.jpg

Another painting of Jesus' baptism was done by Piero della Francesca, "The Baptism of Christ,*" detail (c. 1448-1450). That panel was* **commissioned** *by the Camaldolese abbey of Sansepolcro, originally part of a triptych. Its dating is to* **Piero della Francesca's** *early career and is evidenced by the strong relationship with the "light painting" of his master, Domenico Veneziano, and can be seen at the link below.*

https://en.wikipedia.org/wiki/The_Baptism_of_Christ_(Piero_della_Francesca)#/media/File:Piero_della_Francesca_-_Baptism_of_Christ_-_WGA17595.jpg

Again, this painting does not depict Jesus being baptized but sprinkled with water on his head. In a quick review of early paintings of the baptism of Jesus, I found one of eighteen paintings that correctly pictured Jesus's baptism. That is, Jesus, being baptized and accurately depicting Jesus standing in "waist-high" water about to be immersed. There is something awful here. One might expect that those representing God would be incredibly careful in everything such that there was no question of being truthful. However, in **everything Catholic,** *there is deception; it is evil. Instead of truthfulness being the motive, the Catholic motive seems to be protecting the teachings of Catholicism – at all costs. The evil of torturing and murdering heretics is obvious, but the evil of depicting baptism as sprinkling is devastating to souls – in the next section, this will be made crystal clear.*

Note: The scripture account of Jesus's baptism is below for reference.
Matthew 3:13-17
13 Then Jesus came from Galilee to John at the Jordan to be baptized by him.
14 And John tried to prevent Him, saying, "I need to be baptized by You, and are You coming to me?"
15 But Jesus answered and said to him, "Permit it to be so now, for thus it is fitting for us to fulfill all righteousness." Then he allowed Him.
16 When He had been baptized, **Jesus came up immediately from the water**; *and behold, the heavens were opened to Him, and He saw the Spirit of God descending like a dove and alighting upon Him.*

17 And suddenly a voice came from heaven, saying, "This is My beloved Son, in whom I am well pleased."

More on Catholic art in relation to Baptism and Obedience

Another sidebar before returning to the Catholic Church history seems appropriate. Everything related to the truth will come from the word of God. God always means what He says and the way He says it. Baptism plays a crucial role in the salvation of every conversion. Of course, this is discussed extensively throughout the scriptures and other books by this author such as "God" and "What Is Life All About." Baptism simply means immersion, and thus it would be a severe error to decide to pour water over a person's head and call it baptism. That action would be called pouring water over the head or sprinkling, but it is not baptism. There is much more than symbolism involved here, although the symbolism is powerful and what God intended, and therefore no one should oppose or accept anything different than immersion. Romans 6:3-4 and 17 define the method for eliminating sin and establishing a relationship with Christ and refer to it as **that form of doctrine.**

Romans 6:3-4 and 17

3 Or do you not know that as many of us as were baptized into Christ Jesus were baptized into His death?
4 Therefore we were buried with Him through baptism into death, that just as Christ was raised from the dead by the glory of the Father, even so we also should walk in newness of life.
17 But God be thanked that though you were slaves of sin, yet you obeyed from the heart that form of doctrine to which you were delivered.

Note: Of course, the only fit subjects for baptism are those who believe, have confessed Jesus as the Christ, and have repented. See Chapter 7 for more details.

There is much more than symbolism because there is obedience. It is a symbolism that must be obeyed. God is so incredibly gracious and helpful in providing His word that we know the truth with high confidence.

Consider the battle of Jericho (Joshua 6) and the victory that resulted from the collapse of the very substantial walls. God required several things, and one was marching around Jericho's walls seven times and doing various other things during that march. What do you suppose would have happened if they only went around six times? Would the walls have fallen; would Israel have won the battle?

Consider if Naaman (2 Kings 5) would have only dipped six times in the Jordon river or if he would have dipped seven times in the **Abanah** or **Pharpar** rivers he preferred, would his leprosy have been cured?

Consider Cain's (Genesis 4:1-16) decision to substitute something different for the sacrifice. It did not please God and how that rejection and Abel's acceptance resulted in murder and the subsequent lie. The consequences of a casual consideration of God's directions are severe.

Consider the Sons of Aaron, Nadab, and Abihu (Leviticus 10), who determined to offer a strange (different) fire than God had specified and how that cost them their lives.

You see, obedience matters, and what God says and how He says it does matter. You can see the reason for baptism in its symbolism, and who has the right to change it? Baptism is unique in God's plan and central to His purpose. The components of baptism going down into the water dying to sin (baptized into Christ's death) that is being buried with Christ in baptism and then coming out of the water free from sin, and even so we should walk in newness of life. Of course, the apparent problem of changing the word baptism meaning to immerse and replacing it with sprinkling is disrespecting God's word. Obeying God means receiving the God-designed result, namely the forgiveness of sin. Like Naaman would not have been cured of leprosy had he rejected God's way, so there is no forgiveness of sins if the pattern is changed – if the gospel form of doctrine is not obeyed.

Note: To all those who see this as trivial, silly, and unimportant, it is a perfect way to measure a person's humility. You are so much more open-minded than God, so much more flexible, so much more forgiving, so much more tolerant when it is just your pride. Indeed, God's test is perfect in every aspect, and deep down, you do not like God's ways. God hides nothing regarding how He views those who do not take His word seriously, His calling seriously, and as He says, those who disdain His counsel. The love of God is found in taking the counsel of God *seriously. Whereas rejecting His counsel will be realized when your terror comes like a storm, And your destruction comes like a whirlwind (Proverbs 1:24-27). Indeed God reveals the certainty of **rejecting His counsel** or we could say **rejecting his word,** or we could say **changing His word.***

The things mentioned that occurred in the past were for our learning (Romans 15:4). That is, learning obedience, **learning the seriousness regarding the directions from God.** The gospel message includes the most important of all actions required for salvation, and it is obedience, and God, by His Son's obedience, meets the requirement for reconciliation. Namely, the perfect sacrifice as indicated in the gospel message wherein the obedient person participates in the death, burial, and resurrection of Jesus. The gospel message is the saving message and needs to be obeyed. God perfectly calls it obeying the gospel, and thus it is obeying the death, burial, and resurrection of Jesus as mentioned above in Romans 6:3-4, and 17. Properly referred to as obeying that FORM of doctrine.

This form of doctrine is emphasized throughout the New Testament (i.e., Acts 2:38, Galatians 3:26-29). It is one of the most flagrant, most deceptive abuses to show Jesus being sprinkled and not baptized, yet calling it baptism. Of course, this Catholic deception is related to the Catholic practice of sprinkling and calling it baptism. There is a pattern to Catholic evil, and it is easily observed. In the case of the "Real Presence," they take it literally, but it is a metaphor, and then in the case of baptism, they take it as a metaphor or that the process (immersion) is not essential. **Everything in Catholicism is the opposite of the truth.** Errors occur because humankind attempts to make the rules for God. We have God who is perfect and fits everything perfectly together. We have humanity getting everything wrong and then trying to recover, and they just make everything worse.

*Note: **In this book,** you will see why immersion is literal and needed to forgive sins. Also, you can see that the "Real Presence" is a metaphor. These things are not difficult to understand, and Catholicism's versions are impossible to defend – unless they make the rule that Catholicism has the right to make the rules. Of course, it is more than making the rules since they consistently violate the word of God in their rulemaking.*

[We are leaving the sidebars - Back to the first historical period of Catholicism.]

The Edict of Toleration and the Edict of Milan seemed good for Christianity, but where was Christianity?

Note: The emperor Galerius stops the Christian persecutions in 311 by issuing the **Edict of Toleration**. *Two years later, emperor Constantine declared freedom of religion with his* **Edict of Milan.**

Emperor Theodosius followed Constantine's ways and made Christianity the state religion of the Roman Empire and made church membership compulsory and thus forced conversion. Even before the edicts, the "Christians" of Rome had begun to incorporate idol practices into their beliefs. Now in close proximity to pagan gods, Christianity already weakened by the early church father's deviations from scripture would take on a different character. At this point, between all the false teachings that entered beginning in the latter half of the first century and now all the idolatry, **the Christianity (the church Jesus was building) of the first century had largely disappeared**. One example of the change was in worship that evolved from simple to elaborate, with stately and very imposing ceremonies and outward splendor giving the appearance of the heathen temples. Indeed the building blocks of Catholicism were in place.

Here comes the Pope

The most fundamental change as the spiritual church being built by Jesus evolved to the physical Catholic Church was the **means of becoming a Christian**. There was no longer the emphasis on preaching the gospel and obeying the gospel. When this occurred, the Lord could not add to His body. There is a seriousness regarding everything God does and not to be changed. The church is simple in all its aspects but tampering with anything will have serious consequences. Changing the means of achieving conversions completely destroys evangelism. The definition of elders in their qualifications, in the need for multiple elders is established by God and thus must not be modified. Tampering in this matter would lead to an earthly head of the church. The local churches each had bishops (some incorrectly had just one bishop), but there was no single bishop over all of Christendom. The bishop of Rome did have considerable power, and several of them declared they were the head bishop over all the church. Early church fathers would occasionally mention the idea of a single bishop over all the church. Although it did not exist, there was momentum, and it would be realized in the future. There was an evolution from the bishops being referred to as papa to eventually being restricted to the bishop of Rome. This came to include the concept of universal bishop or the one over all of Christendom. All this is coming to pass about 600 AD or roughly for 600 years there were bishops over the churches but there were no popes. Pope, of course, means papa or simply father.

*Note: Catholics and Protestants know of God's proclamation that (**in a religious sense**) no man has the title father except the Father in heaven. The Catholic pope was the perfect abuse of this verse in Matthew.*

Matthew 23:9

9 Do not call anyone on earth your father; for One is your Father, He who is in heaven.

It is amazing how Catholicism honors the early church fathers in their writings and rejects the God of heaven in His explicit declarations. What were they thinking, not about their souls or the souls of others – quite the opposite of God's focus.

Protestants use this Matthew 23 verse to deny that the pope is the legitimate head of Christianity, and Catholics just ignore the complaint or explain it away. However, God is serious, and having a man wear the title of father being the religious head of the church (the church that has a single head, namely Jesus) is some gigantic blasphemy. In other words, those wearing this title and those supporting such a person have a serious and eternal problem and are the ultimate idolators.

The momentum for a single head of Christianity

We will look at a few men who were the bishops of Rome and begin with Innocent I (402-417), who called himself "Ruler of the church of God." During this period, Augustine wrote his monumental work, "The City of God," where he envisioned a universal Christian empire and favored a universal church hierarchy under one head. It is worthy of stopping and mentioning a few things about Augustine due to his impact on the coming institution of Catholicism. Augustine began writing the "City of God" in 413 and continued writing its many volumes for many years. Augustine (354-430) remains a favorite early church father to the present day and is frequently quoted in support of Catholic doctrine. He was perhaps the most influential of the early church fathers being a renowned theologian and prolific writer. Like all the early church fathers but notably Augustine, when they stayed in the bounds of scripture, their writing and efforts contained value. However, when they wandered away from the things inspired, they were in error. Nonetheless, due to their notoriety, some would claim the desirable aspects of their errant writings to be valid doctrine. An example in Augustine's case would be a universal Christian empire.

Augustine is an excellent example of why God does not allow the changing of His word. God's word settles all spiritual matters. God defines the church, salvation, forgiveness of sins, and so on. Augustine was describing the church per his view – in other words being careless with the scriptures. One cannot be sure, but Augustine's private interpretations were just that, namely what he thought, what he concluded, what he favored but likely never intended to be doctrine. Augustine knew he was not inspired. Nonetheless, as he strayed from the scriptures, he was irresponsible and a contributor to eventual great evil.

*Note: I often wonder if there has been tampering with the writings of the early church fathers. Augustine states that **the Scriptures alone** can instruct human beings about the highest good and the highest evil and that without this guidance, human endeavor has no purpose. Catholicism favors Augustine in things that support their goals, but here is an Augustine belief that supports **the scriptures alone** as being valid, and such strong opposition to Catholic doctrine is ignored. The reference link below is a good, albeit very brief summary of Augustine's "City of God."*

https://www.sparknotes.com/philosophy/augustine/section2/

As we move slightly forward in history, we come to Leo I (440-461) as the bishop of Rome, who some historians believe was the first pope. Leo I proclaimed himself the Lord of the church, advocated the universal papacy, and indicated that any resistance to this was a sure way to hell.

*Note: It is curious that Innocent I, Augustine, and Leo I all favored a universal bishop, which **means that there was no such position at that time**. Thus there is zero validity in Catholics naming 66 popes backward from one who has been **historically recognized** as a first Catholic pope, namely, Boniface III. They would, of course, end this backward movement with Peter, their first pope. It is sad, very ridiculous, actually just a giant lie.*

Gregory I, who reigned from 590-604, is considered by some to be the first pope (others think it was Boniface III, 607). From this point forward, the Roman Catholic Church would grow to be more powerful, and there is a general historical agreement (of the existence of popes). In this first period of Catholicism, in the earlier part from the first century to the beginning of the seventh century, Catholicism is without a pope. However, by the early seventh century, they have their universal bishop. Of course, Catholic history has Peter being the first pope and then back-naming various persons as popes. Some of these "popes" were possibly the local bishops of Rome. Eventually, the bishop of Rome would be recognized as the universal bishop of all of Christendom. Certainly not recognized by God, that is, by the church Jesus started. There is little clarity concerning this history of the early popes. Still, Gregory I and Boniface III were possibilities. Some would suggest that the first universal bishop was Leo I (440-461) because he made such a claim while condemning dissenters to hell. Christianity went from being the truth in the first century under the auspicious of the apostles led by the Holy Spirit to being the early church of the first four centuries with many different versions of the truth (thus not the truth). "Christianity" was influenced by pagan Rome before the Edict of Tolerance and the Edict of Milan, then even more influenced by idolatry after the Edicts. The Christian church went from simple to ornate, lavish, and very pagan in appearance. It would get worse. The presence of a single source of oversight for the church provided momentum and authority for the growth of error.

Consequently, the church belonging to Christ had disappeared. It began to disappear when the gospel was being changed, as Paul mentioned in Galatians. By the time the early church, as described by the early church fathers, had appeared, there were likely less than imagined "in Christ."

Note: It was mentioned that the means of becoming a Christian had disappeared, but that is not entirely correct. Indeed, in major cities such as Rome, that seems to be the case. Yet, there were places in the world where the churches still knew the truth and acted accordingly. I am sure that was the case because God indicated His word would not pass away. Also, there are in history various groups, although relatively small, that followed the scriptures from the first century. These generally remote early churches possessed portions of the scriptures and were aware of some oral statements passed down. Someone might say that such a statement (oral transmission) is essentially accepting tradition. Tradition has always been accepted as long as it is consistent with the scriptures. For example, those who learned the gospel from Paul, passed those things along through their generations. **If they did that correctly without adding to or taking away from what they learned from Paul, then that "tradition" would be valid.** *The validity is always in relation to the truth. Since the scriptures are complete, the message brought by Paul and the other apostles that God wanted to be transmitted through the remainder of history has been included in God's completed word.*

Jesus is building His church, but following the period of inspiration, men were changing the doctrine of Christ to be very different, very physical, very humanlike

If we view the 4th, 5th, 6th, and 7th centuries we have listed below the six rule-making church councils of this early period. The Christianity of the scriptures was gradually disappearing before the first council of Nicaea (called by Constantine). Such councils were a massive violation of the will of God. The organization God designed for the local church was to handle spiritual matters as defined by God. Their focus was on evangelism, and questions of faith should be non-existent since there was a single rulebook and there was a dedication to not changing it, specifically not changing the meaning. The problems arise from those who privately interpret the word of God. The church councils fail before they begin because they open the door to private interpretation. These church councils are ultimately **not important** because they were called by, attended by those who had no association with God. How can we know that? Because they were **by their attendance** opposing the will of God.

- First Council of Nicaea (325)
- First Council of Constantinople (381)

- Council of Ephesus (431)
- Council of Chalcedon (451)
- Second Council of Constantinople (553)
- Third Council of Constantinople (680–681)

*Note: The emphasis of this and my other books in terms of Christianity has been on Roman Catholicism and secondarily on Protestantism. Of course, there is another component. We could call it the Greek or Greek Orthodox church or even the Eastern Orthodox or the Russian Orthodox church or named by many other localities or other conventions. This "Orthodox" church has been in the picture as long as the Roman Catholic Church, and in fact, they grew to be competitive. Constantine recognized both and considered himself in a leadership role over both. When the councils were called, they involved both the Roman and Orthodox churches, at least through the first seven councils. These first seven councils were all called by a Roman emperor. This can be simplified by referring to the churches as the Eastern Orthodox Church and the Western Catholic Church. The Eastern rite goes by several names but includes the word Orthodox. The Western Catholic Church would **eventually** be called the Roman Catholic Church. Amid the evil nature of the councils, I found one thing that appears to have been of value. Namely, the early gatherings of these first seven centuries, particularly the earliest councils, brought together the various "pieces of scripture" from different locations, different local churches. Frequently, they possessed the same information but not always. Thus there was occurring preservation and a complete record of the "New Testament." Eventually, this would be helpful in the development of a Cannon.*

Pause to reflect on the evil of church councils – seemingly so innocent

These church councils represent a significant form of evil. We might say mathematically evil x evil x evil or evil cubed (evil^3). The point here is to show it would be difficult to exceed the destructive nature of this concept. God's word is not to be changed, and here we have all these men debating "spiritual" matters, making determinations regarding the meaning of the scriptures, and as suggested, none may have been Christians. The truth, specifically the gospel message, was lost to these people, and if it were not lost, they would not be participating in such councils. The following is to bring some clarity to the evil nature of these church councils. It would be a continuing evil. The Catholic Church lists 21 church councils, the last one being the second Vatican council (1962-1965). Below are five reasons why these councils are problematic.

First, they are wrong because these councils themselves are inconsistent with God's will. There are three ways the councils are incompatible with God's pattern, and respectively they are the sovereignty of God's word, missing the understanding of the Jerusalem council, and the realization that God had completed His communication with humankind. That is for clarity: The laws of God are not debatable. The so-called council in Jerusalem was quite different as Paul and Barnabas met with the Jerusalem church leadership to discuss a particular matter. The word of God was not yet completed until near the end of the first century. In the time of the Holy Spirit guiding the apostles, there would never be another such meeting. The "end game" God was providing was the completed word of God – no more communication with God. Any future issues would be addressed by that which is perfect in the framework of the God-designed local church.

Second, these bishops do not have a fundamental understanding of the scriptures. The basic principles of God's inspired word are missing over the entire history of the church councils. The early church councils were trying to find some synergy among many competing beliefs, **all of which were inconsistent with the word of God**. The later councils were more interested in validating Catholic doctrine, realizing the scriptures could not validate them.

Third, we can see Constantine's logic in having the first council from his point of view. He wanted to unify Christianity, to settle their differences. It is reasonable to think that there may have never been any church councils if it were not for Constantine. Certainly, Constantine had no spiritual or truth-related reason for the council. There would be no reason for the councils unless there were different private interpretations of the scriptures. If that had not occurred, Constantine would not have seen the significant in-fighting among Christians. It was more than privately interpreting the scriptures in the early centuries. It was the creation of new doctrines typically originating from the early church fathers.

Fourth, it is somewhat nonsensical for these various bishops and other officials to meet to discuss issues that, by their nature, were only symptoms of much deeper problems. The church that Jesus started was spiritual, and it consisted of those obedient who were added to the body of Christ by the Lord Himself. The local church was independent and understood the only rule was the word of God. This independent nature of the church, "builds-in" the separation of even, local churches, i.e., no gathering of the minds among local churches to settle spiritual issues. The population of any one local church is relatively small, and this avoids any grandiose plans of any wayward leadership affecting the whole of Christianity. It would be silly to have many local church leaders meeting to settle various issues when God's guidance points to the local church, specifically the elders holding fast the faithful word.

Fifth, one aspect of the evil of these councils is simply by their existence they confuse God's process for achieving His purpose. God built in many safeguards to His plan to reconcile Himself with humankind. The local independent church was one of those safeguards since it consisted of persons the Lord added to His body by their "humble" obedience. These people were the most likely to continue in obedience, and part of that was a dedication to God's word. The character of the local church as defined by God was not to change the things delivered by inspiration. One of those things was the organization and work of the local church. The leadership of the local church was multiple elders, servant-type elders meeting all the qualifications. All matters concerning the scriptures would be managed locally with an absolute dedication to maintaining God's meaning. The wisdom of God knew that a single head over all of Christendom would be a disaster, and indeed in Catholicism, that would happen. These church councils were meetings of the various local church leaders that should never have occurred. It is not hard to imagine that the councils would eventually lead to power-grabbing, some sort of need for leadership. I do not know the impact of these councils in terms of arriving at a single head over all of Christianity, but I suspect they played a part. These church councils would be places that would facilitate the changing of God's word and, in so doing, when the church was universal (under one leadership), infect the entirety of Christendom.

Note: Christianity in these earliest of times is full of significant differences from the scriptures. These massive deviations in Christians' beliefs were easily observed, and beginning with emperor Constantine there would be church councils to seek resolution. Early confusion came from some reliance on the varied writings of the early church fathers. Only the scriptures can provide unity, but there was little concern about the sacred nature of God's word. That is where the emphasis should have been. Standing in the fourth century, particularly in the area of Rome, the doctrine of Christ was missing. It was a gradual falling away from the word of God that was being replaced by various private interpretations. The issues must have been causing significant disturbances, or Constantine would not have been bothered.

*The church councils, initially called by Roman emperors, were to unify the Christian religion to benefit the Roman empire. Although we refer to this book in terms of the history of Catholicism, it is the history of Christianity. It is a history of Christianity that would evolve **in the eyes of the world** into Catholicism. Christianity never becomes Catholicism but remains pure in a fierce dedication to the word of God, albeit obscure.*

*"Down the road," the Catholic Church will claim the writings of the early church fathers are valid for doctrine. Whereas they only brought conflict resulting in Catholicism. This should not be a surprise as prideful men, and very apparently many not having the serious understanding that **no changes to the word of God were allowed,** would consequently never be able to get God's meaning correct. We have very diverse men from various parts of the world associated with "Christianity," and obviously, they disagreed. How could anyone get the truth from these early church fathers? How could they sort through all the different opinions they had? They could not, but they could pick and choose what they liked, the things that made the most sense to them. Now we have these early men of the churches not agreeing and then another layer of men (typically bishops) at the church councils trying to make decisions of a spiritual nature. These early church fathers and the early bishops of the church councils have zero credibility concerning doctrine. God shut the door on any revelation other than provided by His Holy Spirit, and it is easy to see why.*

God's wisdom is very far advanced from what people think is best. God's design of the church is perfect for accomplishing His purpose, and that design is "local." It is not surprising but even logical that **humankind would think a central rule for the church might work best.** If a person would align with God's purpose, they might better understand God's way and, in this case, better understand the local church. God's desired result is related only to souls, to souls succeeding. A person can read Galatians 1.6-9 and realize the seriousness of changing the gospel message. It was a travesty of monumental proportions, and it is emphasized inasmuch as there is a curse and then a repeated curse. The most serious of problems occurring in the **local independent church** could be managed. In humankind's or the Catholic Church version, the universal church's **deviations from the truth will infect all of "Christianity."** Human leadership of the church fails to see God's wisdom, and bad choices can only be avoided if there is strict adherence to the word of God – there is no other source of truth.

In other words, even in these early days, there was a belief that Christian teachings could be changed, negotiable things among men. The early church fathers, in their speculations and private interpretations, would suggest a ruling leadership over all churches (universal bishop). That idea could be perpetuated in the first church councils of bishops. These councils would be places where the word of God could be changed and simultaneously legitimized. This attitude is still seen today as religions see their power as something that their rulemaking can forever enhance. There is a definite paranoia that has them doing whatever is needed to gain power and maintain it. In whatever way changing the doctrine can support their goals, there is no hesitation. God's word does not change from one generation to the next. God's way emphasizes high quality/character individuals who seek Him and will respect **His word.** Consider how distant these churches are from what God intended after almost 2000 years of abusing the word of God.

Moving forward in the history of Catholicism – Period one continued

It should be no surprise that the church of the early centuries was evolving away from the scriptures and with no meaningful justification for their teachings. This "Christianity," different than the scriptures, needed something to support their changes. The essential component to assure their sovereignty was establishing a single head over all of Christianity. You can see this in the writing of the early church fathers, but it had grown from what some thought was a good idea, to something badly needed. As suggested, the church councils likely promoted this concept of a universal bishop as the bringing together of local bishops would logically require some leadership. At the same time, various bishops of Rome were seeking such sovereignty over all of Christianity – over all the churches. Finally, this happened and was recognized in the early seventh century. Now that their structure included the universal bishop and was located in Rome, Catholicism would protect and grow its brand. A massive power structure was being created that positioned their leaders with the influence that would eventually exert power over nations. They would enact the evilest, threatening, and violent behavior to maintain their control.

It is not a pleasant read going forward as Catholicism is a terror to various nations and anyone **hesitant** in their allegiance to Catholicism. Catholicism became the definition of paranoia. One would think that such a history would be sufficient to turn away every person from Catholicism, and yet it has not. Although we will proceed with a very brief history from the seventh century thru the seventeenth century, we pause to question why there are any Catholics today. The pluses for individuals must outweigh the minuses.

*Pause for why there are Catholics today: One prime negative is the acknowledged evil history of Catholicism. The positives for remaining Catholic are associated with believing there is truth in Catholicism. However, for most Catholics, Catholicism is likely the religion of their family, and it is **expected they will have no reason to change** from infant baptism until their death. All the Catholic Masses, the priests, the popes, Mary and her honor and apparitions, the dramatic singing and instrumental music, the Real Presence, the weddings, the funerals, and of course there is the indoctrination, the propaganda that makes everything seem so right. Catholicism for many has been their life. Catholicism portrays the **present undeniable evils** as, "we all have problems, no one is perfect." We might throw in the optimistic belief that the Catholic Church has a supposed continuation from the first-century church – the church belonging to Christ. We have the apparent alternative to Catholicism being Protestantism, but that religion also has many scriptural problems. Thus, Catholics often remain Catholics. The scriptures provide the answer for everyone caught up in error. Namely, a person needs a love of the truth. The truth is Christianity, but neither Catholicism nor Protestantism is representative of the church started by Jesus.*

Continue from the seventh thru the seventeenth century – an exceedingly brief record of these last 1000 years of this first period of Catholicism

As we reach the early seventh century, the papacy is established. A majority of the current Catholic doctrine was instituted in this first period of Catholicism. In addition to the various random teachings of Catholicism, there have been nineteen church councils. The seventh century also begins with the appearance of Islam, and this new religion is starting to supplant "Christianity" in certain parts of the world. Islam conquers Jerusalem in 636 AD. Another significant event was the coming to power of Roman Catholicism in England (or we might say in Celtic lands) in 664 AD. Roman Catholicism was beginning its sovereignty over what would be many nations.

Note: There is no intention to provide a detailed history of the Christian church. That would be a massive undertaking. However, there is something to be said about the accuracy of recorded history. You should not expect an accurate history from the Catholic Church. It will be exceedingly prejudiced and overseen by a biased hierarchy with a past of deceit. It is possible to find a reasonably unbiased account of the church and validate it by other independent sources. One person who seems to have those honest characteristics and is consistent with many other historians without Catholic ties is Dr. Henry H. Halley. Halley's Bible Handbook is quite good and recommended. The recommendation is only from a historical viewpoint and does not necessarily agree with his Bible conclusions. He correctly sees at a high level the gradual movement from the church Jesus started in the first century to the falling away ending in the Catholic Church. I am not sure he sees how early Christianity disappears in terms of the time of the early church fathers. That disappearance was occurring simultaneously with leaving the doctrine of Christ and very specifically changing the gospel message.

A second note: Jesus provided evidence of who He was in John 5.31-44. In those verses, He mentions that His testimony of Himself has the most negligible value; even having no value is suggested.

John 5:31
31 If I bear witness of Myself, My witness is not true.

*The Catholic Church cannot stand without its **OWN** testimony. Regardless of Catholic history or doctrine, there is no supporting evidence for either **outside their own organization**. Not to be confused, some historians outside of Catholicism have unwittingly accepted Catholic historical documents. After all, there is a massive number of them. A person or group's testimony in support of themselves should always bring into question all documents in their control. Those considering the validity of the early church father's writings should consider the potential for such documents to have been maliciously altered.*
*Jesus, of course, never spoke anything that was not the truth, but He was pointing out confirmation should come **from outside** a person or group. Jesus, in these verses, goes on and provides other sources, witnesses of Himself. Indeed, an organization such as the Catholic Church in their flagrant history of deceit (e.g., naming popes back to Peter and hundreds of*

other lies) and open cruelty and genocide (e.g., Anabaptists, Huguenots, Waldensians and Albigenses) *cannot be trusted. The one thing that has convinced many people of the validity of Catholic lies is, ironically, the magnitude of the dishonesty. That is, the significance and the number of lies. Certainly, everything is not a lie, yet successful liars live in persistent lies.*

Focusing on the prominent popes from the seventh thru the seventeenth century

One way to study the history of Catholicism that simplifies and dramatically shortens this section is to look at the prominent popes during this time. Certainly, the most dramatic results in the late sixth, early seventh centuries were from Gregory I (590-604), and as mentioned, he was considered by some to be the first pope. He was able to bring some stability and thus control over the churches in various countries such as Italy, Spain, Gaul, and England.

Note: Can you see what has happened to the spiritual church of God's Son? It is such a simple requirement to have local independent churches. Once again, the wisdom of God versus the foolishness of substituting something else. The outcome of a single leader over all of Christendom is creating a monster. The Catholic Church is a physical church with a desire to rule over all the churches. They also seek to rule over nations. Catholicism's mission, particularly at this time, had little to no focus on the prime mission of the church Jesus started – namely, souls. It appears the gospel message had long ago been lost.

Bringing the church under the control of the pope and a ruling Roman Catholic hierarchy was the beginning of a rule over nations that would carry on for about 1000 years. It would be a time of significant Catholic Church domination in the countries mentioned above and eventually include many other countries. The Catholic Church would become the Papal States or sometimes called the Temporal Dominion of the popes. The **Papal States** were a series of territories in the Italian Peninsula under the direct sovereign rule of the pope from the 8th century until 1870. These lands and many other favors were the results of various collaborations with the popes. The power of Catholicism is expanding, and it is religious but also very secular. During these times, Catholicism was growing in power, particularly under Charlemagne (742-814), the king of the Franks, and principally in conjunction with Pope Leo III (795-816). During this period, there was a growing belief that the Roman Catholic Church and the pope were a constant since the first century and were indeed the church Christ started. That was quite amazing in the realization of the Catholic history of the time. Yet perhaps understandable to those impressed by prodigious power, by pageantry, by prestige, and spectacular ceremonial rites. In addition, there was terror involved with any opposition to Catholicism, to Catholicism's pope.

The popes and the Catholic Church would sink into what Halley would call the darkest period of the papacy. This period was from 870 to 1050 and featured unimaginable horrors and immorality. This pathetic period of Catholicism can be studied in many historical texts, and there is general agreement. Catholicism seldom alludes to the horror of this period but does not dispute its existence. Finally, Pope John Paul II did formally apologize for much of the terror. I disagree with Halley as the following centuries were only somewhat less devastating and, in fact, in different ways, this "terror" has carried forth to the present time.

One of the genuinely devastating rules of Catholicism that has precipitated endless agony for so many Catholics and Catholic families has been to disallow their clergy from marrying. At the urging of Popes and councils, monastic austerity was gradually forced upon the clergy as a whole. Pope Benedict VIII, in 1018 formally forbade priestly marriages; the prohibition was solemnly extended by the First Lateran Council of 1123. God is clear about prohibiting marriage (1 Timothy 4:1-4) as a sign of departing the faith. Catholicism's character consistently opposes the will of God. It should awaken Catholics to realize God requires elders and deacons to be the husband of one wife, but Catholicism forbids their clergy from marrying. It is not an exaggeration to say Catholicism, in everything, opposes the will of God.

Pope Gregory VII (1073-1085) was determined to address the two primary sins of the clergy, namely immorality and Simony (the purchase of church office), which was the standard way to become priests and bishops. Those titles could lead to a life of comfort and security.

Urban II (1088-1099) declares the first Crusade, bringing more prestige to the Catholic Church. Catholicism was recognized as representative of Christianity in the eleventh century, and there was no other "visible" representative of Christ's church. Innocent III (1198–1216) was called the most powerful of all the popes and claimed to be the "Vicar of Christ," the "Vicar of God," the "supreme Sovereign over the church and the world." His powers included the rule over the Kings of Germany, France, England, and practically all the monarchs of Europe. The Byzantine Empire was also under his control. He ordered two Crusades.

The important things to realize are Pope Innocent III's religious decrees, and they include transubstantiation, confirmed the auricular confession, that the popes can never in any way depart from the Catholic faith, papal infallibility, and he forbade the reading of the Bible in vernacular. His list of atrocities depicts his arrogance. He condemned the Magna Carta, ordered the extermination of heretics, and instituted the inquisition. He ordered the massacre of the Albigenses. The Catholic version of Innocent III is quite a bit tamer, and in one case, despite the atrocities, he is the "true defender of the faith." Catholicism at this time is so far from the truth that they believe Christianity is something to be forced on people. Opposition from anyone denotes them as heretics and thus requires their torture and frequently their extermination. This is precisely why God requires perfect adherence to the scriptures, no changes. The fourteenth, fifteenth, sixteenth, and seventeenth centuries are very similar, with the Catholic Church continuing to be incredibly arrogant and immoral. There are various battles over papal sovereignty with nations under their control, and finally, nations begin to resist. The sixteenth-century brought the Protestant movement, and Catholics intensified the inquisition and brought in the Jesuits led by Ignatius Loyola. He supplies Inquisitional leadership and provides the pope with absolute and unconditional obedience. Luther's break with Catholicism (1517) was for many reasons, including the church hierarchy's great immorality. However, the thing that finally got Luther to act was the well-known indulgences that people could purchase to help their loved ones out of purgatory. This particular push of indulgences offered an irresistible "get out of purgatory free card" as the purchaser's coins could be heard clanging in the bottom of the container, their loved ones would be rising out of purgatory. It was all to build the church of Saint Peter in Rome, today it is known as St. Peters Basilica. St. Peter's Basilica was begun by Pope Julius II in 1506 and completed in 1615 under Paul V.

Catholicism came out of the pack of competitors in the early centuries and was solidified as the dominant powerhouse of Christianity during the early seventh century. Catholicism is a very different church than defined by the scriptures. Historically this period from the seventh century forward was one of tremendous growth for Catholicism. Roughly from the seventh thru the seventeenth century was a time of establishing a feared presence. Indeed it was a very long period of Catholic domination. It was a time of forced participation full of threats, and the place of safety was being Catholic and not causing any trouble. There is no connection between the Catholic Church and the church Jesus built and continues to build. Of course, near the end of this period, the Reformation represented the first real challenge to Catholic dominance. Christianity now has another home called Protestantism and a welcome change from the tyranny of Catholicism. Unfortunately, Protestant doctrines were also opposed to the scriptures and primarily due to their private interpretations. Sadly, they also kept much of the Catholic mannerisms, but the gospel message was also lost to them most regrettably.

Note: The Crusades occurred from 1095 to 1291 and involved eight different campaigns. The reasons are complex but involve religious, political, social, and economic motivations. Participants also had personal motivation as the papacy granted a remission of sins in the 12th century – which will eventually be formulated as the plenary indulgence (a complete remission of punishment). Robert of Clari [a knight from Picardy] talks about the Fourth Crusade, saying people joined because the crusade indulgence was so great. Using the consensus of many who studied the crusades, the number of persons killed was about 5-6 million. The Crusades are just one of the many schemes of the hierarchy of Catholicism "flexing their muscles." Incredibly, this godless institution of Catholicism has the audacity to motivate the crusades' armies with an offer of forgiveness of sins as though they possessed such capability. The following are good references for the crusades:

https://www.historyextra.com/period/medieval/crusades-causes-history-when-how-many-were-there-death-toll/

https://courses.lumenlearning.com/boundless-worldhistory/chapter/the-crusades/

2.6 Second period of historical Catholicism
(eighteenth century thru the mid-twentieth century)

As we move into the eighteenth century, there is more of the same. There seems to be less violence but no lack of proclaiming the Catholic pope as the sovereign over all of Christianity. Pope Pius VII (1800 -1820) issued a Bull against Bible societies. In these times, Catholicism had a great fear of the Bible falling into the hands of the ordinary man. Before the end of the twentieth century, there will be acceptance of and even promotion of Bible use. The Catholic hierarchy had no choice but to allow bible use due to its widespread availability. Fortunately, the timing was good as Catholic apologists devised good arguments for most apparent problems.

Pius IX (1846–1878) was responsible for an incredibly long list of declarations. Catholicism's loss of control over nations in terms of having those nations exterminate their heretics required a change in direction. We can see this in Pius IX's declarations such as the right to suppress heresy by force, condemned the separation of church and state, commanded Catholics to obey the Head of the church rather than civil rulers, denounced liberty of conscience, denounced freedom of speech, declared that Protestantism is no form of the Christian religion. Pius IX also said, "Christ has dictated every dogma of the Roman Catholic Church through His Viceregents on earth."

Centuries passed, and the majestic church building of Rome named St. Peter's Basilica was completed in 1615. Indeed, the Catholic Churches worldwide are elegant, monstrous in size, palatial, and bastions of art with the richest construction. This was not the church of the first century. The Protestants followed Catholicism in the physical majesty of their structures, yet Paul was very specific in Acts 17.

Acts 17:24-27

24 "God, who made the world and everything in it, since He is Lord of heaven and earth, does not dwell in temples made with hands.

25 Nor is He worshiped with men's hands, as though He needed anything, since He gives to all life, breath, and all things.

26 And He has made from one blood every nation of men to dwell on all the face of the earth, and has determined their preappointed times and the boundaries of their dwellings,

27 so that they should seek the Lord, in the hope that they might grope for Him and find Him, though He is not far from each one of us;

God does not dwell in temples made by man. So why do these churches have these ornate buildings, elaborate ceremonies? Why do humankind's worship ideas fill the Christian landscape when the only thing essential to worship is obedience – God's way?

Catholicism has proved itself to be all about ignoring the scriptures. They claim to accept the scriptures but never consider that adding to and subtracting from them rejects the scriptures. It is hard to get to the truth regarding the origins of the Catholic church – historically speaking. The conclusion provided in this book is that Catholicism slowly evolved from as early as the first century as the thing Jesus warned of in Matthew 7:15, "Beware of false prophets, who come to you in sheep's clothing, but inwardly they are ravenous wolves." Then Paul, when he was writing the letter to the Galatians says, "I marvel that you are turning away so soon from Him who called you in the grace of Christ, to a different gospel, which is not another; but there are some who trouble you and want to pervert the gospel of Christ." **So the falling away was occurring even during the time the Holy Spirit was inspiring the scriptures.** The warnings are to God's children, those "in Christ" in the various local churches. The warning below is from Paul to Timothy.

2 Timothy 4:3-5

3 For the time will come when they will not endure sound doctrine, but according to their own desires, because they have itching ears, they will heap up for themselves teachers;
4 and they will turn their ears away from the truth, and be turned aside to fables.
5 But you be watchful in all things, endure afflictions, do the work of an evangelist, fulfill your ministry.

Then there is a warning which refers to a later but undefined time, and it is also to Timothy from Paul.

1 Timothy 4:1-4

1 Now the Spirit expressly says that in latter times some will depart from the faith, giving heed to deceiving spirits and doctrines of demons,
2 speaking lies in hypocrisy, having their own conscience seared with a hot iron,
3 forbidding to marry, and commanding to abstain from foods which God created to be received with thanksgiving by those who believe and know the truth.
4 For every creature of God is good, and nothing is to be refused if it is received with thanksgiving;

Over history, many have said these verses refer to the Catholic Church, and that cannot be proven, although each of the characteristics is Catholic-like. The Catholic doctrine of *mental reservation* fits "speaking lies in hypocrisy" as a means to allow lying to protect their teachings. However, speculation is not fact, and these characteristics are examples of things that would indicate those who departed from the faith. The church that Jesus was building beginning in Acts 2 and defined by inspiration of the Holy Spirit was disappearing. Eventually, what appeared to be Christianity was no longer representative of the doctrine of Christ and would by the early seventh century, become the Roman Catholic Church.

Nonetheless, even though there were few and with an unimportant appearance, the truth and those "in Christ" would continue till the present time. God will get the best of humankind, albeit their countenance in human terms is not impressive. It is like God told Samuel concerning Jesse's oldest sons, "Do not look at his appearance or his physical stature, because I have refused him. For the LORD does not see as man sees; for man looks at the outward appearance, but the LORD looks at the heart." In these verses of 1 Samuel 16, God rejected the seven eldest sons of Jesse, and the youngest and in stature, David, would be selected. In a similar sense, the church Jesus built is very much different than how men see God and the church and humanity. God's church is spiritual and perfect in every way, and the relationship is very personal since each is "in Christ." The church was never intended to be a physical church as such a place could never offer salvation, and indeed the Catholic Church is a massive abomination to God, thwarting the purpose of God

Note: Chapter 13 continues to clarify the origin of the Catholic Church.

Sorting through these turbulent centuries (eighteenth century thru the mid-twentieth century)

Catholicism is desperate to verify its teachings and make them believable. It is interesting, albeit pathetic, how Catholicism uses these early church fathers and their writings and practices to validate what the scriptures do not validate.

In the end, we need to fall back on faith. That is for those that understand faith. That is, **faith only comes from the word of God**. Saying this more directly, we are relying on the word of God to direct us. We can rest in confidence that our sovereign and powerful God not only inspired the biblical writers but has also providentially overseen its preservation in such a way that the Bible we have today is reliable. It is nothing less than the infallible, inerrant word of God. What Isaiah said 2700 years ago will always ring true: *The grass withers, the flower fades, but the word of our God will stand forever,* Isaiah 40.8. Of course, God makes it clear in the New Testament that "Heaven and earth will pass away, but My words will by no means pass away."

More on Catholicism's second period (slowly moving away from the Catholic terror)

In this period, Catholicism transitioned from being a "world power threatening tyrant" to simply **emphasizing** and promoting Catholicism as the only road to heaven. This was, of course, something they always did, but now they needed to be more sophisticated as their power over nations was deteriorating. They had lost their ability to seek out and torture and murder heretics. The Catholic message was that you must be a Catholic to go to heaven. This period would see a lessening of much of the previous terror, apologists would be more prominent, miracles would be central in their story, emphasis on the Eucharist, and Marian doctrine would be used to maintain their power over people. Catholicism emphasizes the Eucharist as that which makes them unique. Unfortunately, their "Real Presence" evidence is non-existent and in opposition to the scriptures.

Nonetheless, they maintain control over their "faithful." Their members are **faithful to the Catholic Church** but, in truth, naïve. Except in the poorest and least educated countries, they consistently lose membership. Although not so obvious, the major stumbling block of Catholicism during the early part of this period (18th century) was America coming into existence as a Protestant nation. Catholicism was very much feared due to their historical rule over nations, and from the beginning of America, Catholics were very limited in public matters. That would gradually be of less concern in the early nineteenth century. By the beginning of Catholicism's third period, this American anti-Catholic sentiment had almost totally disappeared. They even elected a Catholic president.

This second period (as mentioned) was approximately from the **eighteenth century to the mid-twentieth century**. This is a comparatively short time contrasted to the first period. Although much of the early terror regarding heretics, as seen in approved torture and murder, was in decline. The sixteenth-century threat from Protestantism reignited the treachery. Groups such as the Anabaptists, Huguenots, Waldensians, and **Albigenses** were examples of terrible savage persecution. Much of the Catholic treachery against Protestants, Anabaptists, Huguenots, Waldensians, and **Albigenses** occurred, and it seems finally ended in this second historical period of Catholicism.

The Catholic Church called three church councils mentioned below from the sixteenth to mid-twentieth century.

> ➤ **FIFTH LATERAN COUNCIL**
> **Years:** 1512-1517
>
> **Summary:** The Fifth Lateran Council sat from 1512 to 1517 under Popes Julius II and Leo X, with the emperor being Maximilian I. Fifteen cardinals and about eighty archbishops and bishops took part in the council. Its decrees are chiefly disciplinary. A new crusade against the Turks was also planned, but came to naught, owing to the religious upheaval in Germany caused by Luther.
>
> The details of this council can be found at:

https://www.papalencyclicals.net/councils/ecum18.htm

> ➤ **XIX. COUNCIL OF TRENT**
> **Years:** 1545-1563
>
> **Summary:** The Council of Trent lasted eighteen years (1545-1563) under five popes: Paul III, Julius III, Marcellus II, Paul IV, and Pius IV, and under the Emperors Charles V and Ferdinand. There were present five cardinal legates of the Holy See, three patriarchs, 33 archbishops, 235 bishops, seven abbots, seven generals of monastic orders, and 160 doctors of divinity. It was convoked to examine and condemn the errors promulgated by Luther and other Reformers and to reform the discipline of the Church. Of all councils, it lasted longest, issued the largest number of dogmatic and reformatory decrees, and produced the most beneficial results – for Catholicism.
>
> The details of this council can be found at:
> https://www.papalencyclicals.net/councils/trent.htm

> ➤ **XX. FIRST VATICAN COUNCIL**
> **Years:** 1869-1870

Summary: The Vatican Council was summoned by Pius IX. It met 8 December 1869 and lasted till 18 July 1870, when it was adjourned; it is still (in 1908) unfinished. There were present six archbishop-princes, 49 cardinals, 11 patriarchs, 680 archbishops and bishops, 28 abbots, 29 generals of orders, in all 803. Besides important canons relating to the Faith and the constitution of the Church, the council decreed the infallibility of the pope when speaking *ex-cathedra*, i.e., when as shepherd and teacher of all Christians, he defines a doctrine concerning faith or morals to be held by the whole Church.

The details of this council can be found at:

https://www.papalencyclicals.net/councils/ecum20.htm

Note: For your reference, the link below identifies the 21 councils of the church.

https://www.newadvent.org/library/almanac_14388a.htm

The church councils were highly revered events involved in deciding the most serious church matters. The first eight church councils were called by the Roman emperors consistent with the practice began by Constantine. They involved both the Eastern and Western Christian churches until the great schism in 1054. The Catholic popes called the remaining 13 councils. Catholicism justifies the whole process by claiming the councils have some sort of divine oversight. All you have to do is to look at the outcomes from these councils and be stupefied. Why is that? The topics under study and results can be summarized as nonsense and always in opposition to the scriptures. They provide an ever-changing doctrine and with emphasis on maintaining Catholic authority. The Catholic Church councils are indeed massive in the time spent, the subjects covered, the outcomes, and even then, they create more confusion. You might try to read the results of these councils. They are colossal and incredibly confusing, and the wanderings of men trying to make sense of something that is not reasonable – namely Catholicism. **The church that Jesus started is simple. There is the gospel message and the required obedience. His church is spiritual and directed by the understandable word of God as the only rule.** If there is something more obnoxious to God than these councils, then what could it be. The words contained in the encyclical letters that document each of the councils are incredibly blasphemous. The statements coming from these councils is self-adoration of all things Catholic. In case you doubt the Catholic Church, they will declare you are anathema. Here is one of the thousands of statements honoring themselves and condemning everyone who dares object to the Catholic authenticity. The following is from the First Vatican council 1869-1870 (Chapter 2 / Session four, item 5):

*"Therefore, if anyone says that it is not by the institution of Christ the lord himself (that is to say, by divine law) that blessed Peter should have perpetual successors in the primacy over the whole church; or that the Roman pontiff is not the successor of blessed Peter in this primacy: let him be **anathema**."*

Anathema definition:

- something or someone that one vehemently dislikes

- a formal curse by a pope or a council of the Church, excommunicating a person or denouncing a doctrine

For convenience, the word used above, excommunication, should also be defined.

Excommunication is the harshest punishment (in modern times) available to the Roman Catholic Church and essentially means that their community must shun the excommunicated person, and unless they "clean up their act," they will probably be going to hell.

Is there a better way to attack your enemies than to threaten them by using the words anathema and excommunication? For Catholicism, it is either "their way or the highway." Besides the hundreds of things wrong with Catholicism, the attitude of their clergy is appalling and very different from the attitude demanded by the scriptures. Most apparent from the scriptures is the necessity of people making a free will choice – not forced – not from intimidation. This is God's design. The gospel is designed to appeal to those with a good heart, with a love of the truth. The gospel is preached, and if not accepted, then the teacher moves on. There is no animosity, no threats. Look at the requisite character of one who is "in Christ."

Galatians 5:22-25

22 But the fruit of the Spirit is love, joy, peace, longsuffering, kindness, goodness, faithfulness,
23 gentleness, self-control. Against such there is no law.
24 And those who are Christ's have crucified the flesh with its passions and desires.
25 If we live in the Spirit, let us also walk in the Spirit.

Is this the attitude you find in Catholicism? Does this mean these people of leadership bringing such heartlessness, such cruelty, and making the rules for God are not Christian? Their attitudes are supporting factors why they are not Christian but ultimately it is because they never obeyed the gospel. They never obeyed the gospel because they changed the message from God. Their pathetic attitudes represent the things that keep them from obeying the gospel, since in pride, they have a better way.

The Catholic councils make a shambles of the truth and thus condemn many to a terrible fate. They appear like those of authority, as great persons of wisdom, and their ceremonial processes can be intimidating. Catholic leadership is filled with evil in their opposition to the doctrine of Christ, resulting in the destruction of souls. The most fundamental aspect of what God has done in Christ, results in the gospel message. It defines how reconciliation occurs, how souls receive forgiveness of sins. It is the truth that is absent from Catholicism.

2.7 Catholicism's third historical period (modern Catholicism, disguising the evil)

The third period of Catholicism is from the **mid-twentieth century, from about 1950 until the end of time**. This period is more sophisticated and emphasizes Bible use. The Bible was once on the INDEX of books that Catholics should not read. Modern Catholicism tries to deny this opposition to reading the Bible and to penalties for possessing a Bible. However, there was strong opposition to "Bible use" by Catholics in the first two periods of Catholic history but progressively less so entering the third period. A good record of this opposition can be found at these links:

http://www.aloha.net/~mikesch/banned.htm

http://galileo.rice.edu/chr/congregation.html

These documents show the efforts of popes, church councils, and other Catholic hierarchies to control access to the scriptures. The Catholic Index of books (1564 to 1948, a total of twenty editions) contained in the earliest editions various restrictions regarding certain Bibles either on the list or in some way discussed regarding certain dangers of entering the scriptures without a guide – that is without the Catholic Church.

We had previously mentioned the action of Innocent III (1198–1216) in forbidding the reading of the Bible in vernacular, and Pius VII (1800 -1820) issued a Bull against Bible societies. The consideration here is why there was opposition to the scriptures being in the hands of the common person. Catholics argue that people need a guide and the Catholic Church is the guide. The truth is the scriptures reject the doctrines of Catholicism, and they know this, and consequently, their effort to keep the scriptures from the people makes Catholicism exceedingly evil.

Note: For reference, vernacular is the language or dialect spoken by ordinary people in a particular country or region.

Indeed there has been an evolution from Catholics disallowing their members to have the Bible to now encouraging the reading of the Bible. Still, there would be compelling instructions in the Catholic Bibles, warnings regarding interpretation different from the Catholic Church.

Reading a small portion from a Catholic Bible (Douay), the Encyclical Letter of Pope Leo XIII (pope from 1878 to 1903) on the Study of Holy Scripture:

"Wherefore it must be recognized that the sacred writings are wrapt in certain religious obscurity, and that no one can enter into their interior without a guide and most of all that they may understand that God has delivered the Holy Scriptures to the Church, and that in reading and making use of His Word, they must follow the Church as their guide and their teacher." Also continuing, "in things of faith and morals, belonging to the building up of Christian doctrine, that is to be considered the true sense of Holy Scripture which has been held and is held by our Holy Mother the Church whose place it is to judge of the true sense and interpretation of the Scriptures: and **therefore that it is permitted to no one to interpret Holy Scripture against such sense or also against the unanimous agreement of the Fathers.**"

Bible study is encouraged in more modern times, and Catholic Bibles contain an imprimatur or canonical rescript that approves that particular Bible. This amounts to a guarantee that there are no anti-Catholic doctrines in this Bible. Also, a Catholic Bible will have notes and annotations to help you understand the text. These notes may provide alternate readings of unclear passages, help in understanding "plays on words" that depend on knowing the original language, and brief explanations of how the Catholic Church has interpreted the passage.

It is doubtful that the Catholic hierarchy considers their actions that place instructions in their Bibles as evil. Specifically, they define how the Bible is to be used, and the consequences of misuse, and of course, providing the Catholic Church accepted interpretation. These things are private interpretations of God's word and **not God's word**. Catholicism knows they cannot allow Catholics to come to their own understanding of God's word since it would often lead to a very non-Catholic conclusion. There is absolutely nothing in support of Catholicism in the Bible.

Additionally, Catholicism is now **more openly aggressive** in using the early church fathers to justify their practices. This can be in the form of including references to the early church fathers and the mention of church councils in various preaching/teaching opportunities. They are building a familiarity with the "early church fathers and church councils" that was seldom discussed with their laity in previous decades. Catholicism had no choice in this change of direction since Catholics were increasingly using the scriptures, and they would quickly realize the lack of authority and opposition for their practices. There is a giant void, an impossibility of justifying anything Catholic from the scriptures. In addition to their non-biblical justifications, they needed to twist the scriptures more convincingly. The one surprising means they devised was to promote the use of the scriptures more aggressively. This gives the appearance of their teachings being solidly aligned with the Bible. Now a Catholic sees the Bible being quoted much more frequently. This frequent use of the Bible is not only by their clergy but has become common among their laity. The twisting of the scriptures is accomplished by having more people learn and speak the Catholic private interpretations.

Their teaching techniques are more powerful, more refined in gaining support among Catholics and making converts. Interestingly, when they want to bring authority to their teachings, they always wander back to the scriptures. The goal is to keep Catholics believing that the authority in religion is both the scriptures and the Catholic Church. Their methodology is incredibly convoluted and complicated. They effectively overwhelm people such that they do not understand what is being taught. An example of this confusion can be seen in Chapter 5 of this book, "God's simplicity versus Catholic complexity." A subject that should be so simple because it is so important, namely salvation, is badly distorted. The process of salvation in the scriptures is simple, makes perfect sense, and is entirely different than what Catholicism teaches. The problem with the deceit is that their teachings are based on a poor foundation. That is, based on direct opposition to Bible principles. Catholicism in this last historical period more boldly emphasizes early church father's tradition, apostolic succession and their Magisterium plus of course, their equivalency with the scriptures and even in some cases their superiority. This latter capability is due to their claimed ability to explain the scriptures accurately.

Note: It might seem impossible for a Catholic to overcome their indoctrination, and yet it is easily done in the pages of this book, for the reason that the truth is infinitely more potent than Catholic deceit.

During this last historical period, the Catholic populations have fallen in regions where people are more highly educated. However, there is growth in regions where there is less questioning. The physical and mental cruelty used in the first period combined with their world domination was most effective in growth. Islam has never relinquished its physical and mental control over people and consequently consistently demonstrates growth since its beginning. In addition to the Catholic acceptance of and promoted study of the Bible, there has been an unexpected source of support. Namely, the conversion of various Protestants to Catholicism. Their conversion has NOT been due to some campaign seeking out Protestants to become Catholics. Instead, these Protestants (as well as persons from other religions or even atheists) find problems with their current beliefs and start "looking around." One of the characteristics they seek is an ancient religion, and for Christianity, that would seem to be the Catholic Church since they claim a connection back to Peter, their first pope. Catholicism makes the unabashed claim as the only answer for heaven. They have an outward appearance of magnificence, of pomp, of pageantry, of a vast number of devotees, and what appears to be a long and fixed means to succeed. In any case, although Catholics and potential Catholics see problems, there is an attractiveness, a mystery. For many Catholic converts with a Protestant background, it includes life in the Protestant ministry. This phenomenon, with its appearance in this last period of Catholicism, is worthy of study. One thing that was noted early in this document was that these converts seemed more dismayed by their discovery of the many errors in the Protestant doctrines than in any acceptance of Catholicism. Catholicism had now become an option and required its own investigation. Those becoming Catholic traveled that investigative path and found it reasonable. An entire chapter has been devoted to addressing this topic – Chapter 6, "Protestants converting to Catholicism." It is a worthwhile study since it demonstrates how capable Protestants with excellent scriptural knowledge can reach the "Catholic conclusion." To be fair in the **analysis** (Protestant to Catholic), I selected two of the most celebrated Protestant converts in terms of their skills and in terms of their critical investigation of Catholicism. Their thinking is challenged in the videos they produced to explain their conversions.

In addition to this movement of people from Protestantism, there is another movement among Catholics, specifically involving their laity and often includes their clergy. It is a modern social model of aggressive teaching. These self-styled Catholic apologists use various social media, particularly transmissions using (often live) television/radio and frequently in a question/answer format. There must be dozens of these "programs." It is an excellent way to develop a more dedicated laity. Catholics know people's questions, and the answers have been designed for about every typical question/objection. This can be an effective tool for Catholicism to evangelize and fulfill their "new evangelism" goals.

Note: There is again something undeniable about Catholicism in this last period, and it is a different type of deceit and in keeping with modern Catholicism appearing so innocent. The use of Catholic laity in the apologetic movement seems like a good thing. They have a new breed of laity and clergy apologist warriors for the Catholic faith. However, it is not a good thing, since in effect, all they do is provide excuses for their doctrines, justifications for Catholicism's historical problems. Like many Catholics before them, they twist the scriptures to continue the deceit. They defend the Catholic Church and often learn how to do that for the first time. **Those in the Lord's church** *are not typically acting as apologists, although they could be on occasion. The gospel message is simple and requires little or no defense. Their mission is simple, and it is evangelism, the teaching of the gospel message. The distinction between the gospel preacher and the Catholic apologist is staggering if properly understood. Catholics live in defending the complicated, the non-scriptural, the soul-destroying distraction of Catholicism. I am reasonably sure they believe they are doing the right thing. The right thing for those "in Christ" is to preach the word, and that can involve providing a defense from time to time, but it is not a life-work of defense primarily due to its simplicity and the perfect agreement with all scripture. Catholicism is a life-work of defense because of its weaknesses.*

One purpose of this book is to expose the error in all three periods of Catholicism. Essentially that means thoroughly exposing Catholicism, but to some extent being able to associate the error with a certain period of Catholicism, might help. Certainly, overcoming Catholicism in this final period is substantially different than in the previous two periods. The truth about Catholicism is easily exposed, but do people care when they live in such a casual religious world? The Catholic **experience** seems to be alright, **simple in living it**, and not bothersome. Why would anyone move from such a comfortable existence? The "word simple" refers to how the Catholic life might be lived and not the complicated and unverifiable doctrine that is Catholicism. Those who want the truth about life and are deeply concerned about their eternity, will seek God and truth and can succeed.

2.8 Summary of the three historical periods of Catholicism

An unfortunate but realistic possibility is that there were few Christians from the first century onward and perhaps none in the region of Rome as the fourth century approached. We are talking about only having a few who were truly "in Christ." The falling away in the region of Rome essentially eliminated Christianity at the time of the Edict of Milan. The freedom of that Edict was for all religious beliefs but primary gave Christians relief and worth. However, it was for a different Christianity (really not Christianity). Christianity was becoming very pagan and was on the road to becoming the complete opposite of the truth. If one respects God, they respect God's word and will not water down the truth. Christians are not Christian by calling themselves Christian. Thus it is much more than a suggestion that there may have been few Christians in the early church, especially as we approached the fourth century in the region of Rome. Do you respect Matthew 7:21 and 1 John 1:9? If you do, you understand the seriousness of doing the will of God, of obeying the gospel and living by the doctrine of Christ.

Matthew 7:21

21 Not everyone who says to Me, 'Lord, Lord,' shall enter the kingdom of heaven, but he who does the will of My Father in heaven.

2 John 1:9

9 Whoever transgresses and does not abide in the doctrine of Christ does not have God. He who abides in the doctrine of Christ has both the Father and the Son.

After the Edict of Milan, "Christianity" would continue to **get even worse** as there was an emphasis on having a singular head over all of what was called "Christianity." People were no longer obeying the gospel but especially in Rome, as they incorporated more pagan practices. Even Constantine was confused about becoming a Christian and put off his baptism until his death bed and was not immersed. As "Christians" embraced their new freedom, they were open to accepting pagan practices. There was something wrong, and it was a very gradual decay of the local church and the growing emphasis to accept an earthly head. There was no apparent reluctance to accept the council called by Constantine, and the local church bishops attended. All these things and the writings of the early church fathers led to the conclusion that Christianity was different. A different Christianity is not Christianity. Many before the fourth century were "in Christ" and suffered great persecution and death at the hands of the Romans. The **"getting worse"** part would involve the total rejection of the word of God and nothing was more damaging than the growing primacy of the bishops of Rome, leading eventually to the Catholic popes and their rule. This was not the organization of the church designed by God and seen in the apostle's teaching led by the Holy Spirit. Instead of the early church (and early church fathers) being a source that consistently followed the scriptures, it was a place of gradually adding to and taking away from the word of God. Thus this early church period was serving to produce the falling away.

I always must mention something positive about the early fathers of the church, and it was their understanding that **they were not writing by inspiration**. Also, they were in many cases involved in making copies of the scriptures earlier penned during the time of inspiration. In fact, their contribution in this area was significant in having the word of God today. Even though some of these early church fathers were careless in their writings, they were careful in copying scripture. God works providentially to assure His truth will never pass away as it is essential to fulfilling His purpose.

These early fathers of the church recorded the different things the churches were doing, including correct things and things that were not. Some would occasionally include in their writing what **they thought** would be good things for the church, such as having a central leadership, and specifically, some favored a universal bishop over all the local churches. In **some** of their writings, there was the concept of the "Real Presence." None of these things were teachings from the scriptures but THEIR private interpretation of certain verses of scripture. It is likely that some of the early church fathers privately interpreted Matthew 16:13-19, John 6:53-56, Matthew 26:26-28, and 1 Corinthians 10:1-4, and many others. Where else would they get these ideas? The correct meaning of these verses is provided in this book and is exceedingly clear, exceedingly consistent with all scripture, and undeniable for anyone who loves of the truth.

Indeed, there was a gradual falling away and always because the one thing missing was the **respect for God's word** and thus for God. As a result of these many doctrinal innovations, the essential thing disappeared: the gospel message. During these early centuries, the Catholic Church was coming into existence and had effectively left behind the church belonging to Christ. The exact timing of this transition occurred when they left the doctrine of Christ.

After these early centuries (mainly after they had a recognized pope) came the true wrath of Catholicism as they moved to protect what they had wrought. The record of evil was beyond imagination and continues to this day but in ways less subtle than the tortures and murders but as seen in their sexual abuse by pedophile priests and particularly in their "executive" cover-ups that allowed the abuse to continue long after it should have seized. The thing carried throughout pre-Catholicism (error creeping in period) is the loss of the gospel message and in its place is something so confusing that people have no idea the truth is missing. Indeed, Catholicism consists of cunningly designed fables. In all three periods of Catholicism, there was evil with the root reason of creating something that brought power and prestige and then sustained that power. It should be clear that Catholicism is the result of the careless handling of the word of God and an associated disregard for its seriousness. God throughout time made it clear that His word was not to be changed, and this one critical thing was not on the mind of those early church fathers. If there were one thing they could have learned from the Old and New covenants, it would have been the sacred nature of God's word. Certainly, it was emphasized. However, this is where pride enters and when people think their way is better than God's. These are not the people God is seeking. The early church fathers did display an attitude of seriousness toward the word of

God inasmuch as they accurately copied the inspired writings. Yet, in idolatry, they honored their own thinking. They honored their private interpretations and those historically following the early church fathers (popes and associated hierarchy) justified Catholic doctrine based on those private interpretations.

We have this concise history of Catholicism, and it contains a good account of how Catholicism evolved. It points to something very different than the church Jesus was and continues to build. The disregard of scripture is highly obvious, and even from an overview of the history, there are good reasons to abhor Catholicism. What follows in this book uses the word of God to shut the door on any possibility of Catholicism having an association with God.

Note: The falling away began during the time of the inspiration (i.e., Galatians 1:6-9) and gained momentum in the early centuries as the early church fathers strayed from the scriptures. At some point, there would have been very few Christians. This would have been the result of corrupting the gospel message. This central and essential teaching was not being emphasized in the early church father's writings, and in its place were many of their private interpretations. **Unless there is truth, Jesus cannot add those obedient to His body** – *they will not know what to obey. The pattern that follows this abandonment of the gospel message would be the gradual creation of doctrines that opposed the word of God. Indeed, this was the beginning of what would become the Catholic Church. The doctrines of Catholicism practiced to this day originated from this period by very non-Christian persons. Although not necessarily intentional, the early church fathers distort, add to, or subtract from God's word. The outcome of this mess would be a pattern for salvation that defies logic, opposes the scriptures, and essentially assures every Catholic will fail in life.*

Another note: You can be assured that the historical separation between Christian and Catholic is properly affirmed because of the technique used. All other histories are problematic because they are constructed without the appreciation of God's word. There are many keys to properly making the historical separation between Christianity and Catholicism. A couple of examples may help. The church Jesus is building is, first, spiritual. There is no local church without those who are spiritual to be the essence, the members. The local church is designed to be independent of all other local bodies and has a God-defined organization. The local church has only **one** *guide*, *and it is the scriptures. The local church has only **one mission**, and it is spiritual. The local church consists of those "in Christ" and participates in worship, and that worship is mandatorily spiritual - in **spirit and truth**. Thus whenever you see a divergence from God-inspired directives for His church, you see something different than Christianity.*

Interestingly in Catholicism, there are obvious and significant deviations on every point just mentioned regarding God's definition of the church. We can mention them respectively for the items just cited. First, the members are spiritual, but in Catholicism, the church comes first and then the members. Furthermore, there is no way in Catholicism for a person to become spiritual. Since the local churches are independent and follow only the scriptures, there can be no central organization, no dominant head, i.e., no pope, no earthly rulemaking. The churches of the world are involved in many matters, many physical matters and this is seen in the early church and particularly in the early church councils. The "worship of the falling away" is divergent from what God authorized, much like Paul described how the Athenians worshipped. Namely, placing God in temples made with hands and being worshiped with men's hands, and this is the pattern seen early in the falling away. It was accelerated by the integration of "Christianity" with the religions of Rome and their temples and other pagan practices.

*The scriptures perfectly define the history of the first-century church, but they can also be used to demonstrate a divergence from that pattern in the future. As might be expected, when the rules come from humankind (deviation of scripture) instead of God, the church will look much different, completely different. Certainly, by the fourth century **the separation is clear** even without their pope and even without their name, Catholicism was being constructed. The church belonging to Christ would also exist, but the world would believe that Catholicism was Christianity. The world would hold that assessment from the seventh century until the sixteenth century when that perception would change with Protestantism. In the background since the first century, we have those relatively few, largely unknown, who held to the scriptures and the meaning God intended. These are "**in Christ**" and not designated by men/women into some human devised category (Catholic or Protestant) but very personally by the Lord (by their obedience) added to the spiritual body of Christ.*

82

2.9 The history of Christianity

This second chapter is called "The Historical Periods of **Catholicism.**" How would "The Historical Periods of **Christianity**" be any different? In the sense of world history, they would appear to be no different. The Christianity of the first century evolved into Catholicism by the early seventh century. Catholicism and its pope being formally recognized in the early seventh century and then in the early sixteenth century, there would be another "branch of Christianity" called Protestantism. Catholicism and Protestantism both continue to this day. It is fair to say that neither is Christianity. **So, where was Christianity, historically?** It was there in the first century and then continued, albeit somewhat obscure. It is the church that never changed the meaning of the scriptures, and in so doing, the Lord could continue to build His church. On the world stage, the history of Christianity is clear during the time of inspiration in the first century but then appears to be fragmented in the following early centuries. Once the doctrine of Christ is lost, "Christianity" disappears from the "world of historians." Christianity disappears because it is in hiding, rather powerless, and sought out for destruction. It is suggested that Christianity had vanished by the fourth century, if not sooner, particularly in the region of Rome. All the attention is on Rome, on the emperors, on some concessions being allowed for Christians. These significant matters are what interests history. This is where the action is, where the masses of "Christians" are living their lives. The falling away continues (Christianity is no longer present) as the errors "pile up." The next major milestone is the Catholic Church and its pope being recognized in the early seventh century. Catholicism expands to being a force involving the entire world. Still, historians do not understand Christianity has disappeared, or we might say it is insignificant compared to what is happening in the world of religion. History is willing to allow the Catholic Church to be Christianity, and thus the world accepts this, at least until Protestantism suggests differently in the early sixteenth century.

Of course, Christianity has its own history, albeit not in the widely acknowledged public record. Christianity survives the early persecutions of Rome and exists in various locations. The word of God would be carried forward in time by a few. These Christians throughout history would be the enemies of what the world thought was Christianity. Primarily that means the enemy of Catholicism. Catholicism's paranoid behavior has them "snuffing out" any doctrine that opposes the Catholic way.

I would not claim the Anabaptists (beginning 16th century), Huguenots (16th and 17th century), Waldensians (12th century), Albigenses (12th, 13th century) represented Christianity during their early years of existence. However, they did represent **something profoundly different than Catholicism**. They were exceedingly closer to the doctrine of Christ than Catholicism simply because they respected the word of God as the only authority. You can read about the terrible torture and murder of these groups. Catholic and Protestants were both responsible for Anabaptist cruelties and murders. Although these groups mentioned above were typically very docile, humble, and peace-loving, it was necessary for Catholicism to paint a picture that justified their actions. Sometimes the only history available is from the Catholic Church who would indicate the evil ways of these groups to gain acceptance for their treatment. To settle that matter, it is easy to observe who was the aggressor. These groups often purposely lived in remote villages and never sought trouble, but trouble came to them to destroy them. So, who do you think were the evil ones? The crimes of these groups were always the same; namely, they taught differently than the Catholic Church and did not accept the Catholic pope. Certainly, this is worthy of torture, of genocide.

The modern doctrines of these groups frequently changed, and it would be hard to catalog their doctrines over time but compared to Catholicism, they were very different, much more aligned with the word of God. During this time, perhaps some in these groups were Christian. Perhaps they were obeying the gospel and understood the church as God defined it via the Holy Spirit. Throughout time, there were likely those in obedience to God but seldom noteworthy in history. All these deviations from Catholicism were instrumental in producing a more public awareness of Christianity. In a general way, in the rejection of Catholicism, there were emerging people growing in the knowledge of God. This was a declared hope of John Wycliffe that every Christian would have access to the scriptures and not be forced to accept what a few men of Catholicism were teaching. Christianity can be seen in the questioning of Catholic doctrine. It is not particularly important to establish a name for these groups of Christians, for they can be known by their adherence to the word of God, to the doctrine of Christ. They are those added to the body of Christ, His spiritual church by the Lord Himself. There was something evident in this last age, and it is as God promised, "heaven and earth will pass away, but My words will not pass away."

The true history of Christianity is not known following the period of inspiration. That would not be surprising since Christians were being pursued, tortured, and murdered. The Waldensians and the Albigenses were among the first **historically recognized** groups in opposition to Catholic rule. The Anabaptists did not appear until the time of the Protestant reformation but were vehemently not Protestant. Finally, the Huguenots would be considered Protestants in their association with Calvin's teaching. These four groups all exhibited deep respect for the scriptures, and all were the object of the most severe torture and murder. The road back to first-century Christianity was a bloody one. The truth of Christianity came down through the ages thanks to the early century Christians and then to groups like the ones just mentioned. Certain persons withstood the Catholic Church, and their courage and ability to articulate the truth were undoubtedly powerful motivations for many. Two names that stand out are John Wycliffe (14th century) and John Huss (14th and 15th century). They strongly opposed Catholic doctrine. Wycliffe was a priest, an English theologian, and philosopher and considered a forerunner of the Protestant reformation. He is best known for translating the Bible into the common language, specifically the first English translation. He was particularly opposed to the Catholic doctrines of transubstantiation, confessing sins to a priest, celibacy, indulgences, the immorality of clerics, and their judgment by special ecclesiastical tribunals and not secular courts. His opposition was, of course, based on humankind not being authorized to make the rules for God and how Catholic doctrine was in opposition to the word of God. For instance, concerning his objection to private confessions, he would say that Jesus never authorized such, and the apostles never practiced such. Wycliffe's followers were persecuted, and some of them were burned at the stake. After his death, the Catholic Church had his writings burned, and they also dug up his body and burned it. Wycliffe's beliefs were aligned with the scriptures, and in various ways, he made this known. His position can be summarized as follows:

Wycliffe regarded the scriptures as the only reliable guide to the truth and maintained that all Christians should rely on the Bible rather than the unreliable and frequently self-serving teachings of popes and clerics. Wycliffe taught there was no scriptural justification for the papacy's existence and attacked the riches and power that popes and the Church as a whole had acquired.

A John Wycliffe quote demonstrates his fundamental emphasis on the scriptures.

"The gospel alone is sufficient to rule the lives of Christians everywhere, any additional rules made to govern men's conduct added nothing to the perfection already found in the Gospel of Jesus Christ."

The thing the Catholic Church most despised about John Wycliffe was his translation of the Bible into English. They needed to rid themselves of Wycliffe, and he was arrested for heresy and placed under house arrest. There were eighteen charges, church edicts brought against Wycliffe by the papacy. Wycliffe was so popular in England that the Catholic Church feared executing him. Wycliffe died suddenly of a stroke at 54 years old before the authorities could convict him of heresy. Wycliffe was on a path leading to the **restoration** of the first-century church. Unfortunately, his death, it seems, did not allow him to fully appreciate God's definition of the church. Luther, Calvin, and Wycliffe all missed the same thing, and it was the need to **totally reject the Catholic Church** and not try to reform it. However, Wycliffe was very close as he taught there was no scriptural justification for a pope, and Catholic doctrine by doctrine was dismissed on those same grounds. John Wycliffe was an extraordinary man living in a challenging time, being amid great evil. His insight precisely pinpointed the fundamental error of Catholicism as their disrespect for the word of God.

John Huss was a catholic priest who read the works of Wycliffe and aligned with them. He was declared a heretic for his views and his opposition to the Catholic Church. He was burned at the stake at 43 years of age. Interestingly, the Council of Constance (1414 to 1418) sentenced John Huss to be burned at the stake. It seems that now the Catholic Council could be directly associated with the murder of those who opposed the Catholic Church. Of course, the designation of "heretic" and their punishment was a daily chore of the Catholic hierarchy, but the Catholic Church council was directly responsible this time.

Historically, the church belonging to Christ that we call the Christian church, the one containing Christians, is solidly in view in the first century and has been solidly in view in modern times and documented since about the seventeenth century, perhaps much earlier. Once again, this dating of Christianity is not necessary or relevant. The principle of New Testament Christianity is historically rooted within the New Testament itself. The truth is that where the seed of the kingdom (the Word of God) is preached, and men and women obey it, there are Christians. Throughout this book, it is pointed out how Catholicism has corrupted the simplicity of the gospel message. It is no more difficult to understand than what happens when men make the rules for God. We are talking about how God's most basic rule has been rejected, namely, do not change His word.

Christianity was continually in existence since the first century relative to God's commitment that His words would by no means pass away. However, it was not apparent to the world due to its insignificance in appearance and number of adherents and how the Catholic Church undermined every aspect of anything, not Catholic. Thanks to the many who sacrificed (sometimes their lives) in the early centuries and to those over history who were faithful to the word of God, Christianity was kept alive. We mentioned certain groups who **may not have** obeyed the gospel message but suffered in their dedication to God's word and were an important part of Christianity visibly returning, as historically visible. These groups were mentioned as the Anabaptists, Huguenots, Waldensians, Albigenses, and perhaps their notoriety was inadvertently the result of their extreme persecution by Catholicism. Of course, Protestantism was the "sore thumb" that ended the dominance of Catholicism as the only means to Christianity. At 10,000 feet Catholicism and Protestantism have primarily appeared as Christianity to the world. **Yet, neither represent Christianity**. Christianity is represented by the first-century church Jesus built and continues to build, that is, those obeying the gospel message.

In the future, as a result of Wycliffe, Huss, and even Luther and Calvin, some would gain an awareness of the most fundamental of errors of Catholicism. The obvious solution was to **restore** the church of the scriptures. People believed they needed to be told what to do, but that was never God's way. Wycliffe correctly realized God's word needed to be in the hands of every person. He may have been encouraged in reaching that conclusion after seeing the outcome of men, groups of men, committees devising selfish private interpretations of the scriptures. Men had no right or ability to change God's meaning, but there was a need to respect God's sovereignty in the scriptures. The Lord's church exists today since the gospel message is available, and thus the Lord can add the obedient to His spiritual body, the church.

Chapter 3
Catholic folly

Folly may seem to be the wrong word, but it fits, albeit possibly being offensive. It indicates the whole of Catholicism is fraudulent, which means it is not the way to heaven. If you can read this book with a reasonably open mind seeking the truth, that will also be your conclusion. The larger question will be how did all this (Catholicism) happen. People question WHY regarding the various evils currently in the world and in the world past. To a reasonable and somewhat moral person, evil is pathetic. Wars are pathetic, people exhibiting cruelty are pathetic, selfishness is pathetic, greed is pathetic, envy is pathetic, lying is pathetic, immorality is pathetic, and the list of disturbing observances is very long. Folly seems like a kind word as no word accurately describes misleading people to the destruction of their souls. We will show the recklessness of Catholicism in their doctrines, and the bottom line is that precisely zero Catholics will succeed in life. Each component of what we discuss is sufficient to bring about the demise of Catholicism. Altogether, the Catholic Church is overwhelmingly erroneous in every way – enough to take your breath away. This chapter is devoted to exposing Catholic doctrine as false. Other portions of this book involve more detailed discussions of Catholic principles that dismantle the basics of Catholic teaching. This chapter covers four topics discussed from the perspective of the scriptures versus a Catholic perspective.

3.1 Sin

Sin is the God-designed criteria to allow Him to provide perfect justice. Sin is defined as the transgression of God's law. Sin is always associated with disobedience, and salvation is always associated with obedience. The Catholic Church determined to create a sin called *original sin* and place it on every person at birth. Of course, they are saying this is something God did. However, there is no such indication in scripture, and as you understand God as the perfect absence of evil, this would be impossible. God would have to transmit something to each person that is 100% alien to Him, namely something evil. This is the worst kind of blasphemy but is consistent with something seen in the doctrines of humankind. Namely, finding some way to blame God. This make-believe sin then leads to a variety of other inventions beginning with infant baptism and many others. I have covered this subject of Catholicism's original sin on the following web page:

(https://catholicsquestion.com/the-fall-of-catholicism-and-protestantism-in-one-simple-lesson/).

This post includes the Protestant error of "inherited depravity."

So, Catholicism is off to a bad start in the area of sin. Folly or nonsense or deception or gaining power over people are the realities of original sin. Sadly, all of those things are involved and impact the lives of Catholics. I certainly do not know why the original sin doctrine was developed, but it is certain it did not come from God and opposes God's way. We will see that there is God's way, and there is the way of humankind. You will, in all matters, align with one or the other by your choices. If you align with neither, then your association will be with humankind.

Sin is a subject where the scriptures provide great clarity, including how to have sin forgiven. The gospel message, specifically the preaching of the gospel message, contains the solution to sin.

1 Corinthians 1:21

21 For since, in the wisdom of God, the world through wisdom did not know God, it pleased God through the foolishness of the message preached to save those who believe.

Unfortunately, the Catholic Church does not, really cannot recognize this most fundamental concept of the scriptures. The gospel message conflicts with all their teachings on salvation and consequently will result in the eternal failure of every Catholic. Catholicism twists the scriptures, and they have to do this in their support of many false doctrines. Original sin seems in its creation to "**use up**" the doctrine of baptism. They baptize babies to bring them into the Catholic Church. They say this baptism is to erase original sin but more accurately erase the sin they imagined called original. Actually, they sprinkle babies with water. The next new doctrine is a confirmation of these baptized babies when they are somewhat older. Thus Catholic Confirmation represents a commitment for each baptized child and hence their first genuine involvement in Catholicism. They had zero say in their infant baptism. The Confirmation is done with essentially little or no understanding except for the indoctrination they have been receiving. Catholicism has not covered the sins people **commit**, and they have already played their "baptism card." Looking to the Old Testament, there were priests, and their role involved sin and its forgiveness. The New Testament church has no priests, but that is not a problem as Catholicism creates priests and designs various duties for them, one of which is hearing the committed sins of Catholics and providing them forgiveness. The obvious inferences of original sin were quite a dilemma for the Catholic hierarchy. The truth from God fits everything together perfectly, but humankind trying to act as God makes a mess of everything.

Catholicism decides to extend God's definition of sin

The Catholic leadership decided they needed more definitions for sin and began to define the seriousness of various sins. The magnitude of sins seems like such a great idea, although God never does this. God does mention certain things as hated and certain things as an abomination, and one can see that some things in the sin category may be difficult to leave. God focuses more on the motives behind the sins because those things are the real problem. Those characteristics can lead to a person committing any number of different sins. That information for a child of God is invaluable as they can assess their weaknesses. Every child of God wants to avoid sin, please God, and live faithfully to achieve the crown of life. God indicates one must not die in sin, in any sin. Catholics invented the terminology of venial and mortal sins, with the mortal sins being gravely serious and dying in mortal sin means eternal loss. Indeed, this categorizing of sin is a very human idea. That is, let me know which sins are serious and which are less serious. Catholicism gets nothing right. Of course, as a Catholic, all you need to do is go to the priest and confess your sin(s), and all is well. Thus we have this grading of sins and the subsequent assignment of the penance. Penance is the requirement given by the priest as the sinners part in receiving forgiveness. Many of the Catholic innovations come from some perceived need to cover their previous invented doctrines. Original sin spawned all sorts of additional doctrines to address this sin imparted at birth. It was then necessary to do something to address the original sin on each infant. Thus infant baptism was designated to wipe out original sin. Catholicism creates all these problems for itself, and one of the early ones was babies that died before baptism. This problem stayed with Catholicism for a while, and several doctrines were created and then changed. One doctrine created a special place for infants called **limbo** that kept babies out of hell. That did not satisfy "Catholic parents," so the final solution was to say God would handle this, and limbo was no longer a doctrine. Of course, God does not have to address this, since there is no original sin.

Sin and Purgatory

Another problem with Catholicism's management of sin was the lesser sins people commit and then dying with those sins against their souls. Catholicism reasons, they still fall short of satisfying God, and thus something else is needed. Thus, purgatory is invented. Catholics define purgatory as a place or state of suffering inhabited by the souls of sinners who are expiating their sins before going to heaven. Purgatory is unscriptural and, like all of the invented doctrines of Catholicism, can be seen as the opposite of the truth. In addition to the concept of purgatory not being in scripture, God has defined the eternal separation, which disallows any other means. The things we know beyond our realm come from God's revelations. Spiritual things come only from God, and sin is very spiritual in its definition and its resolution. To get life right, one cannot alter God's inspired word. Purgatory is discussed in detail in Chapter 10 of this book.

Note: The Catholic Church is all about changing the word of God. They do this by saying the apostles had this right, and then the succession of the apostles could also make the rules. This *comes from Matthew 16:19, and they also use John 20:23 to support their confession of sins to a priest. These verses are discussed in terms of their meaning throughout this book, particularly in Chapters 6 and 8. Just a brief comment on these verses as they both have the same characteristic. Neither of these verses was understood when Jesus declared them to the apostles. The apostles realized they would have some involvement in bringing the message and knew from John 20:23 that it would involve forgiveness of sins. They had no idea of the mechanics of this process. They would learn the meaning as Jesus indicated when the Holy Spirit came and guided them into all truth. You can imagine all sorts of things concerning these verses (used independently of other scripture), and apparently, that is what Catholicism proceeded to do. We see many such doctrines being suggested in the time of the early church fathers. The scriptures are where truth resides, but at the time of the early church in close proximity to the inspired period, many believed there were still new revelations. The opportunities are endless in terms of creating new doctrine during this time. However, the humble person knows that the correct meaning will come from God, and of course, in the scriptures. In a sense, this is the Catholic problem, the Catholic condemnation, as men decide what God means – the very core of idolatry. At this time of the early church fathers, there was no intention of creating something new – a different church. They were just working with the scriptures they had and, in hindsight, were **at times very careless**. They were trying to excel in this exciting, new "Christianity" of the first century, this real connection with God and the church being built by His Son. Regardless, there is truth, and there is error, and it is the most serious thing in the world to get right. Chapter 12 is devoted to this subject of the early church fathers, tradition, and the Catholic Magisterium.*

God's use of sin is perfect in accomplishing His purpose – A key understanding

We will continue with this idea of Catholicism's folly with sin. The folly can already be seen in the mess Catholicism has made. God in His perfection created everything from nothing and then designed a means to accomplish His purpose that is every bit as perfect. Everything throughout time has been perfectly fitted together. Now, here comes some men wanting to modify what God has done. God was able through His Son to allow humankind to be reconciled back to Him. God was successful in achieving His purpose, long before Catholicism and before the early church fathers existed. **Humankind is incapable** of fitting everything perfectly together, and God knows if humankind becomes inventive with what He so carefully delivered, it will be a disaster for souls. The message of reconciliation will be hindered. Thus we have God's severity in the warning not to change His word, which includes not privately interpreting His word. Earlier it was mentioned that God emphasized the **serious faults BEHIND the sin** instead of defining a hierarchy of sins. It will usually be pride that is behind changing the word of God. It will be in pride that one can see the scriptures a certain way, that is to their advantage. Then they begin to defend THEIR belief aggressively. Let us look at John 20:23 in this regard. A very human view of John 20:23 could mean hundreds of different things. In the current Catholic conundrum with sin, they find an answer in a combination of their priest, their confessional, and defining a method for the forgiveness of committed sins. In ignorance of God's word, they create something with no scriptural support and absolutely the opposite of God's way. In pride, they fail to seek God's meaning and replace it with what they think makes sense. There is a discipline in the scriptures that is missing and it has to do with respecting God and His word. Also missing is the humble attitude, including the fear of the Lord in relation to handling the word of God. John 20:23 is an excellent example of how carelessness in handling God's word allows the creation of wildly different doctrines very far from the truth.

John 20:23

23 If you forgive the sins of any, they are forgiven them; if you retain the sins of any, they are retained."

When this statement was made by Jesus, as discussed above, the apostles did not understand it, as other verses like Matthew 16:19. The understanding would come later as promised by Jesus, specifically as the Holy Spirit guided them into all truth. There were various other things to be revealed **AFTER** the death, burial, and resurrection of Jesus. Everything is completed in the timeframe designed by God. There were excellent reasons, and in Matthew 16:20, Jesus even tells the apostles, "Then He commanded His disciples that they should tell no one that He was Jesus the Christ." It was not yet the time for anyone to know this, or was it the time for the apostles **to understand what they were just told.** Shortly, the things Jesus told the apostles in John 20:23 and Matthew 16:19 would be revealed for their understanding.

Timing is crucial to God in terms of accomplishing His purpose. So, we have people looking at a verse like John 20:23 and making certain claims about it when even the apostles did not understand the meaning of this verse. They could not understand it correctly because they did not have enough information from God. Also, we can now see that the event required to make sense of these verses **had not yet occurred** – namely the death, burial, and resurrection of Jesus.

There are two things emphasized in this book in order to get the correct meaning of scripture, and they are to **understand God** and **understand God's purpose and how He is going about to achieve it**. You will not get the correct meaning of John 20:23 or Matthew 16:19 unless you know that God gradually reveals their meanings in these cases. Again, He is doing this consistent with His pattern of revelation in the New Testament and similarly done in the Old Testament, especially in relation to His purpose. It is why we must correctly understand God's purpose and all He indicates on any subject.

Note: We can go back to Genesis 3:15, and God provided the solution to what had just happened, namely sin entered the world. Although what God said was the truth (of course), the meaning was not revealed until Christ came some four thousand years later, and even then, the understanding would not be complete until after the death, burial, and resurrection of Jesus.

Jesus came preaching the kingdom, and gradually people were beginning to understand the meaning, but not fully until the kingdom came in Acts 2. Even then, additional clarity came during the period the Holy Spirit was working with the apostles, and Ephesians 3:9-11 indicates the mystery no longer exists. When Jesus was teaching the parable of the seed, the meaning was not known; however, in this case, God wanted to reveal the true meaning and did so following His completion of the parable. The details of John 20:23 and Matthew 16:19 were not revealed when they were first declared. The apostles learned they would have some involvement, and it appeared to be of significance from both verses. They had no idea of their roles. Yet a person, perhaps an early church father, can look at these verses and say they know what they mean – AMAZING. Such people did not carefully consider what came shortly after, that clarified the apostle's roles. These people who imagine various meanings for these verses should wonder why the meanings they envision **did not occur** in the scriptures and, more importantly, why there are **scriptural conflicts with their interpretation of these verses**. One might suggest the early church fathers did not have all of the scriptures – not yet in a book, not complete. We are not blaming them because they did not have all the information but about being careless. They were privately interpreting scripture. Many people today live and die on these verses as they stand.

In contrast, the **apostles learned what they meant** via the Holy Spirit and then fulfilled the correct meaning. In Matthew 16:19 and John 20:23, the apostles led by the Holy Spirit brought the message, and whether it be binding and loosening or forgiving or retaining sins, **it was all contained in the gospel message**. What the apostles did in bringing the message fulfills both the verse in Matthew 16:19 and John 20:23. In bringing the gospel message, they fulfilled their roles of binding and loosing and forgiving or retaining sins. **Is there something more important they could have done? Is there something that better addresses God's purpose?** This subject of sin is the perfect example of carelessly handling God's word. God the Father did His part; Jesus came and did His work as did the Holy Spirit, and yet there needed to be the apostles taking the message, or there would be no reconciliation. The message would then continue to be brought till the end of time by those "in Christ." In this book, Chapter 6, "the fifth verse not seen by Grodi," the responsibility of God's children to carry the message is revealed and demonstrated.

The meaning of John 20:23 to the careless, those without a good foundation in the truth

John 20:23

23 If you forgive the sins of any, they are forgiven them; if you retain the sins of any, they are retained."

There are many ways to understand God's meaning, and of course, it begins with the understanding that God used the Holy Spirit to bring the truth. However, the apostles on the day of Pentecost learn from God's Holy Spirit their role. **They will understand that their role is the means, the only means to have past sins forgiven.** They are at the end of the chain in all that God has done but essential. The Holy Spirit will tell them what must be done. It will be the beginning of a great deal of revelation that will be with them for the next 50 plus years. The apostle's work will begin with the gospel message in Acts 2. The local church will gradually be revealed, and each person "in Christ" will have advocacy with Jesus. This advocacy means there is a way to have their "post-initial obedience sins" forgiven and a means to connect to the Father in prayer. They will learn that there will be an end to the revelation, which also ends God's inspired communication with humankind.

*Note: Quite often, people desiring a particular outcome become irrational and careless. If you understand God and His purpose, you will get to the truth and certainly avoid absurdity. The problem is sin beginning in the garden of Eden with Adam and Eve, and God provides the answer in the seed of woman, and Jesus is the fulfillment, a spiritual solution. The apostle's role is not specifically defined in John 20:23. The absurdity would be to think the apostles would decide whose sins would be forgiven and whose would be retained. After all, that is what is said, or is it. The thing missing is HOW this will happen, and THE HOW could carry a completely different understanding from what **seems likely** in the verse alone. God is not trying to fool people but does leave the door open to careless people to arrive at their own conclusions. However, the door is not open very long before He reveals the meaning. The crack in the door no longer exists once God's word brings clarity. Nonetheless, certain proud persons can pick and choose verses and declare their view and not relent. God is exceedingly clear in His meaning, as it was revealed about two thousand years ago. It fits perfectly with all that God is doing concerning His purpose.*

Sin carries a huge weight in determining success and failure for each person and the apostles being Jews, had a good awareness of the seriousness of sin. How would they possibly make correct judgments concerning what might be supposed in John 20:23? Catholicism defines a priesthood for the New Covenant and then invent the confessional. Now people (Catholics) can come and confess their sins to the priest and receive forgiveness. Yes, that must be the answer. We know Jesus could forgive sins while He was on earth. How would these priests have such a capability? God gets things right; He knows the heart of each person. The forgiveness of sins could never be a task for humankind.

God manages sin perfectly

Here is how God manages sin; that is, He manages it perfectly. The gospel is preached, the gospel is obeyed and the Lord adds to His spiritual body those who believe in Him as the Son of God and repent of their sins, and in baptism, their sins are forgiven. God knows the heart of every person, and in that way, there are no mistakes. No one will be reconciled to God, who is not deserving. Along with establishing a relationship with Jesus, the person gains an advocate with the Father, and future transgressions can be forgiven per God's process.

In the "salvation process" defined by the scriptures, there is no Catholic Church, no pope, no priests, no councils, no confessional, and the hundreds of other things devised by humankind. There is no chance of humankind on their own getting this right. However, there was a certainty of getting everything wrong, and in that, they were successful. It is no wonder that people look at religion with doubt, even with malice, as it all appears very humanlike while claiming some divine relationship.

As Catholicism "grasps for straws," they suggest some of the early church fathers had some contact with the apostles, which they claim supports the validity of early church tradition. Of course, the apostles were never given the right or had the responsibility to create or change the will of God. The apostles were blessed with delivering **the message**, specifically the gospel message, to the world. The Holy Spirit guided the apostles into all truth just as Jesus told them would happen. There was no succession of the apostles and no pope. In Chapter 6 (also in Chapter 8), the idea of a pope is wholly and thoroughly and scripturally rejected. The truth is that the early church of the first few centuries is, in some locations, not the church that Jesus started. The "early church" ceased being His church when the doctrine of Christ was changed. This early church with a new set of teachings would eventually develop into what would be called the Catholic Church. Once the gospel message is altered, the inescapable conclusion is that the Lord will no longer be adding people to His spiritual body. The early church that Catholicism depends so passionately on for doctrinal support, at some point contained few and perhaps no Christians.

We are intimating that the Catholic theologians are not thinking. It is a kind way of saying they are not helping anyone to be successful. They have their marching orders, and in whatever they do, Catholicism must be supported. God defines sin and how to have it forgiven. He is precise, and there are many examples, and everything fits perfectly together concerning God achieving His purpose. Then along comes original sin, baptizing babies, Catholic Confirmation, priests, confessing sins to a priest, a hierarchy of sins, purgatory, and hundreds of others. Then to validate this, they look to the early church father's writings, apostolic succession, and the associated right to make the rules. Catholicism sees their new doctrines as additional revelation but seems to overlook that they are in opposition to the inspired word of God. They fail to see the idea of a pope from Matthew 16:15-19 is not in any way what is revealed. Jesus indirectly explains to the apostles how they will understand their role in binding and loosing when He declares He is sending the Holy Spirit to guide them into all truth. You see, it makes perfect sense that humankind cannot make the rules for God, and they could not be the ones making decisions concerning forgiving sins – a very spiritual matter.

One thing (among thousands) that **confirms the folly** of the Catholic church is how they seek validation outside the word of God. Specifically looking to the writings of the early church fathers and claiming the right to make the rules via apostolic succession. Of course, that is not quite right because they hurry back to the scriptures to find an authority to allow rulemaking outside the scriptures – like the case they attempted to make for tradition. Deep down, Catholicism knows that the scriptures are holy, sacred, and designed by God for a purpose. Despite knowing this, Catholicism ignores or blocks out the needed validation and embraces its doctrines. This only makes things worse, and they live in the defensive mode surrounded by very nonsensical doctrines.

*Note: A great deal of Catholic doctrine has evolved from **not** understanding God. In this discussion, not understanding how God gradually revealed various truths according to His timeframe is a stumbling block. Before it was possible to understand a passage correctly, God must complete the required related events. Catholics consider what a Bible passage might mean without using all God revealed for understanding. In John 20:23, the apostles did not understand what it meant when Jesus spoke it. Nonetheless, Catholics or perhaps the early church fathers **suggest the meaning** based on this verse alone. There is no way to understand this verse without the clarification the apostles received. Jesus understood the apostles were in a quandary regarding various things revealed, revealed in part and true, but incomplete. He promised them resolution, and it would come soon as He told them in John 16:13, "However, when He, the Spirit of truth, has come, He will guide you into all truth." In receiving the Holy Spirit in Acts 2, many things became clear to the apostles, and although those things were not always made known by direct scripture, they were seen in the things the apostles did or did not do. Furthermore, they can be verified by the consistent application (e.g., conversions) of what the apostles learned and how God fitted everything perfectly together.*

There is another thing that makes it challenging to explain Catholicism, and it is the fact that what they created is very convoluted. Above it is stated, "Catholics consider what that passage (John 20:23) might mean and create doctrine, specifically confessing sins to a priest." Then they go to the early church fathers for validation. If SOME early church fathers looked at this verse and in some way envisioned the apostles and their successors forgiving and retaining sins, then they have confirmation. The convolution is a "chicken and egg thing." Catholic doctrine seems to largely have evolved from the writings of the early church fathers, and thus going to the early church fathers for validation is rather convoluted. The origin of Catholic doctrine is often from the uninspired early church fathers. My comment on this matter is how simple God's ways are, and thanks to His wisdom, we have the truth, and it makes sense and fits perfectly together with all that God has done. Catholicism in trying to speak for God becomes incredibly complicated, makes no sense, leaves people in some sort of mystery, and, as might be expected, provides zero value for humanity while at the same time destroying many souls.

One might wonder why God revealed some things in part. First, this was a common mode of operation for God and was seen as early as Genesis 3:15. Second, in the case of John 20:23, He was preparing the apostles for the seriousness of their mission. Thirdly, as in many cases, there were necessary things to understand the revelation that must first occur. Typically, it was the completion of Jesus's mission as seen on the cross. In the case of John 20:23, the forgiving and retaining of sins occurred in the message the apostles delivered, when people responded in obedience (forgiveness) or rejected the message (retained).

As we complete this topic of sin, we know sin is evil, but do we understand that sin is holy in view of being defined by God? God sets sin aside as part of His plan for achieving His purpose. God is not involved with any sin (since He is the perfect absence of evil) other than using the concept as part of His determination of each person's success or failure. It would be very wrong for any person to tamper with God's plan and, in this case, tamper with sin. God defines the means of covering sin (forgiving sin). God defines sin itself in terms of those dying in sin not inheriting the kingdom of God. The Catholic Church tampers with every aspect of sin, and that is exceedingly and seriously wrong.

3.2 The church

The Catholic Church has no association with God, it never has, and it never will. The church of the scriptures is as follows:

- Built by Jesus ("I will build my church") … Matthew 16:18
- Jesus is the head
- The church is spiritual, not of this world
- The Lord himself adds each obedient soul via the gospel message to His spiritual body, the church.
- There is a "local physical" church, but only with spiritual responsibilities, and its members are spiritual via their addition by the Lord having their sins forgiven.
- The local church has a God-defined structure that includes elders, deacons, and members, all of which have been added to the body of Christ by the Lord Himself. God includes qualifications for both elders and deacons.
- The local church has one responsibility, as does each person "in Christ," and it is evangelism.
- There is a single rulebook, and it is the word of God.

The Catholic Church is nothing like the church Jesus built and continues to build.

3.3 Catholicism's horrendous misuse of Bible words

Catholicism is so far from the truth on every subject that its carelessness can be seen everywhere. Let me give a **few** examples that demonstrate this lack of concern about the truth.
- Baptism – Baptism is defined as immersion; Catholics sprinkle.
- Father – The Father is God the Father, and no one else can wear that title **religiously**. Catholics have their pope (meaning papa or father). He is referred to as the Holy Father.
- Repentance – Repentance is a turning from sin and part of the conversion process. Catholics use this idea in association with confessing sins to a priest. In its correct usage, it is a critical element in obeying the gospel.

- Bishop or elder – The bishop or elder is a defined position in the Lord's church with certain qualifications. Catholics name persons to this title using a process devised by them and opposed to God's definition.
- Saint – All those added to the body of Christ are saints. Catholics created a very special class of saints and a complicated process for becoming a saint.
- Priest – There are no priests in the New Testament. Catholics create this title to support some of their non-scriptural practices.

This could be a very long list of hundreds of words where Catholicism has changed the meaning of words to suit their purpose.

3.4 The violation of the principles of God

Essentially every principle of God has been violated by Catholicism. We will mention some obvious ones. There is no official list of the principles of God. However, with a bit of effort and good knowledge of the scriptures, you can understand these things are consistent with God's nature. Although each principle is unique, they fit together. They are not contradictory but complementary because we are dealing with perfection, with God.

- Worship must be in spirit and truth. Catholics have no idea what this means, and consequently, **they have never worshiped God**. There is no mystery in what this means. To worship God, you need to be spiritual. Since the reconciliation, a person can be spiritual by obedience to the gospel and therefore added to the spiritual body of Christ. Then the worship itself must be according to God's specifications, that is, according to the truth.
- No one deserves any honor in a religious sense except God. This is covered in detail in Chapter 9.
- There is only one mediator between God and humankind, and it is Jesus. This is also covered in detail in Chapter 9.

- Do not change the word of God. This is key to understanding God and the truth. This is covered throughout this book.

God has carefully delivered His will, and in the process, we learn a great deal about God. Many things could be referred to as the principles of God. A fundamental characteristic of God is that He cannot lie, as would be how God loves His creation. The principles of God are most noble, honorable. The idea that God is perfect in everything is a powerful principle to understand and respect. Such an understanding does not have a person conceiving that God has made any mistakes or that His way of delivering the message to humankind is anything less than perfect/complete.

Chapter 4
Understanding God destroys Catholicism

Catholicism is unreasonable when God is correctly understood. God reveals Himself; His nature, and He is indeed marvelous in every way. The author has done several profound studies of God's nature regarding the subject of good and evil. You can read about these in several places, but the conclusion is that "God is the perfect absence of evil." I was motivated to make these studies since many want to blame God for various things, especially suffering. This is not the case, and hopefully, getting past that particular serious mistruth might help some people to understand God correctly and then get them on the road to heaven. Learn that God is the perfect absence of evil by connecting to this link.

https://heavencoach.com/god-is-the-perfect-absence-of-evil/

Everything we know about God that is true has been revealed by Him. We have that revelation only from His word. It is the "word of truth of the gospel." He tells humankind that heaven and earth will pass away but not His words. God compares the longevity of His word to the frailty of the seemingly immeasurable sturdiness of the physical creation. God wants us to know how highly we should value His message, the scriptures.

One of the most misused words in the Bible is faith. It seems no one ever points out the misuse of this word because the word faith is in some way whatever a person wants it to be. Someone may say my faith is increasing, I now have faith in my religion, or I have faith in Catholicism, or I have accomplished this wonderful thing due to my faith. However, what are they saying? Faith in the scriptures has a precise meaning, and it has to do with its source and its only source. Faith comes from hearing and hearing from the word of God. So, if a person says their faith is increasing, do they mean they are coming to a better understanding of the truth, of God's word. This is probably not what they mean, but instead, they mean whatever they believe has been enhanced. They are likely not talking about the word of God, but that would be great if they were. If they meant their faith increased due to their continued obedience to God, that would be quite a good thing. It would be like Abraham following God's directives, and as he continually did so, his relationship with God was becoming stronger. The world uses faith to mean belief in something, anything, which is fine, but God is not involved. I have great faith in this person or this system, and everyone understands such devotion. In the area of the God of the Bible, faith is always associated with the truth and the truth is always associated with the word of God. The short verse in John 17:17 brings clarity to the association between truth and God's word, "Sanctify them by Your truth. Your word is truth." Truth outside our realm only comes from God's word. Yet, in Catholicism, they claim other sources.

4.1 Continually work at understanding God; it is vital for your eternity

Why is faith important to our discussion about Catholicism? God has tied the truth to His word, or we can say He has connected Faith to His word. Thus, all other sources of faith in God are eliminated. Who is the rule maker for everything? It must be God Himself. The truth about life always comes from God, which has changed somewhat in how it has been transmitted. Initially, God spoke directly to a few persons such as Adam, Abraham, and Moses. Still, later through His prophets and finally, the Holy Spirit guided the apostles into all truth (John 16:13). God summarizes how He has communicated with humankind in the first chapter of Hebrews.

Hebrews 1:1-4

1 God, who at various times and in various ways spoke in time past to the fathers by the prophets,

2 has in these last days spoken to us by His Son, whom He has appointed heir of all things, through whom also He made the worlds;

3 how shall we escape if we neglect so great a salvation, which at the first began to be spoken by the Lord, and was confirmed to us by those who heard Him,

4 God also bearing witness both with signs and wonders, with various miracles, and gifts of the Holy Spirit, according to His own will?

Today and until the end of time, God speaks through His Son. The Son indicated the Holy Spirit would provide the truth by inspiration to the apostles. In that process, God bore witness both with signs and wonders, with various miracles, and gifts of the Holy Spirit, according to His own will. We also learn that Catholics like to refer to faith as a mystery, that is, "God works in mysterious ways." Yet God works in very **non-mysterious ways** per the revelation from God in Ephesians.

Ephesians 3:9-11

9 and to make all see what is the fellowship of the mystery, which from the beginning of the ages has been hidden in God who created all things through Jesus Christ;

10 to the intent that now the manifold wisdom of God might be made known by the church to the principalities and powers in the heavenly places,

11 according to the eternal purpose which He accomplished in Christ Jesus our Lord,

Faith's source is clear – the word of God. God's means to bring about the reconciliation is clear and demonstrated throughout the New Testament. There is no **valid new or additional doctrine** found in the early church fathers in their "tradition." Faith is not associated with doctrine originating by any source other than God, i.e., God's word.

We learn that God planned to end His revelation to humankind and did so in the latter part of the first century. This closed the door to later revelations and effectively on such aberrations as the Catholic Church, which is not found in the scriptures in name or principle. Faith cannot come from the tradition associated with the early fathers of the church – it must come from the word of God. The word of God does not authorize the early church tradition as found in the early church father's writings. The tradition the apostles authorized were the things they were teaching but not yet available as scripture. Tradition is discussed throughout this book, particularly in Chapter 6 in the fourth verse not seen by Marcus Grodi. God was PERFECTLY careful to assure the message came accurately using His divine means, specifically His Holy Spirit. Then men randomly in the early church independent of God's "Spirit-inspired word" created a different message and not only different but in opposition to God's word. It is interesting how John 20:30-31 indicates the things written are such that you might believe. The New Testament points to where the truth can be found and its sufficiency.

John 20:30-31

30 And truly Jesus did many other signs in the presence of His disciples, which are not written in this book;

31 but these are written that you may believe that Jesus is the Christ, the Son of God, and that believing you may have life in His name.

The things "written" are what we need. God places His stamp of approval on what was written.

John 14:26

26 But the Helper, the Holy Spirit, whom the Father will send in My name, He will teach you all things, and bring to your remembrance all things that I said to you.

The Holy Spirit of God would even bring the apostles their remembrance of what Jesus had told them. God is careful in assuring the truth will be recorded and be available for the remainder of history. God's confidence was not in the apostles remembering the things Jesus spoke. The apostles might recall those things (even in principle) differently. Jesus sends the Holy Spirit to assure His final revelation will be accurate.

*Note: There are so many apparent things just ignored by Catholicism. You can observe that the apostles, as men can make mistakes, might get things wrong. They may even misunderstand the things Jesus said and did. God knows this, and in His perfection, He sends His Spirit, the Holy Spirit, to guide them into all truth. The result is the truth. The idea of apostolic succession is absurd for many reasons. One might say it did not happen, but even more so because the apostles never had any knowledge beyond our realm without the guidance of the Holy Spirit. Think of how impossible it would be for the early church fathers to get anything right. They were never with Jesus nor did they have the benefit of the Holy Spirit. If what they wrote is different from the scriptures, it carries no weight, carries no truth. It is often mentioned that the Catholic Church is the **universal physical church**. Thus where do they place their emphasis? Everything for Catholicism is physical. Catholicism trusts men and honors men when TRULY the only one to be trusted and honored is God, which means honoring His word. There is no other source of truth. Everything of the truth is spiritual, beginning with the Lord's spiritual body, that is, those* *added to His body by the Lord Himself. The Catholic Church looks for ways to express itself in physical ways, whereas the church of Jesus is, as He stated, not of this world.*

We mention how Paul said the message of God was being corrupted even when he was recording the letter to the Galatians. **How can anyone believe any different doctrine that came after the word of God was completed?** God knows something that Catholics never realize, and that is **humankind will never get it right on their own**. God was very blunt in this regard in Jeremiah and Isaiah.

Jeremiah 10:23

23 O Lord, I know the way of man is not in himself; It is not in man who walks to direct his own steps.

Isaiah 55:9

9 "For the heavens are higher than the earth, So are My ways higher than your ways, And My thoughts than your thoughts.

Knowing these things, God provides the truth and never leaves it to individuals or groups to determine the meaning. God directs us and does this perfectly because His ways are higher. It is so strange that men think they can decide what God requires, decide which were the valid traditions of the early church fathers, yet they must realize the impossibility of getting this right. However, if they gather a team of bright persons into a council, surely they will get the correct answers. Forgive my facetiousness. Humankind will never get it right, and God has continuously made this clear just as He has in the two verses above.

The **truth must come down in writing,** which means the Holy Spirit works in bringing the message to specific persons by inspiration. In the New Testament, that meant nine different writers. About half of that writing was done by Paul and Luke. Once the message from God was completed, sometime in the latter part of the first century, there would be no more. The scriptures have God's imprint throughout, and without inspiration, there is no validity. One would expect there to be confusion unless there was complete adherence to what was inspired. There were about 60 years during which the New Testament was recorded under the Holy

Spirit's supervision. That is quite a long period and plenty of time for God to get the message across. This is where thinking helps, which means more than having thoughts but being logical and creative in learning and understanding God. God is perfect, and He delivered the truth, completed His communication with humankind, and nothing is missing. We can see how the early church fathers brought **many different things** and thus the confusion. We can also see the considerable conflict with the inspired word when it was privately interpreted. Those interpretations would appear in the writings of the early church fathers. They were careless with Matthew 16, Matthew 26, John 6, 1 Corinthians 10, and many others. They put their twists on scripture. It could be said it was not easy since they did not have all the New Testament in a single place, yet they did have a great deal of the scripture.

Nonetheless, there is no excuse for changing the meaning. The net outcome of the early church father's writings was truth and error, and the obvious thing is that serious error entered early in the church. Catholics assume the "early church father's writings" were the truth when that is only correct if they were consistent with the scriptures. God would not leave such a mess, not when His noble purpose was at stake – your soul! Thus He pleads, do not change His word, His inspired word. You can see Peter providing the wisdom from God when he declares in 2 Peter 1:3, "His divine power has given to us all things that pertain to life and godliness." Peter thought we had all we needed. However, careless men wanted something different, and in pride claim that there is more. The more includes different things and often in conflict with what the Holy Spirit delivered.

4.2 Faith is always present in your search and must be understood

We just talked about faith above in this chapter, and the point was to connect faith with the word of God. In terms of spiritual matters, they cannot be separated. Yet who knows this? As we talk about faith, God has more clarity, and one place is in Hebrews.

Hebrews 11:6

6 But without faith it is impossible to please Him, for he who comes to God must believe that He is, and that He is a rewarder of those who diligently seek Him.

So we see the importance of **seeking God** and doing that diligently. There is **only one place to find God, and it is in the scriptures,** and you will need a diligent effort. Faith is not emphasized in Catholicism as coming from the word of God. That would NOT allow faith to be whatever they dictate. Faith for Catholics is faith in the Catholic Church. That means in their Magisterium, which provides authorized interpretation, the use of writings from the early church fathers, apostolic succession, and the scriptures. Here is the Catholic meaning of their Magisterium.

"The magisterium of the Catholic Church is the church's authority or office to give authentic interpretation of the Word of God, "whether in its written form or in the form of Tradition." According to the 1992 Catechism of the Catholic Church, the task of interpretation is vested uniquely in the Pope and the bishops though the concept has a complex history of development."

What is better than the interpretation of the Magisterium? Infinitely better is the correct meaning, understanding God's word as realized by a person with a good heart who loves the truth. God says His word is truth and provides how that word was delivered with His oversight.

John 17:17

17 Sanctify them by Your truth. Your word is truth.

Colossians 1:5

5 because of the hope which is laid up for you in heaven, of which you heard before in the word of the truth of the gospel,

There is a dramatic difference between the scripture's emphasis on **seeking God** as an absolute core requirement and the Catholic Church being the center of one's life. The Catholic focus is **seeking the Catholic Church** to achieve a relationship with God. Can you see the seriousness of placing the Catholic Church before God, in place of God? What is Catholicism for, what purpose does it serve? The Catholic Church serves as a distraction from the truth to the detriment of billions of souls.

We have Catholicism inventing all sorts of doctrines in opposition to the scriptures and then creating a means to validate their private interpretations of the Word of God. They go further to define the word of God to include both the scriptures AND early church tradition. Thus we can see faith for the Catholic is in the Catholic Church instead of in the word of God.

4.3 Understanding God eliminates Catholicism

We are talking about understanding God and consequently destroying Catholicism. Here is how that happens.

- The word of God is certain and the only legitimate message from God. Everything else is from humankind, and specifically, in our case, Catholicism creates its self-serving message promoting their religion.

- Catholicism does not understand faith, and therefore they create doctrines that oppose the plan of God for reconciliation. Catholic speak is, "I have faith in the Catholic Church."

- We have suggested that a careful study of scripture indicates that God is the perfect absence of evil. The Catholic Church has a history of extreme evil and always promotes the Catholic Church. Catholicism brought suffering, torture, and death to those in opposition. It would be impossible for God to be aligned with such an organization. Additionally, they exerted rule over nations – what was the reason for that? Also, they had nations hunt down their heretics and torture and murder them – what was the reason for that? The clergy (bishops, priests, and other ordained titles, etc.), and the hierarchy within the Catholic Church has long been the purveyors of immorality and every sort of evil.

- The things God demands of those in His body represent the highest qualities possible for humankind. His church is pure, unselfish, and willing to sacrifice even their own lives for others, for the truth. They commit to living for Christ and the gospel as opposed to living for themselves.

- The requirements of an elder are given in Titus.
Titus 1:5-9.

5 For this reason I left you in Crete, that you should set in order the things that are lacking, and appoint elders in every city as I commanded you—

6 if a man is blameless, the husband of one wife, having faithful children not accused of dissipation or insubordination.

7 For a bishop must be blameless, as a steward of God, not self-willed, not quick-tempered, not given to wine, not violent, not greedy for money,

8 but hospitable, a lover of what is good, sober-minded, just, holy, self-controlled,

*9 **holding fast the faithful word** as he has been taught, that he may be able, by sound doctrine, both to exhort and convict those who contradict.*

These are scriptural requirements, the things God requires for elders. God knows the importance of the local church and defines men who will lead as God requires. The organization of God's church must be as God has designated. In God's wisdom, this is what will work. Catholicism invents an entirely different organization. God has high expectations for leaders, as seen in Titus 1:5-9. One can observe the characteristics God requires are very much the opposite in the Catholic leadership.

The better you understand God and His purpose, the less you will want to associate with Catholicism. The bottom line for Catholicism is the need to sell the validity of early church father's traditions, the succession of apostles, their Magisterium, and more simply can be summarized as "their need to rule over all of Christianity." Their organization operates with characteristics the opposite of what God requires of those "in Christ." Those leadership characteristics can be seen in the qualifications for elders of the local church and are missing in the Catholic leadership. God is serious about those qualifications, and they would be present if Catholicism respected the word of God. Consequently, there would be no plotting to murder those who believe differently. Don't you know that those capable of murder are also capable of lying – lying about everything, of creating doctrine to their benefit? Thus understanding God leaves no place for Catholicism.

Chapter 5
God's simplicity versus Catholic complexity

One of the **enemies** of your sought-after life success is the **confusion** brought by religion. Another is the **distractions** brought by religion. This can be summed up as the **complexity** of religion. Very few realize how deadly these things are to their eternity. God is dedicated to bringing simplicity to the solution people need – He wants people to succeed (2 Peter 3:9, 1 Timothy 2:4). The "world of religion" is highly complex in terms of doctrine and then often followed by a reasonably simple means to be faithful. The opposite of these things is true – the doctrine is simple, understandable, and logical while living the life that pleases God can be challenging, requiring serious dedication.

Note: You might have noticed if you are familiar with the scriptures that people were saved, placed on the road to heaven quite easily and in the shortest possible amount of time. It is reasonable to observe the "churches of the world" as having many rules, having all kinds of complexity, and so many different names. The hindrance occurred when people began to make the rules for God. Humankind interfered and brought something different. The good news is that there is no complexity required to become a person having a relationship with the Creator.

Once again, God's way is simple to understand in establishing a relationship with Him, but it can be challenging to conform your life. After all, living for Christ and the gospel is demanding since it means **not living for yourself**. Living as a Catholic is not particularly challenging, just a few requirements – no pressure. Catholics are primarily Catholic from birth and remain "in the faith" due to the early indoctrination, regular propaganda, and a certain number of captivating beliefs and practices. Beliefs like a connection with the first-century church, the indication of being close to Jesus in the Eucharist, and a lifetime of trust placed in Catholic priests and the pope are powerful encouragements. There is an effort to make Catholics dependent on the Catholic Church's hierarchy in their various doctrines, i.e., a priest for confessing sins, for the Mass, and Eucharist. Once a person buys into Catholicism, it can be hard to leave, at least in the beginning. Eventually, unless the Catholic Church can build a relationship with a person, they usually become frustrated and question. Thus they either leave or substantially cut back on attendance. The best Catholics have a cradle-to-grave relationship and completely buy into the Catholic faith. They are labeled devout.

God claims that He is **not** the author of confusion (1 Corinthians 14:33). God provided the truth in simplicity. Catholicism and the "religions of the world" cannot claim to represent God believably to anyone who has a love of the truth. Unfortunately, such persons seem rare, and many do believe in such organizations. One can easily imagine the impossibility of creating such religions when only God knows things outside our realm. In any case, humankind has built an endless number of religions with all sorts of doctrines. Catholicism has created the most intricate, complicated system, with each new doctrine requiring reasonable links to other doctrines. It becomes an unmanageable mess and evident except to the Catholic faithful. This chapter aims to help people differentiate the truth from God, versus the "religions of the world" by their characteristic differences. God provides simplicity and a message that demonstrates God by perfectly fitting everything together from Genesis 1:1 to Revelation 22:21. You can observe the single purpose of God from the beginning and a consistent marching toward that goal with a very spiritual and noble character. Humankind's efforts at religion always appear as selfish endeavors to gain control over others. In their doctrines, they are very physical, from their church buildings to their honor for persons. Their religions end up being confusing and complicated in their teachings, and all their parts are disjointed. Their most apparent fail comes in the thing most important for religion and it is to help people achieve eternal life. They offer a solution, but since it is from humankind's perspective, it may seem worthwhile, but it cannot withstand scrutiny. How can humankind speak of things outside their realm? When the word of God is abandoned even partially, or we might say not respected, or we might say selectively considered, there will no longer be the truth. A consequence of all of humankind's rules is the complexity of doctrine and something that cannot be fitted together. This is the mess we have in Catholicism.

*Note: The "religions of the world" become complicated as they try to make the rules for God. This is somewhat of a relative matter and only realized if there is an awareness of the religion of truth, the religion of God – that is, the truth and simplicity of God's way. There is such power in the truth and how God fits everything together and also makes it simple such that people are amazed and **realize they are dealing with God, with the Creator**. In truth, there is one* *immeasurably powerful thing, and it is the knowledge that existence does not end at physical death. This is much more than an understanding but a dominant certainty like breathing and having a pulse is during our lifetime. Upon achieving a relation with God, you can manage death, both yours and your loved ones, and positively manage your life, and get on with doing good. You have an incredible trust in God that allows you to put life in the proper perspective. It would be unfair to think there will be no difficulties in understanding life and death correctly. There will be challenges, but the knowledge of the meaning of life will be comforting. There is an overwhelming seriousness and certainty about life and death, and "in Christ," you can manage both. Living in the truth, you are not dependent on someone of special religious knowledge, like in Catholicism with their priest. You have the scriptures, and as time passes, there are no doubts but a growing confidence you are dealing with God. There is no history of evil in the Lord's church, no **notable persons*** to attribute the doctrine, no honor for any person, and everything is perfectly logical because you deal with God who is perfect in logic. There is no need for some church leaders to gather to decide issues. There is no change in the teachings due to more "modern times." The doctrine of the twenty-first century is the same as the first century.*

*Note: * Above the term **notable persons** indicates that doctrine is not attributable to any specific person. Someone might want to attribute doctrine to Paul or Peter or Moses or any number of Bible characters, but that is ultimately incorrect. The source of doctrine is God.*

We have created two columns, one representing God's simplicity in terms of salvation and the other the Catholic version of salvation. This comparison might help in realizing God's way (simplicity) versus Catholicism's way (complexity). Salvation is the right differentiator since, in the end, that is all that matters. Salvation is simply forgiveness of sins allowing a relationship with God, and then maintaining that relationship until each person's end. **Salvation** is always associated with the **gospel of Christ** and to be worked out with **fear and trembling** and finally receiving the **end of your faith** – the **salvation of your souls**.

Romans 1:16
*16 For I am not ashamed of the **gospel of Christ**, for it is the power of God to **salvation** for everyone who believes, for the Jew first and also for the Greek.*

Philippians 2:12

12 .... work out your own **salvation** *with* **fear and trembling** *..........*

1 Peter 1:9

9 receiving the **end of your faith**—*the* **salvation of your souls**.

5.1 Salvation Charts: Lord's Church vs Catholic Church

God's version of salvation	Catholic's version of salvation
Gospel preached, obeyed – past sins forgiven, added to the spiritual church by the Lord	Baptized as a baby or as an adult, be baptized
Remain faithful, live for Christ and gospel, and consequently share in the Divine Nature	Confirmed at some "young" age
	Study the Catechism (may take over a year)
	Receive the Eucharist (regularly)
	Confess sins to priest as needed
	Allegiance to the pope
	Obey all the Catholic rules (hundreds and changing)
	Die without mortal sin
	Go to purgatory to clean up any minor sins

The left column above is what those of the first-century church did, and it was simple in its requirements and consistent with all scripture. The right column is the Catholic procedure at present – it could change. Those on the left had their sins forgiven, and continuing in faithfulness will achieve heaven. The ones on the right never had their sins forgiven and will all be lost. We will make a table for God's version of salvation with a brief explanation of each point. Then another table of the Catholic version of salvation with a brief explanation of each point.

God's version of salvation	Explanation
Gospel preached, obeyed, past sins forgiven, added to the spiritual church by the Lord	The gospel is the message of Christ's death, burial, and resurrection, which is exactly what is obeyed in baptism. The candidate believes Jesus is the Son of God and will confess Him as such. Then a person repents of their sins and is Baptized. Sins are forgiven, and the Lord Himself adds that obedient person to His spiritual body, the church.
Remain faithful, live for Christ and the gospel, and consequently share in the Divine Nature	Faithfulness to God is required until your end, which means living for Christ and the gospel and not living for yourself. This way of life is very unselfish with a high consideration for all others.

You might notice that you can become a child of God and be on the road to heaven in very short order. On that first day the gospel was preached, there were about three thousand souls added to the body of Christ.

Acts 2:41

41 Then those who gladly received his word were baptized; and that day about three thousand souls were added to them.

Catholic version of salvation	Explanation
Baptized as a baby or as an adult, be baptized	Babies are baptized in the Catholic church to remove original sin. There is no original sin, but it is an invention of Catholicism. Largely from Augustine and ratified at the council of Trent (1545-1563). Infant baptism was practiced as early as the 4th century. Also, their practice is not baptism but sprinkling.
Confirmed at some "young" age	Confirmation is a sacrament of the Catholic church conferred on baptized persons old enough to understand what they have been taught. Typically this might be about seven years old. This is a sacrament of initiation to the Catholic Church, and they claim the person receives the gift of the Holy Spirit.
Study the catechism (may take over a year)	The Catholic catechism is taught to children at the earliest age and there are many things to learn and many rules. Confusion exists due to complexity, and thus there is no good understanding from an early age. Adults must complete a lengthy catechism instruction before beginning the sacramental process and officially becoming Catholics.
Receive the Eucharist (regularly)	An essential part of Catholicism is the Eucharist, and all Catholics receive the Eucharist and do so routinely. There is a wide range of rules regarding receiving the Eucharist, such as you must have been to confession since your last mortal sin.
Confess sins to priest as needed	Catholic doctrine has you confessing your sins to a priest, and there are defined sins such as mortal and venial to distinguish seriousness, and there are associated explanations regarding each. The priest remits the sins and requires a penance. Of course, the scriptures know nothing of this process, and there are no priests in the New Testament church as defined by God.

Catholic version of salvation (continued)	Explanation
Allegiance to the pope	This has been officially defined, and there are many similar statements to the one quoted here. This one is from the New York Catechism. "The Pope takes the place of Jesus Christ on earth ... by divine right, the pope has supreme and full power in faith, in morals in each and every pastor and his flock. He is the true vicar, head of the entire church, the father and teacher of all Christians. He is the infallible ruler, the founder of dogmas, the author of and the judge of councils: the universal ruler of truth, the arbiter of the world, the supreme judge of heaven and earth, the judge of all, being judged by no one, God himself on earth."
Obey all the Catholic rules (hundreds and changing)	The Catholic Church is a rule-making organization that directly opposes God's commands not to change His word. The Catholic Church itself is the ultimate example of changing God's word. Everything has been changed.
Die without mortal sin	If you want heaven, you need to leave this world without any mortal sins. You have confession to help you and, if necessary, the sacrament of extreme unction (deathbed).
Go to purgatory to clean up any minor sins	The lifestyle of most Catholics is not particularly ethical and moral, and thus most Catholics look to succeed after purgatory. The tag of not particularity ethical or moral is partially due to the **purgatory's concept** and teachings that condone sin in some cases. Sometimes sin is redefined and allows a life exceedingly less in its requirements than the scriptures. Of course, there is no such place or concept as purgatory in the scriptures but the exact opposite – death then the judgment.

God's path to success is quite simple and is the truth, whereas the path of Catholicism is very complicated and fabricated. In the Catholic process, you can see very humanlike thinking. We know of God **and** His nature **and** His ways only because He revealed them. The things of humankind (i.e., Catholic doctrine) are quite different and do not fit together. They might work together in the human mind using human motives, creating something believable. However, there are many holes in the Catholic salvation process, but none as consequential as **sins are never forgiven**. Catholics do not understand God, and this should not be surprising since they have placed their fate in the hands of humankind. They do not understand the gospel message.

Catholics are taught that receiving the Eucharist is necessary for salvation. The concept of the Eucharist is dealt with in this book (Chapter 9) and easily shattered and its evil nature exposed. It is so far from the truth, just another concept of humankind that seems right but falls into the category of the physical church and not the spiritual church of the Lord. Like Judaism and the world and the "world of religion," Catholicism emphasizes the physical. This can be seen in their magnificent structures, various elegant ceremonies, and associated dramatic music. The physical character of Catholicism is also seen in their doctrines. This is the character of religion as seen by the world – that is, a physical character. Religion is aimed correctly when the target is the sin problem. It is a spiritual problem and requires a spiritual solution. The spiritual solution is powerful and requires an attitude that is sufficiently humble to accept God's way. Following initial obedience to the gospel, one must live for Christ and the gospel and not for oneself. Nothing is confusing or mysterious about God's way.

The above statement (in the chart) on **allegiance to the pope** is one of many statements that glorify the popes. It is the height of ignorance, disobedience, error, abomination, and given the scriptures, something that will cost the souls of each pope and all those who follow Catholicism. Indeed, there is no good way to characterize the evil in that statement honoring their pope.

Hopefully, you can see God's simplicity in His plan that allows you to succeed. Not only is it simple and logical and consistent with His desire that you succeed, but it is exactly what people did to be added to the body of Christ. See conversions of the New Testament:

(https://heavencoach.com/conversions-of-the-new-testament/).

Also, see Chapter 7 of this book that discusses the gospel message and contains the table, "Conversions of the New Testament."

Chapter 6
Protestants converting to Catholicism

6.1 Protestant quandary

Two prominent persons have been selected for study, and both were Presbyterian ministers and will allow us to demonstrate their logic in arriving at Catholicism as the truth. Their names are Dr. Scott Hahn and Marcus Grodi. Their reasoning has become helpful in the conversions of Protestants as well as others of different beliefs. Using their Bible perspective, they have developed a stronger apparent weapon in defense of Catholicism that likely was not in the "arsenal" of the Catholic hierarchy. The evidence they produce gives the **appearance of being valid**. That occurs because scripture is frequently used and the presenters are articulate, charismatic, and the teaching is sufficiently complex that it confuses, making it hard to dispute. This might seem like an unlikely formula for convincing people, but it works and leaves followers dependent on their teachers. Thus they have risen to be powerfully convincing instructors of Catholic doctrine. They are appropriately called Catholic apologists. It is worthwhile to understand their thinking. Their conversions have many similarities, and in fact, Marcus Grodi was influenced by Dr. Hahn. In both cases, they were **not** pursued by Catholics to become Catholic, but they both found problems in what they believed – what Protestants believed. They questioned what they, as Protestants, were teaching and in very fundamental ways. The basic tenants of Luther and Calvin were found to be worrisome. In both cases, the **"faith only"** aspect, the **security of the believer,** and doubts regarding sola scriptura, which are the cornerstones of Protestantism, were bothersome. Once they reached this point, there were other substantial issues or questions like why the Protestants believed so differently, which became critical. Dr. Hahn and Marcus Grodi eventually became convinced (100% confident) Luther and Calvin's teachings were not scriptural. Once Sola Fide (by faith alone) was no longer viable, leaving the other sola's and Calvin's TULIP was easy.

Note: A comment regarding Dr. Hahn and Marcus Grodi. These two individuals are wrong concerning the truth. I can only say that it appears to have been a sincere search for truth that ended in their association with the Catholic Church and then an earnest and aggressive effort to promote Catholicism. We live in a world where few are seriously interested in religion, and here are two men who have battled throughout their lives trying to figure out what life was all about. There is an admiration of such by me, yet they landed very far from the truth in this battle. We see things much differently and thus cannot both be right, although both could be wrong. In the case of this book, it is written to help those who love the truth more than what they currently believe. The battle of these two converts ends with an unfortunate outcome. The word of God is simple and so drastically different than the "religions of the world" that it is easy to sort truth from error. Catholicism will be annihilated as a religion by the use of scripture. That does not mean a person will leave Catholicism, but those who love the truth and take their eternity seriously will exit. I would assume that Dr. Hahn, Marcus Grodi, and myself all share an aggressive interest in the souls of humankind. Unfortunately, each person only has the opportunity to succeed when on the side of truth. That is, finding and living the truth.

The next step after leaving Protestantism, at least philosophically, was a growing curiosity about Catholicism. Both Dr. Hahn and Marcus Grodi were well versed in the deceit of Catholicism and had each taught on its evils. Teaching about the history of the popes, the inquisition, the terrible misuse of scripture would mean they believed the Roman Catholic Church was evil. These anti-Catholic teachings were well known throughout Protestantism, and they were often severe.

The immediate issue to enable a favorable consideration of Catholicism would be the terminology used by Protestants in support of Protestant beliefs, namely Sola Scriptura. Catholic beliefs deny this idea of the scriptures being the only guide for faith. In addition to the scriptures, they say the Catholic Church via its apostolic succession (popes) and the tradition of the early church fathers were also valid sources of truth. This would be what Dr. Hahn and Marcus Grodi must address in addition to the many ceremonies and practices (e.g., Catholic mass, Mariology, Catholic confessional, and the Real Presence, to mention a few) to accept Catholicism.

6.2 Dr. Hahn – A Catholic convert from the Presbyterian ministry

One of the helpful things about Dr. Hahn and Marcus Grodi is their prolific use of the Internet, often using videos to present their beliefs. Both are prominent on Catholic television, and Dr. Hahn also with Catholic universities. They are highly respected and desired speakers within the Catholic Church. Dr. Hahn presently teaches at the Franciscan University of Steubenville, a Catholic university in the United States. He is a Professor of Theology and Scripture, author, speaker, and apologist. His title is the Father Michael Scanlan, Chair of Biblical Theology and The New Evangelism.

To be as accurate as possible, we will look at Dr. Hahn's video description of his trip to Catholicism, and this can be seen at these sites:

https://www.youtube.com/watch?v=P-bz4kRtCQI&ab_channel=joboww
Or there is another version, somewhat shorter:

https://www.youtube.com/watch?v=DCD6QF1jCyg&ab_channel=CharlieMike

Dr. Hahn has become a well-known apologist for Catholicism and a highly desired speaker. I would say he is the most talented at presenting the Catholic position. This is quite odd, unless you consider the older generations of Catholic priests and bishops were not well versed in the Bible. What baffled me was how someone with such a strong theology background and a solid working knowledge of the scriptures could reach such an awful conclusion - Catholicism. Dr. Hahn would be just another person with "brilliance" that missed the truth because he had the fundamentals wrong. Despite his high quantities of "apparent evidence," it is easy to dissect his arguments when the basics are wrong.

6.3 Dr. Hahn's conversion story as seen in the above videos

Almost immediately, Dr. Hahn reveals a substantial fatal flaw in terms of a fundamental error. He believes that a man came into his life and "he was sure he was sent by God" to help him along the road to truth. Dr. Hahn thinks that the Holy Spirit was working in a way to bring him to Catholicism. He is keeping this very Calvin idea, and it happens to be a way that Catholics also accept, at least in general. Namely, the Holy Spirit interacting with people related to their conversion. Certainly, Calvin sees this interaction differently from Catholics, but both see the Holy Spirit as active. However, the truth about the Holy Spirit is much different. The truth is that the Holy Spirit completed His mission sometime before the end of the first century. Whenever there are references in scripture to the Holy Spirit playing a part in conversion, leading, witnessing, comforting, strengthening, it is always in relation to the word of God **which He delivered**. This is a massively powerful distinction if a person can make it. It immediately rejects the integrity of all those who claim they have received some sort of message from God. They have not, and in our case, that includes Dr. Hahn. This understanding destroys Protestantism and Catholicism as they rely on this sort of divine contact (from time to time) to direct their lives and even their doctrines. The revelations from God have been completed before the end of the first century – thus there can be no changes, additions, substractions to doctrine after that time. Below is a table I have used in previous books to discuss the operation of the Holy Spirit, particularly in conversion.

God's word in conversion	**Scripture**
Faith comes from the word of God	Romans 10.17
Word of God is perfect in conversion	Psalms 19.7
Word of God enlightens a man's soul	Psalms 19.8
Word of God makes one wise to salvation	2 Timothy 3.15
Word of God furnishes all that as man needs spiritually	2 Timothy 3.16,17
The soul is purified, born again by the word of God	1 Peter 1.22,23
Keeping the word of God (His commands) shows your love	John14.15
Obey the word (the gospel)	1 Peter 4.17, Romans 6.17

It is God's word that guides people **as delivered by the Holy Spirit**. In that sense, the Holy Spirit directs, convicts, enlightens, purifies the soul by the word of God but not personally. 1 Peter 1:22-23

22 Since you have purified your souls in obeying the truth through the Spirit in sincere love of the brethren, love one another fervently with a pure heart,

23 having been born again, not of corruptible seed but incorruptible, through the word of God which lives and abides forever

The operation of the Holy Spirit is one of those things that is very fundamental, and if you get it wrong, there are all sorts of "inventions" that follow. The Holy Spirit was the one that brought "that which is perfect" – the completed word of God. The Holy Spirit's activity since that which is perfect arrived is only through the inspired word. Every case of people claiming the Holy Spirit intervened with them has been a lie, and, if that were possible, there would be conflicts with what God delivered in terms of the means of conversion. Any communication with God is no longer possible except by those "in Christ," and God has no message for you other than what is contained in the scriptures. Seeking God requires a diligent effort, but a person can avoid all the work by saying God or the Holy Spirit spoke to them. If God did such a thing, He would be going against the pattern established for conversion, for communicating with Him, and would make God a respecter of persons, and He declares He is not. Another way of bringing clarity is in Acts 10, where Peter indicates God shows no partiality. Nonetheless, it is a partiality claimed by many, including in our case Dr. Hahn.

Acts 10:34-35

34 Then Peter opened his mouth and said: "In truth I perceive that God shows no partiality.

35 But in every nation whoever fears Him and works righteousness is accepted by Him.

When you understand the operation of the Holy Spirit incorrectly, what follows is a disaster, or we might say the reason for the current state of religion. We have centuries of people building on this "misconception." The truth is the Holy Spirit shut the door on any other doctrine. The word of God is complete. There are no more signs, miracles, gifts of the Holy Spirit, and the word of God has been confirmed. The results of getting this wrong are the creation of conflicts with scripture, assertions of signs and miracles, and all sorts of people claiming some personal interaction with God, Christ, the Holy Spirit, angels, and just about anybody else claimed to be sent from God. In such a world, we have the possibility of all kinds of variances from the truth. That is what we have. God knows this very well and thus provides directions to avoid this, and that can be summarized as "Change Nothing."

6.4 Dr. Hahn and Martin Luther

One of Dr. Hahn's early discoveries related to errors in Luther's *"sola fide"* (i.e., by faith only) and the conclusion that Catholics had this correct (more than faith only) in terms of the need for **doing things beyond some mental belief** in Christ. Martin Luther was a particular hero of Dr. Hahn, and I also viewed him favorably for his courage but not for his doctrine. Dr. Hahn was suddenly thrown into turmoil when he realized Luther was wrong on this most fundamental issue. At this point, the alternative to Protestantism based on the failure of *"sola fide"* and Calvin's TULIP could be Catholicism. Yet, the many problems of Catholicism were significant.

Dr. Hahn is beginning to see that the Old Testament was fulfilled in the New Testament – which of course, he knew but now in different ways. This is one place where Dr. Hahn begins to get seriously off track. He is now seeing **the teachings of the Catholic church** being fulfilled from things of the Old Testament. In any case, this is a theme that dominates Dr. Hahn's teaching and leads him down many wrong paths. We might say he is bringing complexity to simplicity. Dr. Hahn brings a puzzle-like character to understanding God's "apparent hidden" meanings. He now finds many of the teachings of Catholicism that were previously unseen by him, to be in some way exposed in the Old Testament.

Additionally, he is amazed that the early church fathers had previously seen these things and mentions Augustine, Justin Martyr, Thomas Aquinas, or one of the popes. All these "Catholic scholars" had anticipated these novel breakthroughs that Dr. Hahn was now finding in his intense, in-depth scripture study. His classes in a Presbyterian school sounded very Catholic, and his wife said he was becoming Luther in reverse. His students could also see the direction he was headed – but they seemed to like it. Dr. Hahn is going so fast even he cannot keep up, and it would have been wise to slow down. God left no mysteries, no hidden meanings and for a very good reason – He wants people to succeed. God kept it simple.

Protestants have a liturgy, but Dr. Hahn was teaching a liturgy that looked more like the Catholic liturgy. Protestant liturgy was or tried to be very Bible-based. In contrast, Catholic liturgy contained doctrines much broader, including the human-like ideas of their hierarchy, often with a basis from the early church father's selected writings.

Liturgy is defined: a form or formulary according to which public religious worship, especially Christian worship, is conducted.

The Catholic liturgy is centered around the Mass and focused on the Eucharist. Another word for liturgy would be a rite, a formula. An example of what Dr. Hahn brought to his Presbyterian class and to the church he was overseeing was partaking of the Lord's Supper every week. The typical Presbyterian pattern was four times a year. Of course, the scriptures teach "every first day of the week," but Catholicism can even be more frequent. In any case, the people loved this idea. He believed that his studies and discoveries in the scriptures were things that the Catholic Church already understood. He wondered how did they know these things?

A turning point for Dr. Hahn was during a presbyterian theology class, when a student asked, "where does the Bible teach that it is the **only authority** and not also the traditions." "Where does it teach sola scriptura?" Dr. Hahn answered using some verses (Matthew 5:17-19, 2 Timothy 3:16, and Matthew 15 regarding tradition), but none satisfied him (or his class). He began to doubt sola scriptura, which is sad because the Bible is clear regarding it being the only authority, and it is more than a verse here or there. Dr. Hahn should have been grounded in this fundamental principle of God as expressed throughout all scripture.

Dr. Hahn begins to study Catholic books, reads hundreds of Catholic documents, and enrolls at a Catholic college taking theology. Dr. Hahn mentions not getting much help from priests as they seem uninterested in converting a Protestant. Some of the priests he met seemed downright unpleasant in their language and attitude. He also notes a lack of understanding of their beliefs and poor general knowledge of the scriptures. It amazed me that "a light did not go on" for Dr. Hahn, indicating how distant Catholic clergy was from understanding their religion. This was also my experience with Catholicism. Catholic priests were "parish priests" doing Catholic liturgy and other duties but had a poor understanding of the scriptures and thus could not defend their beliefs. As he continued his study of Catholicism, he found many knowledgeable and kind hearts within the Catholic clergy.

Note: It was evil that drove Luther away from Catholicism. Things like the indulgences that preyed on Catholics concerned for their loved ones in purgatory, the general cruelty, and immorality of the Catholic priests and Catholic hierarchy of his time, and he was right to leave. Nonetheless, Luther got it all wrong with his sola's – except sola scriptura.

Looking at Dr. Hahn, there is a constant. It is the complexity he brings in his teaching. He is not taking what God says seriously, he is making a great deal out of the things of the Old Testament and finding how they are fulfilled in the New Testament, but he thinks remarkably fulfilled in Catholicism. He will continue his search and find some Catholic doctrine also "hidden" in the book of Revelation. In this regard, he is overthinking and missing the simple message of salvation. The outcome of this "wisdom of the wise, prudent effort" is something entirely foreign to the scriptures, namely the Roman Catholic Church.

The Eucharist, held in such awe by the Catholic Church, is something none of the New Testament writers inspired by the Holy Spirit ever once mentioned. The "Real Presence" of the actual body and blood of Christ is entirely unknown to them. Those "in Christ" are part of the spiritual body of Christ, and thus **they REMEMBER the savior's death, burial, and resurrection**. The God-defined Lord's Supper has value in weekly (scriptural) recollection of what God through Christ did for them. The Eucharist does fit Catholicism as just another physical aspect of their error-prone, evil institution. It serves no purpose except to make people feel good, whereas the Lord's Supper, properly directed reminds a child of God of what God in Christ did very specifically for them. At the same time, it honors the Son. It is a memorial to the Son. The "Real Presence" is the subject of Chapter 9.

6.5 Dr. Hahn and the gospel message

Dr. Hahn gives the appearance of one obsessed with scholarship – not with bringing the gospel message. This might seem fine to many people, but Christianity to be meaningful has to do with life's purpose: **Life is about the soul**. God has made a simple solution to the sin problem in the gospel message. If you are involved with Christianity, you are engaged with the truth, and there is an overwhelming desire to bring and live the message from God. God's purpose is to share His Divine Nature, and He does nothing to complicate that message and the most essential thing about the message is that it is from God and not to be changed. God used quite a long time, about fifty-plus years, to reveal the New Testament by inspiration. The Holy Spirit inspired certain men, and consequently, the truth for all remaining time was transcribed. That should be (and was) sufficient time to provide the truth in terms of God finishing His message to humankind. It would be lasting because it was written and could be copied and be available "forever." We will see shortly that Marcus Grodi comments that the scriptures referred to in Timothy must be the Old Testament scriptures since that was all that existed – obviously not true. The scriptures were all written in the first century. There was an awareness of this among Christians, such as in the churches Paul had started.

1 Corinthians 15:3-4

3 For I delivered to you first of all that which I also received: that Christ died for our sins according to the Scriptures,
4 and that He was buried, and that He rose again the third day according to the Scriptures,

2 Peter 3:16

16 as also in all his epistles, speaking in them of these things, in which are some things hard to understand, which untaught and unstable people twist to their own destruction, as they do also the rest of the Scriptures.

God, wanting to achieve His purpose, would not allow the message to be unclear. His part would be perfect. Hearsay, verbal communication, and things passed down (tradition) would not be perfect and not flawlessly serve His purpose. As we will see, there was tradition referred to as valid, but to be lasting, there must be a tangible record. A valid tradition was valid being associated with the Holy Spirit's work and would become a written record, or today we would not know its certainty unless it were scripture.

How much **more** do you suppose God had to say after fifty-plus years of the Holy Spirit working with the apostles? You can read about the proper use of tradition in this book, i.e., when it is valid and when it is not, in this chapter as the fourth verse not seen by Marcus Grodi. God delivered His message by inspiration, not by tradition, which would eventually be subjective. Anyone who supports the Catholic concept of tradition must reject God's clear, unambiguous and complete means of delivering the truth. It is the truth that resulted in God's purpose being achieved. Dr. Hahn finds mystery everywhere and does this by making it appear that some of the

Catholic doctrines are validated in the Old Testament. Also, he supports some **select** early church father's writings as a valid support for Catholic doctrine. Some of the primary Catholic doctrines that gain support in Dr. Hahn's theology are related to Mariology, to the "Real Presence" and "as his analysis goes" aspects of these doctrines are "necessitated" by this history (Old Testament, early church father's writing). Thus to Dr. Hahn, it is not surprising to find these things in the Catholic Church doctrine. Indeed, it is all very mysterious, but of more interest would be the **WHY of these Catholic doctrines**. God has a purpose, and the things He does to accomplish that purpose are very straightforward. Much (likely all) of Catholic doctrine plays no part in God's purpose, especially since **the scriptural things resulted in God's purpose being fulfilled**. God's purpose is fulfilled perfectly in the manner of the gospel message. Also, despite making these ridiculous connections with the Old Testament and some of the early church father's writings, his analysis/conclusions are very obviously in opposition to the inspired word of God. **We will demonstrate this throughout the book.**

Dr. Hahn accepts the early church father's writings as valid scripture or as valid as the scriptures. If there is any doubt, he accepts Catholic doctrine such as Vatican II, which places scripture equivalent to the Magisterium of the Catholic church. He ignores the solid truths of scripture and agrees with the pronounced **scriptural problems of Catholicism, i.e., a pope**. Those things that keep Catholicism from having any association with God he somehow overlooks. The most important declaration of scripture is, of course, the thing that brings reconciliation. It should be the centerpiece of every Christian's life and work, and it is the gospel message. Where do discussions of the Real Presence, Mariology, confessing sins to a priest, infant baptism, the mass, purgatory, the pope, and hundreds of other Catholic inventions fit? Why do they exist? They only serve to distract, to confuse the simplicity from God that allows you to share in His Divine Nature.

6.6 Dr. Hahn on Paul's conversion

The problems with Dr. Hahn and the Catholic Church are also seen in a short video on what he refers to as the feast of Saint Paul's conversion. You can see it at:

(https://www.facebook.com/Dr.ScottHahn/videos/437207160658937).

131

Again with this topic, Dr. Hahn gets off to a bad start by honoring Paul in some religious manner. Indeed Paul is a saint, but so are all Christians. Dr. Hahn's intention (being a Catholic) implies he accepts the idea of creating this special category of a saint. Thus he agrees with the Catholic process of making saints, which is truly bizarre. In Catholicism, when the lie is accepted, what follows is building on that lie. As a result, their teachings become even more inexplicable, and this pattern is the hallmark of Catholicism. The name saint is designated by God and used by Paul in reference to those "in Christ." Thus this designation cannot have another use. Paul would sometimes address them as saints in writing to the churches, such as his letters to the Philippians and Corinthians. Saints are those in the spiritual body of Christ, added there by the Lord while they are alive. That is the Godly process of conversion, and it carries the name saint and the idea of having been separated for God – three examples where Paul references those in the local church as saints are given below:

Philippians 1:1

1 Paul and Timothy, bondservants of Jesus Christ,

To all the saints in Christ Jesus who are in Philippi, with the bishops and deacons:

Similarly, in the first and second letters to the Corinthians.

1 Corinthians 1:1-2
1 Paul, called to be an apostle of Jesus Christ through the will of God,
and Sosthenes our brother,
2 To the church of God which is at Corinth, to those who are sanctified in Christ Jesus, called to be saints, with all who in every place call on the name of Jesus Christ our Lord, both theirs and ours:

2 Corinthians 1:1
1 Paul, an apostle of Jesus Christ by the will of God, and Timothy our brother,
To the church of God which is at Corinth, with all the saints who are in all Achaia:

Continuing with this celebration day for Paul, there can be an important lesson. The most fundamental thing **about God** is that no person or thing is to be honored, revered religiously – only God! Dr. Hahn has arrived at Catholicism and is participating.

*Note: Not to be confused, **honor religiously** belongs only to God. However, there is a distinction to be made. 1 Peter 2:17 says, "Honor all people. Love the brotherhood. Fear God. Honor the king." The short version of this truth is that those "in Christ" are to honor all persons, and in this case, it is best to understand this as "respect all persons." In the Christian life, a child of God thinks more highly of others than themself. Also, we see Paul saying, "knowing the terror of the Lord we persuade men." Paul can say this because he respects all persons, and God knows the salvation of the world is in the hands of those in His body, and we need to have an attitude like Paul. That is, showing this high respect for each person, specifically a concern for their souls. The feast day for Paul is a religious honor and **quite different** than having respect for Paul, the kind of respect we are to have for all people. In this case, there is this special day commemorating his conversion. Why are they remembering Paul? Jesus is remembered on each first day of the week, and God designates this. Catholicism is very physical and filled with all sorts of things that people might appreciate, such as honoring Jesus's birth or honoring Paul's conversion, yet neither of these is authorized. The world of the scriptures is a world of things authorized by God, and the "world of religion" is a world that honors the things humankind thinks are important.*

It is noble always to think the best about people, but I am suspicious of how this story of Paul's feast day is presented. When I saw the title of this video, I was very interested in how it would be discussed. Dr. Hahn avoids how Paul was converted because that might be a problem. At the beginning of his talk on Paul's conversion, he mentions three particular scriptures on this subject, namely three chapters in Acts (9, 22, and 26). He fails to return to these chapters in his discourse to talk about the actual conversion of Paul. The truth of Paul's conversion (forgiveness of sins) is in the verses of Acts 9 and 22. They detail how Paul's sins were forgiven, and it is consistent with all Bible conversions. It is nothing like how Catholics claim to become Christians. Of course, they never become Christians. Leaving out these verses because they are problematic would not be an issue for any apologist since they can explain any problem – this is what apologists of all religions do. Below is the scripture from Acts 22 and is complete in the details of Paul's conversion.

Acts 22:9-16

9 "And those who were with me indeed saw the light and were afraid, but they did not hear the voice of Him who spoke to me.

10 So I said, 'What shall I do, Lord?' And the Lord said to me, 'Arise and go into Damascus, and there you will be told all things which are appointed for you to do.'

11 And since I could not see for the glory of that light, being led by the hand of those who were with me, I came into Damascus.

12 "Then a certain Ananias, a devout man according to the law, having a good testimony with all the Jews who dwelt there,

13 came to me; and he stood and said to me, 'Brother Saul, receive your sight.' And at that same hour I looked up at him.

14 Then he said, 'The God of our fathers has chosen you that you should know His will, and see the Just One, and hear the voice of His mouth.

15 For you will be His witness to all men of what you have seen and heard.

16 And now why are you waiting? Arise and be baptized, and wash away your sins, calling on the name of the Lord.'

The conversion of Paul, that is, his receiving forgiveness of sins, occurs consistent with the other conversions of the New Testament (see https://heavencoach.com/conversions-of-the-new-testament/). Since the death, burial, and resurrection of Jesus, there is a consistent process that brings about the reconciliation. **God does not violate that process by saving Paul** when "suddenly a light shone around Paul from heaven and he fell to the ground." Instead, He sent Paul to Damascus, where he would be told what to do. Ananias first instructs Paul to "Arise and be baptized, and wash away your sins, calling on the name of the Lord." Again, see the document "Conversions of the New Testament" - https://heavencoach.com/conversions-of-the-new-testament/ and therein is a brief explanation of "calling on the name of the Lord." There is quite a lesson here in how Paul received forgiveness of sins as it demonstrates how **even Jesus**

respected the pattern that was established for having sins forgiven. Catholicism will violate God's pattern of salvation and thus brazenly disrespect God as they do with all of God's word.

6.7 That which is perfect (1 Corinthians 13.10)

It turns out to accept Catholicism, Dr. Hahn emphasizes the early church father's writings, their associated valid tradition and consequently rejects the word of God. Undoubtedly, he is not fully aware of the latter, but he should be. Dr. Hahn is not alone in missing the meaning of "that which is perfect," for if he got that right, it would be hard to be a Catholic or a Protestant. The revelation from God to man is over, and we have what God wanted us to have – the truth. Anything coming after this in terms of truth, different or added to or subtracted from God's completed word, is wrong. All the things that come after "that which is perfect" have no added value as God has completed His revelation. The timing is perfect since the pattern required for reconciliation was revealed and the reconciliation with God has occurred in some.

1 Corinthians 13:10
10 But when that which is perfect has come, then that which is in part will be done away.

*Note: That which is perfect is discussed throughout this book to bring the correct understanding to this significant revelation from God. It is discussed in Chapter 9 under the topic of "The Catholic position" (9.6) and "Making the powerful distinction of **that which is perfect**" (9.7) and also in Chapter 15.*

6.8 Ask what is missing, and it will be the spiritual versus physical

The thing that seems to be consistently missed is the same thing missed by the Jews, now missed by Catholicism and by the "churches of the world," is the spiritual nature of the church – the spiritual nature of everything. The world's religions still seek signs, and there are no signs, although we might, in a sense, say the signs are all spiritual – the word of God. People will never get over needing signs despite Jesus placing the idea of needing signs into a very bad category, namely, sought by an evil generation. In Luke, the rich man in Tartarus was told his request to have Abraham go to his brothers would not be fulfilled.

Luke 16:29-31

29 Abraham said to him, 'They have Moses and the prophets; let them hear them.'

30 And he said, 'No, father Abraham; but if one goes to them from the dead, they will repent.'

31 But he said to him, 'If they do not hear Moses and the prophets, neither will they be persuaded though one rise from the dead.'

The things that can move people (like Lazarus's brothers) to live correctly are the things God so designates, and Abraham points them to the word of God in terms of the teachings of Moses and the prophets. People want signs, but God always points people to His truth, to the word of God.

Thus this brilliant, articulate theologian is right about some things, mainly the reasons Luther and Calvin, Knox, and so on were wrong. Then they jump into accepting everything Catholic and are back into terribly wrong. One might hope that Dr. Hahn will find his way free from Catholicism, but he has dug himself a very deep hole. It is not only a hole concerning the truth but also, as is so often the case, one of personal reputation. It is a hole we all have trouble overcoming because certainly, we are not proud – being facetious as pride is common but varies greatly in magnitude. One way to conquer pride and ego is to be honest when asking oneself how badly I want heaven – badly enough to humble myself before God, before God's will, before God's word.

6.9 Marcus Grodi: A convert from the Presbyterian ministry

We will discuss three aspects of the conversion and beliefs of Marcus Grodi. He can be seen on EWTN Catholic television, and one particular program he hosts is called "The Journey Home." Marcus Grodi founded the Coming Home Network International and is a frequent contributor/speaker for various Catholic programs and conventions such as "Deep in History." He is the author of multiple books. In reviewing his available internet **material, I settled on discussing his most representative talks to reveal his beliefs and conversion.** They are:

- Marcus Grodi said there were ten bible verses that he had not seen properly, and he provided them and their part in bringing him to Catholicism.

  The *ten Bible verses* used to convince Marcus Grodi, a Presbyterian, to be a Catholic:

https://www.youtube.com/watch?v=DJDVKSF7Hjo&ab_channel=EWTN

- Next, he mentions the one key verse that brought him to Catholicism.

  Marcus Grodi on authority and the ONE verse that brought him to Catholicism:

1 Timothy 3:14-15

https://www.youtube.com/watch?v=OonbbY7bbcw&ab_channel=TheComingHomeNetworkInternational

- Finally, Marcus Grodi discusses, "What must I do to be saved."

https://www.youtube.com/watch?v=k7IJGzQlo1w&t=1508s&ab_channel=TheComingHomeNetworkInternational

*Note: I provided links to the three videos above by Marcus Grodi, but it is only necessary to discuss two of them since the second one, namely the ONE verse that brought him to Catholicism, is also one of the **ten Bible verses** covered. Like all of the verses to be discussed, but perhaps especially this one (1 Timothy 3:14-15), if correctly understood, should cause a person to move **quickly AWAY from Catholicism.***

We begin with a special episode of "The Journey Home" that Marcus Grodi calls "**the ten verses of holy scripture he "never saw"** when he was a Protestant. He discusses these ten verses: Proverbs 3:5-6; 1 Timothy 3: 14-15; 2 Timothy 3:14-17; 2 Thessalonians 2:15; Matthew 16:13-19; Revelation 14:13; Romans 10:14-15; John 15:4 and John 6:56; Colossians 1:24; and Luke 1:46-49. I am sure "never saw" relates more to "**never correctly understood."** Some of the verses he now "**sees**" relate to problems with Protestant beliefs but primarily to considering things that support the Catholic view.

6.10 The ten verses Marcus Grodi never saw

The first verse Marcus Grodi never saw

Proverbs 3:5-6
5 Trust in the LORD with all your heart,
And lean not on your own understanding;
6 In all your ways acknowledge Him,
And He shall direct your paths.

These verses are very fundamental and, of course, true as they are read. Marcus Grodi seems to be recalling these verses that have always held significant meaning for him. Proverbs 3:5-6 have been solid ground for Marcus Grodi because **it is where truth is found** such that you can trust the Lord with all your heart. Marcus Gordi initially believed that the scriptures were the only place truth resided. However, he rightly observed that people claiming only to follow the scriptures could believe very differently. He became concerned regarding who was right. This is all very logical so far. However, the most obvious answer for Marcus Grodi was to look for the **additional revelation** that cleared up this situation. Unfortunately, this led Him to study writings that were not scriptural. The thinking was to look at scripts available from the earliest centuries. That was when many factions were contending for the leadership of Christianity. Did God leave more than the things being recognized as the word of God? An essential discernment from God's word is that it has been completed. However, Catholics and Protestants both miss this critical understanding. This was the right time to complete God's word, to complete His message to humankind since God has fulfilled His purpose. We might say God the Father completed His part, Jesus completed His part, and the Holy Spirit completed His part. All that was left was for humankind to properly respond to all that had been done for them. Humankind has been provided the best possible thing, that which is perfect - the completed word of God. Also, very obviously, they should not tamper with the word of God, but in this matter, they will struggle.

The Holy Spirit emphasizes that no scripture is of any private interpretation. That is, there is one meaning, and thus in that, there is unity – people believing the same. Indeed the current Protestant and Catholic teachings are due to **privately interpreting the scripture differently than God's meaning**. We have all these beliefs, and for Protestants, we go back to Luther and Calvin (and many others of the Protestant movement) and their private interpretations. They were all very wrong, and of course, building on those errors, there is a continuum of many diverse beliefs. People can believe the same using the scriptures, and because many do not, it does not mean it cannot be done.

It is sad because these verses in Psalms emphasize, "Trust in the LORD with all your heart, And lean not on your own understanding." **Marcus Grodi would go forward, trusting his ability** to find something that answered his questions no matter where he needed to go. When men become involved in doctrine, they do not trust the Lord. In all the ten verses (often sets of verses) that Marcus Grodi was now seeing differently, he may have indeed seen them differently, but still, in each case, he saw them incorrectly. In this first verse, he saw differently; his original view was correct, and it is hard to envision seeing it any different than it reads. **His problem was not with this verse but that others of the Protestant belief also believed this verse and yet had many different beliefs.** Thus he thinks if they were all trusting in the LORD with all their heart and leaning not on their own understanding and allowing God to direct their paths, why do they believe very differently? It turns out there are many reasons for this, but he chooses a reason that was the worst possible choice. He began to question if the word of God was all that was needed. This book clarifies why these Protestants believed differently, given all agreeing with Proverbs 3:5-6. Let me mention one reason: they had many different **private interpretations** of the scriptures.

The Second verse Marcus Grodi never saw

1 Timothy 3:14-15

14 These things I write to you, though I hope to come to you shortly;

15 but if I am delayed, I write so that you may know how you ought to conduct yourself in the house of God, which is the church of the living God, the pillar and ground of the truth.

Catholics use this verse to prove that the sole source of truth is **not** the Bible. Instead, they say it is the church. Of course, they mean the Catholic Church. The church is the pillar and ground of the truth. Indeed, the pillar and ground of truth is the church. However, Marcus Grodi does not understand the church, and thus he cannot understand 1 Timothy 3:15.

Here is what Marcus Grodi does not understand. There is but one church, and it is spiritual, and it is that to which the Lord personally adds the obedient. It can be referred to as the body of Christ. **It is not a physical church** where rules are made and dictated by humankind, but the body of Christ is the pillar and ground of the truth. The pillar and ground of truth consist of things delivered to the apostles by the Holy Spirit – the truth. Jesus told the apostles the Holy Spirit would guide them into all truth. The things of God were inspired by the Holy Spirit to be distributed to the world, initially by the apostles. Those "in Christ" would take the things of God seriously, and it could be said those things were written on their hearts. That is, they **acted in accordance with the will of God – the word of God was exceedingly meaningful to them**. God was overseeing the process such that the word of God would be available to all of humankind. Peter would write that we have all things pertaining to life and godliness. What else do we need? The local church, which was gradually revealed during the first century, consists of individuals in the body of Christ. They would carry the message to the world, and being the church, they were to bring the message contained in their hearts. Of course, the message exists in writing. Otherwise, there would be no way for individuals to know the truth, believe it, and make it part of their lives. It is the message inspired by the Holy Spirit and recorded, and those "in Christ" are in effect the pillar and ground of the truth. They are the pillar supporting the word of God as the only rulebook. Originally, there were laws written on stone, but now in the spiritual church, the word of God needs no physical depository. Jesus said He would build His church, and He has been doing that since the gospel was first preached on the day of Pentecost following

His death, burial, and resurrection. We might say that initially, the apostles were the pillar and ground of truth, and then those converted. The rulebook is the New Testament, the word of God as delivered by the Holy Spirit, and unless this message is on the hearts of those in the body of Christ, it is indeed just words on paper. God's purpose can only be fulfilled if those "in Christ" take the message to the world. God's care of scripture is such that no person is ever involved in its creation.

2 Peter 1:20-21

20 knowing this first, that no prophecy of Scripture is of any private interpretation,
21 for prophecy never came by the will of man, but holy men of God spoke as they were moved by the Holy Spirit.

Practically speaking, there needs to be a physical record, and the Spirit of God assures what we have is correct. God's oversight, as seen in His promise that His word would by no means pass away, ensures the scriptures come down through history, and indeed we have them today. Yet, the important thing is that the word of God resides in the hearts of those "in Christ." It reaches those hearts from the written word of God by an individual's dedication to God, and we might say to a love of the truth. If the written word of God sat in some dingy room and was never read, never understood, and especially never taught, it would be meaningless as the pillar and ground of the truth. The word of God needs to be in the hearts of humankind. The reality of being in the hearts of those "in Christ" is demonstrated by bringing the gospel message to the world. The spiritual body of Christ, His church, is the pillar and ground of the truth. The overwhelming problem of Catholicism that makes it easily identifiable as the error is its character as the physical church. This characteristic is seen in everything Catholicism does, beginning with an earthly head and then claiming that the church (the Catholic Church) is the pillar and ground of the truth. This faulty foundation claims to have ownership of the truth. Peter can write the verses below to those saints he is addressing because they obeyed the truth. They heard the gospel message, and it would be very much like Peter spoke on that first day of the kingdom. Regardless of who brought the message, it came from one "in Christ," and it was what they believed (written on their heart). The word of God has been recorded, and those who follow it incorporate it into their lives. I am not talking about memorizing it, although it is natural for those "in Christ" to think of that as helpful in their evangelism. Peter emphasizes the nature of God's word as being incorruptible, meaning able to accomplish what God intended, it will not die. This whole process is at the center of God's purpose and allows a rebirth without sin, through the word of God, which lives and abides forever. There is nothing else like the word of God, not the traditions of men, not the councils of men, or simply said not the Catholic Church.

1 Peter 1:22-23

22 Since you have purified your souls in obeying the truth through the Spirit in sincere love of the brethren, love one another fervently with a pure heart,

23 having been born again, not of corruptible seed but incorruptible, through the word of God which lives and abides forever

The word of God is not some corruptible paper, but God's word is sufficient to purify the souls of those who obey. Thus, in every way, the church, the spiritual body of Christ, is the pillar and ground of the truth. The flawed conclusion that the Catholic Church is the pillar and ground of truth has hundreds of problems beginning with the fact there is no such thing as the Catholic Church in terms of having an association with God. Catholics would have the pillar and ground of truth be physical, changing, and changeable, which does not sound like a pillar. The pillar and ground of truth should be unchangeable, i.e., the truth, very singular. God emphasizes His word must not be added to or taken away from, or changed in any way. The body of Christ is the spiritual church, and it consists of those souls that honor God's word by not changing it.

The **local church** that consists of those in the body of Christ has a platform that is spiritual and has a single rule book, the Bible. The local church cannot change God's word, and thus as we view the spiritual church (individuals that the Lord, Himself added to His body) and the local church, they can be considered the pillar and ground of the truth. The local church qualifies as the pillar and ground of truth since it is made up of the spiritual body of Christ and would never allow changes to the word of God. To be very precise, it would never allow private interpretations of the word of God. God's word is not negotiable, and it is not the object of councils of people to interpret the meaning. The body of Christ knows that God means what He says and means how He says it. The church referred to in 1 Timothy 3:15 is the spiritual body of Christ and is infinitely distant from any physical body of rule-making people. Those "in Christ" making up the local church are dedicated to not changing God's word. We might clarify and emphasize that again by saying not changing God's meaning.

The truth, according to Jesus, is in the word of God. "Sanctify them by Your truth, Your word is truth" (John 17:17). Again, if that word is changeable in its meaning, it would not be much of a pillar. It is the Bible that defines the church and not the other way around. God defined the organization of the local church, and all things were done to assure the gospel message was not altered. Paul in Galatians the first chapter warned about the gospel being changed and then pointed out how he received it from Christ. "But I make known to you, brethren, that the gospel which I preached is not according to man. For I neither received it from man, nor was I taught it, but it came through the revelation of Jesus Christ" (Galatians 1:11-12). The word of God is the one solid thing and not some human-devised church – the Catholic Church. The thing that God's people are to support (pillar) is "the truth." Those "in Christ" being the pillar and ground of truth support the truth.

Note: The written word of God is everywhere. The Bible is by far the most available book ever, with copies throughout the world. However, its principles are seldom followed, and it is disputed, changed in its meaning, and even vilified. However, as it is written on the hearts of those "in Christ," it is powerful in achieving the only thing that matters in life – the soul's success. Very simply the spiritual body of Christ, His church is the pillar and ground of the truth. Those "in Christ" have Christ living in them, and they are the temple of God, having the Spirit of God dwelling in them. Indeed, this would be the place for God's word to dwell, the place for God's word to be supported.

God's children have no authority over His truth because it is *His* and not *theirs*. They have no authority to change it, legislate it, or manipulate it. It exists independent of those "in Christ" and is not theirs for tampering. Jesus is the foundation of the church (1 Corinthians 3:11). The church is the product of truth. In other words, the truth is what begot us, resulting in us being born again (James 1:18; 1 Peter 1:22-23, 25). Those "in Christ" support the word of God and indeed are the pillar and ground of the truth.

Why do men feel they have authority over the truth? Why do we hear of "*the church*" (of England, Catholic, etc.) amending or making laws? Who has authority over the law in a kingdom, the citizen or the king? The "*household of God*" is not a democracy but a kingdom. As citizens of the kingdom, we cannot feel that we have any power over the truth. However, those "in Christ" support the truth. The truth predates them. The truth begot them. Let us be content to receive, live, and share the truth with others being products of its power. If the Catholic Church were the pillar and ground of truth, it would be defending the word of God as the only source of truth and protecting it against any changes.

A little more about 1 Timothy 3:15 – more clarity

Catholics use 1 Timothy 3:15 to claim they have the authority to legislate in divine matters. Here is a quote from "Father Smith Instructs Jackson" regarding the authority of the Catholic Church, page 35; The Question Box, page 96 "...The church of the living God, the pillar and mainstay of the truth" to prove that the church is invested with authority to legislate in divine matters." This is the stated belief of Catholicism concerning 1 Timothy 3:15 and thus the consistency of Catholicism's universal misunderstanding of the nature of the church.

The phrase "pillar and ground of truth" does **not** mean that the church is the originator of truth or that it can make or change the laws of God. It simply means that it is the upholder, defender, and proclaimer of the truth. There is not a single verse in all of scripture that indicates the church has the authority to originate truth or in any way change it.

We have said the truth is written on the hearts of those "in Christ" and seen in their proclamation of the gospel. The local church has one mission, and it is evangelism – to bring the gospel message to the world. The local body of Christ (all "in Christ") has been defined in organization, and its aspects are all spiritual. In a sense, it might seem difficult to differentiate the local church from its members. The sense is that in their unity, they are the pillar and ground of truth both in the singular and plural being dedicated to the sanctity of the word of God. A characteristic of those "in Christ" is humility, as demonstrated in their obedience. The local church has a divinely specified organization led by qualified elders whose qualifications include "**holding fast the faithful word**." If there is one obvious differentiator regarding accepting God's way and dedication to God's way and, in this case, the sanctity of God's word, it is humility. If there is one characteristic of those who changed the word of God, it is pride, having things their way, ruling over others, and such people built the Catholic Church and maintained it with savagery. The early church bishops of Rome often sought preeminence, and they finally got it in the early seventh century. They should have been seeking souls, but this was never a consideration or a meaningful discussion in their early church councils. There is every reason to believe that these "high" bishops never obeyed the gospel. They were never part of the body of Christ. They certainly never had an emphasis on the gospel message, and thus, not recognizing the church as spiritual, they continually sought to build a very earthly, physical church.

1 Timothy 3:15 teaches much more than the guardian of truth is the church, but the essence of the truth and the church as spiritual. God left nothing concerning the truth in the hands of humankind. All this time since Genesis 3:15, all the suffering then culminating in the death of His Son, all of God's plans to accomplish his purpose, and it would be less than perfect if anything in God's plan were left to humankind. God completed His part perfectly and did not leave us in confusion, in complication, at the whims of humanity. The Lord's church is spiritual, consisting of spiritual persons dedicated to the truth. Those in the body of Christ are the church and appropriately referred to as the pillar and ground of the truth.

*Note: In 1 Timothy 3:15, it mentions how you ought to conduct yourself in the house of God, and the physical churches of the world might think that means how you should conduct yourself in some religious building. However, this is much more important and, as might be expected, related to God fulfilling his purpose. The **conduct of those in the body of Christ is always on display** and must be consistent with how God defines the character of those "in Christ." Indeed, they are the light to the world carrying the truth, carrying the gospel message.*

The third verse not seen by Marcus Grodi

2 Timothy 3:14-17
14 But you must continue in the things which you have learned and been assured of, knowing from whom you have learned them,
15 and that from childhood you have known the Holy Scriptures, which are able to make you wise for salvation through faith which is in Christ Jesus.

16 All Scripture is given by inspiration of God, and is profitable for doctrine, for reproof, for correction, for instruction in righteousness,

17 that the man of God may be complete, thoroughly equipped for every good work.

Marcus Grodi begins by saying he **used** these verses to defend *sola scriptura*. Then he indicates that Paul could only be referring to the Old Testament when he says the Holy Scriptures. Of course, that is not the case since Paul's use of scripture would include anything God inspired in the past or future. Indeed these profitable qualities are those ONLY found in the word of God and accurately stated as follows, "All Scripture is given by inspiration of God and is profitable for doctrine, for reproof, for correction, for instruction in righteousness, that the man of God may be complete, thoroughly equipped for every good work." **What other thing can take the place of the scriptures in providing the profit indicated**? Nothing else could replace the scriptures in delivering these attributes. Thus, all other things are eliminated. It would seem the scriptures are the only source of truth, and of course, one would expect the entire message from God to confirm that conclusion, and of course, it does.

The first mention of scriptures in these verses was undoubtedly referring to the Old Covenant since Timothy was a child. However, the second use of the word scripture (verse 16), which is important to the point being made, is a reference to all scripture. It would be silly to think that the things inspired by God in the future would not fit this definition of scripture. Paul was at the center of revelations from God via direct interaction with Jesus (Galatians 1:12) and associated involvement with the Holy Spirit, guiding him, even directing him to certain localities. **Paul was amid God's final revelation**, and those things being revealed would be in the category of all scripture (verses 16 and 17 above).

Note: Earlier in the discussion of Dr. Hahn, we mentioned that the scriptures of the New Testament were (to a varying extent) available to those living during the time scriptures were being written, as seen in 1 Corinthians 15:3-4 and 2 Peter 3:16.

Paul tells Timothy that you have known the Holy Scriptures since childhood, which can make you wise for salvation through faith in Christ Jesus. Paul tells him to continue in the things you have learned and been assured of, knowing from whom you have learned them. Although, there were no scriptures except the Old Testament writings for Timothy as a child. The Old Testament pointed to Christ. Then as Timothy grew up, he was experiencing firsthand the New Testament revelations. Timothy was learning them from Paul, an apostle and thus authorized to teach the truth. Paul would have been committing the truth to the written word, thus creating scripture due to the inspiration of the Holy Spirit. We can see how God is **carefully delivering** the truth through His Spirit and emphasizing its value versus humankind's willingness to accept what non-inspired men have written about things they cannot possibly understand. Indeed, the Holy Scriptures make one wise unto salvation and thus are the key for God fulfilling His purpose. It is frightening that anyone could think anything other than God's word could provide eternal benefit. The doctrines of Catholicism must **look outside the scriptures** for confirmation, which in effect is an admission of rejecting God's word. "**Looking outside the scriptures**" for Catholicism means accepting some things written by select early church fathers, creating a single leader over the church, and then a succession of that leader allowing a perpetual rule-making authority. Not only are these means outside the scriptures, but they are in opposition to the scriptures.

In a rush to validate beliefs, God's perfection is not respected

Marcus Grodi again tries to make the case that the **Bible is not the only source for truth**. His reasoning is consistent with the argument commonly used for many things, and such reckoning is always in error. When God declares something as truth (and that is all that God ever declares), that eliminates all other possibilities. God does not have to list all the other things and ways that truth can be discerned. Scripture is God's way, and it *is* profitable for doctrine, for reproof, for correction, for instruction in righteousness, that the man of God may be complete, thoroughly equipped for every good work. Marcus Grodi wants God to state that only the scriptures are authorized. God does exactly that when He indicates that all scripture is given by the inspiration of God.

Marcus Grodi wants God to mention all the other possible ways **that are not legitimate** that could be profitable for doctrine, reproof, correction, instruction in righteousness, that the man of God may be complete, thoroughly equipped for every good work. God defined "all scripture" to eliminate anything else that could produce these things. Marcus Grodi must think he is dealing with some human being and not with God.

147

The fourth verse not seen by Marcus Grodi

2 Thessalonians 2:15

15 Therefore, brethren, stand fast and hold the traditions which you were taught, whether by word or our epistle.

Marcus Grodi associates his conversion experience from Protestantism to Catholicism in large part to seeing certain scriptures differently. He believes this verse (2 Thessalonians 2:15) demonstrates the validity of the tradition of the early church fathers. Undoubtedly, he has other reasons, but let's focus on what we know was essential for him in this verse. At the same time as promoting tradition, he needs to be rejecting the scriptures as the sole source of authority. He intended to do this using 2 Timothy 3:14-17 in the third verse he did not see correctly. However, we have shown those verses teach very much the opposite, validating the scriptures as the sole source of authority. That alone makes any claim relative to the authority of tradition from the early church fathers meaningless. Then he seems in desperation to repeat, "where in the Bible does it say truth can ONLY be found in the Bible." "If the Bible is the sole authority for the truth, then it should say that, and it doesn't." Marcus Grodi has ignored the most fundamental directives from God. We are dealing with God, and saying God should say this or that a certain way is careless and disrespectful. Instead, he ought to try to understand God's meaning. That meaning is clear since when God specifies something, that eliminates all other means to accomplish that matter – unless God would provide an exception. God could, of course, indicate other means, but He did not. Marcus Grodi assumes God was not as straightforward as He should have been. Therefore, Marcus Grodi concludes the scriptures are NOT the only source of truth. Earlier in the "second verse, Marcus Grodi did not previously understand," we explained the real issue was that Marcus Grodi did not understand the church, particularly the spiritual nature of the church. There is nothing more fundamental than the **sole authority of the scriptures** and the **spiritual nature of the church**. Failure to get these things right leads to all sorts of potential innovations, and one of these is seeing the traditions of the early church fathers as authoritative. There will be no authority for tradition if all authority resides in the scriptures.

Nonetheless, we will look at 2 Thessalonians 2:15 and 2 Thessalonians 3:6 on their own merits. These would be the two prime verses Marcus Grodi would use to validate the tradition of the early church fathers. It is difficult to discuss this idea of tradition given violating the basic principle of "all scripture" (2 Timothy 3:14-17) that God has provided to humankind. Marcus Grodi has abandoned scripture in his reasoning, but we cannot get to the truth if we do the same. We will present this rebuttal to validating the traditions of men to justify Catholic doctrine by considering four aspects of this issue.

First, the fundamental principle regarding God's word

God's word is not to be added to or taken away from, or we might say changed in any way. We have God's word by inspiration, and it comes from God through the Holy Spirit. Thus any teaching, doctrine in opposition or different than the scriptures would be wrong. One thing of note would be **how** the means of salvation were carefully delivered by inspiration. God provides the means of communicating with humankind as the scriptures, and that eliminates all other ways. **How** is salvation communicated or, in this case below, referred to as purifying your souls? Well, of course, by the scriptures, the word of God, and by what other way might this happen? There would be no other way based on God specifying the means in these verses.

1 Peter 1:22-23

*22 Since you have purified your souls in **obeying the truth** through the Spirit in sincere love of the brethren, love one another fervently with a pure heart,*
23 having been born again, not of corruptible seed but incorruptible, through the word of God which lives and abides forever

Second, an end to the communication from God to humankind

God's word is complete by the end of the first century, and we have all we need. It is referred to as that which is perfect, that which is complete. No other communications are coming from God. He has revealed everything, and nothing else is needed. The Catholic Church must think more is required and create an entirely different doctrine in opposition to the scriptures. Of course, **God had fulfilled His purpose,** and the things He put in place would allow His purpose to be fulfilled continually. This significant topic of "that which is perfect" is further discussed in Chapters 9, 12 and 15.

Third, the two senses of tradition in the scriptures – first the unfavorable use
(the fourth point will discuss verses where tradition is talked about favorably in the scriptures)

Marcus Gordi does correctly understand the word tradition is used in two senses in the scriptures. First, it negatively indicates things devised by humankind and thus **cannot** be followed as though they were the directives of God. Examples would be:

Matthew 15:3

*3 He answered and said to them, "Why do you also transgress the commandment of God because of your **tradition**?*

Matthew 15:6

*6 then he need not honor his father or mother.' Thus you have made the commandment of God of no effect by your **tradition**.*

Mark 7:9

*9 He said to them, "All too well you reject the commandment of God, that you may keep your **tradition**.*

Colossians 2:8

*8 Beware lest anyone cheat you through philosophy and empty deceit, according to the **tradition** of men, according to the basic principles of the world, and not according to Christ.*

1 Peter 1:18

*18 knowing that you were not redeemed with corruptible things, like silver or gold, from your aimless conduct received by **tradition** from your fathers,*

Thus there is a substantial bank of cases where tradition is strongly condemned. There is also a verse that does not use the word tradition, which makes a powerful statement regarding worship. Matthew 15:9, "And in vain they worship Me, Teaching as doctrines the commandments of men." The things that come from God are "solid" in their certainty and their consistency. In other words, God is seriously displeased about men following anything other than His direction. The point of Matthew 15:9 is that some doctrines had **originated from humankind** and they might be called tradition or the commandments of men. Any source other than God's inspired word produces error and must be avoided, but it is exactly what has happened in Catholicism.

Fourth, the second sense of tradition, positive or favorable use

Before we go to the verses that support tradition as valid, consider why these verses containing the word tradition mentioned above were strongly rejected. They were in opposition to the word of God, to God's commandments. They were the traditions of men, and in the case of 1 Peter 1:18 mentioned above, they originated from aimless conduct handed down as tradition. One becomes very pessimistic and subsequently cautious in understanding the dangers of tradition. Such traditions must not become doctrine as they have in the Catholic Church. One should be careful whenever tradition is mentioned favorably. Yet below are two cases where that happens, but these are easily qualified. The following two verses speak of traditions in a positive light.

2 Thessalonians 2:15

*15 Therefore, brethren, stand fast and hold the **tradition**s which you were taught, whether by word or our epistle.*

2 Thessalonians 3:6

*6 But we command you, brethren, in the name of our Lord Jesus Christ, that you withdraw from every brother who walks disorderly and not according to the **tradition** which he received from us.*

These traditions were specific teachings received from the apostles, and if they were valid, they were things provided to them by the Holy Spirit. Catholicism uses this **idea of tradition** to allow things **DIFFERENT than received by the apostles from the Holy Spirit to be valid**

151

doctrine. Catholicism would imply anything an apostle spoke to be a valid tradition. However, the apostles on their own **have NEVER been the originators of doctrine**. All they know has been delivered to them by the Holy Spirit. The things for posterity would be recorded as scripture.

In 2 Thessalonians 2:15, the specific teaching is not mentioned, but it is in the 2 Thessalonians 3:6 verse. In this first case, the discussion was regarding the salvation they received through sanctification by the Spirit and obedient response to the truth resulting from them being called by the gospel. That was likely the tradition being referred to or some associated matter regarding salvation. The chances of this thing referenced as tradition being written or was soon to be written are very high. **The tradition mentioned to those being addressed was something evident in the teaching they were receiving.** God is perfect and leaves nothing confusing as that would be in opposition to achieving His purpose.

Note: It is indicated above that the specific thing taught was not mentioned in this verse, but as suggested, it very well may have been what Paul just said in the preceding verses and is now, in fact, recorded as scripture.

2 Thessalonians 2:13-14
13 But we are bound to give thanks to God always for you, brethren beloved by the Lord, because God from the beginning chose you for salvation through sanctification by the Spirit and belief in the truth,
14 to which He called you by our gospel, for the obtaining of the glory of our Lord Jesus Christ.

In speaking positively in these verses regarding tradition, Paul could do this because he knew the source. It will always be the source that makes tradition approved or disapproved. Paul via the Holy Spirit was the source and what he was teaching was from God, and indeed these things should be handed down (the meaning of tradition). **Paul is not providing a reason to allow tradition, IN GENERAL, to be considered truth.** He only uses tradition favorably here because it involves things he had taught them. The Holy Spirit led Paul, and he even mentions that what he taught came through the revelation of Jesus Christ (Galatians 1:12). Yes, of course, carry on these things handed down to you as indeed they are the word of

God. God emphasizes the things that were written, and everything likely referred to positively regarding tradition was also recorded (as scripture).

John 20:31

*31 but **these are written** that you may believe that Jesus is the Christ, the Son of God, and that believing you may have life in His name.*

God has provided everything necessary for your salvation, and the Holy Spirit has inspired it, and it is called scripture. There is nothing beyond the completed word of God – that which is perfect. God did not leave man in such a predicament to be at the bidding of humankind to make the rules and change the laws of God. There is an emphasis on the inspired word of God, that is, the things written because they are not open to questionable teachings, to something that might be **considered** valid tradition. A frequent phrase is, "it is written," and it is a way of emphasizing validity. The scriptures provide assurance since they are from God via the inspiration of the Spirit of God. You will find the whole of the Catholic Church contained **in things NOT written**, but located in tradition (without validation), found in the writings of men, and always in opposition to God's written inspired word. The Catholic **confirmation** of their doctrines comes from the councils of men, namely, for example below, the second Vatican council where they declare, "therefore both sacred tradition and Sacred Scripture are to be accepted and venerated with the same sense of loyalty and reverence."

From the second Vatican Council (1962-1965)

"Hence there exists a close connection and communication between sacred tradition and Sacred Scripture. For both of them, flowing from the same divine wellspring, in a certain way merge into a unity and tend toward the same end. For Sacred Scripture is the word of God inasmuch as it is consigned to writing under the inspiration of the divine Spirit, while sacred tradition takes the word of God entrusted by Christ the Lord and the Holy Spirit to the Apostles, and hands it on to their successors in its full purity, so that led by the light of the Spirit of truth, they may in proclaiming it preserve this word of God faithfully, explain it, and make it more widely known.

Consequently it is not from Sacred Scripture alone that the Church draws her certainty about everything which has been revealed. Therefore both sacred tradition and Sacred Scripture are to be accepted and venerated with the same sense of loyalty and reverence."

This statement from Vatican II should be called "how to validate the terrible lies of Catholicism." Fortunately, the validation only works for those who are naïve, for those who do not love the truth, for those who have been effectively brainwashed. If Catholicism cannot make **the rules of validation,** there will be no validation of their teachings.

Desperately searching for justification

The scriptures do not open the door to anything **men would teach,** claiming it to be valid doctrine from God. In their typical desperate mode, Catholic theologians say that because some of the apostles may have known some of the early fathers of the church, they passed along things that the early church used, and those "traditions" were authorized apostolic traditions. Of course (once again), authority never originated from the apostles but from the Holy Spirit-directed apostles. Nonetheless, the Vatican council designated such early church father's writings to be equivalent to scripture and, in some cases, to be better than scripture. One sense where Catholics hold their traditions greater than the scriptures is saying the truths of the faith are **clarified by tradition** or claiming that only the **Holy See** can correctly interpret scripture through the Magisterium (the Catholic church's authentic teaching office).

*Note: Holy See defined: The **Holy See** is the central government of the Catholic Church. It is the jurisdiction of the bishop of Rome, that is, the pope. The Vatican City State was established by treaty in 1929, providing the Holy See with a small territorial base and consequent recognition as an independent sovereign entity in international law.*

Catholics know there is no way to justify their beliefs using the scriptures. In desperation, they go back to the scriptures to find ways to justify **extensions of the truth** from other sources (like tradition). Thus, they promote a verse like 2 Thessalonians 2:15 and claim tradition is acceptable – that is desperation, ridiculous, and they must think that it is better than nothing.

The other source they want to justify is a continuing line of apostolic succession with the head being a single individual and he will be called the pope. He will be the father of the church, the head of the church, and this will happen beginning with Peter, the first head or pope, and the line of popes will continue until the end of time. The early church fathers make some references to such a leader, which becomes a continuation of the acceptable tradition due to 2 Thessalonians 2:15. There will also be some early church references to the "Real Presence" and other soon-to-be Catholic doctrines. Of course, these are not inspired things coming from God, but it is the best they can do in terms of validation. Then in the framework of their various councils, they solidify or validate their lies. There is not even a nanometer of any truth in Catholicism. Yes, they have made it very confusing with all their propaganda but again, not to one who loves the truth.

Even the naïve being fooled by the complexity of the Catholic Church can understand the many massive holes in the doctrines of the Catholic Church. Let me mention a few things for anyone caught up in the Catholic web.

- The things referred to in the scriptures as acceptable traditions were all related to things taught by the apostles, and there is no reason to believe we do not have all those things in the scriptures.
- We do not see the existence of an earthly head or apostolic succession in the scriptures.
- There is a specified end to the message from God, and it was sometime in the late first century.
- There are numerous **conflicts** between the scriptures and the doctrines of the Catholic Church.
- Catholicism has systematically destroyed God's plan for salvation in their pattern of salvation - no Catholics can be saved.
- The Catholic Church has hundreds of things that directly oppose the will of God.
    - Councils
    - Popes
    - Priests
    - Creation of saints other than consisting of all those in the body of Christ
    - Religious honor for and even praying to anyone other than God through Christ
    - "Endless" others

- Among the big misses, the colossal misunderstanding of the Catholic Church is the most fundamental thing, namely that the church Jesus built and continues to build is spiritual.

Approved apostolic examples and necessary inferences

The source for truth is from the things written, certainly, it is **not tradition** unless it was explicitly things that the apostles had revealed. In those cases, we might call them approved apostolic examples (2 Timothy 1:13, 1 Corinthians 11:1) or even necessary inferences when the Holy Spirit was working with the apostles, guiding them into all truth. Truth consists of the wisdom of God as contained in the scriptures. The approved apostolic examples and the necessary inferences are things validated by the scriptures. The things called acceptable tradition have all come down in the scriptures, but at the time, they were touted as valuable because they came from the apostle's teaching – not written yet. How else could Paul emphasize at that time they should follow the things that were taught (before they were written)? He would say, "brethren, stand fast and hold the **tradition**s which you were taught." That is not the case after the first century, as **all essential things are in the scriptures**. So to avoid any confusion, some use the term approved apostolic example to teach doctrine, which would be correct. An approved apostolic example would be the record showing the apostles gathering on the first day of the week to break bread and drink the fruit of the vine in remembrance of the Lord's death. It is not a direct command but an approved apostles example. Of course, in God's perfection this weekly remembrance is supported by previous revelations regarding this event (also see Chapter 9.2 – True meaning of the Lord's Supper).

We can likewise make necessary inferences from scripture, which is essential to arrive at the truth. The inferences we make from Scripture **must be necessary.** The inference has to actually be there, and the conclusion drawn from it must be logically unavoidable. One thing God expects from those "in Christ" is the ability to think, which means handling the scriptures carefully. Again, there is nothing complicated in making good decisions, and a good example is being accurate in using necessary inferences in our modern world. One might say that abortion, pornography, gambling, and drug abuse, among many others, are not explicitly mentioned in the scriptures. Yet God condemns specific categories of sin, and thus sin by different names is necessarily inferred.

Galatians 5:19-21

19 Now the works of the flesh are evident, which are: adultery, fornication, uncleanness, lewdness,

20 idolatry, sorcery, hatred, contentions, jealousies, outbursts of wrath, selfish ambitions, dissensions, heresies,

*21 envy, murders, drunkenness, revelries, **and the like**; of which I tell you beforehand, just as I also told you in time past, that those who practice such things will not inherit the kingdom of God.*

Notice in verse 21 it says, "**and the like**." In our logical thinking in the framework of the scriptures, we can infer the following concerning moral issues:

- Drug abuse is a sin because it "fits" into the category of drunkenness (5:21). Pornography fits into the category of "lewdness" (5:19). Gambling is nothing more than a form of covetousness (Ephesians 5:5), and abortion is an apparent lack of natural affection (Romans 1:31 "unloving"). To conclude that the unborn baby is a human being, and thus abortion is murder, one can draw necessary inferences from Scripture (Psalm 139:13-16; James 2:26).

I mention these things to point out the completeness of God in delivering His message. All the truth that is needed is contained in the scriptures, the wisdom of God. One can even infer, as shown, that modern names for sin are managed within the scriptures. Can you imagine all the writings of the early church fathers and those that followed (eventually the Catholic Church) subjectively deciding which writings to accept and naming them as valid traditions? There would be innumerable conflicts with the word of God, and indeed that is what we have.

In the previous verse, Marcus Grodi had not seen (2 Timothy 3:14), "continue in the things which you have learned and been assured of, knowing from whom you have learned them," it was shown that the opposite of what Marcus Grodi is trying to prove was validated. **Paul puts the stamp of approval on the things learned from the apostles.** There is this continual warning in the scriptures, and Paul relates it to the danger of false teaching, and its source might be philosophy, deceit, tradition, the principles of the world, versus what comes from Christ. It is safe to say what comes from Christ is what comes to the apostles from the Holy Spirit.

Colossians 2:8

8 Beware lest anyone cheat you through philosophy and empty deceit, according to the **tradition of men**, *according to the basic principles of the world, and not according to Christ*

Colossians 2:8 perfectly defines what Catholicism tries to use to validate its doctrines and is appropriately called in this verse 'the tradition of men."

The entirety of the scriptures points to itself as what must be heeded, and in 1 Timothy 4:16, it is evident where salvation exists. As usual, that eliminates any other source.

1 Timothy 4:16

16 Take heed to yourself and to the doctrine. Continue in them, for in doing this you will save both yourself and those who hear you.

Think about what Catholicism has done. They use the idea of tradition to make authoritative the writings of these early church fathers and, in the process, create a new religion and one that is opposed to the scriptures. God carefully delivered the truth, and then some uninspired men wrote some things that would become the Catholic Church's doctrine. We see authorized traditions (2 Thessalonians 2:15) were found in the scriptures and were things taught that Paul (a proper authority being led by the Holy Spirit) said they should follow. If important, they would end up as scripture. To think that whatever those things that Paul supported as tradition would open the door to **whatever others in the future would write** is pretty implausible, ridiculous. In this case, no words can describe such evil.

The fifth verse not seen by Marcus Grodi

Perhaps the most important verses for Catholicism are these verses where they have developed the idea of a pope and Peter being the first pope. In the history of literature, there has never been more incredible carelessness. Indeed, these are important verses going back to God speaking to Satan in the garden. Catholics would say these verses are essential in starting their church, with Peter being the pope. The truth is that God is revealing Jesus is the Son of God. Then Jesus reveals that He will build His church, and the basis is His Sonship with God.

Matthew 16:13-19

13 When Jesus came into the region of Caesarea Philippi, He asked His disciples, saying, "Who do men say that I, the Son of Man, am?"

14 So they said, "Some say John the Baptist, some Elijah, and others Jeremiah or one of the prophets."

15 He said to them, "But who do you say that I am?"

16 Simon Peter answered and said, "You are the Christ, the Son of the living God."

17 Jesus answered and said to him, "Blessed are you, Simon Bar-Jonah, for flesh and blood has not revealed this to you, but My Father who is in heaven.

18 And I also say to you that you are Peter, and on this rock I will build My church, and the gates of Hades shall not prevail against it.

19 And I will give you the keys of the kingdom of heaven, and whatever you bind on earth will be bound in heaven, and whatever you loose on earth will be loosed in heaven."

These verses in terms of Marcus Grodi's comments will be discussed in this section. However, these most important verses will also be discussed in "Chapter 8: It is easy to scripturally reject Catholicism" from a different perspective with the same outcome. Catholicism fails everywhere in its doctrines, but it has the most brutal fall in these verses, and it occurs in their most essential and cherished verses.

Marcus Grodi says God the Father gave Peter this insight, that Jesus was the Son of God, which is correct and was a blessing for Peter to be the one first to know and verbalize this. Marcus Grodi then diverts to building a case for Peter's leadership. He says Peter held the first church (as he calls it) business meeting by presiding over it. Strangely, he is trying to build the case for Peter before discussing the Matthew 16 verses. However, in Acts 15, Paul did not bring the issue to Peter but the apostles and elders in the Jerusalem church. Peter spoke, but so did James, and in fact, it was James' suggestion that was followed. No one in the Jerusalem church knew the concept of a pope or any such leader over the church. They did know the requirement for multiple qualified elders, of which Peter was qualified and was one of the elders.

Note: Here is just another of hundreds of quandaries in Catholic doctrine. Peter was an elder in the Jerusalem church, and that means He was the husband of one wife. This is a qualification for eldership. Yet Catholicism teaches Peter was never married.

Perhaps the **most significant private interpretation** of scripture done by Catholicism is from these Matthew 16 verses. Marcus Grodi emphasizes the name Peter and the Greek words petra and petrus, and the differentiation between a rock and a small rock. This is just a diversion to bring complexity to the clear message **that has nothing to do with Peter**. Nonetheless, we will look at Marcus Grodi's argument on this word rock in terms of Greek and Aramaic.

First, Peter's name means stone, the Greek word for Peter is Petros. Jesus did not use the same word for Peter as He did for rock but used petra (Greek). Thus different words for Peter and rock in Jesus' statement. Next, Catholicism says Matthew was originally written in Aramaic, where the two words are the same. However, no Aramaic version of Matthew exists. The International Standard Bible Encyclopedia addresses this issue as follows:

"One thing which seems certain is that whatever this Hebrew (Aramaic) document may have been, it was not an original form from which the present Greek Gospel of Matthew was translated, either by the apostle himself, or by somebody else ... Indeed, the Greek Matthew throughout bears the impression of being not a translation at all, but as having been originally written in Greek."

Also, the Zondervan Pictorial Encyclopedia of the Bible makes the following statement:

"It must be admitted, however, that no fragment of an Aramaic Matthew has ever been found and a Greek edition is more plausible than a Greek translation. Matthew's gospel does not give evidence of being a translation, which is one of the weak evidences for the Aramaic theory."

In any case, much more can be said about this, such as the Latin Vulgate preserves the different genders of the two words.

*Note: Pope Pius XII (1939-1958) indicates the Latin Vulgate "in the sense in which the Church has understood and understands it, to be **free from any error whatsoever in matters of faith and morals**; so that, as the Church herself testifies and affirms, it may be quoted safely and without fear of error in disputations, in lectures and in preaching."*

Of course, why are the pope and the Catholic hierarchy deciding on the authenticity of anything? Later, they would choose to create a new Vulgate as they must have found some possible conflicts with their teachings. The standard rule of Catholicism must always be present; namely, it must be complicated. Making everything complicated is not some written goal of Catholicism, but it is a by-product of making the rules for God and trying to fit everything together.

The Bible teaches the meaning of the rock, and it is not Peter, but it is Peter's proclamation given to him by the Father that Jesus is the Son of God. Peter is not, cannot be what the church is built on, but Jesus is the rock on which the church has meaning. We will see that this is the truth and see how that is exactly what happens. There is no such position as an earthly head of the church, and Peter is never mentioned having such a role.

There are a few more things we can say about this idea of the rock of Matthew 16:18. Who or what does the Bible identify as the rock? Instead of the Catholic claim of Peter being the rock with no substantiation, we have the scriptures defining Jesus as the rock. First, we see Paul saying Jesus is the rock.

1 Corinthians 10:1-4

1 Moreover, brethren, I do not want you to be unaware that all our fathers were under the cloud, all passed through the sea,

2 all were baptized into Moses in the cloud and in the sea,

3 all ate the same spiritual food,

4 and all drank the same spiritual drink. For they drank of that spiritual Rock that followed them, and that Rock was Christ.

So instead of any Bible confirmation of Peter being the rock, we have Paul stating the rock was Christ. A considerable amount of scripture indicates that Jesus is the rock, the foundation, the cornerstone. Thus, it is appropriate for Jesus to point to the one and the only thing on which the church can stand, which is on His Sonship. There had been about 4000 years since God indicated a solution was coming from the Seed of woman. The rock is the solution.

*Note: There is another obvious problem with the thinking of Catholicism to justify their existence. They assume that the rock is a reference to the head of the church and then say it is Peter. The rock is not meant to point to the head but **first** to point to the solution, and we will see that the rock is the solution to sin that allows for the reconciliation. The rock must be spiritual to solve the spiritual problem of sin. The solution to sin is Jesus, the Son of God, incarnate to be the perfect, sinless sacrifice for sin. Peter cannot be the solution as he cannot do what Jesus is about to do. Jesus is the solution inasmuch as what He does. He is the solution and thus the rock of Matthew 16:18. Jesus builds the church based on Him being the Son of God. Jesus is spiritual, and His headship of the spiritual church is taught in the scriptures. If we summarize the things wrong with Catholic thinking, they would be:*

- *Thinking the rock has to do with being the head when it is fundamentally the solution. Of course, we learn as the solution Jesus is also the head of the church (Ephesians 5:23, Colossians 1:18).* **If there were no solution, there would be no need for a head.**
- *Thinking Peter is the rock when even in the context of the verse he is not.*
- *Thinking the church needs a physical head when the church is spiritual.*
- *The Catholic Church fails to see that individuals are added to the church by obedience.*
- *Failure to see that in the entirety of the scriptures, God's purpose, character, and plan make the Catholic invention of Peter as the head of the church, ridiculous!!*

Continuing to show Peter is not the rock

Along the historical path leading to Jesus's arrival, Isaiah mentioned the Messiah and referred to Him as the foundation. Indeed, God was bringing a spiritual solution to the spiritual problem of sin. It is appropriate to refer to Jesus as the spiritual rock. Could Peter be the spiritual rock? No, but Jesus was more than a man. He was the Son of God – the spiritual solution. Before the church was initiated on the day of Pentecost after the death, burial, and resurrection of Christ, Jesus would no longer be physical but be at the right hand of God to begin ruling over His kingdom. Indeed, the kingdom was about to begin. It was the church. Like many things referred to in the scriptures, especially during the lifetime of Jesus concerning the mystery, they were not yet fully revealed. But in the fullness of time, they would be revealed. The one significant event that would allow the "closing of various previous statements made without full disclosure " was the death, burial, and resurrection of Jesus. Statements like John 3:16 were not fully understood in terms of what "believe" would include until that time. In Matthew 16:20, Jesus tells His apostles not to tell anyone that He was the Christ. It was not yet time for this to be known except to the apostles. The event that just occurred in Matthew 16:13-19 was the central most important acknowledgment in human history – the Son of God was among them; the Messiah was there in the person of Jesus. Someone was to be blessed to receive the message from God the Father concerning the nature of Jesus, and this same person would bring that solution first to the Jews and then to the Gentiles. Peter was so blessed. However, there was nothing of note in terms of prominence related to him. If there were, it would be revealed in the fullness of time following Jesus' death, burial, and resurrection. In Acts 2, there is clarity in the disclosure regarding Jesus as the Christ, the Son of God, and the apostle's role as alluded to in Matthew 16:19 and the church Jesus will be building.

Yet, there is no indication of a special role for Peter because there was nothing to be revealed. Peter, the apostles, and the entirety of what was encompassed in the Holy Spirit's guiding the apostles into all truth never includes some special role for Peter. God does not miss a single thing. He wants humankind to succeed. He completed and clarified things that were previously mentioned purposely without full disclosure. There were reasons for the mystery, and usually, they related to Jesus completing His mission. Following the revelation of Jesus as God's Son and the church in Matthew 16:13-19 to the apostles, Jesus directed them to not speak of what was just disclosed. It was not yet time.

Matthew 16:20

20 Then He commanded His disciples that they should tell no one that He was Jesus the Christ.

More regarding Jesus as the rock, the foundation, the cornerstone

Isaiah 28:16

16 Therefore thus says the Lord GOD:

"Behold, I lay in Zion a stone for a foundation,

A tried stone, a precious cornerstone, a sure foundation;

Whoever believes will not act hastily."

Next, we have Peter quoting Isaiah and applies it to Jesus.

1 Peter 2:4-8

4 Coming to Him as to a living stone, rejected indeed by men, but chosen by God and precious,

5 you also, as living stones, are being built up a spiritual house, a holy priesthood, to offer up spiritual sacrifices acceptable to God through Jesus Christ.

6 Therefore it is also contained in the Scripture,

"Behold, I lay in Zion

A chief cornerstone, elect, precious,

And he who believes on Him will by no means be put to shame."

7 Therefore, to you who believe, He is precious; but to those who are disobedient,

"The stone which the builders rejected

Has become the chief cornerstone,"

8 and

"A stone of stumbling

And a rock of offense."

They stumble, being disobedient to the word, to which they also were appointed.

Could Peter make it any more apparent who the chief cornerstone is? Peter declares Jesus to be the "rock to be acknowledged" and knows Jesus to be the solution. Jesus is the "stone of stumbling" and the "rock of offense" since He requires people to choose. The solution to sin He brings as the rock requires obedience and cannot be avoided – doing nothing is disobedience. Thus a person cannot go through life casually avoiding God, the God of the Bible, and expect anything but failure. Indeed, to the world, Jesus is a stone of stumbling and a rock of offense. Jesus is forcing a decision from each person to fulfill His purpose. Perhaps a more straightforward understanding of a stone of stumbling and a rock of offense would be how Jesus caused these things to be problems for the Jews. The Jews would **stumble** over the things Jesus did (Matthew 13:54-57). Also, the Jews were **offended** by what Jesus said (Matthew 15:10-12).

The message from Isaiah is that Jesus is the stone, the chief cornerstone, and the rock. None of the New Testament writers ever refer to Peter as the rock. Peter, the apostles, never conceived of an earthly head of the church. Paul again clarifies that Jesus is the church's foundation, and there can be none other. Paul would have been touting Peter as the rock and having a leadership position, but that never happens. Paul, Peter, and the other New Testament writers delivered the scriptures at the direction of God's Holy Spirit. For God to achieve His purpose, the message for humankind had to be provided with great clarity, remarkable consistency. God has done this perfectly, and yet humanity can look to Matthew 16:13-19 and think Peter is in some way central to God's plan.

Additionally, the whole of the scriptures from Genesis defines the solution to sin in precise ways. Everything from Genesis is part of bringing God's answer for sin. Four thousand years pass before the solution arrives. That solution will meet every aspect of God's definition, as mentioned in various prophecies over this long period. God's purpose is to be fulfilled in Jesus. All God has done can be considered the foundation, and there can be no other foundation laid. Jesus is the foundation, rock, and solution and meets every requirement that allows God's purpose to be achieved. Paul, via the revelation of God, brings clarity in Corinthians.

1 Corinthians 3:11
11 For no other foundation can anyone lay than that which is laid, which is Jesus Christ.

We have God the Father directing Peter to acknowledge Jesus as the son of God. Jesus then indicates the basis for the church is His Sonship. Isaiah, Paul, and Peter (Acts 4:8-12) all acknowledge Jesus as the rock and thus eliminate anyone else being the rock. We have no such office for Peter in the scriptures, and Peter never assumes such an office. There are about fifty-plus years of scripture (Holy Spirit active in inspiration), and there is a blank page regarding the concept of a pope and Peter being the first pope. The following verses should make a person realize that the Catholic Church that designates Peter as the rock, conflicts with Peter, who proclaims that Jesus is the rock.

Acts 4:8-12

8 Then Peter, filled with the Holy Spirit, said to them, "Rulers of the people and elders of Israel:

9 If we this day are judged for a good deed done to a helpless man, by what means he has been made well,

10 let it be known to you all, and to all the people of Israel, that by the name of Jesus Christ of Nazareth, whom you crucified, whom God raised from the dead, by Him this man stands here before you whole.

11 This is the 'stone which was rejected by you builders, which has become the chief cornerstone.'

12 Nor is there salvation in any other, for there is no other name under heaven given among men by which we must be saved."

Note: Catholics will never give up arguing about Peter being the pope despite the massive, overwhelming evidence. The meaning of Matthew 16:18 has always been a "game of words" for Catholicism. In desperation, they seek some way to validate their organization. In this case, they will try to use Greek words, Aramaic words saying the Greek word used in verse 4(1 Peter 2:4-8) for stone is lithos, but then in verse 8, petra is used for rock which is the same word used in Matthew for rock. Indeed, Catholics in desperation grab at words, translations, languages to find some way to justify their existence. The meaning of these verses is consistent throughout the scriptures and involves the most basic revelation from God, as He reveals His plan to accomplish His purpose. Tampering with the word of God is indeed a violation of the highest order. It falls in the category of deserving the most severe wrath of God. The truth is that Jesus is the solution, is the head of the church (Ephesians 5:23), and He is the Son of God, as revealed in Matthew 16:18. These things are the basics of God's message to achieve His purpose and are consistent throughout the scriptures.

Peter in Matthew 16:16-18 is only the vehicle used by God the Father to relay the message to the apostles. The message withheld from the apostles up to this moment is that Jesus is the Son of God. Jesus then indicates how Peter is blessed by the Father to bring this message. Four thousand years have passed since the promise in Genesis 3:15. Now the solution to the reconciliation is beginning to be revealed. Jesus says that upon this rock, I will build my church. The rock is Jesus but more specifically is the proclamation that Jesus is the Son of God. Essentially, that means the rock is the Son of God and is this special person of God incarnate. The rock is Jesus. The rock is the **proclamation that will be made throughout history** that Jesus is the Son of God. On that, the church can be built, not on Peter. At this time, we do not know HOW Jesus will build His church, but soon it will be revealed. The salvation of souls, the forgiveness of sins can be built on what Jesus, the spiritual rock, will soon accomplish. In that process involving the death, burial, and resurrection of Jesus, a form of doctrine will be revealed where people can be reconciled to God. As this process is completed by individuals being obedient to the gospel, Jesus will add them to His body, His spiritual church.

Continue to understand Matthew 16:15-19

It turns out that Peter is highly blessed inasmuch as he made the proclamation received from the Father. Peter is also the one who will bring the gospel message the first time on the day of Pentecost in Acts 2. Did Peter know the gospel message? Of course not, but NOW having received the Holy Spirit along with the other apostles, they know what to say. On that day, they could speak such that those present of different languages and dialects understood. It was not the speaking in tongues (in languages) that was important, but it was the message being delivered. People heard the message in their own language/dialect. In Acts 2:14-38, the gospel is preached. People respond, and Jesus begins building His church in Acts 2:47. There is nothing of God, of God's directions known by humankind unless God reveals it. Peter continues to be blessed by being the first to bring the gospel message to the Gentiles. Until the time of Cornelius and his family's conversion, the only ones in the body of Christ were Jewish. To fulfill the promise to Abraham in Genesis 12:1-3 that in Abraham all the families of the earth shall be blessed, there would be fulfillment in the Gentile household of Cornelius's (Acts 10).

Binding and Loosening – Catholicism continues its disrespect for God

Jesus goes on to tell the apostles in Matthew 16:19 that the things they "bind on earth will be bound in heaven, and whatever you loose on earth will be loosed in heaven." A possible assumption is that these men will be making rules and decisions of a spiritual nature for God. However, there is no such indication of people making the rules for God. How would they know

167

what to say, what should be done? They could not know, but they could make a terrible mess. Jesus was very clear about this and would shortly reveal **HOW they would bind and loose**. He indicates that the apostles would be guided into all truth by the Holy Spirit (John 16:13). It was never God's intention to have humankind make the rules. **Someone had to bring the message to humankind, and in that sense, the apostles were binding and loosening.** It was not their message; it was God's message, and they were blessed to bring it. Peter was blessed to convey the message the first time to the Jews and then to the Gentiles. Paul knows this and proclaims it to the Romans. The binding and loosening done by the apostles were perfectly defined and represented by God's power to save as contained in the gospel message.

Romans 1:16

16 For I am not ashamed of the gospel of Christ, for it is the power of God to salvation for everyone who believes, for the Jew first and also for the Greek.

Paul is declaring to the Romans how God saves, and it is by the gospel preached which is God's power to save. Then Paul indicates salvation began with the Jews and then also for the Gentiles. After all this time since Genesis, God was starting to unveil His plan in Matthew 16 for the reconciliation. God's Son is announced to be Jesus and represents the solution for sin since He is the rock. Jesus continues by indicating the place for the saved would be something He will build. All that Jesus has been preaching for the previous three years as the kingdom will be the church – the church He will build. It will have the characteristics of the kingdom He has been teaching, but now it is something Jesus will build for salvation. The church is the place, **a spiritual place** where those responding to the gospel message will reside. Jesus in the Parable of the Sower indicated the seed of the kingdom was the word of God, and now we see that specifically, it is the gospel message, and in a broader sense, it is the doctrine of Christ.

Following the promised (John 16:13) interaction with the Holy Spirit in Acts 2, the apostles understand their role, and Peter delivers the gospel message. The core of the message is what the Father spoke to Peter in Matthew 16:17 that Jesus was the Son of God. Peter presents that very powerfully in Acts 2:36.

Acts 2:36

36 *"Therefore let all the house of Israel know assuredly that God has made this Jesus, whom you crucified, both Lord and Christ."*

We continually make the point that we know the things of life, things outside our realm **only if God reveals them – not from flesh and blood**. Peter just declared in Matthew 16:17 that Jesus is the Son of God. Then Jesus immediately makes the source of that information known, "Blessed are you, Simon Bar-Jonah, for **flesh and blood has not** revealed this to you, but My Father who is in heaven." **This is the only way someone knows the will of God.** Jesus is setting the course for God's message, and it will NOT come from flesh and blood but God. Indeed, the apostles receive the gospel message from God's Holy Spirit, and Peter preaches that long-awaited message of reconciliation. **The messages that originate from flesh and blood are not true.** All those who think they can speak for God – the Catholic Church, the "churches of the world" are a terror for souls. Humankind will never understand God, God's ways, and the attempts to understand the meaning of binding and loosing is a good example. Humankind could guess, try to be logical, and be "scientific" in the method to arrive at the meaning – and never get it right. If you love the truth, all that is necessary is to look to God's word and understand the meaning. The apostles are binding and loosening in their preaching the gospel message. The acceptance of or the rejection of the message determines if there is binding or loosing.

Talking about the KEYS that Jesus refers to in Matthew 16:19

The evidence in the scriptures for the church being built on Jesus as the Son of God is overwhelming. The evidence for the church being built on Peter is non-existent. The apostles bring the gospel message beginning in Acts 2. God designed the binding and loosening to be contained in His message provided to the apostles by the Holy Spirit. Let me bring some clarity. The binding and loosening are included in the gospel message, with a person's response determining the binding or loosening. The truth from God is focused, and God is always focused on His purpose. This can help the understanding of those who love the truth. Everything in Matthew 16:13-19 is regarding God's purpose of sharing His Divine Nature – the salvation of souls, the forgiveness of sins. The nature/definition of those things would not be left to the apostles but was in the mind of God since the beginning. God's purpose would be served by His Son, and the apostles would have a part, **a critical part, namely bringing the message**. All the things God was doing to achieve His purpose would not result in any sharing in the Divine Nature without the message. So who holds the KEYS? Jesus tells the apostles He is giving them the **keys to the kingdom of heaven**. He is handing them the last step in the process. The work done by God the Father is complete. The work of Jesus will **"essentially"** come to an end in his death, burial, and resurrection. Then, the Holy Spirit will be working with the apostles throughout most of the remaining first century.

The apostles will have the keys once God's Holy Spirit empowers them. They are given the message, the truth needed for reconciliation. We will see that the keys to the kingdom of heaven will be given to all those the Lord adds to His body, that is, those "in Christ." The apostles are the first to have the keys, and they uniquely, supernaturally receive the message from the Holy Spirit. Then the Holy Spirit will continue working with them in completing God's communication with humankind. During that time, the word of God is confirmed (Hebrews 2:3-4). In relation to the keys, the apostles are special in how they receive them and their ongoing work with the Holy Spirit. Those "in Christ" carry the keys since that amounts to carrying the truth, the gospel message, and they understand these things correctly since they obeyed the gospel and are spiritual. Each has been added to the body of Christ by the Lord Himself. Unlike the apostles, they have the **completed** word of God as a result of the Holy Spirit finishing His work of inspiration in the latter part of the first century.

The keys are the message, the truth from God that allows Him to accomplish His purpose. The keys remain active until the end of time in possession of all those "in Christ" as they preach the word. Indeed, the church is the pillar and ground of truth inasmuch as it upholds the truth, the scriptures. It is not a message from "flesh and blood" but from God and is the key to the kingdom of heaven. **Is there anything more important than the message from God that fulfills His purpose?** The apostles bring for the first time the means to transform a person from the **power of darkness** to the **kingdom of God's Son** – His church.

Colossians 1:13-14

*13 He has delivered us from the **power of darkness** and conveyed us into the **kingdom of the Son** of His love,*

14 in whom we have redemption through His blood, the forgiveness of sins.

The Catholic Church looks at the keys of Matthew 16:19 and claims the right to make the rules when the rules have already been made and God in Christ has accomplished the reconciliation. The Catholic Church is indeed the universal physical church and entirely incapable of solving the spiritual problem of sin. The message from God, the gospel message, is the only answer to salvation, and by that means, those **obedient** are bound over to God, and the one bringing the message does the binding in preaching. That same message, when rejected, results in loss because there is no other way for sins to be forgiven. When the message from the apostles fails to achieve its goal, the opposite of binding occurs; namely, there is a loosening. They are letting loose of the opportunity for a successful life. The message brought initially by the apostles can bind or loose a person, but that occurs by each person's choice. Thus the apostles only indirectly are binding and loosening by the message with the final decision made by each person. This is God's way of free will. Another way of saying this is that the apostles are not directly determining who is being bound and loosed but indirectly by the message there is binding and loosening. The outcome is bound or loosed in heaven.

The simple meaning from God (Matthew 16:19, John 20:23, and John 6:53-54)
(Quick reference verses for this section)

Matthew 16:19
19 And I will give you the keys of the kingdom of heaven, and whatever you bind on earth will be bound in heaven, and whatever you loose on earth will be loosed in heaven."

John 20:23
23 If you forgive the sins of any, they are forgiven them; if you retain the sins of any, they are retained."

John 6:53-54
53 Then Jesus said to them, "Most assuredly, I say to you, unless you eat the flesh of the Son of Man and drink His blood, you have no life in you.
54 Whoever eats My flesh and drinks My blood has eternal life, and I will raise him up at the last day.

What happens in Acts 2 and the entire time the apostles are preaching? They are binding and loosening (Matthew 16:19). In the sense of John 20:23, they are forgiving and retaining sin. Also, in the process of preaching the gospel, **each obedient person** is metaphorically eating the flesh and drinking the blood of Christ as they are participating in the death, burial, and resurrection of the savior (John 6:53-54). These verses have some things in common. Namely, they are related to the forgiveness of sins, to salvation, and as mentioned, they are all occurring in response to the gospel message. They all have many "flesh and blood" explanations resulting in complicated doctrines and, of course, all wrong, all misleading. In truth, these verses are all straightforward. So simple that they all have the same understanding with outcomes occurring in the obedience to the gospel. They are spiritual things that bring about the reconciliation with God, fulfilling God's purpose. The wisdom of humankind is not needed in any of these matters. There is no human intervention, no practices, no special doctrine. The doctrine is the gospel message, and it elicits a response.

Certainly, the apostles understood the honor of being given the keys of the kingdom but had no idea what this work of binding and loosening entailed. Keys often signify authority, but as one examines God's purpose for humankind, it has to do with providing a successful afterlife for people, albeit deserving persons, which means unselfish, humble persons. How can such people take advantage of God's offer of eternal life? The **KEYS,** when considering all things, opens the door for salvation. Specifically, the key will be the gospel message as this is the means to enter the kingdom and the apostle's role is to bring that message. The keys can be considered in simple terms to be the truth, the gospel message, the solution to sin. The keys are not the authority given to the apostles **to make the rules** for Christianity. This is the claim of the Catholic Church leading to inventing apostolic succession and the pope and finally the means to justify the authority of the Catholic Church.

When we talk about binding and loosening, what is being bound and loosed? Those doing the binding and loosening are not the ones creating what is to be bound and loosed. They are simply executing the directives from "heaven." It is the most important thing for each individual since their eternity hangs in the balance. The Holy Spirit provides the message to the apostles, and the apostles are to deliver the message to the world. Those who accept the message are bound by it, whereas those who reject it are loosed. In the process of preaching, binding and loosing take place. We might say that God's purpose is achieved in both cases.

The apostles are the initial caretakers of the keys. The oversight of the keys is passed on to all those who the Lord adds to His spiritual body. Those things bound or loosed on earth will be bound or loosed in heaven. In other words, the gospel message is taught and obeyed, resulting in sins being forgiven. God knows the record of obedience; indeed, Christ confirms that by personally adding each person to the church, His spiritual body.

Among all the nonsense and blasphemy of Catholicism in perverting God's meaning of Matthew 16:13-19, they infer the Catholic Church has oversight in the matters of God. God is revealing the centerpiece of the reconciliation in Jesus, His Son. Jesus reveals the church He will build and an essential role for the apostles. All that is done in Matthew 16:13-19 has to do with God's purpose, with souls, and not with some future earthy hierarchy.

What happened following Matthew 16:13-19

There is this giant, infinite leap between the doctrine from God and the teaching originating from humankind, and it is the difference between truth and deceit. It is the difference between the gospel message saving and some human-designed message misleading people to eternal loss.

I wrote a document many years ago and published it in the appendix of one of my books. The article demonstrated the rock of Matthew 16:18 was the **declaration** just provided by God the Father to Peter. THEN seeing exactly how this "played out" in the remaining message from God is evidenced by God fitting everything perfectly together. I have copied that below; it shows how God leaves no loose ends in confirming the nature of the church. On the other hand, there is no such confirmation of an earthly head of the church and Peter being the first head.

It is Peter's declaration that Jesus is the Christ, the Son of God that the church is built on, and God's emphasis is on that idea throughout the entire New Testament (there is absolutely no indication of Peter being the rock).

The following are some verses that powerfully demonstrate that the ***acknowledgment of Jesus*** as God's Son is the rock upon which the church is built. Jesus is always at the center of conversion – the solid thing that allows salvation.

John 3:15-16

15 "that whosoever believes in Him should not perish but have eternal life.

16 "For God so loved the world that He gave His only begotten Son, that whoever believes in Him should not perish but have eternal life.

The revelation of the long-awaited reconciliation with God is about to occur. After the Holy Spirit fell upon the apostles, Peter delivers the gospel message for the first time.

Acts 2:29-47.

29 Men and brethren let me speak freely to you of the patriarch David, that he is both dead and buried, and his tomb is with us to this day.

30 Therefore, being a prophet and knowing that God had sworn with an oath to him that of the fruit of his body, according to the flesh, He would raise up the Christ to sit on His throne.

31 he, foreseeing this, spoke concerning the resurrection of the Christ, that His soul was not left in Hades, nor did His flesh see corruption.

32 "This Jesus God has raised up, of which we are all witnesses.

33 "Therefore being exalted to the right hand of God, and having received from the Father the promise of the Holy Spirit, He poured out this which you now see and hear.

34 "For David did not ascend into the heavens, but he says himself:

'The Lord said to my Lord,

"Sit at My right hand,

35 Till I make Your enemies Your footstool." '

36 "Therefore let all the house of Israel know assuredly that God has made this Jesus, whom you crucified, both Lord and Christ."

37 Now when they heard this, they were cut to the heart, and said to Peter and the rest of the apostles, "Men and brethren, what shall we do?"

38 Then Peter said to them, "Repent, and let every one of you be baptized in the name of Jesus Christ for the remission of sins; and you shall receive the gift of the Holy Spirit.

39 "For the promise is to you and to your children, and to all afar off, as many as the Lord our God will call."

40 And with many other words he testified and exhorted them, saying, "Be saved from this perverse generation."

41 Then those who gladly received his word were baptized; and that day about three thousand souls were added to them.

42 "And they continued steadfastly in the apostles doctrine and fellowship, in the breaking of bread, and in prayers.

43 Then fear came upon every soul, and many wonders and signs were done through the apostles.

44 Now all who believed were together, and had all things in common,

45 and sold their possessions and goods, and divided them among all, as anyone had need.

46 So-continuing daily with one accord in the temple, and breaking bread from house to house, they ate their food with gladness and simplicity of heart,

47 praising God and having favor with all the people. And the Lord added to the church daily those who were being saved.

The message is, "Let all the house of Israel know assuredly that God has made Jesus, whom you crucified, both Lord and Christ." It is what Peter proclaimed (coming from God the Father) in Matthew 16:16-17 and the rock on which Jesus said the church would be built. Now Peter declares it again, being led by God (Holy Spirit) to tell these Jews on this first day of the kingdom, the church. Indeed we see the Lord adding to the church on this basis in Acts 2:47.

Jesus is at the core of salvation; we might say the rock of salvation.

Acts 4:8-12

8 Then Peter, filled with the Holy Spirit, said to them, "Rulers of the people and elders of Israel:

9 "If we this day are judged for a good deed done to a helpless man, by what means he has been made well,

10 "let it be known to you all, and to all the people of Israel, that by the name of Jesus Christ of Nazareth, whom you crucified, who God raised from the dead, by Him this man stands here before you whole.

11 This was the stone, which was rejected by you builders, which has become the chief cornerstone.'

12 Nor is there salvation in any other, for there is no other name under heaven given among men by which we must be saved."

Now, does Peter understand that **he is not the rock** of Matthew 16:16-19? Yes, of course, and he knows there is no other name under heaven given among men by which we must be saved (Acts 4:12). It is exactly what Peter stated in Matthew 16:16 and upon which the church belonging to Christ is being built. The church built by Jesus is centered on Him being the Son of God.

Acts 16:31

31 So they said, Believe on the Lord Jesus Christ, and you will be saved, you and your household.

It will **always** be Jesus at the center of salvation. **He is the solution, the rock upon which the reconciliation is built.**

Galatians 3:26-29

26 For you are all sons of God through faith in Christ Jesus.

27 For as many of you as were baptized into Christ have put on Christ.

28 There is neither Jew or Greek, there is neither slave or free, there is neither male nor female; you are all one in Christ Jesus.

29 And if you are Christ's, then you are Abraham seed, and heirs according to the promise."

Once again, Jesus is at the center of salvation, or we might say the rock that salvation is built upon. Jesus points to Himself as the One who must be trusted, or they will die in their sins.

John 8:24

24 Therefore I said to you that you will die in your sins; for if you do not believe that I am He, you will die in your sins.

People need to make the same declaration that Peter received from God the Father.

Romans 10:9-10

9 That if you confess with your mouth the Lord Jesus and believe in your heart that God has raised him from the dead, you will be saved

10 For with the heart one believes unto righteousness, and with the mouth confession is made unto salvation

Peter revealed that Jesus was the Christ, the Son of the living God, which is the basis for salvation. The church exists for the saved. This is so simple, and God is very thorough in pointing to Jesus as the answer to the reconciliation. Paul clarifies that the central ingredient for being in the church was the recognition of Jesus as the Christ, the Son of the living God. The church very simply is built on Jesus as the cornerstone, and those who make up the building are those called by the gospel. They have called on Jesus, recognizing Him as the Christ, the Son of the living God. It is a beautiful thing as the gospel of Christ calls individuals (2 Thessalonians 2:13-14), and then they choose to call on Jesus as Lord (Acts 2:21, Acts 22:16).

Matthew 10:32

32 Therefore whoever confesses me before men, him I will also confess before my Father who is in heaven.

All these verses give witness to the core nature of what Peter expressed in Matthew 16:16. **Missing from all scripture is any indication of Peter being the basis for the church**. Of course, in all the years after Jesus' death, Peter never assumed such a position. Peter was a fellow elder in the **local** church in Jerusalem. The rock cannot be both acknowledging Jesus as God's Son and be Peter! The church of the scriptures stands on Jesus being recognized as God's Son and the "called out" being those that make such a confession. In no conceivable way could God have the church built on Peter.

The emphasis from God is always in terms of achieving His purpose, and that purpose is to share His Divine Nature, or we can say His purpose is YOU and YOUR success. God can accomplish His purpose as a result of His Son's obedience. The Holy Spirit leads the apostles into all truth and specifically brings them the Keys of the kingdom, namely, the gospel message. The apostles would preach the gospel message, and one obedient soul at a time, the Lord adds them to His body, His spiritual body, the church. Jesus is building His church, and that continues to this day. Today, those "in Christ" carry the message as they are indeed the pillar and ground of truth.

There is no place, **no need for an earthly physical church**. Essentially there is no Catholic Church. What would its purpose be? God is accomplishing His purpose as a result of the apostles bringing the gospel message. That message continues to be carried by those converted ("in Christ"), as is the scriptural pattern. It is the responsibility of those "in Christ" and the local church designed by God to do the work of evangelism. In the next section below, **twelve scriptural examples** emphasize the importance of equipping the saints for the work of the ministry, of being teachers. Three are examples of the work being done by the saints, and two are instances of Jesus talking about the role of those who will be in the kingdom being "lights to the world" and showing appreciation for how they have been blessed. The remainder focuses on the need to become skilled teachers and the seriousness of this work. Indeed, God focuses on achieving His purpose, and there is an emphasis on the work of the saints in evangelism.

About 6000 years ago, Adam and Eve had a relationship with God in the Garden of Eden, and then due to sin, it vanished. The promises of Genesis by God required the terrible suffering and death of Christ for fulfillment – now it was done. Yet, there had been no reconciliation. Christ's part is complete, and now the Holy Spirit will provide the truth. The truth includes how a person can participate in what God has done in Christ. There is one more thing needed to achieve reconciliation. Namely, the apostles will learn the gospel message when they are filled with the Spirit of God and then deliver it. Finally, in obedience to that message, there can be the reconciliation. One might wonder what happens after all the apostles die. As time passes in the first century, the final will of God is gradually revealed as complete. In that word, we see how the message will go forward without the apostles. The saving message will be carried by those "in Christ." Those individuals working in the local church will be responsible for the truth people need. They are not alone but have the perfect completed word of God, the wisdom of God. Below are some passages that describe the work of bringing the message by the body of Christ.

The responsibility for carrying the message is that of the church consisting of those "in Christ."

Catholics think it is up to them, to the Catholic Church, to continue to bring the message. It is one of the problems when you build doctrine on error, fundamental error. There is nothing more fundamental in terms of error than the Catholic Church. As it turns out, the church Jesus is building has no successors to the apostles, but as shown, those "in Christ" continue to carry the message. The Catholic Church must have a line of succession back to the first century, or they can claim no authority.

Indeed, the message is conveyed by those "in Christ" who associate with a local independent church. That church is organized precisely as God defined it, such as the qualifications for elders and deacons. The local church's work (elders, deacons, and members) is primarily evangelism. As a group, they worship God in specified spiritual ways, and all are edified, and there may be benevolence for certain members. All of this is quite simple and all under the larger "heading of evangelism." You can see how God carefully and in detail defines the duties of those "in Christ." This responsibility could not be left without definition! There is no aspect of the reconciliation left to chance but well defined from the events bringing Christ after forty-two generations, to His preaching, to His death, burial, and resurrection, to the gospel message conveyed by the Holy Spirit to the apostles, to the apostles bringing the message, then finally the church (the kingdom) continuing to carry the message (that is those "in Christ"). Indeed there is a continuum, and we can see how the message has been carried and how that will persist. Here are just a **few** verses where the responsibility for carrying the message is demonstrated in this last age by those in the kingdom.

1 Peter 3:15

179

15 But sanctify the Lord God in your hearts, and always be ready to give a defense to everyone who asks you a reason for the hope that is in you, with meekness and fear;

Philippians 2:14-15

14 Do all things without complaining and disputing,

15 that you may become blameless and harmless, children of God without fault in the midst of a crooked and perverse generation, among whom you shine as lights in the world,

Colossians 4:5-6

5 Walk in wisdom toward those who are outside, redeeming the time.

6 Let your speech always be with grace, seasoned with salt, that you may know how you ought to answer each one.

1 Peter 2:9

9 But you are a chosen generation, a royal priesthood, a holy nation, His own special people, that you may proclaim the praises of Him who called you out of darkness into His marvelous light;

Matthew 5:14-16

14 "You are the light of the world. A city that is set on a hill cannot be hidden.

15 Nor do they light a lamp and put it under a basket, but on a lampstand, and it gives light to all who are in the house.

16 Let your light so shine before men, that they may see your good works and glorify your Father in heaven.

Luke 12:48

48 But he who did not know, yet committed things deserving of stripes, shall be beaten with few. For everyone to whom much is given, from him much will be required; and to whom much has been committed, of him they will ask the more.

Ephesians 4:12

12 for the equipping of the saints for the work of ministry, for the edifying of the body of Christ,

Acts 8:1-4

1 At that time a great persecution arose against the church which was at Jerusalem; and they were all scattered throughout the regions of Judea and Samaria, except the apostles.
2 And devout men carried Stephen to his burial, and made great lamentation over him.
3 As for Saul, he made havoc of the church, entering every house, and dragging off men and women, committing them to prison.
4 Therefore those who were scattered went everywhere preaching the word.

1 Thessalonians 1:8

8 For from you the word of the Lord has sounded forth, not only in Macedonia and Achaia, but also in every place. Your faith toward God has gone out, so that we do not need to say anything.

Ephesians 3.10

10 to the intent that now the manifold wisdom of God might be made known by the church to the principalities and powers in the heavenly places,

Acts 11:25-26

25 Then Barnabas departed for Tarsus to seek Saul.
26 And when he had found him, he brought him to Antioch. So it was that for a whole year they assembled with the church and taught a great many people. And the disciples were first called Christians in Antioch.

Hebrews 5:12

12 For though by this time you ought to be teachers, you need someone to teach you again the first principles of the oracles of God; and you have come to need milk and not solid food.

God's purpose has been fulfilled and what is left is God's perfection that can result in the remaining conversions

Before the end of the first century, the word of God has been completed and the apostles and various others working with the apostles have brought the word of God throughout much of the accessible world. During this time, the Holy Spirit worked with the apostles in bringing the truth. There was confirmation in terms of "signs and wonders, with various miracles, and gifts of the Holy Spirit, according to His own will."

The miraculous things are over, ceased, and as God has indicated, we have something much better than signs/miracles. The completed word of God is perfect. The church will go forward, the local church consisting of those "in Christ" (His spiritual body, His spiritual church) and take the gospel message to the world. This will continue until the end of time when Christ returns in the air and takes those "in Christ" to be with Him forever. All things physical will be destroyed, and then the judgment. During this intervening time before His return, any living person can succeed in their positive response to the gospel message brought by those in the body of Christ. Humankind might think there needs to be a more powerful, more aggressive means of bringing the message. One thing understood by those "in Christ" is the perfection of God in achieving His purpose. God is perfect in everything, and His means to accomplish His purpose is perfect. God will get **the right ones to share in His Divine Nature**. There is indeed a heavy weight on those in His body, and certainly, they will be held accountable. In Luke 12:48, above, Jesus is speaking of the kingdom. He alludes to those who have been given much (now those "in Christ" in the kingdom) will necessarily be required to do much. We could correctly say doing much as part of living for Christ and the gospel. Understandably, one lives for Christ, which means following His ways, which would mean distancing oneself from sin, living as directed in Galatians 5:22-25 and Philippians 4:8 and 2 Peter 1:5-9, among others. Jesus points out the necessity to live for Him **and the gospel**.

Mark 8:35-36

*35 For whoever **desires to save his life** will lose it, but whoever loses his life for My sake and the gospel's will save it.*

36 For what will it profit a man if he gains the whole world, and loses his own soul?

Living for Christ indicates not living for yourself, but why the emphasis on living for the gospel. Realize that by God emphasizing living for the gospel, it is something of grave importance. As pointed out, those "in Christ" are the last link in bringing the gospel message to the world. It is the reason the world continues because God's purpose can continue to be fulfilled in every soul who obeys the gospel and continues to live faithfully. Jesus reveals a lot in these two verses above, and this is a devastatingly profound understanding for everyone who "**desires to save his life**."

Think about Matthew 16 in terms of what it means – quite wonderful

Think about the magnitude of what God revealed to Peter in Matthew 16:16. How often does God the Father "speak" or we might say reveal something to a person? It is quite rare, and this most important of things began back in Genesis 3:15 and is now reaching culmination after about 4000 years. It is the announcement of Jesus as God's Son. It is **NOT** naming a person to head the Catholic Church, but that Jesus is the solution to a very spiritual problem. Jesus reveals that He will build His church. Is it Peter's church? Is Peter at the center of Jesus's revelation, or is Jesus the solution and the head of the church? The church is spiritual consisting of those who are spiritual. Indeed the scriptures refer to Jesus as the head of the church in Ephesians 5:23, and He is the chief cornerstone (Acts 4:11), and for clarity, Jesus is the rock, the solution. Salvation can only be achieved if the spiritual problem is resolved.

The church of Catholicism has a physical nature and offers no solution to the spiritual problem. They claim the right to make the rules, and in the area of salvation, they devise something exceedingly different than the gospel message. Catholicism states that you must be a Catholic to go to heaven. Of course, as the creator of the rules, that can be changed. I have heard it taught that only Catholics could know for sure they are going to heaven. I have also heard it taught that, of course, by grace, anyone could be saved. In twelve years of Catholic education, it was always you must be a Catholic to go to heaven. There is not a nanometer of truth in Catholicism.

Let me share a few more thoughts on Matthew 16:19. Early in this section, this verse was discussed and shown that the apostle's binding and loosening were **not related** to their wills being imposed as doctrine. **In truth, they would be instructing people in the will of God guided by the Holy Spirit.** This would include what they would teach and what certain ones were directed to write. In any case, it is as the Holy Spirit indicates in 2 Peter 1:20-21, "knowing this first, that no prophecy of Scripture is of any private interpretation, for prophecy never came by the will of man, but holy men of God spoke as they were moved by the Holy Spirit." This should be a compelling statement to those who love the truth, that is, "for prophecy (inspired declaration of divine will) never came by the will of man." The apostles were **not binding and loosening their will** but delivering the will of God to the people. That makes perfect sense and is consistent with all scripture.

There is no need for the Catholic Church to exist, and it should not exist for billions of reasons (all souls). God's purpose is perfectly fulfilled in the scriptures. The Catholic Church serves the purpose of **leading people away from the truth** and is the enemy of God. In the whole of the New Testament, there is no indication of the Catholic Church and its doctrines. There is no office of a pope, and Peter remains an elder in the church in Jerusalem, and the last scriptural evidence of Peter's location is in Jerusalem. The Catholic Church is not alone, but the "churches of the world" are similar in deceiving souls. The Catholic Church and the other "so-called Christian churches," serve as a distraction from the truth people need. There is truth, and it is Christian, but it is neither Catholic nor Protestant.

Stop and think. God planned a solution to sin and fulfilled that spiritual need. If you look at the Catholic Church, it has no purpose. The Bible reveals God's purpose is sharing in His Divine Nature, which is accomplished perfectly in the gospel message. Nothing more is needed, but look what Catholicism has brought. Namely, all sorts of human-devised teachings and glory, prestige, honor to various religious leaders of Catholicism. There is not a single grain of value related to heaven in Catholicism, but many continue to be eternally damaged.

The sixth verse not seen by Marcus Grodi

Revelation 14:13

13 Then I heard a voice from heaven saying to me, "Write: 'Blessed are the dead who die in the Lord from now on.'"

"Yes," says the Spirit, "that they may rest from their labors, and their works follow them."

Here Marcus Grodi realizes that his Protestant belief in faith alone is problematic regarding their teaching on works. However, there are dozens of verses that destroy the faith alone/security doctrine. The entire character of God and His purpose oppose this fundamental belief of Protestantism. Thus this argument against Protestantism appears for Marcus Grodi, but it will be one of many he comes to "finally" see clearly. It is almost like he is creating a list of plus and minus values for and against Protestantism compared to Catholicism. The positive values for Catholicism are growing. He points out the extreme nature of the "faith only" position when he says Protestants downplayed the need to grow in holiness. Their version of security guaranteeing eternal success was a way of minimizing the fear of the Lord and diminishing the growth that God demands. Marcus Grodi sees the fallibility of men such as Luther and Calvin in terms of not being inspired, and thus THEIR doctrines have problems. Marcus Grodi gets this right but then fails to make the same application to Catholicism. He cannot see that Catholicism originates from fallible men. He honors the "early church fathers" and what they write and justifies this by saying they had some connection with the apostles. Indeed, **it seems** some like the apostle John, likely had some contact with a few of the "early church fathers." This is the kind of second-hand, circumstantial, hopeful information that Catholicism wants to turn into doctrine. Knowing some of the apostles in no way allows the leap to accepting some of the things the early fathers suggest in their writings.

*Note: I said "it seems" there was some contact with John and perhaps other apostles with the early church fathers. This is based on a number of different accounts. Admittedly the early church father's association with an apostle may or may not be true – it does not matter. It does not matter because the **apostles never originated doctrine** but received the truth from God through the Holy Spirit, and only the scriptures have validity. Catholicism builds its case on many different things that are not scripture and then builds on those erroneous things. There is only one solid place for the truth, and it is God's inspired word.*

Certainly, the early church father's work during about the first five centuries did contribute to copying the documents we know as the New Testament. It is likely all of the New Testament can be found in their writings. The early church fathers knew that their writings were not scripture (inspired), and Marcus Grodi also knows that. However, Catholics look at these men and their writings and relate them in some way to an ongoing apostolic revelation. They add to this by saying the things they wrote contain tradition that is equivalent to the scriptures. Some of the early church fathers would claim that certain bishops were successors to Peter. There would also be references in the early church father's writing that suggest the concept of apostolic succession. Catholicism builds on this and creates a succession of popes from Peter. Catholicism claims some of these endeavors of the early churches were things God intended for His church. Also, Catholicism implies observances or practices conducted by the early church were at the oversight of apostolic authority. Catholicism can find early century writings that indicated the Real Presence of Jesus in the Lord's Supper, and thus they claim it validates the practice. All this leads to the Catholic teaching that the Bible is not sufficient in matters of faith. The thing most hated by God, namely the **changing of His word**, becomes Catholicism's primary mode of operation. Then the bold claim is made that a person needs the Catholic Church AND the Bible to have the faith God requires. However, God is clear **there is one solid thing, and it is the word of God.** This was the only way to assure the very singular truth - the gospel message reaches humankind. Once any person or group of people insert themselves into this process of defining the truth, something horrendous occurs. In the Catholic case, it would be building a belief system on a deceitful and erroneous foundation that evolves to be the opposite of God's message.

When Marcus Grodi is correct, it can be verified in the scriptures such as Revelation 14:13. The scriptures provide the evidence in which men and women can find comfort. We might say be exceedingly comfortable in the scriptures because God has fit all things perfectly together. However, the things Marcus Grodi finds favorable in Catholicism are always inconsistent in consideration of all that scripture provides on that subject. They are also not consistent with God's purpose, with God's nature. This goes back to the poor foundation of Catholicism and how everything needs defending. Many of the errors are built on errors that were created in defense or support of the primary error. Catholic infant baptism is an excellent example of a doctrine built on the error called original sin.

The seventh verse not seen by Marcus Grodi

Romans 10:14-15

14 How then shall they call on Him in whom they have not believed? And how shall they believe in Him of whom they have not heard? And how shall they hear without a preacher?

15 And how shall they preach unless they are sent? As it is written:

"How beautiful are the feet of those who preach the gospel of peace,

Who bring glad tidings of good things!"

Marcus Grodi makes a wrong turn on this verse as he finds the need for an authority to send people to preach. Finally, he thinks the answer is in the Catholic Church which has a process for sending people (to preach) via their priests and bishops. It is a process that requires training and then approval. He thinks in this process they will all teach the same thing. Of course, since he does not understand the most fundamental aspects of God's message, he could never get this right. I wonder if he considered "Catholic taught" persons could all go out and teach the SAME WRONG THING.

He reasons and observes that although some are ordained in Protestantism, they go out and teach hundreds of different things. Who sent them, who sent him and ordained him to be a Protestant minister, and by what authority was he sent/ordained. Amid his logic, he indicates that not just anyone is meant to be a preacher. A person cannot suddenly decide to preach and go off and begin teaching whatever he likes.

*Note: There is a brief discussion regarding who has the responsibility to teach, to preach in the section named, "The fifth verse not seen by Marcus Grodi." It points out **all those in the body of Christ** have the responsibility to teach the gospel message. The local church is responsible for evangelism, and elders will make sure the body is edified, continually encouraged, and growing in the ability to teach.*

The fundamentals confound Marcus Grodi, and thus he draws poor conclusions

Marcus Grodi's real problem is that he does not understand the church, either the body of Christ (spiritual) or the local church. Thus he will always have hundreds of problems concerning church organization, duties, and everything else. What a mess when people miss the fundamentals as we see people layers deep in the nonsense of things that do not matter and then working fervently on those details. Such people are "sweating out" the details of meaninglessness. Marcus Grodi's understanding of the church and the correct view of the church were explained in this chapter in the section called "the second verse Marcus Grodi never saw." We will define the local church as the Holy Spirit communicated it to the apostles. Once the local church defined by God is understood, Marcus Grodi should no longer have any concerns regarding qualified teachers and teaching the same thing.

The **local church** was gradually revealed in the first century. Since Acts 2, there would be those qualified to be in the local church due to their obedience to the gospel. The local church consisting of those "in Christ" was designed by God **to allow His purpose to be continually fulfilled**. The **local church** has certain duties, and they can be seen as spiritual. The local church organization is well defined by God.

- Structure: There are elders, deacons, and members
- All have been added to the body of Christ (spiritual) by the Lord
- The elders and deacons must meet certain qualifications, and these are given in 1 Timothy 3:1-7 and 1 Timothy 3:8-13
- Another title that the scriptures use is that of evangelist, teacher, preacher. The qualifications are, of course, being a member of the body of Christ who possesses good skills with the word of God. All the members have this responsibility of evangelism, and each is striving to become a good ambassador of the truth to the world. The elders could designate a person to the routine duties of evangelism or preaching and thus carry the informal title of evangelist or preacher. Often, if they agree, such a person could take on the responsibility of edifying the local church. There is always the need to grow in knowledge to carry on the work of evangelism. The prime work of the entire local church meaning each individual is evangelism, and the preacher/evangelist does **not** fulfill this requirement for the other members. Each person in the local church has this responsibility, and a located preacher and the elders, deacons, and all members assist each other in becoming effective at evangelism.

There is a strong emphasis for those "in Christ" to be good teachers, which necessarily means handling well the word of God.

Hebrews 5:12-14

12 For though by this time you ought to be teachers, you need someone to teach you again the first principles of the oracles of God; and you have come to need milk and not solid food.

13 For everyone who partakes only of milk is unskilled in the word of righteousness, for he is a babe.

14 But solid food belongs to those who are of full age, that is, those who by reason of use have their senses exercised to discern both good and evil.

Marcus Grodi is putting the cart in front of the horse, putting the processes before the truth – The problem is not the variation in doctrine being taught, but first, there must be the truth

Marcus Grodi observes the problem in Protestantism as being so many different doctrines, and he blames this on non-uniform instruction. Also, there is no formal process (across all of Protestantism) for qualifying teachers / preachers / evangelists. It must seem inconceivable to him that this could ever be resolved considering all the different divisions (denominations) within Protestantism. In Catholicism, he sees a consistent doctrine via consistent Catholic teaching from the Catholic Catechism, universities, and their hierarchy featuring councils as needed and at the highest level their Magisterium. Catholicism has a process that qualifies men, ordains men. They had similar ordination means in the different denominations of Protestantism, but they taught many different things. Catholicism seems more "organized." This thinking is very logical, but it is **not** God's way. God's way is perfect to achieve His purpose. Both Protestantism and Catholicism are physical religions. They think humankind needs physical organizations with rulemaking, highly educated persons of theology, detailed methods of developing qualified persons who can be certified, i.e., ordained. Marcus Grodi wanted to find out who did this the best. The truth from God is much different than people conceive. The church is spiritual and works when there is one rulebook – the word of God. It works best when the **teachers have a love of the truth, a good heart, and dedication to the scriptures**. The teachers are those in the body of Christ and their attitude was initially demonstrated in seeking God followed by obedience to the gospel. In obedience to the gospel, they have put away past sins. God requires those "in Christ" to live for Him and the gospel.

189

Consequently, they become dedicated to the truth, to spreading the gospel message. It is the combination of the right people using only the scriptures that is meaningful in evangelism. This is God's way and "light-years" from the complexity of humankind's religious institutions. Another obvious miss for Marcus Grodi is that he does not compare the simplicity of God's message to the complexity of humankind's religions. Whether it is Catholicism or Protestantism, the teachings are different from the scriptures, and it is always due to private interpretations. God has a meaning in the scriptures, and it can easily be understood if you love the truth but is never understood if there is prejudice. Neither the "churches" of Catholicism and Protestantism teach the truth, and therefore, concern over them teaching differently and how they qualify teachers is genuinely pointless. Marcus Grodi finds some order in Catholic teaching and the process of certifying teachers. Unfortunately, the consistency is that they are all consistently wrong.

There is a divinely defined organization for the local church, and it includes elders, deacons, and members. There are no priests, bishops, archbishops, cardinals, or popes. The Protestant denominations generally have some sort of non-scriptural organization and share somewhat similar functions for their various "titles." Functions such as superintendent, teaching manager, physical plant, benevolence, teaching plan, growth plan, logistics, finance, youth director and many others represent the very physical organizations of these "churches." There is nothing apparently wrong with all these positions except they are defining something different than the local church and its truly spiritual nature. The outcome of all this stuff will undoubtedly be the wrong focus. If you consider Marcus Grodi's issue it is really related to seeing the church in a very corporate manner, a very worldly view of this rather full-service organization whether it is called Catholic or Protestant.

The eighth verse not seen by Marcus Grodi

Marcus Grodi uses two different verses to explain a single point concerning the "Real Presence."

John 15:4

4 Abide in Me, and I in you. As the branch cannot bear fruit of itself, unless it abides in the vine, neither can you, unless you abide in Me.

John 6:56

56 He who eats My flesh and drinks My blood abides in Me, and I in him.

Marcus Grodi claims that to abide in Christ, you have to literally eat His flesh and drink His blood. Everything Marcus Grodi and Catholicism teaches is like a discovery, like a puzzle, like a mystery, and finally, there is the answer. Those of Catholicism's leadership spend endless hours trying to find ways to support their teachings in areas where the questions never end. This is necessary because the scriptures do not support Catholic doctrine, and despite their various creative ways to validate their teachings, many remain uncomfortable with their exceedingly weak evidence. Catholicism is in a terrible plight as so many of its fundamental doctrines were developed by very unstable leaders sometimes over a thousand years ago. These persons did not understand the scriptures but had a singular focus to rule over Christianity. Some of these were the early popes. Some go back further to the early centuries of Christianity. Seldom does the early church mention the respect needed for the word of God. Looking at their councils, this critical issue of God's word and not changing it, not privately interpreting it, is missing. There are all sorts of "physical church matters," but not the spiritual church. In any case, it is such a mess that after the Bible became acceptable for Catholics to read, there were few solid answers to the many questions. Time and effort by Catholic apologists eventually provided reasonable answers. Nonetheless, as mentioned continuously in this book, Catholic explanations are complicated, disconnected. This is especially true in the most critical aspect, namely salvation.

Consider Jesus' statement in John and how it is associated with His flesh and blood.

John 6:53-54:

53 Then Jesus said to them, Most assuredly, I say to you, unless you eat the flesh of the Son of Man and drink His blood, you have no life in you.

54 Whoever eats My flesh and drinks My blood has eternal life, and I will raise him up at the last day.

It seems like Jesus is associating salvation (eternal life) to eating His flesh and drinking His blood. **Indeed, He does that, and there is no mistake in the answer of Acts 2:38.** In the process of Acts 2:38, sins are forgiven, and one receives the gift of the Holy Spirit. Thus one in their obedience to the gospel eats the flesh and drinks the blood of Jesus. They do this inasmuch as Jesus gave His actual body and blood, and that allowed the reconciliation. Can you imagine all the complications brought to the simplicity of the gospel message by Catholic supposition? In obedience to the gospel, each person is partaking in the actual body and blood of Jesus. Does Catholicism not know that those people were "saved." They did what Jesus said was necessary to have life, to have eternal life. It is a spiritual thing, and then the Lord adds them to His spiritual body, the church. There is something utterly amazing and pathetic about the incredible hierarchy of Catholicism and all its rules, councils, ceremonies, pageantry, and miracles compared to the simplicity of the gospel. It is their movement away from the scriptures that eventually leads to missing God's clear meaning and in this case how John 6:53-54 is fulfilled.

One could go on "forever" with all the incorrect statements from Marcus Grodi in this matter. He says those listening to Jesus took John 6:56 literally, and many left Him. They thought what Jesus said was literal, and thus they departed. Most walked away, and they were the ones who were there for the free food (John 6:26). His disciples did not leave Him as they knew Jesus was speaking the truth, **although they did not understand His meaning**. As seen above, a person eats the flesh and drinks the blood metaphorically in their obedience as **verified by their receiving what Jesus promises,** namely eternal life. To clarify, eternal life would not be possible without eating the flesh and drinking the blood of Christ. Now we learn this is done in their obedience to the gospel, that is, by obeying the death, burial and resurrection of Jesus. Also, to be precise, those obedient are "in Christ," in His spiritual body, the church, and now have the **possibility** of receiving the end of their faith – heaven, sharing in the Divine Nature or, as mentioned, eternal life. Indeed, unless one eats His flesh and drinks His blood, eternal life would not be possible. Throughout the scriptures, it is clear that those "in Christ" **must remain "faithful unto death"** to receive the crown of life, eternal life.

We will also see that Jesus' reference to eating His flesh and drinking His blood at the Last Supper (Matthew 26:26-29) is a metaphor. At no point in the scriptures do the apostles led by the Holy Spirit speak of the Real Presence (also Eucharist to Catholics) concerning the Lord's

Supper. The Lord's Supper stands alone as a remembrance, as a memorial to God's Son. Chapter 9 addresses the "Real Presence" in detail and the meaning intended by the Lord.

The ninth verse not seen by Marcus Grodi

Colossians 1:24

24 I now rejoice in my sufferings for you, and fill up in my flesh what is lacking in the afflictions of Christ, for the sake of His body, which is the church,

Just when you think Marcus Grodi cannot become any more careless, he takes another tangent. Again, this is the result of not having the fundamentals, and then anything goes. Marcus Grodi made a good personal observation when he had no place to put suffering. I assume he meant this was a conflict with the Protestant "works" belief. Of course, there are conflicts with Protestant "works" doctrine throughout the scriptures. Here is where it gets strange as Marcus **Grodi implies that the work of salvation is not completed but is completed in Paul's suffering** for the sake of the body, His spiritual church. **Salvation was completed in Christ,** and each person is saved from past sins in obedience to the gospel. **Nothing is missing.** Nothing is lacking in the afflictions of Christ concerning a person's salvation. Paul could have died immediately after obeying the gospel and would have received the crown of life. Paul's suffering was done for the sake of the body of Christ. Jesus obeyed the Father and did all He could, but He cannot save a single person unless the gospel is preached and obeyed. The Holy Spirit brought the message, and the apostles delivered it. In delivering the message, Paul happened to suffer, and this was not an unusual thing at that time and can even be common today. Suffering is normal in every life, but the scriptures define a certain type of suffering, and it can be called suffering as a Christian. That is, suffering in the process of doing the will of God. This is what Paul was doing, and we can see that he mentions the things he suffered in the process of evangelizing.

2 Corinthians 11:22-28

22 Are they Hebrews? So am I. Are they Israelites? So am I. Are they the seed of Abraham? So am I.

23 Are they ministers of Christ?—I speak as a fool—I am more: in labors more abundant, in stripes above measure, in prisons more frequently, in deaths often.

24 From the Jews five times I received forty stripes minus one.

25 Three times I was beaten with rods; once I was stoned; three times I was shipwrecked; a night and a day I have been in the deep;

26 in journeys often, in perils of waters, in perils of robbers, in perils of my own countrymen, in perils of the Gentiles, in perils in the city, in perils in the wilderness, in perils in the sea, in perils among false brethren;

27 in weariness and toil, in sleeplessness often, in hunger and thirst, in fastings often, in cold and nakedness—

28 besides the other things, what comes upon me daily: my deep concern for all the churches.

Paul is saying that what was missing is preaching **the gospel message** *"and fill up in my flesh what is lacking in the afflictions of Christ"* and what was lacking was the bounty of souls that comes by preaching, and in Paul's case, there was a great deal of suffering involved.

Paul is aware that unless the gospel message comes to the world, Christ's effort will be for naught. Those the Lord sent out, including Paul are in a sense necessarily suffering as they bring a **message that is not well accepted** and in fact, often violently opposed. They suffer, and the reward is souls that respond to the message. Christ's suffering has been completed, and the door is open to reconciliation. Paul is suffering (in this case) for the Colossians in Christ (Colossians 1:24), and in fact, everywhere he goes, there is opposition. Jesus did all He needed to do to bring the reconciliation, but the gospel message is not well received by many and might result in suffering such as in Paul's case. This is not what God wants for them, but like with Jesus, there was much opposition. The opposition is to the truth as **people do not like the truth if it clashes with what they want**, and typically the scriptures conflict with how people want to live and what they currently believe. It is important to distinguish between suffering in a person's natural life and what Paul and others endure for the gospel.

1 Peter 4:14-16

14 If you are reproached for the name of Christ, blessed are you, for the Spirit of glory and of God rests upon you. On their part He is blasphemed, but on your part He is glorified.

15 But let none of you suffer as a murderer, a thief, an evildoer, or as a busybody in other people's matters.

16 Yet if anyone suffers as a Christian, let him not be ashamed, but let him glorify God in this matter.

Jesus learned obedience by the things He suffered (Hebrews 5:8). There is an aspect of suffering for those "in Christ" that is also associated with their obedience, especially with their mission (initially Jesus' mission) to seek and save that which was lost. Jesus told the apostles that "If they persecuted Me, they will also persecute you," and Jesus never desired this for Himself or for those who follow Him. The world did not like the message, not then and not throughout history. Jesus said, "Do not think that I came to bring peace on earth. I did not come to bring peace, but a sword," and this was mentioned in terms of having unfavorable relationships with people. There will be suffering in the life of those who do God's will, and it is connected to the message they bring and can be called "suffering as a Christian." Also, we learn that "For whom the LORD loves He chastens, and scourges every son whom He receives (Hebrews 12:6-11). God provides a great deal regarding suffering as a child of God and emphasizes the short period of affliction versus the eternal weight of glory (Romans 8:18, 2 Corinthians 4:17). However, God never ties a person's suffering to their salvation that Christ did not complete in His suffering. Christ perfectly completed His part such that all that remains is a person's obedient response to the death, burial, and resurrection of the Lord and, of course, their continued faithfulness.

The tenth verse not seen by Marcus Grodi

Luke 1:46-49

46 And Mary said:

"My soul magnifies the Lord,

47 And my spirit has rejoiced in God my Savior.

48 For He has regarded the lowly state of His maidservant;

For behold, henceforth all generations will call me blessed.

195

49 For He who is mighty has done great things for me,
And holy is His name.

Here Marcus Grodi extrapolates Mary being called blessed by future generations to mean that she is in some way spiritually his mother and to be honored. A fundamental principle of scripture is that only God is to be honored in a religious sense, to be revered. Only Jesus is the advocate to the Father. Like Peter, who never becomes the pope, Mary never receives honor in the inspired word of God. Mary deserves the title of blessed because God so indicates, but likewise do those of Matthew 5 who are blessed for various reasons. There is a separate chapter (Chapter 11) describing what has come to be known as Mariology.

A final thought on Marcus Grodi's "things he did not see"

One has to wonder why Marcus Grodi does not indicate the ten things he never saw in the traditions of the early church fathers. He never will because he knows those are not inspired writings. He also knows that those writings are a vast collection of the writings of what men believed, and he knows of their variability across many different early church fathers. It would be impossible to sort the massive number of documents written over many centuries and reach some consensus – they wrote many different things that amount to what they thought. None of the early church father's writings represent any authoritative doctrine. It is easy to realize God knew humankind could never present the things of God correctly – thus the Holy Spirit. One would be committing a terrible wrong to look at the writings of the early church fathers as what God intended. God provided what He intended, inspired by the Holy Spirit, and completed His message for all time. It would be inadvisable to add to or take away from what was delivered.

6.11 Marcus Grodi on salvation in the Catholic Church

Before we leave Marcus Grodi, let us look at the "end-all issue for every person," and Marcus Grodi discusses this, namely salvation.

https://www.youtube.com/watch?v=k7IJGzQlo1w&t=1508s&ab_channel=TheComingHomeNetworkInternational

Marcus Gordi's subject is, "What must I do to be saved?"

One might think this is a good topic since, for most people, this is the bottom line. If you are Catholic, then this is how you were saved and became a Catholic. This is also what must be done to be saved when you want to become a Catholic. You might also think that this conversion process should not take very long to explain. You might think that if you look at the conversions of the New Testament (https://heavencoach.com/conversions-of-the-new-testament/), there will be some synergy with what Marcus Grodi teaches. Of course, different people have different backgrounds, and the conversion process may take longer to explain. Peter's first sermon took several minutes based on the record. The conversion discussion of Phillip and the Ethiopian eunuch was of unknown length but seemed to be short. Phillip explained to the eunuch the text he was reading from Isaiah. Paul's conversion process was very short, as were several others per the available accounts. The time to provide what people need is unimportant, but it could be very quick considering the requirements. However, Marcus Grodi included a history lesson of Israel and Christianity and featured their parallel structures as he taught salvation. In the video link above, before addressing the subject of salvation in the Catholic Church, he describes the primary problems with Protestantism and indicates the superiority of Catholicism.

His talk was designed to lead one to the conclusion that only Catholicism was valid. That conclusion has a basis in the deficiencies of Protestantism. Specifically, this resulted from Protestants failing to recognize the tradition of the early fathers of the church and the succession of the apostles in the form of a valid head, the Catholic pope.

Marcus Grodi's talk on salvation is quite lengthy and complicated. After about one hour of high-speed speaking and about thirty very detailed visuals, I still wondered how one would become a Catholic. I might understand becoming a Catholic, but I did not know what that meant in terms of salvation. Based on what I know of Catholicism, their Catechism, and Marcus Grodi's explanation, I created what appears to be the pattern for salvation and discuss it in Chapter 5, "God's simplicity versus Catholic complexity." One could come to believe Catholics do not have a pattern for conversion but just a "bunch of stuff" that evolved over a considerable period of time by a "bunch of men" trying to create something that made some sense. Of course, their message seems to change a lot. It would be fair to say that no person of Catholicism has ever been saved. Their concept of original sin and all that follows muddies the waters of their salvation. Actually, it leaves no opportunity for salvation.

The talk by Marcus Grodi has been well thought out, and there is something to be learned as the pattern of the Old Covenant is compared to the New Covenant. It is one of those talks that with all the material and the flow of how God acted relative to the Jews and then the similarities with the New Covenant, there is a satisfactory knowledge of the covenants. Thus at a high level, this is good background information when it is consistent with the scriptures. One might think that the conclusions will also be logical and even the truth. Unfortunately, although the explanation of the Old Covenant is reasonably correct, the New Covenant explanation is very non-biblical. Nonetheless, the shadow of the Old can be seen in the New. Of course, this is exactly what the scriptures indicate, for instance, throughout Hebrews.

Hebrews 10:1

1 For the law, having a shadow of the good things to come, and not the very image of the things, can never with these same sacrifices, which they offer continually year by year, make those who approach perfect.

The discussion of the New Testament was done assuming the Catholic Church is in the center of the New Testament. Thus at this point, it is clear that the conclusions regarding salvation will be terribly wrong. Overall the technique used is common to Catholic persuasion, namely make it complicated and lengthy, and thus surely it must be right. It is like a Catholic saying, "I am so glad we have these wonderful men of God because I could never understand all this. I trust my priest, bishop, and the pope." The truth is you need to understand what you believe; you cannot have someone else understand it for you. In Marcus Grodi's entire talk, you never get what is needed for salvation – the gospel message. Marcus Grodi's approach to the subject of salvation is targeted at accepting the early church father's teachings of their traditions and the idea of apostolic succession. Everything is designed to point to the Catholic Church as the only source of salvation. Marcus Grodi confirms the various essential Catholic beliefs in his talk. Rituals are highlighted, as is the Eucharist, the validity of scripture and tradition, the Catholic hierarchy, and priests, as is original sin. Even from the Catholic perspective, I was not clear what was being taught for salvation.

For many Catholics, the distinction will be blurred between what is scripture and what is tradition. An example might be original sin and the associated infant baptism being thought to be in the scriptures. One of the Catholic declarations is that you could never understand what God intended if not for the early church's tradition. You can hear Catholics making such statements, but you learn they will say anything that supports Catholicism. Catholicism is so distant from the truth that they had to go to extremes throughout their history to maintain their theology. Those extreme measures have varied over history to include fanatical violence at one extreme. Then, in more recent times to develop better apologetics in defense of apparent scriptural opposition to their doctrines. They cannot succeed since, in rejecting God's word, they reject God. As they win new converts and maintain their current members, those victories will ultimately be losses – eternal losses.

God can and did deliver the truth and did it in every way perfect. He completed His revelation for humankind, and it is validated in many ways. His words will not pass away. However, as people accept human ideas and human tradition as valid, there will be confusion and inconsistency. This is the complication seen in the Catholic Church. Through the Holy Spirit, God worked with the apostles for fifty-plus years, and even though God was perfect somehow during that time (according to Catholicism), God could not get the message across clearly. Catholicism is exceedingly disrespectful to God. Of course, they have no choice since they do not exist without their ability to make the rules.

Salvation cannot be found in the Catholic Church

Several times, it is mentioned that a Catholic has never had their sins forgiven. In the scriptures, sins were forgiven when the gospel was obeyed, but no Catholic ever obeyed the gospel. Their salvation is an incomprehensible mix of original sin, confession to a priest, the rules of Catholicism, including taking the Eucharist, benefitting from indulgences, and finally somehow (in most cases) enduring the suffering of Purgatory to achieve heaven. None of this is scriptural but opposed to God on every point. People believing in God know that He is the creator and He spoke everything into existence, but they do not understand how. Catholics can grant God the creation but cannot believe He can deliver the truth in the **manner He designated** or do a perfect job in that **delivery**. Yet the creation is just the stage and players to allow God to achieve His purpose. God did "salvation" perfectly. To get the right persons to share in His

Divine Nature, He was every bit as careful as in the creation, perfectly careful in His plan. He was also perfectly protective of His plan by requiring humankind to never change His word, by telling them if they speak, it should be as the **oracles of God** (God-breathed speech, i.e., the word of God), by informing them that there must be **no private interpretations** and in fact that the word of God never came by the will of man, but holy men of God spoke as the Holy Spirit moved them.

Finally, to those who love the truth and can rightly divide the word of God, He informs them through the Holy Spirit that when that which is perfect has come, then that which is in part will be done away. It is just another thing that Catholics in the middle of their human-devised religion never saw and is another teaching that Protestants also never saw. God informs humankind that He has brought an end to all those things they like so much, like signs, miracles, and so on. The thing remaining is His word, and it is the most potent thing in God's arsenal to achieve His purpose. Catholics act in opposition to God's completed word and its implications. Again, they must do this because otherwise, they have no way to validate their doctrines that are consistently in opposition to God's word. How did the Holy Spirit inform those who love the truth that the word of God was complete? The same way we know everything from God, even knowing how to purify our souls, that is, by the Spirit through the word of God. It is only by the scriptures that we know the things of God.

1 Peter 1:22-23
22 Since you have purified your souls in obeying the truth through the Spirit in sincere love of the brethren, love one another fervently with a pure heart,
23 having been born again, not of corruptible seed but incorruptible, through the word of God which lives and abides forever

Catholicism has essentially built a new religion, and it is not Christianity. They will create and validate their teachings via their Magisterium (teaching authority of the Roman Catholic Church as exercised by bishops or the Pope). The Magisterium considers the scriptures, the tradition of the early church fathers and the succession of the apostles as factors to validate teachings. The Magisterium outcomes are considered as ***equivalent to*** or ***as important as*** or in some cases even ***better than the scriptures***. Catholic doctrine indicates you must be a Catholic to go to heaven. Marcus Grodi, with no explanation, indicates that you still might be saved by the grace of God, although you can never be certain of salvation unless you are Catholic. It is hard to say what Catholicism teaches on this subject of salvation, but it is different than the gospel message.

6.12 Dr. Hahn and Marcus Grodi – Miss the mark

In this chapter, both Dr. Hahn and Marcus Grodi have been discussed concerning their conversions to Catholicism and their subsequent aggressive promotion of the Catholic faith. There were things to be admired about Martin Luther and likewise about Dr. Hahn and Marcus Grodi. There is, however, a higher court, and people are judged regarding their alignment with the scriptures. Dr. Hahn and Marcus Grodi are still alive at this writing, and thus their outcome is still to be determined. One is not allowed to specifically suggest any person in relation to their soul's final destination. It is simply, preach the word, and if the seed falls on good ground (a good heart), there can be a good eternal result. However, suggesting certain **categories of people,** such as those dying in sin or those who did not obey the gospel, are going to fail is allowed. If you look at the world, there are few people with a sincere and active interest in the truth, even only a few with an uncompromising interest in heaven. Dr. Hahn and Marcus Grodi have a deep interest in God, in eternal matters, in salvation. However, they have it terribly wrong, and at the root cause level, they have convinced themselves that the Catholic Church is the truth. However, there is truth, and there is error, and the latter brings devastation.

Catholics often remain faithful to the Catholic Church because it can be harrowing to leave, and the most painful part could be swallowing their pride. However, in the case of Dr. Hahn and Marcus Grodi, they have done this before in leaving Protestantism. I certainly do not know about their pride, but I do know **that is why people fail in general**. My deep concern is for those billions of people who follow Catholicism (also who follow Protestantism) believing there can be good eternal outcomes. God's gospel message is clear, and that is why it is easy to see error and confidently oppose the damage it does. To succeed, you will need a love of the truth.

Continuing to address Dr. Hahn and Marcus Grodi

Dr. Hahn is an influential Catholic teacher, perhaps the best of any Catholic apologist. His writing and speaking need to be examined because they are compelling in supporting Catholicism to Catholics and Protestants, and others. However, his beliefs are problematic, even silly to many outside Catholicism. To those in the body of Christ, they appear as a terror to souls. One thought that might help both him and Marcus Grodi is to consider that God would not make achieving His purpose complicated, mysterious in any way. God wants to accomplish His purpose, which means as many as possible will be sharing in the Divine Nature. In some way, both of these men must think they are helpful, needed to explain God in ways the average person cannot understand. God did not design the truth such that it required such men of exceptional skills, but the people God seeks realize the truth due to having good hearts, a love of the truth, a humble character, unselfish and are very different from persons of pride and ego. Such people can build on the correct foundation and gain a deep and truthful understanding of God and life.

The New Evangelism of the Catholic Church

Once again, like Marcus Grodi, we have a person who does not know the fundamentals of God's message. Dr. Hahn's talk on The New Evangelism is layers deep in misconception. You can see Dr. Hahn speaking on The New Evangelism at the links below.

https://www.youtube.com/watch?v=i_oJF7qhqWM&ab_channel=St.PaulCenter

https://www.youtube.com/watch?v=sZRy0f2KJDg&t=5192s&ab_channel=MountSt.new TestanMary%27sSeminary%26SchoolofTheology

Indeed, Dr. Hahn makes everything complicated, which is the character of Catholic teachings. When you associate with Catholicism, you connect with confusion, and all of your resulting beliefs will be confusing and wrong. Dr. Hahn is brilliant as he speaks intelligently about Christianity but draws the wrong conclusions from partial truths. Paul warned of those like Dr. Hahn who possess great wisdom, but it is the "wisdom of the wise" that is, their own pride speaking. God emphasizes the importance of humility in everything but especially in accepting His ways, and in the case of salvation accepting the gospel message.

Additionally, there are those prudent in their analysis with much "over-study" to reach **their desired conclusion**. To see things their way, they overthink everything and consequently miss the simple message from God. There were people back in Paul's time, in the time of the early church fathers, and to this day who possess such characteristics, and Paul warns of them. I see this particularly in Catholics as frustration of always needing to defend what they believe. The root cause is that they do not have the truth, and after all this time of human intervention into the will of God, Catholic teachings remain quite preposterous. The truth of the scriptures fit perfectly together as one might expect due to God's perfection and from one who stresses He is not the author of confusion. **There is a simplicity in the truth that reveals divinity**. One thing in the verses below is how Paul emphasizes the simplicity of the saving message from God. This is in contrast to those who provide penetrating consideration before action, filtering God's word, over analyzing it, and usually with the desire to arrive at something different.

1 Corinthians 1:18-19

18 For the message of the cross is foolishness to those who are perishing, but to us who are being saved it is the power of God.
19 For it is written: "I will destroy the wisdom of the wise,
And bring to nothing the understanding of the prudent."

This new evangelism of the Catholic church is not related to the conversion of non-Catholics. It is an evangelizing of existing Catholics. When Pope John Paul II created this notion it was undoubtedly his awareness of the typical Catholic which is one of "insufficient commitment" to the Catholic Church. The Catholic Church in many parts of the world is dying, and he wanted to stop this and prevent it from starting in places where there is growth. There needs to be a change such that Catholics have a deep commitment to Christ or really to the Catholic Church. Whatever steps can be taken to gain this commitment must be developed. According to Dr. Hahn, evangelism belongs to the Catholic Church. The Catholic Church creates

203

a link between evangelism and the Eucharist, as seen in the holy sacrifice of the Mass. They would say the two cannot be separated. Dr. Hahn and Marcus Grodi are fixated on how the New Testament is an outgrowth of the Old Testament, which they then use to validate Catholic teaching. They make the clear message from God seem like a mystery, a puzzle to be figured out. Fortunately, on the day of Pentecost and the other conversions of the New Testament, there was no quiz, there was no mystery, but just the truth presented and obeyed.

How can someone like Dr. Hahn or Marcus Grodi, who have a good familiarity with the scriptures, not realize Catholicism's doctrines are not in God's word but very much the opposite? Of all the poor scholarship of these two, their acceptance of the Catholic teaching of Matthew 16:16-19 is unfathomable. This book points out in many different ways the horrendous error of Catholic teaching of these verses. When I consider the complexity taught by these two men and the Catholic Church given the scriptures, it is a wonder how Matthew 16:16-19 in its straightforward simplicity is so badly misunderstood. These verses and the entirety of the scriptures fit together in a way to allow a single conclusion, a single meaning from God. Catholicism is based on these verses, and indeed they are central to what God has planned since Genesis. Many things have happened since Genesis, and at this time, Jesus had been bringing the message of the kingdom. God is beginning here in Matthew to reveal how He will achieve His purpose. Throughout this book, there is extensive material on these verses indicating their clear meaning. Nonetheless, let us look once again at Matthew 16:16-19.

Matthew 16:16-19

16 Simon Peter answered and said, "You are the Christ, the Son of the living God."

17 Jesus answered and said to him, "Blessed are you, Simon Bar-Jonah, for flesh and blood has not revealed this to you, but My Father who is in heaven.

18 And I also say to you that you are Peter, and on this rock I will build My church, and the gates of Hades shall not prevail against it.

19 And I will give you the keys of the kingdom of heaven, and whatever you bind on earth will be bound in heaven, and whatever you loose on earth will be loosed in heaven."

These verses are discussed in two places (Chapter 6 - The fifth verse not seen by Marcus Grodi, and then further discussed in Chapter 8) and various chapters throughout this book. Peter was given by the Father the answer to Jesus' question. Peter's statement is the central piece in fulfilling God's purpose. Namely, that Jesus was the Son of God, and then Jesus declares He would build His church on what the Father just delivered to Peter. Peter never became the Catholic pope, or was there such an office. The emphasis of the verse is on Jesus, and then Jesus introduces the church and Himself as the solution planned by God. The church would be a spiritual entity and have a spiritual head and all to solve the spiritual problem of sin.

Jesus lived a perfect life in every way, whereas Peter was just a man, far from perfect. Peter would be the kind of person who would benefit from what Jesus was about to accomplish. Peter and the apostles would certainly have a vital role, and without them, there would be no salvation because **someone had to bring the message and record it**. The apostles would initially bring the message from the Holy Spirit to the people. They were the first to do this and followed in bringing the message by those who the Lord added to His spiritual body, the church. Of all the things being discussed, the one thing that baffles me about Dr. Hahn and Marcus Grodi is how they can think Peter is the rock of Matthew 16:18. The verse does not indicate this. The scriptures do not validate this but confirm Jesus being the Son of God as the basis for the church. The construction of the verse does not point back to Peter but to what Peter just declared. The church is a spiritual entity and requires no earthly head, and the head can only be Jesus because He is spiritual. Jesus was about to do something that allowed Him as the Son of God to be the spiritual answer to the spiritual problem of humankind. Peter in no way has any credentials to be the head. If you can understand the scriptures with a reasonable appreciation of God's seriousness, you cannot conceive that Peter is the head of the church. Chapters 6 (this chapter) and Chapter 8 go meticulously through Matthew 16:16-19. Unless a person's mind is closed, they must admit that Peter is in no way recognized as an authority in these or any scriptures. Peter was blessed to announce for the first time that Jesus was the Son of God. The apostles were blessed as a group to have a substantial role in God's plan. They would bring the message for the first time. Again, what Jesus said in these verses related to the church and the binding and loosening was not (yet) understood. It is mind-boggling that these two ex-Presbyterians can believe Peter is the rock. If he were, there would be no reconciliation, no salvation (forgiveness of sins), no church.

At the risk of overkill on the "rock," there is something incredibly important about Matthew 16:18. It is not related to Peter but the rock. The rock in this verse is at the center of all that God has done to fulfill Genesis 3:15. The rock is necessary for reconciliation. It is important that **God the Father** Himself reveals it to Peter. Think of the most essential thing in God's purpose, and it is not Peter, that would be meaningless. Peter just revealed this marvelous thing that Jesus is the Son of God. Then Jesus completes the revelation by indicating that **the Father's revelation would be the basis for salvation**. Somehow salvation will result in what Jesus will very shortly accomplish. The church is also revealed for the first time and is something Jesus will build. Indeed, these verses reveal the essence of God's plan as the Messiah is acknowledged to be Jesus. The rock is not tied to Peter but Jesus, the church, and thus to salvation. These matters of the church and salvation will be clarified throughout this book. We will see that every aspect of these things is spiritual, providing the solution to the spiritual problem of every person, namely sin.

One more aspect of Dr. Hahn and Marcus Grodi

One interesting thing about Dr. Hahn and Marcus Grodi is that they found problems with Sola Scriptura (the sole source of authority being the scriptures), which essentially made everything about the Luther/Calvin view questionable. If we look at the five sola's of Protantism below and give a very brief description of each, it will help make the point at the end concerning Dr. Hahn, Marcus Grodi, and the Catholic view. The Five Sola's are:

- Sola scriptura ("by Scripture alone")
- Sola fide ("by faith alone")
- Sola gratia ("by grace alone")
- Solus Christus or Solo Christo ("Christ alone" or "through Christ alone")
- Soli Deo gloria ("glory to God alone")

Sola scriptura ("by Scripture alone")

The inerrant Scripture (the Bible) is the sole source of written divine revelation, which alone can bind the conscience. The Bible alone teaches all that is necessary for our salvation from sin and is the standard by which all Christian behavior must be measured. It is denied that any creed, council, or individual may bind a Christian's conscience, that the Holy Spirit speaks independently of or contrary to what is set forth in the Bible, or that personal spiritual experience can ever be a vehicle of revelation.

Sola fide ("by faith alone")

Justification is by grace alone through faith alone because of Christ alone. In justification Christ's righteousness is imputed to us as the only possible satisfaction of God's perfect justice. Our justification does not rest on any merit to be found in us, nor upon the grounds of an infusion of Christ's righteousness in us, nor that an institution claiming to be a church that denies or condemns sola fide can be recognized as a legitimate church.

Sola gratia ("by grace alone")

In salvation we are rescued from God's wrath by his grace alone. It is the supernatural work of the Holy Spirit that brings us to Christ by releasing us from our bondage to sin and raising us from spiritual death to spiritual life. It is denied that salvation is in any sense a human work. Human methods, techniques or strategies by themselves cannot accomplish this transformation. Faith is not produced by our unregenerated human nature.

Solus Christus or Solo Christo ("Christ alone" or "through Christ alone")

Our salvation is accomplished by the mediatorial work of the historical Christ alone. His sinless life and substitutionary atonement alone are sufficient for our justification and reconciliation to the Father. It is denied that the gospel is preached if Christ's substitutionary work is not declared and faith in Christ and his work is not solicited.

Soli Deo gloria ("glory to God alone")

It is affirmed that because salvation is of God and has been accomplished by God, it is for God's glory and that we must glorify him always. We must live our entire lives before the face of God, under the authority of God and for his glory alone. It is denied that we can properly glorify God if our worship is confused with entertainment, if we neglect either Law or Gospel in our preaching, or if self-improvement, self-esteem or self-fulfillment are allowed to become alternatives to the gospel.

Note: The above definitions are attributed to this reference: https://www.theopedia.com/five-solas

*The author does not necessarily agree with these definitions, and in my search, I found dozens of different albeit similar meanings for these "Sola's." Of course, the Sola's are all the inventions of humankind, and thus considerable variation would be expected. Admittedly, they all **imitate some aspect of truth**, especially Sola Scriptura. However, there is nothing quite as perfect as "the wording and connectivity" by which God delivers the truth. Faith comes from the word of God and never by the creative ways humankind tries to express the things of God.*

Four of the five sola's violate the scriptures. Creating additional doctrine by reconfiguring the scriptures is risky and, at best, exceedingly unwise. People like to put what they believe about God from the scriptures in their own words, maybe combining several beliefs into new teachings. This is the case of these sola's, and they are often wrong, as are four of the five sola. They may even contain some truth, but it is exceedingly unwise – let the Bible speak for itself. Creeds are also in this category as in the case of the early church councils. Sola Scriptura in its most basic definition; "*Sola scriptura* means that Scripture is our only authority." This seems harmless as it is just another way of saying the word of God is our only authority. I do not like sola scriptura as a term even if it is correct because it is not a Bible term, and thus people can and have assigned different meanings. There are other ways this has been said, such as, "speak where the Bible speaks and be silent where the Bible is silent," This is good advice but also not a Bible phrase. There are several man-made statements that end up reaching this conclusion, and thus sola scriptura is correct when the definition is included, and it is just another way stating, "speaking where the Bible speaks and being silent where the Bible is silent." The correct Bible understanding is God's declaration throughout scripture to not change His word. God defines the value of scripture (2 Timothy 3:16-17), eliminating any other means of achieving that same value. Peter's statement that the speaking forth of the mind and counsel of God never came by the will of man is declaring the only source of truth (2 Peter 1:21). Peter would also say that if any man speaks, let him speak as the oracles of God (1 Peter 4:11). We are talking about God-breathed speech, and that means from the word of God. There is an associated verse in terms of God's seriousness about His word, and God is very blunt when He says, "let God be found true and every man a liar" (Romans 3:4). In any case, Dr. Hahn and Marcus Gordi reject "sola scriptura," the only correct sola. Sola scriptura does point out the level of respect needed in handling the word of God since there are no other means of knowing the truth.

It is critical for Dr. Hahn, Marcus Grodi, and Catholicism that sola scriptura is not true. First, they find that salvation by faith only is not true, and likewise, Calvin's five points (TULIP). However, the reason these Protestant doctrines are false is not the fault of "sola scriptura" but because Luther, Calvin, and others changed the meaning of the scriptures. It is not a difficult study to realize four of the sola's and the associated TULIP of Calvin are wrong simply by correctly understanding God's meaning. In some way, Dr. Hahn and Marcus Grodi independently (for the most part) use the clearinghouse approach and dump all of the sola. This would be a critical mistake for their souls and those who follow them. This is what they should have done: Namely, they know Protestantism is wrong, and realizing the scriptures are the only guide, they would also reject Catholicism. Now, they are getting close. They know the doctrine of Protestant "works" is false, and they know the history of Catholicism is filled with evil actions and non-scriptural doctrines, and those should be strong reasons to be wary of these religions. They also know to trust the inspired pattern of the apostles as the Holy Spirit was guiding them. Thus they should consider the following:

- How were people reconciled to God by the apostles, and how incredibly different is the process of salvation in the Catholic Church
- Consider the **spiritual perspective** of Christ and His church in all things
- What was the nature and organization of the "Holy Spirit defined local church," and how drastically different is the Catholic Church
- Live knowing that God is perfect in everything and have complete trust in His word

Unfortunately, Dr. Hahn and Marcus Grodi run off to the only alternative to Protestantism, namely Catholicism. Somehow it never strikes them that both religions are terribly wrong. A good place for them to start would be to look at Matthew 16:16-19 and see something they never saw before (using Marcus Grodi's terminology of previously unseen things) and see the rock was Peter's declaration of Jesus as the Son of God. That would be a good start and then to realize that rejecting four out of five sola's was correct, but not "sola scriptura."

My bewilderment with Dr. Hahn and Marcus Grodi

My brief analysis of these two applies to all those who have good knowledge of the scriptures and end up in the wrong place. There are (at least) eleven pivotal matters that might explain the problem, that is, the problem with sincere individuals "getting it all wrong." These are not in order of importance. First, thinking Christianity has only two broad possibilities – Catholic or Protestant. Second, failure to appreciate the perfection of God, particularly in how He fits everything together. Third, the significance of the gospel message. Fourth, God's seriousness regarding the church as He defined it. Fifth, the simplicity of God's saving message. Sixth, the difficulty of living for Christ and the gospel. Seventh, the absolute requirement to never change God's word. Eighth, God's seriousness about the precision of His commands, including the details. Ninth, understanding God's love concerning keeping His commands. Tenth, realizing we are in the last age and have "that which is perfect" – God's completed word. Eleventh, in a world where churches have "endless" objectives, God has only one needed to accomplish His purpose – evangelism. Although I am sure there are more "pivotal matters," each of these requires a person's contemplation. The outcome of a thoughtful reflection should be moving away from the "religions of humankind" to the place you can qualify to share in the Divine Nature.

Chapter 7
Where did the gospel message go?

7.1 Reconciliation

Finally, in Acts 2, we have the long-awaited reconciliation between humanity and God. Everything has been about bringing this event, and now with the death, burial, and resurrection of Jesus, it is possible. Jesus spoke of this in terms of the kingdom He began to preach about three years earlier. Characteristics of the kingdom have been provided in many different ways. The seed of the kingdom was taught to be the word of God. There was a message coming from God, and those with good hearts would receive it. We need to realize that Jesus was a Jew, was amid Jews, and was their awaited Messiah. He was meant for them and, as far as they knew, only for them. After all, that was how it had been since their establishment, namely the separation of Jews and Gentiles. There is a singular message coming from God in Genesis 3:15 and Genesis 12:1-3, and it relates to the answer for sin. The solution would involve Jews and Gentiles (all nations).

Genesis 3:15

15 And I will put enmity

Between you and the woman,

And between your seed and her Seed;

He shall bruise your head,

And you shall bruise His heel."

Genesis 12:1-3

1 Now the LORD had said to Abram:

"Get out of your country,

From your family

And from your father's house,

To a land that I will show you.

2 I will make you a great nation;

I will bless you

And make your name great;

And you shall be a blessing.

3 I will bless those who bless you,

And I will curse him who curses you;

And in you all the families of the earth shall be blessed."

These verses in Genesis three and twelve speak of Jesus as the answer to sin, the answer to reconciling humankind back to God. Jesus is the Seed of woman, and the blessing for Abraham would be that God would make him a great nation, and in his name, **all nations** would be blessed. The blessing would be Jesus coming through the lineage of Abraham, and then God extends the blessing to include all the families of the earth. In just a few verses in Galatians, we can "jump ahead" and see the fulfillment.

Galatians 3:26-29

26 For you are all sons of God through faith in Christ Jesus.

27 For as many of you as were baptized into Christ have put on Christ.

28 There is neither Jew nor Greek, there is neither slave nor free, there is neither male nor female; for you are all one in Christ Jesus.

29 And if you are Christ's, then you are Abraham's seed, and heirs according to the promise.

Despite the Jews in Jesus' time not realizing the blessing was for all nations, they also looked for a different Messiah. They wanted a more dominant Messiah that would restore Israel as a powerful nation and relieve the present agony with Rome. They never appreciated the Messiah as spoken of in Genesis 3:15. This would not be surprising at that time, but they might have noticed from verse 15 that He would be a suffering Messiah (And you shall bruise His heel). They could have also realized the suffering that would accompany their Messiah from Isaiah 53.

Isaiah 53:4-5

4 Surely He has borne our griefs And carried our sorrows; Yet we esteemed Him stricken, Smitten by God, and afflicted.

5 But He was wounded for our transgressions, He was bruised for our iniquities; The chastisement for our peace was upon Him, And by His stripes we are healed.

The more important problem was failing to realize that the Messiah had the most significant of missions. It was necessarily a **spiritual mission** to solve a spiritual problem – the problem of Adam and Eve, of all of humankind. The distinction is spiritual versus physical, and the Jews never see this, and neither does the Catholic Church. Catholicism is truly the universal **physical** church with a **physical** head of a **physical** rulemaking organization. Being physical, they cannot solve the spiritual problem, and in their rulemaking, they assure sins will never be forgiven.

7.2 Where did the gospel message go?

First, what is the gospel message, and what did it accomplish. The gospel message was in the mind of God since Genesis 3:15 (actually before). How do we know that? Because that is what happened to bring about the reconciliation. Jesus spoke of the gospel prior to it being fully revealed. Jesus would refer to it as the gospel of the kingdom, and when the gospel is mentioned, it was in the sense of it being preached. It takes on a different character after the death, burial, and resurrection of Jesus. One thing that is different is the use of the term **obey the gospel** or **obey the truth** (2 Thessalonians 1:8, 1 Peter 4:17, 1 Peter 1:22).

Jesus used the terminology of **preaching the gospel** in His ministry. There are different definitions of the gospel, and in its simplest form, it is God's message, and it is a good message for humankind. We can say that the gospel Jesus was preaching in His ministry was largely in the form of parables of the kingdom, which was perfect for His gradual revelation. It will evolve to something to be obeyed after the death, burial, and resurrection of Jesus. When the gospel is fully revealed, it will have the characteristics spoken of by Jesus in the parables of the kingdom. It will be in its obedience the means to enter the kingdom. It is a spiritual kingdom and properly called the church.

Matthew 4:23

23 And Jesus went about all Galilee, teaching in their synagogues, preaching the gospel of the kingdom, and healing all kinds of sickness and all kinds of disease among the people.

Jesus provides another insight into the nature of the gospel in Matthew 24, indicating how it will be preached in all the world before the end shall come.

Matthew 24:14

14 And this gospel of the kingdom will be preached in all the world as a witness to all the nations, and then the end will come.

There have been various things that Jesus revealed that were purposely incomplete, including Matthew 16:19, John 20:23, and John 6:53-54, to mention just three. Certainly, the gospel was also only partially revealed. These partially revealed things needed to be revealed entirely to be understood, and that would occur after Jesus' death, burial, and resurrection. These verses (just mentioned above) and the gospel message are intimately related, and that will become clear as promised by Jesus. Jesus tells the apostles He is sending the Holy Spirit to guide them into all truth. Following Jesus' resurrection, He spends about forty days on earth and speaks to His disciples of the things about the kingdom before rising to the Father to sit at His right hand. Jesus had told the apostles that all authority had been given to Him in heaven and on earth. He is in the position of being King over His kingdom, which is about to begin. Jesus told the apostles His promise of the Holy Spirit was near, and this meant they were about to gain a better understanding of the kingdom, of their roles, and they should wait in Jerusalem to receive the power.

Acts 1:8

8 But you shall receive power when the Holy Spirit has come upon you; and you shall be witnesses to Me in Jerusalem, and in all Judea and Samaria, and to the end of the earth."

In Acts 2, the missing comprehension would be revealed to the apostles, and the reconciliation with God after four thousand years would occur. The apostles no longer had to

214

wonder what their part in the binding and loosening and in forgiving and retaining would be as those things would happen in their role of bringing the gospel message. There was no longer any misunderstanding regarding eating the flesh and drinking the blood of Jesus as it was accomplished in an individual's obedience. The gospel message itself was now something to be obeyed and was obeyed in Acts 2. The Holy Spirit would continue to work with the apostles for the next fifty-plus years, gradually revealing all God wanted to pass on to humankind. The things God was now revealing were in no way "in part" as it was the final revelation. We have a proper definition of the gospel as the death, burial, and resurrection of Jesus.

1 Corinthians 15:1-4

*1 Moreover, brethren, I declare to you the **gospel which I preached to you**, which also you received and in which you stand,*

2 by which also you are saved, if you hold fast that word which I preached to you—unless you believed in vain.

*3 For I delivered to you first of all that which I also received: that **Christ died for our sins** according to the Scriptures,*

*4 and that **He was buried**, and that **He rose again** the third day according to the Scriptures*

The gospel is the death, burial, and resurrection of Jesus. This is the gospel message by which people are saved. The gospel message is something to be obeyed.

2 Thessalonians 1:8

*8 in flaming fire taking vengeance on those who do not know God, and on those who do not **obey the gospel** of our Lord Jesus Christ.*

1 Peter 4:17

*17 For the time has come for judgment to begin at the house of God; and if it begins with us first, what will be the end of those who do not **obey the gospel** of God?*

1 Peter 1:22-23

*22 Since you have purified your souls in **obeying the truth** through the Spirit in sincere love of the brethren, love one another fervently with a pure heart,*

23 having been born again, not of corruptible seed but incorruptible, through the word of God which lives and abides forever

How does one obey the gospel? In Acts 2, for the first time, people obeyed the gospel and had their sins forgiven. They questioned Peter about what they should do, and having received His answer, they responded in obedience.

Acts 2:36-38

36 "Therefore let all the house of Israel know assuredly that God has made this Jesus, whom you crucified, both Lord and Christ."

*37 Now when they heard this, they were cut to the heart, and said to Peter and the rest of the apostles, "Men and brethren, **what shall we do?**"*

*38 Then Peter said to them, "**Repent**, and let every one of you be **baptized** in the name of Jesus Christ for the **remission of sins**; and you shall receive the gift of the Holy Spirit.*

A person who believes (Jesus is the Christ, the Son of God) and then repents of sin is a candidate for the next step of baptism and receives forgiveness of sins in this last step. So how does a person obey the gospel? They obey the death, burial, and resurrection of their savior, and that occurs in baptism.

Romans 6:3-4

3 Or do you not know that as many of us as were baptized into Christ Jesus were baptized into His death?

4 Therefore we were buried with Him through baptism into death, that just as Christ was raised from the dead by the glory of the Father, even so we also should walk in newness of life.

A person **dies to sin** as they are **buried** in the watery grave and then **rise** without sin. Indeed, they have obeyed the gospel, and therein their past sins have been forgiven. They have

obeyed that form of doctrine (Romans 6:17) corresponding to Jesus' death, burial, and resurrection. They obeyed the gospel.

One who qualifies to be baptized (Acts 8:37) and is baptized has obeyed the gospel, obeys the death, burial, and resurrection of Jesus, and their sins are forgiven. Just one thing is missing, and the Lord Himself takes care of this for the obedient person. Jesus said He would build His church, and now that begins on this first day of the kingdom. He adds those obedient to His spiritual body, the church. The church is spiritual, Jesus is spiritual, and now the one who obeyed is spiritual.

Acts 2:47

47 praising God and having favor with all the people. And the Lord added to the church daily those who were being saved.

Everything is now moving very quickly as the apostles do their work of binding and loosening and forgiving and retaining as they bring the gospel message. Indeed for each obedient person in their submission to the will of God, reconciliation occurs. One might pause to realize the **partial information regarding these duties** would never have been conceived as they turned out. We only know the things of God as He reveals them. That is why the ideas of humankind concerning God will always be wrong, and God in great seriousness points out, "let God be found true and every man a liar." In Catholicism, you have the early church fathers, the pope, the hierarchy of Catholicism, and they are all men and all wrong to the cost of billions of souls. The good thing for any person who loves the truth is that they can see Peter is NOT the rock. Such a person can also see that the saving, perfect gospel message is missing, changed, or replaced by what men think is a better way, albeit in its various forms complicated and provides no value. Not only is the gospel message simple and easily understood, but it is also the thing that fits perfectly together all that God has done since creation to achieve His purpose.

7.3 Conversions of the New Testament

God generously provides via His inspired word a sampling record of first-century conversions. We could say those **who obeyed the gospel**. Below is a record of these conversions:

Conversions of the New Testament

Conversion	Hear	Believe	Confess	Repent	Baptized
Pentecost, Acts 2	Yes	Implied Not Stated	Not stated	Yes	Yes
The 5000, Acts 4	Yes	Yes	Not stated	Not stated	Not stated
Simon, Acts 8. 4-13	Yes	Yes	Not stated	Not stated	Yes
Ethiopian Acts 8.26-40	Yes	Yes	Not stated	Not stated	Yes
Saul, Acts 9	Yes, from Ananias	Not stated	Not stated	Not stated	Yes
Cornelius, Acts 10	Yes	Yes	Not stated	Not stated	Yes
Lydia, Acts 16.14,15	Yes	Not stated	Not stated	Not stated	Yes
Jailer, Acts 16.29-34	Yes	Yes	Not stated	Not stated	Yes
Corinthians Acts 18.1-8	Yes	Yes	Not stated	Not stated	Yes
"John's baptism" Acts 19.1-5	Yes	Yes	Not stated	Not stated	Yes
Saul, Acts 22.12-16	Yes	Not stated	Yes	Not stated	Yes
Galatians Gal. 3.26-29	Inferred	Yes, by faith	Not stated	Not stated	Yes

You can see this table and a detailed explanation of the conversion process at:

https://heavencoach.com/conversions-of-the-new-testament/

This table, in its responses to the gospel message, represents what the apostles were teaching. The scriptures do not provide all the details of each conversion, but knowing the pattern for obeying the gospel message, everything required would have been included. A person would not reach baptism without the preceding steps. The website reference provides helpful information about the conversion process. For example, one might think confessing Jesus (Romans 10:9-10) is missing in the conversions since it is seldom mentioned, yet that is an action that can be included in verbally stating their **belief** in Jesus as the Son of God.

In this process of bringing the gospel message, the apostles were binding and loosening, forgiving, and retaining. It is all contained in preaching the gospel message and those who respond in obedience are forgiven (and those who do not obey have their sins retained). It is the message that provides salvation upon obedience, that is, provides forgiveness of sins. It is the message that the apostles are to carry and will be carried by those "in Christ." It is a message wherein God declares sin can be forgiven and only by this means. It is the message brought by the apostles and results in the table of **examples** of some obedient to the gospel in the first century. Salvation is possible because Jesus obeyed the Father, and individuals obey Jesus in their obedience to the gospel since they obey His death, burial, and resurrection.

Hebrews 5:8-9

*8 though He was a Son, yet **He learned obedience** by the things which He suffered.*
*9 And having been perfected, He became the author of eternal salvation to all **who obey Him***

This is how Jesus built and continues to build His church one obedient soul at a time. God carefully provides the means for salvation, and it is simple. People hear the message and can choose to obey the gospel. Where is the gospel message in Catholicism? It is not there, and neither is salvation. Catholicism provides their version of salvation that comes in some way as a result of being Catholic. They also offer all sorts of distractions such that a Catholic never understands the truth. Catholicism's rejection of God's inspired word as the **sole source of truth** means no Catholic will achieve eternal life since the gospel message is never preached.

The gospel message has disappeared in the "world of so-called Christianity." It is a world without any Christians who are referred to as Catholic and Protestant. Protestants came into existence to protest Catholicism but unfortunately accepted enough things Catholic that they never understood the gospel message. However, **if** they had been determined to **restore** the first-century church (not **reform** the Catholic Church), the gospel message would be as defined in the scriptures, and they would have succeeded. Catholic and Protestant religions live on and are known as Christian but, in reality, contain no Christians. The evidence for the truth of the gospel exists, and those acknowledging the scriptures as the only source of truth are in the body of Christ per their obedience. They have the awareness and subsequent dedication not to change the word of God and are in their obedience to the gospel, Christians.

What a wonderful deception to have Catholics focusing on venerating Mary, confessing sins to a priest, believing in original sin, considering their connection with the Eucharist, praying to Catholic designated saints and Mary, considering purgatory's place in their life, honoring special feasts of Catholicism and following all sorts of rules and none of it having any spiritual value. Maybe if Catholics understood God's purpose and His singular focus on achieving His purpose, they might realize that none of the "things Catholic" have such a focus. God's focus is souls. It is on sharing in the Divine Nature. It is on seeking and saving that which was lost. It is, as we emphasize, "life is about the soul" and absolutely about nothing else.

Chapter 8
Scripturally, it is easy to reject Catholicism

If you want to be on solid ground concerning your denial of Catholicism, it is quite easy. The most important proof-text for Catholicism is Matthew 16:15-19, and it is absolutely all that is required to reject Catholicism confidently. Of course, Catholicism uses various other valued verses, but they all assume their version of Matthew 16:15-19 is true. Those other verses also provide zero evidence favoring Catholic doctrine. Although it would be easy to disprove all the other Catholic "proof texts," it is unnecessary once the Matthew 16 verses are exposed. Remove their source of authority, and consequently, their pope and Catholicism will disappear.

Matthew 16:15-19

15 He said to them, "But who do you say that I am?"

16 Simon Peter answered and said, "You are the Christ, the Son of the living God."

17 Jesus answered and said to him, "Blessed are you, Simon Bar-Jonah, for flesh and blood has not revealed this to you, but My Father who is in heaven.

18 And I also say to you that you are Peter, and on this rock I will build My church, and the gates of Hades shall not prevail against it.

19 And I will give you the keys of the kingdom of heaven, and whatever you bind on earth will be bound in heaven, and whatever you loose on earth will be loosed in heaven."

Note: The subject of these verses has already been covered in Chapter 6 under the title of "The fifth verse Marcus Grodi did not see." That discussion completely discredits the Catholic claims of a pope, and it will be done again in this chapter somewhat differently with the same outcome.

8.1 Begin at the beginning

The question is, "what is the rock Jesus references in verse 18?" We have arrived at revealing the central issue for humankind, and it goes back to Genesis.

Genesis 3:15

15 And I will put enmity

Between you and the woman,

And between your seed and her Seed;

He shall bruise your head,

And you shall bruise His heel."

There is little or no disagreement since the New Testament was completed about the meaning of this verse. God was bringing a solution for sin, which had entered the world through Adam and Eve. That solution would emanate from the Seed of woman. It would be Jesus whose heel was bruised, which refers to the suffering and death of Jesus. Now in Matthew, God the Father reveals to Peter that Jesus is His Son. The key element of this long-awaited revelation was not understood until then. The central building block for what God was doing is apparent and consistent with God's solution. Jesus continues following Peter's declaration and introduces the means for reconciliation by saying **He** will build **His church**. This is not understood in any specific way at this point. However, at a high level, the solid things from Matthew 16:15-19 at this point are:

- Jesus is going to build His church
- The basis of the church is that Jesus is the son of God and in the language of the text this is the rock upon which the church will be built. Can the church stand on Jesus being the rock, the foundation of the church? Yes! What else could be the rock on which the reconciliation with God could be achieved?
- Very little is understood at this point about the church or about HOW the apostles will be binding and loosing, but that will be understood shortly in the only way it can be understood, by God revealing it.

Pause to clarify the church

If we look at what Jesus has been preaching concerning the kingdom, it is clear that the kingdom is spiritual – not of this world.

John 18:36

36 Jesus answered, "My kingdom is not of this world.

There is no question that Jesus will build His kingdom and that it is spiritual. Who can rule over a spiritual kingdom, and where should the king or head of that kingdom reside? Jesus must rule over the kingdom, and the rule should be from heaven, i.e., the right hand of God. Jesus reveals His location in Mark.

Mark 16:19

19 So then, after the Lord had spoken to them, He was received up into heaven, and sat down at the right hand of God.

Jesus is ruling over His kingdom, His spiritual church. This is exactly what Jesus revealed in Matthew 28:18, "And Jesus came and spoke to them, saying, "All authority has been given to Me in heaven and on earth.""

*Note: Although the **kingdom is the church,** or we might say the establishment of the word "church" flows seamlessly from the word "kingdom." Beginning with Jesus introducing the word "church" in Matthew 16:18, there was more clarity brought to the kingdom Jesus had been preaching. Unfortunately, some religious groups have made a mess of the words "kingdom" and "church" in various ways, some even claiming that the kingdom has not arrived, and thus insinuating Jesus failed. Understanding the church and the kingdom is very basic, and therefore I created a short document called "The church is the kingdom."*

https://catholicsquestion.com/the-church-is-the-kingdom/

Although similar, another document simply called "Church" also addresses the question of the kingdom as the church.

https://catholicsquestion.com/church/

The value of an earthly kingdom

What is the value of an earthly kingdom? There is no value when the problem is spiritual. There is no need for a physical kingdom, which is exactly what men have built in the Catholic Church because that is all they know. The truth is spiritual and only comes from God. We might ask, over whom is God ruling? They would be the ones who Jesus added to His spiritual body, the church He is building. Is He ruling over the rest of humankind? Of course, He is not. The King rules only over His kingdom.

Colossians 1:13-14

13 He has delivered us from the power of darkness and conveyed us into the kingdom of the Son of His love,

14 in whom we have redemption through His blood, the forgiveness of sins.

In the gospel message obeyed, we are conveyed into the kingdom as we are now without sin. Our King is in heaven at the right hand of God.

Another blunder in Catholic thinking is to have a succession of the earthly head of the church. Where did that idea originate? Is it some logical need to maintain power after Peter dies? Yes, it would seem to be. Of course, Jesus is the head of the church and the only head until the end of time. Jesus will remain at the right hand of God until He returns in the air to take those "in Christ" to forever be with Him and then destroy all things physical followed by the judgment.

8.2 Giving Peter a role of authority over the church is irrational and inconsistent with everything in God's plan

These verses in Matthew 16 do not indicate any specific role for Peter different from the other apostles. The role specified for all the apostles is that of binding and loosening. Peter was blessed by God inasmuch as He was the one who revealed Jesus as the Son of God – the rock upon which the church would be built. Jesus and His Sonship is the solid rock and consistent with all scripture. The understanding of Matthew 16:15-19 will improve with the revelations shortly to come to the apostles, and as always in God's perfection, all things will fit perfectly together.

The eventual Catholic doctrine will be that the church was built on Peter, and he is something called a pope (or father, even holy father) and via Matthew 16:19 has the right to make the rules. Additionally, there will be a succession of this head of the church – many popes. This Catholic Church becomes a very **physical church** quite different from the spiritual body that Jesus would build. We have come four thousand years to this point in Matthew 16, and somehow the route to reconciliation ends up going through Peter. Of course, Peter never held such a position as pope but was an elder in the local church in Jerusalem (1 Peter 5:1 and Galatians 1:18). There is no such position as pope in everything delivered from God, and Peter or Paul or any of the other New Testament writers never mention such a concept. We also learn that the mystery from Genesis 3:15, which God refers to as a mystery, has been revealed. This was truly the only mystery God discussed because it was central to all He was doing for the reconciliation. Jesus was the mystery person of Genesis 3:15 who would destroy Satan and bring about the reconciliation. Of course, the mystery is concerning salvation, and Peter wrote of how the prophets inquired and searched carefully (1 Peter 1:10-12). Once again, there is this gradual revealing of the salvation mystery. The critical part of the mystery was revealed in Matthew 16:18 when Jesus introduced the church He would build, and we know from an earlier revelation it would be a spiritual church – His kingdom will not be of this world. Paul writes about these things in Ephesians 3:9-11 as the Holy Spirit directs. We learn there is no longer a mystery but even more surprisingly that the manifold wisdom of God is made known **by the church** to the principalities and powers in the heavenly places. God's wisdom is on display through the agency of the church. God's plans were even hidden to the principalities and powers in the heavenly places. The mystery is no longer beneficial because the reconciliation has been accomplished in the obedience of the Son to the Father and the subsequent obedience of those who respond to the gospel message. God adopted a plan to save the world from sin through His spiritual body, the church.

Note: Many things in the scriptures become clear when there is a study by one who loves the truth. As God reveals the mystery of salvation and how it baffled the prophets of God and was not known to the principalities and powers, it should be evident that things outside our realm are not understood unless God reveals them. In Catholicism, we have people much less than the prophets than the principalities and powers in heavenly places in the form of, for instance, the early church fathers. They are given credibility in what they wrote. God manages the truth, and in the case of achieving His purpose, He does that perfectly by sending His Spirit to deliver the truth.

Ephesians 3:9-11
9 and to make all see what is the fellowship of the mystery, which from the beginning of the ages has been hidden in God who created all things through Jesus Christ;
10 to the intent that now the manifold wisdom of God might be made known by the church to the principalities and powers in the heavenly places,
11 according to the eternal purpose which He accomplished in Christ Jesus our Lord,

The things of God are perfect, and if you can remove your prejudice (be open-minded to what might be the truth), you can uncover the truth. What could be more obviously wrong than having a physical church, a physical head, and a rulemaking body to solve the spiritual problem of sin. The simplicity of God's solution, the beauty, and the perfection of that solution will appeal to those who love the truth. The truth is a spiritual solution to the spiritual problem of sin. Indeed, people had their sins forgiven when the gospel message was preached and obeyed in Acts 2 and subsequently all those who obeyed the gospel message. There was no Catholic Church, and there was no pope. As God reveals Himself and His purpose, we can see the logic and reasoning in His plan – everything fits perfectly together. Truly, various pieces are extraordinary such as how the message is available to all, but only those with a good, humble heart and a love of the truth will appreciate how God is accomplishing His purpose in obedience to the gospel.

The Catholic Church exhibits its physical character in its doctrines that are particularly damaging to salvation. The character of its leaders was historically and often still can be characterized by greed, pride, anger, envy, arrogance, and selfishness. They exhibit in-fighting in their rulemaking and historically out-fighting as they battled with other religions and even nations. The church belonging to Christ has a focus on solving the spiritual problem of sin. What else does the church built by Jesus have as a focus? Absolutely, nothing else. The Catholic Church has an evil character since they mislead people to the worst possible end. Catholics think they are on the road to success. The church that Jesus built contains souls that repented to reach the point where their sins were forgiven in baptism. Jesus personally adds them to His body following their obedience. The character of those "in Christ" was and needed to continue to be gentle, true, helpful, kind, and entirely unselfish. These good souls were not empire builders, receiving honor and making rules but often suffered to death in the early days of the church. We have said God is the perfect absence of evil, and with a bit of thought, one can see He could never have an association with the Catholic Church.

Correctly understanding Matthew 16:15-19 is all that is needed to realize that the rock could only be the Son of God. The evidence of a pope, of Peter being that first pope, is non-existent. There is no indication of an earthly rule for the church Jesus built and continues to build. It would be meaningless.

8.3 The circumstantial case for Peter

The Catholic Church tries to build a circumstantial case for a pope and Peter being the first pope. They do this by looking at how Peter was special in terms of the other apostles. Peter did receive special attention and was blessed in this regard. Those things were his selection by the Father to divulge the true nature of Jesus, his preaching the first sermon (the gospel message) both to the Jews and the Gentiles, and there were additional instances where he was favored, but so were others. John was the apostle Jesus loved. Paul was the apostle to the Gentiles and traveled the world carrying the message. Paul suffered for Christ far more than any apostles and wrote more of the New Testament than any other apostle. Paul was unique inasmuch as He was dramatically selected by Jesus and met the apostolic qualification of an actual encounter with Jesus after His resurrection. The point is that various persons, including Peter, stood out, and none of them were chosen as the Catholic Church claims – in fact, there was nothing for which to be chosen. None of this circumstantial evidence qualifies Peter for a non-existent job called the pope. Peter was very much like all people since he sinned, and his denial three times of Jesus was a weak point, and there were undoubtedly more. Some persons have pointed to Peter's humility as a reason he was chosen to be the first pope. However, there would only be one way to be a pope, and that would be God creating such a position and then naming that person and then specifying a continuum for that position. **None of that happened**. God brings clarity to everything, while the Catholic Church, without any apparent authority, must work in the shadows, in mystery and suppositions. They do this by claiming that after God's word was completed, there was a valid truth different from the scriptures found in the early church traditions. Apparently, in those fifty-plus years the Holy Spirit worked with the apostles, guiding them into **all** truth; there was still more to be said. Not only more to be revealed, but essential things that conflict with the scriptures. As they say, adding insult to injury, they declare their tradition to be equivalent to scripture and create an infallible body of teaching called the Magisterium.

*Note: A thought on humility. Since some have made a case for Peter being the first pope based on (for one thing) his humility, it might be worthwhile to point out the desperation and sadness of such an idea. The truth from God is powerful in its ability to convert souls such that God can accomplish His purpose. There is not a shred of truth associated with the Catholic invention of a pope. People need to move from error to truth so that they can achieve heaven. It turns out that humility is a **vital ingredient of EACH PERSON'S salvation**. Catholicism is the fortress of complexity, but the "little things such as humility" are unimportant and not emphasized in the Catholic Church. It is fair to say that without humility, you will never become a child of God. The reason is that you need to obey the gospel, and obedience requires humility. It requires a continuing humility to live for Christ instead of yourself. Peter's humility is not atypical of what is needed by all who choose to obey the gospel.*

*It will require humility to leave the Catholic Church because living in the opposite, namely pride, closes your mind to anything different. I am Catholic, I am right, my family was right, the popes are right, and you think it is what God wants. However, pride may not even allow you to seek the truth because you already have it. Thus as the scriptures say, "pride comes before destruction," and "whosoever exalts themselves shall be humbled, and whosoever humbles themselves shall be exalted." **It is painful to talk about Catholicism**. It would be better to preach the gospel. Yet, for some, it might help, and especially in exposing the deceit that is so obvious. In pride, some people will find excuses, but there are none – you need a love of the truth.*

Continuing with Catholic circumstantial evidence regarding Peter

Jesus mentioned Peter feeding His sheep as one thing that would happen with Peter. Indeed, Peter would become an elder in the Jerusalem church.

John 21:17

17 He said to him the third time, "Simon, son of Jonah, do you love Me?" Peter was grieved because He said to him the third time, "Do you love Me?"
And he said to Him, "Lord, You know all things; You know that I love You."
Jesus said to him, "Feed My sheep.

One of the duties of an elder is to shepherd the flock among them, including their spiritual growth. A very common problem with Catholic logic is looking at verses and using them to make their point even though that verse alone was only in part. Peter never understood from the verse above what the implication was for him. The Holy Spirit was gradually (after Acts 2) revealing the local church, and that included the designation of elders. That title carried with it the role of shepherding the flock as part of the revelation of the Holy Spirit. Now Peter would know the meaning of what Jesus told him in John 21:17.

1 Peter 5:1-4

1 The elders who are among you I exhort, I who am a fellow elder and a witness of the sufferings of Christ, and also a partaker of the glory that will be revealed:
2 Shepherd the flock of God which is among you, serving as overseers, not by compulsion but willingly, not for dishonest gain but eagerly;
3 nor as being lords over those entrusted to you, but being examples to the flock;
4 and when the Chief Shepherd appears, you will receive the crown of glory that does not fade away.

Once again, we have the Catholic Church teaching, implying that when Jesus spoke to Peter about being a shepherd over His flock, He meant being a shepherd over the Catholic Church, as their pope. Catholics claim Peter was the pope, but it never happens. He was an elder in the church in Jerusalem and indeed that is where the scriptures indicate he was fulfilling his duty of shepherding over the flock. That is truth instead of imagination.

Jesus was pointing to Peter's being an elder in the church. The world might think that being an elder in a local church was not something of great importance such that it would be worthy of Jesus' mentioning it concerning Peter. It is not the grandiose position of lording over all the churches. The elders were not to lord over the flock entrusted to them but to be examples (1 Peter 5:3). As always, it is the physical church of Catholicism versus the spiritual church Jesus was and is building. Instead of saying what someone thinks should be important to Jesus, believe what He says is important. The physical church is interested in their numbers, their thousands, millions, and even billions of members. Jesus builds His church one soul at a time via their obedience to the gospel and adds them to His spiritual body – the church. The elders of the local church are a key design element in God fulfilling His purpose. The physical churches of the world will never understand God even when He is perfectly clear. **Believe Jesus when He tells Peter to feed my sheep, and then when Peter becomes an elder, see the fulfillment.** There is another thing here if one does not appreciate the role of an elder in the local church as "all that important." The physical Catholic Church is exceedingly distant from the truth. Catholicism envisions a massive worldwide Catholic Church with their guidance over all Christians. The head is their pope. Jesus points to the importance of Peter knowing he will be an elder. Jesus knows the true value of elders in their humility, in their example, and in their mission of **holding fast the faithful word**. Jesus knows His sacrifice will be in vain unless the message is carried to the world. God's very purpose is at stake. Catholicism focuses on physical matters such as ceremonies, relics, buildings, rulemaking, and honor for their hierarchy, especially their pope. The spiritual church is always focused on souls, and indeed the elders in each independent local church are critical to God's plan.

It would be possible to make a good or better case for Paul, James, or John to be the pope. However, as Peter, Paul, James, and John all know, there was no such intention of God to have an earthly rule, and as we see, there was not one - it would be nonsense. The one thing you can see from Peter, Paul, James, and John and all the apostles is an emphasis on the word of God directing them and never being directed by any person. The church of the New Testament is spiritual, with each person being added to the body of Christ by obedience to the gospel. Jesus is building His church one obedient soul at a time.

Continue to shut the door on this idea of a pope

We can continue to quickly fill in the pieces to Matthew 16:15-19 as God reveals them. Jesus' statement to the apostles in John 16:13 provides the answer to the binding and loosening. The Holy Spirit who inspires will lead the apostles into all truth. The apostles would have no idea what to do. As a sidebar, it could be said that the early church fathers would also have no idea what to do – the things outside our realm only come from God! The scriptures provide how a person becomes part of the spiritual body of Christ, His spiritual church, beginning in Acts 2. This pattern is then repeated throughout the scriptures (see conversions of the New Testament).

https://heavencoach.com/conversions-of-the-new-testament/).

Catholics never have their sins forgiven; all fail in life! There is no reason to debate the Real Presence, Mariology, the pope, Catholic confession, the Mass, the sacraments, Purgatory, and hundreds of other Catholic inventions. The Catholic Church is infinitely distant from God, which means it has no association with God. Exactly **what does not happen** in the inspired word of God is the Catholic Church. It turns out that every Catholic Church doctrine is wrong and typically, if not always, the exact opposite of the truth.

Peter or any person could never be the head of the church. Peter plays a significant role in revealing the message and then fulfills the role of all apostles in bringing the message. However, the core creation of the reconciliation process is outside our realm, is holy, with **all aspects** belonging to God. First, it is a spiritual church and requires a perfectly sinless individual to be the head of the church. Jesus is the only one to be designated as the head of His church. There is nothing more obnoxious than creating a physical church with a physical head, and it is pathetic because it opposes what God did in Christ and massacres the souls of all its followers.

Colossians 1:18
18 And He is the head of the body, the church, who is the beginning, the firstborn from the dead, that in all things He may have the preeminence.

Jesus is the spiritual head of the spiritual church and rules from the right hand of the Father.

Ephesians 1:22-23

22 And He put all things under His feet, and gave Him to be head over all things to the church,
23 which is His body, the fullness of Him who fills all in all.

What is wrong with the Catholic Church? Everything, absolutely everything, is wrong. Everything is in error. There is not a single thing of value. It may be the most hated thing by those pulled-in under its influence and now spending eternity in the lost state. I suspect one of the most regretted aspects for a Catholic losing their soul will be how **obvious** it was in its error, in its inventions, and its terror brought to so many in their earthly existence. If people in the lost condition have use of their memories, it may amaze them how they could ever conceive of the rock of Matthew 16:18 being anything different than the **acknowledgment** of Jesus as the Son of God.

God's perfection allows the decision to obey the gospel to be made in confidence

The church Jesus has and continues to build incorporates a process in the form of the death, burial, and resurrection of Jesus to achieve forgiveness of past sins. Jesus is directly involved with the salvation of each soul. It would be difficult to miss the pattern designed by God to reconcile humankind back to Him. The justification or the thing allowing the reconciliation with God would be that sins are forgiven. We have that pattern repeated throughout time since Jesus' death, burial, and resurrection. Perhaps the most amazing thing in substituting the directions from God with something utterly foreign to the word of God is that Catholicism effectively eliminates any possibility to have sins forgiven.

The Catholic Church begins in Matthew 16:15-19 and ends in Matthew 16:15-19. In other words, since Peter is not the rock, there is no Catholic Church. In the religious sense, Catholicism is an evil force opposing the purpose of God and an utter abomination. The things of God are perfect, and God wants to accomplish His purpose and has done that, and now near the end of the first century, He closes the communication with humankind. It is staggering to realize all that God has done to provide humankind every chance to succeed. Indeed, He did not leave a single stone unturned that could help. Yet somehow, as God's word is completed, He does not mention a human head for His church or is there **any aspect of Catholic doctrine** in the scriptures. Instead, all that occurs is evidence of salvation's association with the saving church built on Jesus. A long list of verses demonstrates this in Chapter 6 (the fifth verse not seen by Marcus Grodi). God leaves no mystery, but clarity and simplicity, as seen in the gospel message. Catholicism creates a historically brutal and venerated organization with doctrines supporting their religion, and none of it makes any sense given the scriptures. Therefore, Catholicism has to eliminate the scriptures, minimize them, and claim they exist only because of them. They create alternative paths to truth and develop a core of apologists to defend all the problems. In their early history, they bring fear/threats/brutality to any that even appear to oppose them. They have done all of those evil things and exceedingly more than we know. Catholicism brings confusion and complication because their human-devised doctrines that supposedly address spiritual matters are nonsensical – without the foundation of the scriptures. Humankind, in their wisdom, cannot invent solutions to a spiritual problem. If they try, it will require considerable explanation and, as we see additional doctrine to cover all the problems. Catholic teaching creates confusion and complication, as seen in their organization, councils, and paranoid hierarchy focused on exalting the Catholic Church.

In conceiving and maintaining their religion, they have devised doctrines that assure every Catholic will fail in life. It is so sad and pathetic that the simple gospel message was changed to something so complicated, and the bottom line is "billions" of souls are lost due to a complicated scholarship. Yet, no one has to fail. It will be the choice of each individual. Although Catholic scholarship is complicated, the gospel message is easily understood and obeyed. You can move quickly from the power of darkness (which is a condition of sin) and have Christ convey you to His kingdom, having received redemption through His blood, the forgiveness of sins. This all happens in obedience to the gospel message, and then you are added to the body of Christ by the Lord Himself. This is possible because Jesus is the rock of Matthew 16:18, and the subsequent simplicity of the gospel message is assuring.

One thing a Catholic must face is Catholicism's absolute deceit. It can be seen in their history, in their rejection of God's word, in the evil of their early leaders, and in their focus on many things different than God's purpose. Catholics will be devastated by the truth, and arriving at that place (devastation) is a good thing because it is a religion you must leave to succeed.

As a person becomes serious about the truth of life, one distinction will be compelling, and it is between a physical church versus one that is spiritual. Humankind creates churches and beliefs that can be seen as physical, but God's church is in every way spiritual. There are a variety of things which will amaze a person coming in contact with the truth. One of those things will be a variety of questions for God. Such things as, "how did God allow this mess to happen?" Regardless, of the question the answer exists as you come to the correct understanding of God and His purpose. It is fair to say that God has graciously provided those answers and indeed they will make perfect sense.

Chapter 9
The "Real Presence"

The Real Presence is discussed in several places in this book. However, it deserves special attention. Perhaps the greatest lie ever told is Catholicism and their popes. The reason for the success of the Real Presence is that it has a supernatural quality. Jesus is present, and you are partaking of His actual body and blood. One constant in religion is the desire for signs, seeking some real, provable association with God. The Eucharist is a very attractive sign, and some scriptures appear when twisted or misunderstood to validate the Real Presence. Besides the "pope lie" in Catholicism, there are many sub-lies, and the greatest among them is the Real Presence. First, let us define the Real Presence based on Catholic usage.

REAL PRESENCE Definition:

(https://www.catholicculture.org/culture/library/dictionary/index.cfm?id–35978)

"The manner of Christ's presence in the Holy Eucharist. In its definition on the subject, the Council of Trent in 1551 declared that "in the sacrament of the most holy Eucharist is contained truly, really, and substantially the body and blood, together with the soul and divinity, of our Lord Jesus Christ" (Denzinger 1636, 1640). Hence Christ is present truly or actually and not only symbolically. He is present really, that is objectively in the Eucharist and not only subjectively in the mind of the believer. And he is present substantially, that is with all that makes Christ, Christ and not only spiritually in imparting blessings on those who receive the sacrament. The one who is present is the whole Christ (totus Christus), with all the attributes of his divinity and all the physical parts and properties of his humanity."

There are many definitions of Real Presence, but I have tried to choose one most consistent with most of them. Fundamentally, it is not difficult to understand, although it is challenging to accept its character and understand its purpose. The bread and the wine of the Lord's Supper simply become the actual body and blood of Christ in the Catholic consecration process. Of course, they do not claim the elements are scientifically the actual body and blood of Christ.

Then what are they? They must be the bread and fruit of the vine. It becomes a matter of faith or, more accurately, another mystery of Catholicism. **Faith in God comes from the word of God and absolutely from no other place.** There is no faith in believing in the Real Presence since it is not in the Bible.

9.1 Catholic justification for the Real Presence

As we begin to discuss the Real Presence, I choose a relatively brief **Catholic statement** that uses some Bible verses to **justify the concept** of the Real Presence. The link below is from the Catholic News-Herald:

(https://catholicnewsherald.com/faith/198-news/faith/faith-facts/4920-the-real-presence-of-christ-in-the-eucharist).

"The Real Presence of Christ in the Eucharist is a doctrine – an official teaching of the Catholic Church – and a profound mystery. With the words of consecration, the whole of Christ is truly present – Body, Blood, Soul and Divinity – under the appearances of bread and wine.

The doctrine is based upon the words of Jesus Himself when He instituted the Eucharist. Jesus took the bread and said, "This is my body" (Mt 26:26), and He took the cup filled with wine and said, "This is my blood" (Mt 26:28). When Jesus said, "This is my body," He declared that the bread actually is His Body, and that He is really present.

We accept and believe what Jesus said as a matter of faith. There is no scientific evidence, definite proof, or factual explanation. We take Jesus at His word because He is truth (Jn 14:6), He came into the world to testify to the truth (Jn 18:37), and the words that He spoke are spirit and life (Jn 6:63). St. Cyril of Alexandria wrote, "Do not doubt whether this is true, but rather receive the words of the Savior in faith, for since He is truth, He cannot lie."

Indeed, Jesus cannot lie, but clearly, the bread and the fruit of the vine in Matthew 26:26 and Matthew 26:28 were not His actual body and blood. In this narrative, there is the bread, and separate is His body - they are not the same. There is the fruit of the vine, and there is His blood, and they are distinct. The elements represent His body and His blood.

Consider all the writing done by Catholicism on the subject of the Real Presence – a massive amount of apologetics in defense of this doctrine. How can a simple non-theologian rebuttal conceive of possibly refuting all that "stuff."

My chain analogy is used to overcome seemingly huge obstacles. You have a massive chain with eleven massive links, each made of the best high-quality alloy steel and weighing five pounds each. You are trying to pick up a pound of butter that is rigidly attached to the end link. You must pick it up using the link at the other end of the chain. However, the link in the middle of the chain is a single strand of freshly cooked angel hair spaghetti. This is called the weak link analogy. It would be impossible to pick up the butter. The apparent strength of the chain (except for one link) is impressive. Many doctrines fit the weak link analogy in this discussion of the Real Presence and involving everything Catholic. Despite the appearance of the chain's strength, ultimately, there is truth and error. Catholicism's strength in appearance is useless if the butter (salvation) cannot be lifted (achieved). That thin spaghetti noodle could be many things in Catholicism. We can say for sure it is the claim of tradition, apostolic succession, and their Magisterium being valid sources of authority. If you do not see the weak link, then Catholicism can appear very impressive. Certainly, this impressive church can provide salvation. However, the weak link is there, and consequently, there is no salvation in the Catholic Church.

Now, this analogy fits Catholicism in every way. The Catholic Church is a powerful organization that is mighty in its appearance with all the pomp and glory, hierarchal titles, and massive structures and teaching organizations with all those theologians. The weak link for every Catholic doctrine is no scriptural evidence, and we might say that usually means the need to change God's meaning. In the case of the Real Presence, this Catholic doctrine is easily dismissed as something very oppositional to God's intention and a real obstacle to the important aspect it plays in God accomplishing His purpose. The scriptures themselves powerfully reject this concept of the Real Presence. There are two instances of Jesus using the terminology "eating His flesh and drinking His blood." Both are metaphors and easily provable as such – in different ways. I made a point earlier in this book ("The eighth verse not seen by Marcus Grodi"), and I will repeat it here.

John 6:53-54

53 Then Jesus said to them, "Most assuredly, I say to you, unless you eat the flesh of the Son of Man and drink His blood, you have no life in you.
54 Whoever eats My flesh and drinks My blood has eternal life, and I will raise him up at the last day.

It seems Jesus is attaching salvation (eternal life) to eating His flesh and drinking His blood. Indeed, He does that, and yet there is no mistake in the answer of Acts 2:38. In that obedient process, sins are forgiven, and one receives the gift of the Holy Spirit. Coincidently, in that process, one eats the flesh and drinks the blood of Jesus. They do this since Jesus gave His actual body and blood, and that allowed the reconciliation. Can you imagine all the Catholic complications brought to the simplicity of the gospel message? Do you not know that those people were "saved." As mentioned previously, "there is something utterly amazing and pathetic about the incredible hierarchy of Catholicism and all their rules, all their councils, all their ceremonies, all their pageantry, all their miracles, compared to the simplicity of the gospel. Since those people in Acts 2 were saved and are in a position to receive eternal life, **they did eat the body and drank the blood of Jesus – in their obedience**. Essentially Jesus was indirectly revealing in the context of their salvation the meaning of John 6:53-54. It was always characteristically a metaphor, but what happens here in Acts 2 and all subsequent conversions represents the consistency of God, or we might say how God fits everything together perfectly. There is a sense where it is not a metaphor inasmuch as it was Jesus' actual body and blood that allowed the reconciliation. Yet, it is a metaphor in relation to the Lord's Supper. The Lord's Supper is worship and thus requires "spirit and truth" to be valid. Thus the Lord's Supper is for those "in Christ" since they are spiritual (those in the body of Christ), and it will be done in the kingdom as a remembrance. Those in the kingdom, the spiritual Church consist only of those added to the body by the Lord. **Recalling** the death, burial, and resurrection would be the correct worship since it is spiritual, as are all the things done in honoring God by His spiritual body, the Church.

There is an undeniable problem using John 6:53-54 as evidence for the Real Presence. John 6:53-54 is defined and included in what happened in Acts 2:38 since people were saved. Those who heard Jesus speak these verses in John did not understand them, including the apostles. **Now the fact that people were saved by preaching means they ate the body and**

drank the blood. Genesis 3:15 was not understood until God achieved it in Christ's sacrifice, and then the reconciliation occurred in Acts 2. The apostles did not understand Matthew 16:19 but Jesus indicated the meaning was coming (John 16:13). Then in Acts 1, the apostles learn the Spirit of God was coming with power, which occurs in Acts 2, and now, the apostles understand Matthew 16:19, and **we learn its meaning by the apostles' actions**. They are the ones bringing the message. We **only know the things of God** (spiritual things) when He reveals them. In many ways, there needs to be **no more discussion** of the Real Presence. However, to be thorough, let's complete the analysis of the Real Presence.

9.2 True meaning of the Lord's Supper

As you might expect, the Lord's Supper is quite simple and not worthy of all the complications brought by Catholicism. The Real Presence is more than a complication but is a distraction from the thing that is important. Those "in Christ" have the assurance they are on the road to heaven because they already know God in a real way. The scriptures assure them of Christ's presence from when they were added to the Lord's spiritual body – however, they know they must remain faithful. The Lord's Supper is a weekly memorial recalling the death of the Savior. We know the Lord's Supper is weekly because it was the pattern of the first-century church to remember the Lord in the breaking of bread and fruit of the vine on the first day of the week. How many first days of the week are there? Thus on each first day of each week, those in the body of Christ remember the death, burial, and resurrection of the Lord. The Lord instituted this memorial before His death in the upper room during the Last Supper.

Matthew 26:26-29
26 And as they were eating, Jesus took bread, blessed and broke it, and gave it to the disciples and said, "Take, eat; this is My body."
27 Then He took the cup, and gave thanks, and gave it to them, saying, "Drink from it, all of you.
28 For this is My blood of the new covenant, which is shed for many for the remission of sins.

29 But I say to you, I will not drink of this fruit of the vine from now on until that day when I drink it new with you in My Father's kingdom."

In Luke's account, the partaking was to be done in remembrance.

Luke 22:19

19 And He took bread, gave thanks and broke it, and gave it to them, saying, "This is My body which is given for you; do this in remembrance of Me."

Also, we learn that we are proclaiming the Lord's death till He comes.

1 Corinthians 11:26

26 For as often as you eat this bread and drink this cup, you proclaim the Lord's death till He comes.

We are learning a lot about the partaking of this bread and the drinking of this cup. It will not happen until it is done in the Father's kingdom, it is a remembrance, and it will be a proclamation until He comes. That is saying quite a bit, and again, it will not happen until it is done in the Father's kingdom. That kingdom is just a few weeks away from Jesus' statement at the Last Supper (about 53 days). Jesus came preaching the kingdom was at hand, and now it is close, and in that kingdom, Jesus' death, burial, and resurrection will be remembered. Peter says it this way, "Therefore let all the house of Israel know assuredly that God has made this Jesus, whom you crucified, both Lord and Christ," and it cut at the hearts of those present. It is the Lord and Christ who was crucified who is to be remembered. In his detailed preaching that day in Acts 2, Peter brought to the crowd something very recent for them to recall and now in the Lord's Supper that will be remembered each week by those "in Christ." In the context of this breaking of the bread and drinking of the fruit of the vine, it is mentioned this remembrance will continue until Jesus returns. In other words, it will continue to the end of time.

Note: The scriptures provide considerable detail concerning this weekly remembrance, as noted just above. Yet amid all this detail, there is no reference to what Catholics claim is the event's centerpiece – the Real Presence.

Understanding God's purpose brings clarity

The following verse evokes the idea of sharing. That is a group of those "in Christ" sharing the elements and together proclaiming the death of Christ in a memorial manner and realizing they will be doing this together until He comes at the end of time.

I Corinthians 10:16

16 The cup of blessing which we bless, is it not the communion of the blood of Christ? The bread which we break, is it not the communion of the body of Christ?

The Lord's Supper is a remembrance with no indication of anything more, and in this sense, it is spiritual – not in any way physical. The Lord's people have this huge responsibility to bring the gospel message, and God always has a reason for what He does, and being perfect it would be a perfect reason. He wants to keep what He did in Christ before those "in Christ." It would be a reminder of what they have received – forgiveness of past sins. The Lord's Supper is a weekly reminder of our authentic relationship with the Son of God. It is, of course, first a memorial for God's Son as we are "called back" to the suffering of Christ, and we honor the Son. Keeping our relation with God before us at all times is needed, and this requirement (Lord's Supper) is a God-designed opportunity. We must not forget; we have an advocate with the Father for prayer and for seeking forgiveness as needed for future sins. One cannot help but realize God's intention to aid in our faithfulness in this weekly remembrance – He wants us to succeed.

One thing you can understand about God is His focus, and here is where Catholicism has no clue, no idea of what God is all about. So many things, maybe everything regarding God, come back to His purpose to share in the Divine Nature. The Real Presence developed by Catholicism is very much out of focus in terms of its purpose. What is the purpose of the Real Presence, how is it helping? Does it make the Catholic person feel better? How could that be promoting God's purpose? Is it worshipping God, no, because it is not in spirit and truth (admittedly, Catholics do not understand this requirement for worship)?

On the other hand, the Lord's Supper, as God defines it contributes to achieving God's purpose. Those "in Christ" know how they entered the kingdom and realized it was through the sacrifice of Jesus. They follow the directions from God and remember the death, burial, and resurrection of their Savior. The Lord's Supper is on each person's mind, and they honor Jesus, the one they are living their life for and for His mission. It is the mission of all those in the local body to bring the gospel message to the world. Jesus is also the one who resides in them continually, not only at the moment. Indeed, this event is a memorial, and it keeps the minds of those "in Christ" on their mission, God's purpose. One might say it is a weekly opportunity to re-focus or continually keep the great task left in their hands before them. It is a task that cannot be achieved without the gospel message being preached. Is it any wonder God devised this weekly event as part of His plan to fulfill His purpose?

9.3 Early church fathers and the Real Presence

Catholics call this process of the elements of the bread and the fruit of the vine becoming the actual body and blood of Christ to be transubstantiation. They use Matthew 26:26-29 (see verses above) to make this claim.

Jesus says in these verses, "This is my body" and "This is my blood." The evidence this is figurative was indicated above concerning those being saved in Acts 2. That alone makes these verses figurative when used either in John 6 or here in Matthew 26. Catholicism tries to make its case since some early church fathers **mentioned the idea** or even taught the Real Presence. Yet, not all of the respected early church fathers such as Tertullian, ca 200 A.D. supported this concept. He wrote *Against Marcion*, IV.40 saying:

"Taking bread and distributing it to his disciples he made it his own body by saying, 'This is my body,' that is a 'figure of my body.' On the other hand, there would not have been a figure unless there was a true body."

Thus we again see the problem with tradition in the early writings. There were all sorts of differences of opinion. Tradition has many issues, but the overwhelming one is that tradition is not scripture.

Thinking about the Real Presence - scripturally and rationally

Jesus said, this is My body while holding the bread, but clearly, the bread and His body were different. Jesus said, this is My blood while holding the cup and referred to the contents as the fruit of the vine. His blood was present in His body and not the same as what was in the cup. The words of Jesus are precisely the way one establishes a metaphor, and that seems obvious.

Now, if we look at Jesus's mission as He states it to be seeking and saving "that which was lost," what part does the "Real Presence" play? Whether in John 6 or in the upper room at the Last Supper, there should be just one emphasis: it is souls. The Catholic Church Real Presence seems designed to keep Catholics excited about being Catholic, and that is the conclusion compared to God's purpose for the Lord's Supper. God's reason for this remembrance (see section 9.2) is related to souls and to bring honor to the Son.

The thing involved in accomplishing Jesus' mission was obedience to the Father, requiring a perfect sacrifice. Jesus would give His body and blood to achieve the atonement. In John 6, the time was approaching, and in Matthew 26, the time was just hours away at the Last Supper. In about 24 hours, it would be over, and **that meant Jesus would have given His body and blood literally**. The Lord's Supper featuring the elements of the bread and fruit of the vine would follow the kingdom's establishment and be **only for those in the kingdom**. That is, those added to the kingdom upon their obedience. Does God have a purpose in the Lord's Supper for those "in Christ?" Yes, that purpose aligns with all God has done concerning His creation: to share in the Divine Nature. Those "in Christ" are now in the kingdom, the church but have not received the end of their faith, the salvation of their souls. **One thing to keep before their minds is the sacrifice that brought them into the kingdom.** God wants His saints every week to remember the source of their spiritual relationship with Jesus. The partaking of the bread and the fruit of the vine is there for this remembrance. **Do not forget what God has done for you in Christ's sacrifice.** God is focused on your success, and that involves your mind and is a spiritual thing. How vibrant is the Lord's Supper? Indeed the bread represents the body, and the fruit of the vine represents the blood of Christ, and that is pretty vibrant. You did eat the body and drink the blood when you had your sins forgiven and thus fulfilled, "Most assuredly, I say to you, unless you eat the flesh of the Son of Man and drink His blood, you have no life in you. Whoever eats My flesh and drinks My blood has eternal life, and I will raise him up at the last day."

This is the intimate relationship you have with Christ, and based on your obedience, the one who provided His body and blood adds you to His spiritual body, the church. Strangely, those who celebrate the Eucharist, claiming to partake in the actual body and blood of Christ, are the ones who never have benefitted from the sacrifice of the Son. They have never obeyed the gospel and thus have never had their sins forgiven.

It is not the actual body and blood of Jesus – that happened one time on the cross. The world of physical churches can never give up the idea of physical things, and thus they say each person is partaking of the actual body and blood of Christ. As just mentioned, those who do so are, interestingly not in the kingdom, the church. They are not in the kingdom because they did not obey the gospel to have their sins forgiven. They do not understand the gospel message because they have not rightly divided the word of God. They cannot differentiate when Jesus was speaking literally and when He was using metaphors. This distinction is only made by respecting the meaning of God's revelation.

God's revelation was gradual from when it began with the "appearance" of the Holy Spirit in Acts 2 until all was completed towards the end of the first century. The Holy Spirit delivered the truth to the apostles, and one thing was the record of the events at the "Last Supper." Then the Holy Spirit documents those in the kingdom partaking of the Lord's Supper, and it would be a remembrance on the first day of the week. The Holy Spirit **never** alludes to the idea of the Real Presence. He does reveal in Galatians 2:20, Romans 8:9, and 1 Corinthians 3:16 (all seen below) that there is a permanent indwelling of God within the child of God. **The Lord is present in those added to His spiritual body (the church) and not in some temporary fashion when one partakes of the elements.** The elements are, of course, just the representation of the Lord's body and blood. The Lord no longer possesses a physical body, and as the scriptures indicate, He made the sacrifice one time for all time (Hebrews 9:28, Hebrews 10:10). In many cases, the "world of religion" still strives for the physical, which is the opposite of the truth, which is spiritual in every way. The remembrance is spiritual and "on purpose" for God. The sense Jesus was portraying in speaking of eating His body and drinking His blood was always **indicating the seriousness** of what Jesus was about to do for each of us. In remembrance, we see what Christ did, and it is very real as we recall the events of that day. The commemoration of this very real event will never leave the mind of those "in Christ." As always, the things done by God are related to achieving His purpose of sharing in the Divine Nature. Those "in Christ" are in the spiritual body of Christ, His church, and the local church consisting of those "in Christ" have a spiritual mission (evangelization), and their work is in every way spiritual. They are edified in the word of God. They sing spiritual songs making melody in their heart. They give as purposed in their heart. They partake of the Lord's Supper by remembering His sacrifice. In Catholicism, one error leads to another, and it begins with the pope and rulemaking. They invent the Real Presence and now need a way to turn the physical elements into the actual body and blood of Christ, so they invent the Catholic Mass. They need priests and similar functionality to the Old Testament priests, so they ignore the organization established by the Holy Spirit and add priests. They invent original sin and then invent baptizing babies and destroy any hope of obeying the gospel. The obedience to the gospel is how God forgives past sin. Since there is no Catholic way to have committed sins forgiven, they use their priests to have people supposedly receive forgiveness in confession. Indeed, the Catholic Church is the opposite of the church Jesus built and is truly the universal physical church and the living holding place for those souls who will fail in life.

Note: It might be reasonable for someone to ask, why does anyone care if Catholics believe the elements of the Lord's Supper are the actual body and blood of Jesus. I could indicate it does not matter. After all, is there any harm in such a belief? There is harm because it is not the truth, and lies are always problematic, and as in many Catholic teachings, they serve as distractions to the truth. However, the real problem is Catholics have been deceived in this matter. The word of God has not been properly divided. The Real Presence is just another teaching of Catholicism that is confusing but enticing in its appeal. The same type of reasoning exists for all of the Catholic doctrines. It is a reasoning that is focused on protecting Catholicism at all costs. Regardless, if it is related to salvation or the Real Presence or Marian doctrine or purgatory or a hundred other things, Catholicism is without any scriptural support. The persons who point out the errors of Catholic doctrine do so in the hope that in the obviousness of those errors, there will be a realization of Catholicism's lack of connectivity with God. Thus the genuine concern is, as always, and in all matters, the soul.

Continuing discussion of the Real Presence

This teaching of the Real Presence is divisive in the anguish it brings. So many people have been deceived into thinking they are doing as they should, and feel fortunate to contact God. Many things about the Catholic Church can provide a sense of security but nothing more than those who believe in the "Real Presence." The word terror (knowing the terror of the Lord, we persuade men) fits very well with the awakening of those who die in Catholicism. The Real Presence in terms of the modern language used in marketing could be spinning a story, being deceptive. Still, there is something very different about this "Real Presence con," which provides credibility. Namely, this con has been going on for well over a thousand years. Someone might consider the term "con" despicable, but those who know Christ established this event as a remembrance might think this designation is too mild. Deception is always eventually bitter.

When we discuss any essential doctrine of Catholicism and show it to be false, it should be apparent that Catholicism fails as a religion. The Real Presence is just another invention of Catholicism, and some Protestants also include a version of it in their teachings. There is no reason for the Real Presence. Does it make a person feel good that the wafer and the fruit of the vine are the actual body and blood of Christ? **The truth is Christ is already present and continually present if a person is "in Christ."**

Galatians 2:20

20 I have been crucified with Christ; it is no longer I who live, but Christ lives in me; and the life which I now live in the flesh I live by faith in the Son of God, who loved me and gave Himself for me.

Romans 8:9

9 But you are not in the flesh but in the Spirit, if indeed the Spirit of God dwells in you. Now if anyone does not have the Spirit of Christ, he is not His.

1 Corinthians 3:16

16 Do you not know that you are the temple of God and that the Spirit of God dwells in you?

Again, what is the harm in believing in the Real Presence? First, it is not true and is adding to God's word. Also, it is part of the deception of Catholicism that keeps people loyal to their organization. The Real Presence is a step down because **the child of God, "in Christ," always has God in them – much better and the truth.**

When people fail to take God seriously, they move from the truth, and it will not be long before they move further away with other invented doctrines. This is the story of the "religions of the world" as they change God's meaning to suit their needs, and then it never stops. As a result of false teaching, there is often a need to create or change doctrine because of necessary inferences. The result is the creation of many new religions or religious practices, and the outcome is very far from the truth – thus the loss of souls.

9.4 Catholic mysteries versus full disclosure

The "Real Presence" is the most revered thing within Catholicism. It is truly the most physical of all the things in the universal physical Catholic Church. It is among many ridiculous things, the most ridiculous. It is pure nonsense. Everything God did was about accomplishing His purpose. The obedience to the Father meant Jesus would have to die the terrible death. The sending of the Holy Spirit to the apostles provided the message of truth that God's purpose was to be fulfilled in those who would be obedient. They needed the truth. God requires that worship must be in spirit and truth. Those added to the body of Christ by their obedience are in the spiritual body and are spirit. Worship is always doing things God's way, and that can be said to be obedient things. Worship in whatever form requires a person to be spiritual. Even evangelism requires such a person. A spiritual person brings the truth. As a group (local church), they honor God on the first day of the week in remembering Jesus' death, burial, and resurrection. There is a reason, and of course, it has to do with God's purpose, namely keeping what God has done before those "in Christ" to encourage their faithfulness in doing God's will. The Lord's Supper is a spiritual event; it is a remembrance, a memorial of a past event.

The bread is bread. The fruit of the vine is the fruit of the vine. The Real Presence never occurred in the New Testament, or it would have been recorded under the inspiration of the Holy Spirit. There was no pope recorded in the New Testament record. The essential things of

Catholicism are somehow not present. That is, God did not include them in His holy and perfect record. In terms of God's purpose, there is no reason for the Real Presence as the sacrifice of Jesus has been completed. It cannot be for worship because all worship is related to **doing what God directs**. There is no indication from God that Christ's body and blood are actually being partaken except perhaps in a spiritual remembrance sense. That is, the sense that Jesus shed His actual body and blood. Those who partake in memorializing Jesus do so with the knowledge that the bread represents the body of Christ and the fruit of the vine represents the blood of Christ. In that sense, they appreciate, they honor Jesus' sacrifice. They will not forget that Jesus gave His actual body and His actual blood. Therein is the power of this memorial since it strengthens those already "in Christ." The horror of all the lies of Catholicism is that people believe them and never have their sins forgiven.

If you think about John 6 for a moment and how Jesus tied together eating His body and drinking His blood to eternal life, then like the apostles, you would know from these verses that something was missing. The apostles must have been relieved about many things when Jesus said He would send the Holy Spirit to guide them into all truth.

John 6:53-54

*53 Then Jesus said to them, "Most assuredly, I say to you, **unless you eat the flesh of the Son of Man and drink His blood, you have no life in you**.*

54 Whoever eats My flesh and drinks My blood has eternal life, and I will raise him up at the last day.

*Note: Catholicism makes such a mess in its doctrinal creations. This verse above points to a **single event** that is necessary for a person to achieve eternal life. That event we learn is their obedience to the gospel. Catholicism's private interpretation of the verse has the Catholic regularly eating His actual body and drinking His actual blood. John 6:54, with a **bit** of thought, is pointing to a one-time event that is necessary to qualify for eternal life. That apparent **one-time event** (from the verse) occurs when they obey the gospel. Once again, the Catholic invention of doctrine, i.e., the Real Presence, makes it more ridiculous by continually having Catholics partake in the Lord's Supper and believing they are fulfilling John 6:54. Since God tied eating His flesh and drinking His blood to eternal life, does Catholicism think that the*

Lord's Supper is in some way providing salvation? The point here is that whenever humankind gets involved in making the rules for God, it will be a mess, and there is no way "everything" will fit together. When we frequently say God has fit everything perfectly together in His word, we mean everything from Genesis 1:1 to Revelation 22:21.

God's plan is very timely; that is, it occurs in the fullness of time

John 16:13 "begins" as the apostles received the Holy Spirit in Acts 2, and the ongoing process of guiding them into all truth would continue for 50 plus years. In Acts 2, they preached the gospel for the first time, and people were added to the church, the kingdom, and with sins forgiven, they were on the road to eternal life. Of course, without sin, they now qualified to be included in the body of Christ, and the Lord immediately adds them. They need to live faithfully to receive the end of their faith – the salvation of their souls (1 Peter 1:9). Now they were spiritual and could, for instance, contact the Father through the Son. **Thus, did they eat the flesh, drink the blood of Jesus? Yes, they did, as it was a requirement for eternal life for having this spiritual relationship.** At the time of John 6, Jesus could not reveal the gospel message because it had not yet occurred. It would be meaningless and not according to God's timing to talk about the death, burial, and resurrection before it happened. Yet very soon, it would be possible to obey the gospel, that is, obey the death, burial, and resurrection of the Lord, resulting in sins forgiven and establishing a spiritual relationship with Christ who would be living in them.

Until the time came (after Jesus' death, burial, and resurrection), Jesus spoke in parables of the kingdom. As the time grew near, He was revealing more. He indicated the nature of the work for the apostles in Matthew 16:15-19, and before that, **another thing only partially revealed** occurred when He spoke of eating His body and drinking His blood. These things were not to be understood until the right time. Even when there was clarity brought to these verses (John 6:53-54 and Matthew 16:15-19) in Acts 2, there were those (like the early church fathers) who **look back to these verses WITHOUT THE CLARITY brought by the Spirit of God** to find support for their doctrines. In doing so, Catholicism creates a pope, an earthly ruling class, and the Real Presence, among many other things. The net result is the destruction of the gospel message designed to save souls. The scriptures reveal the meaning of these verses, and they are no longer mysteries. They now represent the truth not earlier understood in Matthew 16:15-19 and John 6:53-54. Even though we now know their meaning, Catholicism returns to those verses and declares their meaning differently than what has been revealed. God did not intend certain things understood until the "fullness of time," and now, looking back to those verses, they can be properly understood. Roman Catholicism claims Matthew 16:15-19 was teaching that Jesus was giving authority to Peter over the church. Of course, there is no indication of that in the scriptures, and that is not what happened. The church has its foundation in Jesus being the Son of God, and Jesus is the head of the body, His spiritual church.

Note: The fullness of time defined: It is a terminology that refers to being the right time for something. Galatians 4:4-5 "But when the fullness of the time had come, God sent forth His Son, born of a woman, born under the law, to redeem those who were under the law, that we might receive the adoption as sons." In our case, the fullness of time was the appropriate time for certain things to occur, allowing the proper understanding of (for example) Matthew 16:15-19 and John 6:53-54. Even though the truth could now be understood, that will only happen if a person has a love of the truth. If a person considers only those verses, they will not have all that God revealed on those subjects and most certainly get it wrong.

9.5 The Catholic Mass

There would be something missing in discussing the Real Presence if there was no mention of the Catholic Mass. The Catholic Mass is the vehicle for turning the elements of bread and wine into the actual body and blood of Christ, and it is called the transubstantiation process. The other term that refers to the Real Presence is the Eucharist.

Catholic Mass defined: The Mass is the central liturgical rite in the Catholic Church, encompassing the Liturgy of the Word and the Liturgy of the Eucharist, where the bread and wine are consecrated and become the actual body and blood of Christ.

Vatican II puts the Catholic position succinctly:

"At the Last Supper, on the night He was betrayed, our Savior instituted the Eucharistic Sacrifice of his Body and Blood. He did this in order to perpetuate the sacrifice of the cross throughout the centuries until he should come again, and so to entrust to his beloved spouse, the

Church, a memorial of his death and resurrection: a sacrament of love, a sign of unity, a bond of charity, a paschal banquet in which Christ is consumed, the mind is filled with grace, and a pledge of future glory is given to us" (*Sacrosanctum Concilium* 47).

https://www.catholic.com/tract/the-institution-of-the-mass

9.6 The Catholic position

The Catholic Church teaches that the Mass is the re-presentation of the sacrifice of Calvary. It does not teach that the Mass is a re-crucifixion of Christ. That is, He does not suffer and die again in the Mass. Yet, it is more than just a memorial service. John A. O'Brien, writing in *The Faith of Millions*, said, "On the cross, Christ really shed his blood and was really slain; in the Mass, however, there is no real shedding of blood, no real death; but the separate consecration of the bread and the wine symbolizes the separation of the body and blood of Christ and thus symbolizes his death upon the cross. The Mass is the renewal and perpetuation of the sacrifice of the cross in the sense that it offers [Jesus] anew to God . . . and thus commemorates the sacrifice of the cross, reenacts it symbolically and mystically, and applies the fruits of Christ's death upon the cross to individual human souls. All the efficacy of the Mass is derived, therefore, from the sacrifice of Calvary."

The problems are always the same with Catholicism, namely "inventing doctrine" to cover the lies. This time the invention is the Mass, which becomes the primary means of worship in Catholicism. Catholics go to Mass, meaning going to worship, meaning going to church. During this process, the priest consecrates the physical bread and wine into the actual body and blood of Christ. Of course, there were no priests in the new testament, so the Catholic Church retreats to the Old Testament priesthood and their connection with God and sin and sacrifice. Indeed, the Old Testament was this very physical worship and occurred with the priests offering very specific sacrifices. Catholicism fails because they continue the physical worship, which was imperfect. The old law was a shadow of what was to come, but Catholicism continues the Old Testament style of worship. Everything in their worship is physical and complicated, and the complication is due to their rulemaking, making the rules for God.

Of course, there was no mass, no priests, no "Real Presence" in the scriptures, and thus Catholicism fails. However, they failed long before instituting these things and even long before they had a pope. Their point of failure was when certain persons moved away from the doctrine of Christ. The most obvious thing would be changing the gospel message, which means none could be Christian. The root cause was carelessness in handling the word of God.

There was no Catholic church in the early centuries, but the seeds of Catholicism were being planted. Eventually, there would be this religion called Catholicism that fulfilled the falling-away predictions. The Catholic Mass comes from the private interpretations of certain scriptures in John and Matthew relating to the body and blood of Christ. There needed to be a way of changing the elements into the actual body and blood of Christ. To fulfill this need, the Mass is invented, priests are invented, consecration or transubstantiation is invented, and a ceremonial style sacrifice was devised. All of these things are alien to the scriptures. Catholics consider the Real Presence as the central event of their worship. Unfortunately, God did not include the Real Presence in what the Holy Spirit delivered as the truth. God defined worship to be in spirit and truth. In spirit means those worshipping must be spiritual. That is not surprising because a person in sin cannot approach God in any way, cannot pray to God*, would not be suitable to worship God, and ultimately cannot share in the Divine Nature. Not to confuse, it is sinners who God seeks. Specifically, those who can face up to their sin and in humility obey the gospel. Then they can approach God as mentioned in prayer, in worship, and receive the end of their faith – the salvation of their souls.

Note: *"Cannot pray to God" refers to being without a relationship with God that allows prayer to be meaningful. The scriptures indicate God does not hear the prayer of the sinner (James 9:31), but the prayer of a righteous person (without sin) avails much (James 5:16). Nonetheless, seeking God, that is, seeking a relationship with God, is necessary, and that means appealing to God, **praying for this relationship** is needed. The author recognizes the subject of prayer in this context can be confusing, but only because some of humankind's ideas about prayer are accepted. God's definition and use of prayer are very straightforward. The following may bring clarity for some:

https://heavencoach.com/miracles-healing-and-prayer/

In truth (worship must be in spirit and truth) means the method of worship is authorized and that primarily means "not of men's devising." If someone determined to build a massive edifice to praise God and have a large musical ensemble play wonderful music, it would not be in truth. It would be an abomination. **The truth in worship means doing as God directed**. Matthew 15:9 states, "in vain they worship me teaching for doctrines the commandments of men." God is worshipped when the gospel message is taught. It honors Him and His Son because it is done by one "in Christ," and the truth is taught. The Catholic Mass is in no way a form of worship but is vain and an abomination. It is amazing how Catholicism searches out the early church fathers and their tradition and, in their assumed apostolic succession, adds their Magisterium to justify their teachings. God has been generous with His revelations about Himself, about His purpose, and the meaning of life. There is such clarity and convincingly so as He fits everything together perfectly. The Catholic teachings are the opposite of the truth and obviously so, and only held together by clever apologists.

Note: There is one other thing that, if understood, would also negate any possibility of the Real Presence – not that anything else is needed. Yet this thing has consequences throughout various Catholic beliefs that negate many, if not all, of their beliefs. It is that God has completed His communication with humankind. This occurred near the end of the first century and God speaks of this as "when that which is perfect has come." ***Nothing else is needed if humankind has the completed word of God – certainly not the Catholic Church.*** *Throughout the scriptures, people want evidence in terms of signs, miracles, and at times God has obliged. Perhaps it suited God's purpose because the revelation was not complete or because it was timely for God to demonstrate Himself as God. Now God has drawn a line in the sand with His perfect word. His word is perfect in every way, perfect in conversion, and thus perfect in fulfilling His purpose. As always, humankind wants signs, miracles, some direct communication with God. However, those things have ceased commensurate with the coming of "that which is perfect."* ***If this were understood, the Real Presence and many other doctrines of the physical Catholic Church would be pointless.*** *Actually, they would be impossible because the will of God has been completed, and many Catholic teachings have a miraculous association. Catholicism grossly underestimates the power, the perfection of the scriptures.*

9.7 Making the powerful distinction of that which is perfect

1 Corinthians 13:10

*10 But when that which is perfect has come, then that which is **in part** will be done away.*

The various things that were "in part" were things people love, but there was always something better. God now provides that which is better, provides that which is perfect – His completed word. God, Himself is no longer interacting with humankind directly but provides perfection in that which Catholicism diminishes – the word of God.

There seem to be two senses of "in part." Both relate to achieving God's purpose, both relate to conversion, and both are concluded in the perfection of God's completed word. In the context of 1 Corinthians 13, God will be eliminating the use of supernatural things that confirmed who He was, who Jesus was, and were used when timely for God's purpose. Specifically, these things were in the supernatural category, meaning God's involvement, such as with Moses to support the Israelites escape from Egypt. The ten plagues, the parting of the Red Sea, were miraculous. The miracles of Jesus, His resurrection, and His ascension to the right hand of God demonstrated who He was. The scriptures are filled with God's supernatural interactions with humankind, and it includes God speaking to humankind in various ways. The last of these supernatural actions was the Holy Spirit confirming the word of God as documented in Hebrews. During the time the Holy Spirit spent with the apostles guiding them into all truth (a period above 50 years), there was a confirmation of what would be the final revelation from God.

Hebrews 2:3-4

3 how shall we escape if we neglect so great a salvation, which at the first began to be spoken by the Lord, and was confirmed to us by those who heard Him,

4 God also bearing witness both with signs and wonders, with various miracles, and gifts of the Holy Spirit, according to His own will?

Indeed, signs, wonders, various miracles, and gifts of the Holy Spirit are no longer "available" since sometime near the end of the first century. The terminology of 1 Corinthians 13:8, chronicles the end of miraculous things.

1 Corinthians 13:8

" .... But whether *there are* prophecies, they will fail; whether *there are* tongues, they will cease; whether *there is* knowledge, it will vanish away."

These prophecies, tongues, and knowledge are supernatural and serve as confirmation of God's word. It was a special time as it was the completion of God's communication with humankind. Interestingly, once the inspiration was completed, miraculous things were no longer needed. The perfection, the power of God's word, is infinitely more potent than the signs so cherished by humankind.

Verse nine of 1 Corinthians 13 goes on to say we will no longer KNOW **in part**. Much more can be said here about the comparative staying power of love and so on, but the thing to realize is that the change is occurring for humankind's remaining time. These miraculous ways of discerning God have stopped AND what is remaining is much better. Who could believe that the completed word of God is better than experiencing miracles, communicating directly with God? The answer is **those who love the truth,** and those are the ones God seeks and who seek Him.

All those claiming some communication with God or receiving some supernatural message are lying or are delusional. They may very well be in some mental breakdown, and that would be sad, but **do not let them mislead you.** Such communications are no longer in existence. God has powerfully in the process of ending "signs, etc." essentially emphasized to humankind the importance, the potency of His word. Yet, the word of God is soundly rejected and disrespected by the Catholic Church and by the "churches of the world." Until the return of Jesus at the end of the world, people will cry out for signs, but not those that love the truth.

The second sense or characteristic of "**in part**" when God's word was completed is the end of any partial revelations such as Genesis 3:15 or Matthew 16:19. We have seen that Jesus in the parables was revealing characteristics of the kingdom that only allowed for a limited understanding – the big picture was not yet revealed. In this book, we have seen how certain persons, groups have used things partially revealed by God and created doctrine in opposition to **all that was revealed** in the fullness of time. Four specific partial revelations made by Jesus to the apostles were concerning the rock of Matthew 16:18, the eating of the body and drinking of the blood of Jesus of John 6:53-54, the forgiving/retaining of sins of John 20:23, and the binding/loosening of Matthew 16:19. These revelations were "**in part**," but now, with the word of God completed, there is nothing left "**in part**." It seems God's truth is now open to humankind in its fullness but not appreciated by humankind, or we might say not taken seriously by humankind. This is a significant milestone in God's plan, yet in almost two thousand years of having God's completed word, the religions of humankind remain far from the truth.

*Note: As you understand God, it might be obvious why God would end His communication with humankind. Many of God's early communications were incomplete. There was often something else coming concerning achieving God's purpose. We are talking about something else to be done to complete the message. In that sense, there was often a mystery until more was revealed. The most significant example is what was meant by Genesis 3:15. With Genesis 3:15 revealed, the reconciliation accomplished, and the form of doctrine **known** to achieve salvation, there was no reason for further communication. The Holy Spirit would continue to complete God's revelation till near the end of the first century to assure ongoing opportunities for individuals. The "heavy lifting" was done in what Jesus had accomplished, and the apostles were doing their part by bringing the message. Gradually, the local church was established in detail, including its mission. The Holy Spirit would work with various persons recording the gospels and the letters to the churches. God even reveals the end of all things. No more revelation is needed. Also, as we have learned, there is perfection in the means of achieving conversion. What could be better than God's word in completed form? Everything humankind needs to know is laid out before us and is understandable. To help us grasp how powerful God's word is we are informed that there is no longer any need for signs or miracles. We have something much better. We have the entire plan of God from creation, and we understand God and His purpose. There is no question about how we must live, and we are encouraged by what is coming.*

Before beginning this section, the point was made that although the Real Presence was entirely unscriptural that "all revelations following the work of inspiration" could be discredited by a single understanding. That understanding was that God completed His communication with humankind, and thus any new or changed doctrine would be from man and not from God. Furthermore, those miraculous aspects such as signs, miracles, and direct communication from God to man would no longer happen. The scriptures were completed – never again would there be any inspired communications from God. Thus Peter could say, "His divine power has given to us all things that pertain to life and godliness." Peter could not be more explicit as he wrote this sometime in the latter part of the first century. Of course, he could never imagine the position that would be created for him as the head of the church, the Catholic Church. How much more has the Catholic Church and the "churches of the world" brought as doctrine? How many changes have those organizations brought that destroy the gospel message? This most "holy" of Catholic Church teachings called the Real Presence is without merit in the scriptures.

Chapter 10
Purgatory

Why should purgatory be discussed? The concept is not in the Bible, but Catholics refer to this place as **suggested** in the Book of Maccabees, an apocryphal book of the Old Testament never recognized by the Jews. The two books of Maccabees are historical and provide a significant amount of the history for this period. Portions of Maccabees are considered religious propaganda regarding how the sin of a nation is the cause of divine punishment.

Roman Catholics believe in purgatory from their interpretations of passages such as 2 Maccabees 12:41-46, 2 Timothy 1:18, Matthew 12:32, Luke 16:19-31, Luke 23:43, 1 Corinthians 3:11-15, and Hebrews 12:29. They also believe these verses support praying for purgatorial souls. Those souls are believed to be within an active interim state for the dead undergoing purifying flames (which could be interpreted as an analogy or allegory) after death until purification allows admittance into heaven.

10.1 Catholicism devises means to maintain control

Much of the general Catholic "distortions" still exist today in a more civilized and believable presentation. Indulgences are an example where just some subtle differences, giving the appearance of a "logical" idea, now result in little or no questioning. As early as Pope Pascal I (817), popes used indulgences to remit suffering in purgatory for a price. The one thing that was so outrageous to Martin Luther was the selling of indulgences by John Tetzel in 1517. Tetzel, working with Pope Leo X, devised a scheme for collecting large sums of money to build the church in Rome into the massive edifice it is to this day. Tetzel was carrying certificates signed by the pope offering pardon of all sins to buyers. Tetzel would tell the people, "As soon as your coin clinks in the chest, the souls of your friends will rise out of purgatory into heaven." John Tetzel was a German Dominican friar and preacher and the inquisitor for Poland and Saxony and later became the Grand Commissioner for indulgences in Germany. The inquisitor worked making the inquiries for the inquisition. The inquisition was a Roman Catholic tribunal for the discovery and punishment of heresy. The characteristics of the investigation were conducted with little regard for individual rights, including severe questioning, torture, and murder.

Behind indulgences was the associated doctrine of purgatory. This doctrine is of questionable origins, but people have discussed such a place since as early as the second or third century. The Catholic Church proclaimed it an article of faith in 1439 at the Council of Florence and then confirmed it at the Council of Trent in 1548. There is no such concept in the Bible as purgatory, and in fact, it stands in direct opposition to the teachings of scripture.

Indulgences purchased by Catholics pay for some of the time spent by departed souls in purgatory. The Church of Rome told those who had lost dear ones they could reduce their time in purgatory for a price. Today there are still indulgences, and they may be in the form of prayers worth so many days out of purgatory. There are various indulgence-like offerings for Catholic masses offered for the dead, typically concerning purgatory. At a lower cost, one can light some candles in the church for a similar purpose or for any reason to receive some benefit related to the request. As a child, I remember purchasing various small cards with pictures of the saints or Mary or the "sacred heart of Jesus," and usually on the opposite side was a prayer that, if said, provided you an indulgence of so many days out of purgatory.

10.2 Purgatory: Dissecting its nature

The scriptures indicate an eternal separation along the lines of being "**in Christ**" or **not** being "**in Christ**." The separation is in terms of being in sin or not being in sin.

2 Thessalonians 4:15-17

15 For this we say to you by the word of the Lord, that we who are alive and remain until the coming of the Lord will by no means precede those who are asleep.

*16 For the Lord Himself will descend from heaven with a shout, with the voice of an archangel, and with the trumpet of God. And the dead **in Christ** will rise first.*

17 Then we who are alive and remain shall be caught up together with them in the clouds to meet the Lord in the air. And thus we shall always be with the Lord.

There is a contrast between Catholicism and the scriptures – nothing true versus the scriptures, where everything is true. These verses in 2 Thessalonians represent something that will happen at the end of time, and those dead "in Christ" will be raised first, and then those who are alive "in Christ" will be gathered when Christ returns. They shall always be with the Lord. Paul is writing to the saints in Thessalonica, expressing to them how God will handle the end. Of course, there is no purgatory in these final events, but in fact, our final destination is determined when we die, and that final condition for those "in Christ" will be to eventually share in the Divine Nature. **There is only one way into Christ, and it is by obedience to the gospel.** Hebrews accurately defines our end as, "it is appointed for men to die once, but after this the judgment." Paul also describes the end for those **not "in Christ."**

2 Thessalonians 1:7-9

7 and to give you who are troubled rest with us when the Lord Jesus is revealed from heaven with His mighty angels,

*8 in flaming fire taking vengeance on those who do not know God, and on those **who do not obey the gospel** of our Lord Jesus Christ.*

9 These shall be punished with everlasting destruction from the presence of the Lord and from the glory of His power

Everything fits perfectly together in the scriptures, and these end-of-life outcomes result from the choices people make. God wants people to succeed and thus positively fulfill His purpose. All this is determined by God's perfectly designed test that allows God to make the separation. Again, it is a separation that is the result of the choices people make. Strangely, people exhibit opposition to God, make bad choices, and consequently lose their souls. There are many reasons for their poor decisions, but one is related to God's definition of sin. People cannot accept anything that opposes **what they want**. God's way is perfect, and people reveal their true character and make it easy for God to sort good from evil. So much is at stake for each person, and easing the concern is something purgatory provides for Catholics. Thus it is a distraction from the truth and provides a sense of comfort when there needs to be a serious search for truth and living accordingly. Purgatory represents the highest level of deception because of its cost.

There is no scriptural mention of purgatory, but instead, judgment is according to what you have done in the body (2 Corinthians 5:10) and your relationship to Christ. Catholics point to an *apocryphal* book called 2 Maccabees that, at best, very vaguely and indirectly provides them with something (really nothing) they use to justify purgatory. Then they start their human logic beginning with **the need for such a place**. God did not leave this oppositional teaching amid His revelation. God is precise, and by defining the end in detail, there can be no differences.

Catholic logic regarding purgatory

Catholic "speak" would be that no one is perfect; you must be perfect to go to heaven. Therefore, except for some saints named by the Roman Catholic Church, most everyone will have to spend time without God in purgatory. The truth is you could never become perfect or acceptable to God in any place, with any amount of suffering. Suffering, depression, or any other thing you could do or endure could never remit a single sin. Yet your sins are forgiven in the eyes of God, if you do what is required to be "in Christ." Purgatory violates the most basic principles of scripture and the associated logic as mentioned below:

- The seriousness of sin required Christ's terrible suffering and death. The price for sin was the blood of Jesus (Acts 20:28). Catholicism would seem to understand this. Yet, it does not bother Catholicism to diminish this with their rules by believing there are other means to have sins forgiven (confession to a priest, purgatory, and baptism for the non-existent original sin).

- *The scriptures indicate* there is no other payment for sin except Christ's sacrifice.

- God's children have Christ living in them. Are His children headed for purgatory?

- Humankind does not have to achieve perfection to go to heaven in any way man perceives perfection, but God sees those *"in Christ"* as perfect since sins have been covered. There is no way for man to have a higher status in the "eyes of God" than being *"in Christ."* Perfection has to do with eliminating sin, and Christ is the solution for sin.

- People seem to want purgatory, just as they want a confessional so they can sin in life and recover. God requires valid repentance, which means committing to leave sin and putting it out of their life. If you genuinely do that, it will not be a continual return to sin. Simon, the sorcerer, sinned after becoming a Christian and was told, "Repent therefore of this your wickedness, and pray God if perhaps the thought of your heart may be forgiven you." God knows our hearts. It is ridiculous to think people can sin, go to confession and have their sins forgiven, sin, go to confession and have their sins forgiven, sin, go to confession and have their sins forgiven. First, of course, a Catholic's sins have never been forgiven since they never obeyed the gospel. Also, in their process of sinning, receiving forgiveness, and returning to sin, it makes God seem foolish – He is not. There is a godly process mentioned that might seem like it is equivalent to sinning, being forgiven, sinning, and so on. However, it is quite different, and like all things with God, it is perfect. Since in case of one "in Christ" returning to sin, it can be forgiven but at God's discretion knowing a person's heart and thus the validity of their repentance.

Man will die, and after that, the judgment. There is great clarity in this statement. God places nothing between your death and the judgment of your eternity.

Hebrews 9:27

27 And as it is appointed for men to die once, but after this the judgment,

If you are "in Christ," living acceptably, you will go to heaven; and if you are not "in Christ," you will be lost eternally. At the judgment, those in the household of God "will scarcely be saved" – 1 Peter 4:17-19. Some who obeyed the gospel may fall from grace and never repent of the sin that removed them from a relationship with God. God's children have Christ as their advocate, but if they return to the world, their end will be worse than if they had never known the way of righteousness (2 Peter 2:20-22). It is the perfect deception to have people in the Catholic confessional and believing in purgatory and never understanding the eternal danger. Catholics think they can live a predominantly "worldly life" and still "squeak" into heaven. When Jesus says that few will take the narrow road to life, it is not what God wants, but what God knows will happen. Ultimately, many will be lost because they accept things (like purgatory) that allow them to live how they want. Nothing "fits the bill" for deceiving people about eternity better than Catholic doctrine and specifically purgatory and the Catholic confessional.

A little about 2 Maccabees

263

The book of 2 Maccabees is a non-scriptural book of the Old Testament used by Catholics to provide some potential credibility for purgatory. Below are the verses they use in support of purgatory.

2 Maccabees 12:41–45

41 So they all blessed the ways of the Lord, the righteous judge, who reveals the things that are hidden;

42 and they turned to supplication, praying that the sin that had been committed might be wholly blotted out. The noble Judas exhorted the people to keep themselves free from sin, for they had seen with their own eyes what had happened as the result of the sin of those who had fallen.

43 He also took up a collection, man by man, to the amount of two thousand drachmas of silver, and sent it to Jerusalem to provide for a sin-offering. In doing this he acted very well and honourably, taking account of the resurrection.

44 For if he were not expecting that those who had fallen would rise again, it would have been superfluous and foolish to pray for the dead.

45 But if he was looking to the splendid reward that is laid up for those who fall asleep in godliness, it was a holy and pious thought. Therefore he made atonement for the dead, so that they might be delivered from their sin.

There is little reason to examine any of the seven extra books of the Old Testament added to the Catholic Bible. Jesus, the apostles, the Jews and even the majority of the early church fathers and for a long period also the Catholic Church rejected these books. Finally, the council of Trent (1545-1563) officially pronounced these books canonical, and the First Vatican Council (1869-1870) reaffirmed the council of Trent. This is one of those things where I am tempted to say, "what is all the fuss about." There is nothing of significance in these books, but it would be very wrong to place them among the inspired books as that would be very deceitful. Catholicism likes them for their possibility of supporting various matters concerning life after death. However, the scriptures are very clear about those matters. This chapter deals with what God has delivered about the next life, and it conflicts with the claims made by Catholicism.

Here is a good reference on the subject of the added Catholic books.

(https://www.lavistachurchofchrist.org/cms/the-extra-catholic-books/).

A sidebar: When Catholic evidence is insufficient, they revert to this

There is another point here that the readers should have an awareness. The Catholic Church likes to claim that the Bible exists because of them. This is something I got used to hearing as their apologists were losing in a debate. Here are a couple of references:

"The church...exercising the authority given her by Christ, fulfilling her duty as custodian and champion of the written word, separated the true from the false, the divine from the human, and gave men the New Testament, as it is today. And this in the year 397 A.D. -- nearly 400 years after Christ. Thus the Bible came from the church!" (Paulist Correspondence Course, No. 2, pp. 55-56).

Another reference:

"Now we have seen that the complete divine revelation is transmitted to us from Christ through the Apostles in the divine tradition of the Church. Hence the only certain guide as to the inspiration and canonicity of all the books of Sacred Scripture is the authoritative pronouncement of the Church" (The Teachings of the Catholic Church, Vol. I, p. 30).

If you believe the Catholic Church is why we have the scriptures, One would disagree, namely God. God has provided the scriptures, assured their accuracy by inspiration and how the message would be delivered. There were copies made by various persons of the originals, and in some way, the word of God has come down correctly through history. God promised His words would not pass away, and He keeps His promises. We might see difficulty correctly getting the scriptures through time in our human minds, but we might also see difficulty creating everything from nothing. God, not the Catholic Church, saw we have the scriptures. There is a "solid way to truth," and God provides it through His word. The preservation of the New Testament is living evidence of the unmatched power and providence of God. We have the completed word of God in the latter part of the first century, and everything else concerning spiritual matters is speculation. You would be right to think it is a grievous abomination to claim the Catholic Church is the reason we have the scriptures.

Note: God is perfect in every way, and one thing seldom, if ever, noticed is the providential care of His word. God has preserved His word throughout time, and thus we have it today. People change His word by changing God's meaning and typically not God's word, God's inspired words. It is in the hands of humankind to get the meaning right. Those who honor God's word search the scriptures to assure they have the correct meaning, whereas those who search for their desired meaning privately interpret scripture to prove their points. Those who love the truth will find God's meaning and find assurance in how everything fits perfectly together.

10.3 Addressing Bible verses claimed to justify purgatory

(Luke 16:19–31, 1 Corinthians 3:10-15)

We will discuss Catholicism's two most frequently used Bible verses to validate purgatory. The verses in 2 Maccabees are not discussed here since it is not a valid book of scripture. Maccabees has many problems in the manner of the writing – much different than scripture. It fails the standard Canonical tests except those used by Catholicism. Catholics like this book since it provides several verses having an extremely remote possibility of supporting their concept of purgatory. This Purgatory concept is alien to the scriptures and in opposition to the basic principles of God's word relating to the afterlife. The Catholic attempt to "squeeze out" the concept of Purgatory from Bible verses is addressed below for Luke 16:19-26 and 1 Corinthians 3:10-15. Neither of these verses **or any other Bible verses or the verses in 2 Maccabees** supports the concept of purgatory. Still, the second verse mentioned is the one Catholics believe has the most credibility. This second set of verses in 1 Corinthians 3 displays the pathetic scholarship of Catholicism, or if they understand these verses correctly, then there is malicious deceit in how they purposely twist the verses to their benefit.

Luke 16:19-31 – as a case for purgatory? Lazarus and the rich man

Luke 16:19-31

19 "There was a certain rich man who was clothed in purple and fine linen and fared sumptuously every day.

20 But there was a certain beggar named Lazarus, full of sores, who was laid at his gate,

21 desiring to be fed with the crumbs which fell from the rich man's table. Moreover the dogs came and licked his sores.

22 So it was that the beggar died, and was carried by the angels to Abraham's bosom. The rich man also died and was buried.

23 And being in torments in Hades, he lifted up his eyes and saw Abraham afar off, and Lazarus in his bosom.

24 "Then he cried and said, 'Father Abraham, have mercy on me, and send Lazarus that he may dip the tip of his finger in water and cool my tongue; for I am tormented in this flame.'

25 But Abraham said, 'Son, remember that in your lifetime you received your good things, and likewise Lazarus evil things; but now he is comforted and you are tormented.

26 And besides all this, between us and you there is a great gulf fixed, so that those who want to pass from here to you cannot, nor can those from there pass to us.'

27 "Then he said, 'I beg you therefore, father, that you would send him to my father's house,

28 for I have five brothers, that he may testify to them, lest they also come to this place of torment.'

29 Abraham said to him, 'They have Moses and the prophets; let them hear them.'

30 And he said, 'No, father Abraham; but if one goes to them from the dead, they will repent.'

31 But he said to him, 'If they do not hear Moses and the prophets, neither will they be persuaded though one rise from the dead.' "

These verses tell the story of the rich man and Lazarus and give some insight into life immediately after death. The rich man is in Hades, and Lazarus is in Abraham's bosom and can be considered paradise. There is no indication of a temporary punishment that releases one from sin, and in fact, there is no passageway between these realms since a great gulf is fixed. No one can pass from one realm to another. This would be consistent with Hebrews 9:27, "And as it is appointed for men to die once, but after this the judgment." **A person's fate is sealed at death and thus the urgency, the importance of the message.** If there were relief, the rich man would not be pleading with Abraham for his brothers. There will be an eventual movement from Hades (torment) to the lake of fire – the final hell.

Note: Hades can be clarified as being the realm of the dead and appears to be divided into two parts. One is the bosom of Abraham and can be thought of as paradise. The other is a place of torment. This place of torment is not the same as the final hell that is spoken of in Revelation 20:13-15.

1 Corinthians 3:10-15 is used by Catholicism to validate purgatory

These verses in Corinthians do not teach purgatory. People who think they do are very careless and possess an attitude that insinuates God provides truth by innuendo. The truth is NOT hidden like a puzzle as though there is some mystery. God straightforwardly provides the truth, and indeed it is in a perfect manner. God wants to accomplish his purpose, and that requires the correct message to reach humankind and not some coded message.

Note: To clarify, God, as indicated in this book, did provide over history various information, for instance, to the apostles but insufficient for their complete understanding. However, He would eventually provide full disclosure. This delay always fits with God's purpose. Since God's revelation is complete, all those things left initially without their complete meaning have been revealed. This was the case as detailed for Matthew 16:15-19 and John 20:23 and Genesis 3:15, among others. Purgatory, if true, would be something essential to human awareness concerning how a person should live. If purgatory existed, you could live casually, and despite some carelessness, there is a place of recovery. In truth, you must live very seriously consistent with God's ways, and there is no escape clause. God accurately defines a person's success as being "in Christ," which is how His communication to humankind ends.

All the Catholic Church teachings are consistent with a very human-devised physical character and, as we suggest, confusing and mysterious. That is why it is easy to differentiate the truth because it is simple, understandable, and with solid evidence contained in the word of God. 1 Corinthians 3:10-15 is used by Catholicism to promote the idea of purgatory. Like so many verses, one might believe there is some validity to their claim at first glance. However, a closer examination reveals the meaning of these verses, and it is very different than Catholicism proposes. It exposes a genuine carelessness, real desperation to find some way to support purgatory.

1 Corinthians 3:10-15

10 According to the grace of God which was given to me, as a wise master builder I have laid the foundation, and another builds on it. But let each one take heed how he builds on it.

11 For no other foundation can anyone lay than that which is laid, which is Jesus Christ.

12 Now if anyone builds on this foundation with gold, silver, precious stones, wood, hay, straw,

13 each one's work will become clear; for the Day will declare it, because it will be revealed by fire; and the fire will test each one's work, of what sort it is.

14 If anyone's work which he has built on it endures, he will receive a reward.

15 If anyone's work is burned, he will suffer loss; but he himself will be saved, yet so as through fire.

These verses in 1 Corinthians 3:10-15 in no way have any relevance to purgatory. The context of Paul's speaking here is that he is laying a foundation (Romans 15:20). The foundation is always the gospel message. The foundation is critical, but it is not the whole building. In verse 9 (of 1 Corinthians 3), Paul states that God's workers are God's building. God's workers carry the same message, and yet the responses received can be different. Peter also uses this illustration of **Christians** being stones in a building (1 Peter 2:4-5). Yet, we know that becoming a Christian is not a guarantee of salvation. Whether a man's work endures will not be known until the day of judgment (1 Corinthians 1:8, 2 Peter 3:10). The fire in the verses above is the test of the materials, and some are very fire resistant like gold, silver, precious stones, and some are less resistant or in no way resistant like wood, hay, and straw. The fire tests each man's work, and each Christian faces trials throughout their life. **Paul was talking about Christians who will not endure to the end.** Those preaching the gospel brought people to Christ, but some converts go back to the world, such as Demas (2 Timothy 4:10). The Christian life can be difficult, and thus the idea of being tested by fire. God explains the seriousness of living the faithful life in 1 Peter and 2 Peter.

1 Peter 4:17-18

17 For the time has come for judgment to begin at the house of God; and if it begins with us first, what will be the end of those who do not obey the gospel of God?

18 Now, "If the righteous one is scarcely saved, Where will the ungodly and the sinner appear?"

2 Peter 2:20-21

20 For if, after they have escaped the pollutions of the world through the knowledge of the Lord and Savior Jesus Christ, they are again entangled in them and overcome, the latter end is worse for them than the beginning.

21 For it would have been better for them not to have known the way of righteousness, than having known it, to turn from the holy commandment delivered to them.

With this background, let us understand what Paul is saying in 1 Corinthians 10 and why. It is fair to realize how Paul felt about those he converted and his responsibility and concern for them. Throughout the letters of Paul, there is this concern for their continued faithfulness, and he consistently mentions his prayers for them in this regard. Here is one of many examples:

1 Thessalonians 3:5-13

*5 For this reason, when I could no longer endure it, I sent to know your faith, lest by some means the tempter had tempted you, and **our labor might be in vain**.*

6 But now that Timothy has come to us from you, and brought us good news of your faith and love, and that you always have good remembrance of us, greatly desiring to see us, as we also to see you—

7 therefore, brethren, in all our affliction and distress we were comforted concerning you by your faith.

8 For now we live, if you stand fast in the Lord.

9 For what thanks can we render to God for you, for all the joy with which we rejoice for your sake before our God,

10 night and day praying exceedingly that we may see your face and perfect what is lacking in your faith?

11 Now may our God and Father Himself, and our Lord Jesus Christ, direct our way to you.

12 And may the Lord make you increase and abound in love to one another and to all, just as we do to you,

13 so that He may establish your hearts blameless in holiness before our God and Father at the coming of our Lord Jesus Christ with all His saints.

Paul understands the delicate nature of those "in Christ" due to the persecution of the times and the temptation to go back into the world. Notice how he has a concern that **our labor might be in vain**. He is referring to those with him who share in the preaching. In 1 Corinthians 3:10-15, Paul is talking with his fellow workers in the gospel and tells them as distraught as they may be if some leave the faith, they need to realize if anyone's work is burned (that is the teacher), he will suffer loss; but he will be saved, yet so as through fire. There is a godly principle here that Paul understood, and it is the seriousness of bringing the truth and the consequences of not bringing the message. Paul transmitted that principle to his fellow workers. Ezekiel makes the same point that Paul is making both in Ezekiel 3 and 33. Verse 21 of Ezekiel 3 says, ***"Nevertheless if you warn the righteous man that the righteous should not sin, and he does not sin, he shall surely live because he took warning; also you will have delivered your soul."*** Verse 9 of Chapter 33 says, ***"Nevertheless if you warn the wicked to turn from his way, and he does not turn from his way, he shall die in his iniquity; but you have delivered your soul."***

Ezekiel 3:17-21

17 "Son of man, I have made you a watchman for the house of Israel; therefore hear a word from My mouth, and give them warning from Me:

18 When I say to the wicked, 'You shall surely die,' and you give him no warning, nor speak to warn the wicked from his wicked way, to save his life, that same wicked man shall die in his iniquity; but his blood I will require at your hand.

19 Yet, if you warn the wicked, and he does not turn from his wickedness, nor from his wicked way, he shall die in his iniquity; but you have delivered your soul.

20 "Again, when a righteous man turns from his righteousness and commits iniquity, and I lay a stumbling block before him, he shall die; because you did not give him warning, he shall die in his sin, and his righteousness which he has done shall not be remembered; but his blood I will require at your hand.

21 Nevertheless if you warn the righteous man that the righteous should not sin, and he does not sin, he shall surely live because he took warning; also you will have delivered your soul."

Ezekiel 33:1-9

1 Again the word of the LORD came to me, saying,

2 "Son of man, speak to the children of your people, and say to them: 'When I bring the sword upon a land, and the people of the land take a man from their territory and make him their watchman,

3 when he sees the sword coming upon the land, if he blows the trumpet and warns the people,

4 then whoever hears the sound of the trumpet and does not take warning, if the sword comes and takes him away, his blood shall be on his own head.

5 He heard the sound of the trumpet, but did not take warning; his blood shall be upon himself. But he who takes warning will save his life.

6 But if the watchman sees the sword coming and does not blow the trumpet, and the people are not warned, and the sword comes and takes any person from among them, he is taken away in his iniquity; but his blood I will require at the watchman's hand.'

7 "So you, son of man: I have made you a watchman for the house of Israel; therefore you shall hear a word from My mouth and warn them for Me.

8 When I say to the wicked, 'O wicked man, you shall surely die!' and you do not speak to warn the wicked from his way, that wicked man shall die in his iniquity; but his blood I will require at your hand.

9 Nevertheless if you warn the wicked to turn from his way, and he does not turn from his way, he shall die in his iniquity; but you have delivered your soul.

It is chilling to understand how seriously concerned those who love the Lord feel about the lost. They are warned of the need to bring the message. They succeed in some cases, and then some of those converts fail in their faithfulness. Indeed as Paul says, "If anyone's work is burned, he will suffer loss; but he will be saved, yet so as through fire."

It is a very **sick and careless insinuation** that suddenly, these verses support the idea of purgatory. This is the accurate and consistent evil of Catholic teaching as they build on nothing and create doctrine. As can be expected when the foundation is so weak, people create doctrines that make their teachings even more ridiculous. Such would be the case with original sin and many others and, in this case, with purgatory. They hold out purgatory as a relief for Catholics instead of the absolute **necessity** of living their life for Christ and the gospel. Of course, it is even worse because, in their system of purgatory, this period of temporary suffering is for those with just minor sin issues. A Catholic has never had a single sin forgiven since there are no valid means to allow that to happen. Thus in the Purgatory system (if it existed), there would be no Catholics. Foundational errors (like purgatory) make everything very nonsensical. However, it is much worse since people need to understand the seriousness of living for Christ and the gospel. Purgatory provides Catholics a "get out of a failed life card," allowing them a casual lifestyle.

10.4 Thinking about purgatory

The information above refutes the doctrine of purgatory. The concept of purgatory provides an excellent opportunity for some common sense if there is a good Bible understanding. The efforts to validate purgatory are typical of Catholic teachings since there is no justification in the scriptures. The format for validation is to go outside the scriptures to the early church fathers, apostolic succession, and then to their teaching arm, which is their Magisterium (infallible when certain conditions are met). Additionally, in the case of purgatory, Catholicism goes to an apocryphal book to justify purgatory. Also, two of the most used scripture verses by Catholics supporting purgatory were addressed and provided no justification for purgatory. Catholicism knows the scriptures are valid, and thus they must twist them to support their doctrines as we have just seen to support purgatory. It is the carelessness of necessity since not a single doctrine of Catholicism can be validated by the scriptures.

Now, let us do a little thinking. The scriptures provide a single means of having past sins permanently forgiven. The gospel message includes the process of receiving forgiveness, and the cost was the death, burial, and resurrection of Jesus. In the scriptures, sins are sins, and there is no differentiation as they all need to be forgiven. Catholics want you to think that God has this other means of forgiving sins. Sins can be "worked off" if they are of a lesser nature by spending some time in purgatory by some sort of suffering. I would suggest that if any sin can be handled differently, then the process defined by God requiring Jesus' suffering and death would not have been required. Another way of saying this is that evil is evil, and God can have no association with evil. Evil cannot be removed if those created in His image suffer. It requires a great deal more. The suffering and death of His incarnate Son, who lived a perfect, sinless life, was needed.

Chapter 11
Mariology

11.1 Mariology defined

"Mariology, in Christian, especially in Roman Catholic theology, is the study of doctrines concerning Mary, the mother of Jesus; the term also refers to the content of these doctrines. The primary methodological problem of Mariology is the very limited mention of Mary made in the New Testament and the relative, although not complete, silence about Mary in the early church." (Source: The Editors of Encyclopedia Britannica)

Indeed, this subject has been one of the more significant distractions in the "Christian" religion. Protestants look at "Mary worship" as something very far from the truth and an abomination to God as only God deserves to be worshipped, and in fact, idolatry is a most grievous offense. Of course, the Catholic responds with, "we do not worship Mary." The deceptive Catholic response would be as given below from the reference provided.

Do Catholics worship Mary?

https://www.thereligionteacher.com/do-catholics-worship-mary/

"No, Catholics do not worship or adore Mary. Catholics hold Mary in a special place of honor and venerate her with special devotions such as the Rosary. The first point of confusion related to this issue is terminology.

Only God deserves worship and adoration. Worshiping Mary or the other saints would clearly be idolatry. To venerate is to "honor" or "respect" someone.

We venerate Mary because of the special grace that is within her."

The Catholic narrative is that they do not worship Mary but venerate her. Let us define venerate.

Definition of *venerate:*

transitive verb

1: to regard with reverential respect or with admiring deference

2: to honor (an icon, a relic, etc.) with a ritual act of devotion

Synonyms for *venerate*

- adore
- deify
- glorify
- revere
- reverence
- worship

11.2 What veneration of Mary looks like

"Veneration for Mary is based on the reference in the Gospel of Luke to Mary as the selected handmaid of the Lord who is greeted and praised by both Elizabeth and the angel Gabriel. God's work is further illuminated in the Marian dogmas of the Roman Catholic Church, such as the Immaculate Conception and the Assumption. In the Roman Catholic view, Marian doctrine is part of the apostolic tradition and divine revelation. Catholics distinguish veneration from worship." See the link below:

https://en.wikipedia.org/wiki/Veneration_of_Mary_in_the_Catholic_Church

Instead of belaboring the point of **worship versus veneration**, let us look at the Catholic teaching on the subject of Mary. We cannot do that in a comprehensive manner because it would require many hundreds of books larger than this one. The quantity of writing in honor of Mary is quite amazing in consideration of having no special honor for Mary in the scriptures. Indeed, she is blessed among women for being chosen to be the mother of Jesus, and that is an acknowledgment of who she is, but not an authorization to worship, venerate.

We might begin by looking at a **few** of the titles for Mary as designated by the Catholic Church. There is quite a good deal of carefully selected information regarding Mary from a Catholic viewpoint at the same source as noted just above.

Some of the common titles for Mary include:

Mother of God

Queen of Heaven

Mother of the Church

Mediatrix

Co-Redemptrix

Our Lady

Now let us consider some statements from Catholics regarding Mary.

https://libguides.stthomas.edu/Mary

We will begin with a tweet from Pope Francis on August 14, 2014.
"Mary, Queen of Peace, help us to root out hatred and live in harmony"

Then just some random selections regarding Mary:

"Mary is 'Queen of the Apostles' without any claim to apostolic powers: she has other and greater powers."
Hans urs Von Balthasar

"The Marian principle is that subjective spirit found in Mary and lived out dynamically in all that leads to the Church's sanctity."
Chiara Lubich.

"Never be afraid of loving the Blessed Virgin too much. You can never love her more than Jesus did."
Saint Maximilian Kolbe.

"There is no more direct road than by Mary for uniting all mankind in Christ."

Pope St. Pius X "Ad Diem Illum."

"O sweetest Star of Heaven! O Virgin, spotless, blest, shining with Jesus' light, guiding to Him my way! Mother! beneath your veil let my tired spirit rest, for this brief passing day!"
St. Therese of Lisieux

"Mary's fidelity to the grace of her conception makes her the most perfect model, after Jesus Christ, of fidelity to grace."
Blessed William Joseph Chaminade

"About Mary, one can never say enough."
St. Bernard of Clairvaux

"Let us call the Church by the name of Mary; for she is worthy of the double name."
St. Ephrem, Second Century.

One of the more famous books of Catholic literature is *Glories of Mary* by Liguori. It contains many statements regarding Mary, which few Catholics would deny. To the best of my knowledge, it has never been refuted by Catholicism. I doubt it could be refuted because it is typical of many statements found throughout Catholicism in hundreds of books. The following quotes are from the Glories of Mary by Liguori with page numbers from the book in parentheses.

"Whoever asks and wishes to obtain graces without the intercession of Mary, attempts to fly without wings" (page 189).

"Very glorious, oh Mary, and wonderful, exclaims St. Bonaventure, is thy great name. Those who are mindful to utter it at the hour of death, have nothing to fear from hell, for the devils at once abandon the soul when they hear the name of Mary" (page 163).

"The devils have presented my sins before the tribunal of the Lord, and already they were dragging me to hell, but the holy Virgin came and said to them: 'Where are you taking this youth? What have you to do with one of my servants who has so long served me in the congregation?' The devils fled, and thus I have been saved from their hands" (page 667).

"Father Bernardine de Bustis relates that a hawk darted upon a bird which had been taught to say *Ave Maria*; the bird said *Ave Maria*, and the Hawk fell dead" (page 96).

"Wherefore those who are servants of Mary, and for whom Mary intercedes, are as secure of paradise as if they were already there" (page 280).

"What poor sinners we should be if we had not this advocate, so powerful and so merciful, and at the same time so prudent and so wise, that **the judge, her Son, cannot condemn the guilty, if she defends them**. ... Precisely the same thing does Mary continually in heaven, in behalf of innumerable sinners: she knows so well how to appease the divine justice with her tender and wise entreaties, that God himself blesses her for it, and as it were thanks her, that thus **she restrains him from abandoning and punishing them as they deserve**" (page 220).

"God was also subject to her will" (page 201).

"And therefore, says St. Peter Damian, **the Virgin has all power in heaven as on earth**" (page 201).

"She seems to command rather than request" (page 202).

"Thou, then oh **Mary, being Mother of God, canst save all men by thy prayers**, which are enforced by a mother's authority" (page 211).

"But now, if God is offended with any sinner, and Mary undertakes to protect him, she restrains the Son from punishing him and saves him" (page 133).

"She possesses, by right, the whole kingdom of her son" (page 280).

"St. Bernardine of Sienna does not hesitate to say that **all obey the commands of Mary, even God himself**" (page 202).

"Holy Virgin, Mother of God, succor those who implore thy assistance. Turn to us. But, **having been deified**, as it were, hast thou forgotten men?" (page 331).

It is easy to consider these quotes ridiculous in their honor for Mary if they were not all very typical of Catholic literature. We have popes, saints, Catholic clergy, and well-known persons from religious history proclaiming Mary as exceedingly special (an understatement).

11.3 Deceived, then trying to help

A former Catholic nun writes an excellent document on the subject of Mary. She spent a significant portion of her life in devotion to Mary. She would say her time was spent worshipping Mary. Finally, she realized that this was wrong and wrote a convincing document refuting the Catholic teaching on Mary. The entire refutation is done with a good understanding of the scriptures. You can find the document at:

https://bereanbeacon.org/mary-worship/.

I will use three short arguments from her work and include my comments.

First, Pope John Paul II shows his allegiance to Mary

If you want to see what a person's real priorities are, then watch what they do when their life, or the life of a loved one, is in danger. When Pope John Paul II was shot, while the ambulance was rushing him to the hospital, the pope was not praying to God or calling on the name of Jesus. He kept saying, over and over, "Mary, my mother!" Polish pilgrims placed a picture of Our Lady of Czestochowa on the throne where the pope usually sat. People gathered around the image, and the Vatican loudspeakers broadcasted the prayers of the rosary. When the Pope recovered, he gave Mary all the glory for saving his life, and he made a pilgrimage to Fatima to publicly thank her.

Second, there is a belief in the Catholic Church that Mary is the Co-Redemptrix

Pope Benedict XV said of Mary that "One can justly say that she herself redeemed mankind with Christ." Pope Pius IX said, "Our salvation is based upon the holy Virgin… so that if there is any hope and spiritual healing for us, we receive it solely and uniquely from her."

A lay movement called "Vox Populi" ("Voice of the People") gathers signed petitions to send to the pope, seeking to have him officially declare that Mary is Co-Redemptrix. Over six million signatures have been sent to him, representing 138 countries and all seven continents. This doctrine is supported by over 40 cardinals and 600 bishops worldwide.

Thus we owe our salvation to Jesus and Mary. The only good thing about this is that it is so ridiculous that perhaps some will realize all of Catholicism is nonsensical. More importantly, they may realize there is no salvation in the Catholic Church.

Third, Mary lived a sinless life

ALL HOLY – Mary, "the All-Holy," lived a perfectly sinless life. (Catholic Catechism)

Romans 3:23 *says, "For all have sinned, and come short of the glory of God."*

Revelation 15:4 *says, "Who shall not fear thee, O Lord, and glorify thy name? For thou only art holy."*

Romans 3:10 *says, "There is none righteous, no, not one."*
Jesus is the only person who is referred to in Scripture as sinless.

Hebrews 4:15 says, "For we have not a high priest which cannot be touched with the feelings of our infirmities; but was in all points tempted like as we are, yet without sin."

2 Corinthians 5:21 says, "For he hath made him to be sin for us, who knew no sin; that we might be made the righteousness of God in him."

1 Peter 2:22 says, "Who did not sin, neither was guile found in his mouth."

In contrast, Mary said that God is her Savior (Luke 1:47). If God was her Savior, then Mary was not sinless. Sinless people do not need THE Savior. In the Book of Revelation, when they were searching for someone worthy to break the seals and open the scroll, the only person who was found to be worthy was Jesus. Nobody else in heaven or on earth (including Mary) was worthy to open the scroll or even look inside it (Revelation 5:1-5).

St. John Henry Newman – Perspective of Mary

https://www.thecatholicthing.org/2016/01/01/fitness-glories-mary/

John Henry Newman (1801-1890) was made a cardinal by Leo XIII in 1879, beatified by Benedict XVI in 2010, and canonized by Pope Francis on October 13, 2019. He was among the most important Catholic writers of the last several centuries.

Newman gives this description of Mary

"Nothing is too high for her to whom God owes His human life; no exuberance of grace, no excess of glory, but is becoming, but is to be expected there, where God has lodged Himself, whence God has issued. Let her "be clad in the king's apparel," that is, let the fulness of the Godhead so flow into her that she may be a figure of the incommunicable sanctity, and beauty, and glory, of God Himself: that she may be the Mirror of Justice, the Mystical Rose, the Tower of Ivory, the House of Gold, the Morning Star. Let her "receive the king's diadem upon her head," as the Queen of heaven, the Mother of all living, the Health of the weak, the Refuge of sinners, the Comforter of the afflicted. And "let the first amongst the king's princes walk before her," let angels and prophets, and apostles, and martyrs, and all saints, kiss the hem of her garment and rejoice under the shadow of her throne."

Of course, Catholics say they are not worshipping Mary

Catholics claim they do not worship Mary, and yet they pray to her. Prayer, praying as used throughout the New Testament, in Greek, is the word *proseuchomai*. *Proseuchomai* means to request or ask favors **of God**. Catholicism wants to use prayer differently in allowing people to pray to Mary. The accepted concept of prayer is praying to God, and thus praying to Mary is praying to God. They know this and only claim otherwise when there are objections, such as saying they worship Mary. **They give Mary the status of God**. We see this in her titles and the claims made about her, like being the Co-Redemptrix and Mediatrix.

They elevate Mary to a height far above the woman who gave birth to Jesus. There is another thing overlooked in Catholicism in their doctrine of praying to Mary or the saints. Mary and the Catholic saints are dead, yet Ecclesiastes 9:5-6 indicates that praying to them would be impossible.

Ecclesiastes 9:5-6

5 For the living know that they will die;
But the dead know nothing,
And they have no more reward,
For the memory of them is forgotten.
6 Also their love, their hatred, and their envy have now perished;
Nevermore will they have a share
In anything done under the sun.

People like to think there can be contact with the dead, but in truth, there is no contact with the dead.

11.4 Bible speaks concerning Mariology

The scriptures do not indicate honoring Mary as a form of doctrine. She is God's choice to be the mother of Jesus, and this is an extraordinary distinction, or we could say a blessing. The closest thing to honoring Mary comes from Luke, who records Mary's statement that "henceforth all generations will call me blessed." Certainly, the one chosen by God would be blessed among all women for this privilege.

Catholics have a pattern of building up certain **persons** in such a way as can benefit Catholicism. Peter as their pope is the critical invention for Catholicism as it gives Catholicism a place of continuing power, of authority. Peter is the first pope but never so mentioned in the scriptures. As indicated in this chapter, Mary is honored in many ways, but she never has any awareness that she is to be "venerated." Catholics invent the Real Presence, but it is not in the scriptures. Mariology and the Real Presence keep Catholics thinking they are unique. All this and much more are necessary since the scriptures do not support their beliefs or Catholicism's existence. In the case of Mary, **Catholics violate the three most significant aspects of God's nature**, and they do this using the most hated thing by God. They lie. The **first thing** is a special honor for Mary, really they **worship Mary,** and they say they do not, but given her titles and the attention she gets, it is worship. The **second thing** is almost inconceivable in making her the **co-redeemer with Jesus**.

In some cases, Catholicism suggests God should listen to her. The scriptures are crystal clear that only God should be worshipped, and there is **no religious honor for any except for God**. The following verses are a sampling of where praise and worship belong.

1 Timothy 1:17

17 Now to the King eternal, immortal, invisible, to God who alone is wise, be honor and glory forever and ever. Amen.

Revelation 14:7

7 saying with a loud voice, "Fear God and give glory to Him, for the hour of His judgment has come; and worship Him who made heaven and earth, the sea and springs of water."

Exodus 20:1-4

1 And God spoke all these words, saying:

2 "I am the LORD your God, who brought you out of the land of Egypt, out of the house of bondage.

3 "You shall have no other gods before Me.

4 "You shall not make for yourself a carved image—any likeness of anything that is in heaven above, or that is in the earth beneath, or that is in the water under the earth;

Matthew 4:10

10 Then Jesus said to him, "Away with you, Satan! For it is written, 'You shall worship the LORD your God, and Him only you shall serve.' "

Luke 4:8

8 And Jesus answered and said to him, "Get behind Me, Satan! For it is written, 'You shall worship the LORD your God, and Him only you shall serve.' "

Acts 12:21-23

21 So on a set day Herod, arrayed in royal apparel, sat on his throne and gave an oration to them.

22 And the people kept shouting, "The voice of a god and not of a man!"

23 Then immediately an angel of the Lord struck him, because he did not give glory to God. And he was eaten by worms and died.

1 Chronicles 16:29

29 Give to the LORD the glory due His name;

Bring an offering, and come before Him.

Oh, worship the LORD in the beauty of holiness!

God is very clear about the honor and worship that He is to receive, and at the same time, none other can receive such glorification. Although inconceivable, Catholicism claims that Mary shares the redemptive process with Jesus (as the Co-Redemptrix). The **third thing** or violation of God's nature is placing Mary in a position where she receives prayer. That is, she is a mediator and referred to as the Mediatrix since she is the object of prayer that she takes to Jesus. The reality is Catholics pray directly to Mary and look for her to answer their prayers as two popes have done in this chapter. The Catholic inventions are not well thought out, but there is no concern when you have a limitless supply of apologists. They will find a way to convince Catholics and perhaps others but never fool one who loves the truth. Since there is zero scriptural authority for Mariology, there will always be blunders. Apparently, Jesus was not sufficient in the roles of redemption or mediator. The proper characterization for Mariology, in a word, is idolatry.

1 Timothy 2:5

5 For there is one God and one Mediator between God and men, the Man Christ Jesus,

Only those "in Christ" can go to God in prayer via one mediator, and only they have an advocate with the Father, namely Jesus. Jesus is the one mediator in prayer and is the advocate in relation to a child of God seeking forgiveness of sin.

2 John 2:1-2

1 My little children, these things I write to you, so that you may not sin. And if anyone sins, we have an Advocate with the Father, Jesus Christ the righteous.
2 And He Himself is the propitiation for our sins, and not for ours only but also for the whole world.

Since Jesus added those obedient to His spiritual body, He knows who they are and can allow the transmission (prayer) to the Father. Jesus knows the heart of each person, and Mary, of course, does not. Catholicism fails in everything because they do not respect the word of God and do not understand the perfection of God in everything. You see when God declares there is one mediator between God and man, that eliminates any other way, any other being.

In Catholicism, there is a grand disregard for the scriptures as they are always trying to find a way to change the clear meaning. One mediator means one mediator. I often refer to the things written for our learning from the Old Testament (Romans 15:4). Many of those things emphasize God's seriousness, even the seriousness of the **details** of His directions. In terms of worship, the case of Nadab and Abihu is for your understanding of God.

Leviticus 10:1-2

1 Then Nadab and Abihu, the sons of Aaron, each took his censer and put fire in it, put incense on it, and offered profane fire before the Lord, which He had not commanded them.
2 So fire went out from the Lord and devoured them, and they died before the Lord.

The sons of Aaron, priests themselves, decide to change the type of fire specified (likely an unauthorized incense), which was unacceptable. God means what He says and that includes the detailed description of the fire. God means one mediator and all the apologetic excuses; all the Catholic reasoning will not change this.

The instance above regarding Pope John Paul II's allegiance to Mary and Pope Francis praying to Mary demonstrates Catholicism's claim they do not worship Mary is a lie. The popes have zero knowledge of the truth and zero respect for the word of God. They all know 1 Timothy 2:5 very well but do not honor it and consequently do not honor God. There is only one way to reject Catholicism: that is to reject all of Catholicism – there is no truth there.

11.5 Penalty for Idolatry

Revelation 21:8

*8 "But the cowardly, unbelieving, abominable, murderers, sexually immoral, sorcerers, **idolaters**, and all liars shall have their part in the lake which burns with fire and brimstone, which is the second death."*

A person might consider Mariology as not important. Like so much of Catholicism, Mariology is a distraction from what people need. Mariology is a sub-distraction as Catholicism is the prime distraction. Yet any of these sub-distractions such as Mariology, the "Real Presence," purgatory can overcome a person. **It is not just Mary. It is not just the pope. It is not just any one thing. It is everything. It is idolatry. Idolatry equals Catholicism.** It is the opposition to the God of the Bible, to our Creator.

Distractions hide the truth because people think they have the truth. It is easy to observe that Catholicism does not have an association with God – they never have and they never will. The most fundamental aspect of the message from God does not exist within Catholicism, although "many, many other things do." The "many, many other things" are all the additions and subtractions to the word of God. Since Catholicism does not have a correct understanding of the gospel message, there has never been an eternally successful Catholic. Idolatry is much more than having some namable other gods. Idolatry is 2 John 1:9, "Whoever transgresses and does not abide in the doctrine of Christ does not have God. He who abides in the doctrine of Christ has both the Father and the Son." So a person who does not have God but claims to have God has another god. The differentiator is those who have the doctrine of Christ and those who do not. Revelation 21:8 points to a bad ending and you can call it idolatry, lying or unbelieving, or all of them.

11.6 The core issue of Mariology

The subject of Mariology addresses the honor, respect, worship of Mary. In a religious sense, only God is to receive worship, religious honor. There is a strict manner of approaching God, and it is specified. We have discussed how God was gracious in revealing so much about life and Himself. We have suggested and shown that God is the perfect absence of evil, which means He cannot share His Divine Nature with sin (evil). Much of our understanding of God's test requires this understanding and then seriously seeking God and truth. Sometimes we need to stop and realize we are dealing with God, and it would be an infinite understatement to say we are not in His league. The two verses that follow are easily understood but seldom grasped in their magnitude.

Isaiah 55:9

9 "For the heavens are higher than the earth, So are My ways higher than your ways, And My thoughts than your thoughts.

Jeremiah 10:23

23 O Lord, I know the way of man is not in himself; It is not in man who walks to direct his own steps.

The magnitude that is not understood is how much higher are God's ways. Infinitely higher would be one way to express this. How close is humankind to being able to direct their own steps? **Even the apostles were not able to direct their own steps**. Jesus sent them the Holy Spirit. The **early church fathers** were exceedingly distant from being able to direct their own steps. The things they wrote should only be considered valuable if they are consistent with the word of God.

Indeed, God's ways and thoughts are infinitely higher, and we can only have the correct understanding of life and post-life if He reveals those things. God is approachable, but only in the way He specifies. If we consider the route to God in prayer, it would be as a child of God, one "in Christ" praying to God the Father and doing that via the mediator, that is by Jesus. The prayer **to the Father** ends in the **name of Jesus,** that is, by the authority of Jesus. You might see the difficulty in fitting Mary into this picture. Indeed, God's way is formal and straightforward, and there is no other way. We are dealing with God, the Creator, and nothing is casual about such an excellent relationship. It is careless, disrespectful to God to suggest any other route to Him. Those who invented these "Mariology things" had an abysmal foundational understanding of God. Only Jesus could be the head of His spiritual church. Only Jesus, by His addition of one to His body (in their obedience), can allow that "now sinless person" to approach God in prayer. God opened the door allowing those "in Christ" via their obedience to the Son of God to access Him directly by the mediator. It is enough to make one tremble with humility, knowing the love of God toward us personally.

Note: A point of clarity regarding obedience. There is the obedience of Jesus in relation to the Father and the obedience of those obeying the gospel in gaining a relationship with the Son. In two short verses, there is a good understanding of this.

Hebrews 5:8-9

8 though He was a Son, yet He learned obedience by the things which He suffered.

9 And having been perfected, He became the author of eternal salvation to all who obey Him

This chapter could be very long in showing the poor scholarship of Catholicism in justifying the special honor for Mary. However, it is not needed since all that is required is to understand two principles from God. As you might expect, it would be good not to violate the principles of God. The first principle is God's sovereignty and the subsequent respect required, and the second is God's defined means to access Him. That means of access is by His Son, and that eliminates all other ways.

Mary is a blessed person, and that blessing continues since Mary announces in Luke 1:48 that *"all generations will call me blessed."* Yet, there is no particular honor paid to Mary in the scriptures.

1 Timothy 2:5

For there is one God and one Mediator between God and men, the Man Christ Jesus,

Can someone make a case for praying to Mary? Of course, that is what apologists do! All one has to do is disrespect the God of heaven in His declaration made in 1 Timothy 2:5.

11.7 Mariology – one last thing, Dr. Hahn

I completed this chapter and, in fact, this book when I came across a video (below) by Dr. Hahn on Mary. It touted the honor and worship of Mary, even including Mary as Co-Redemptrix Mediatrix and Advocate. It is worth a brief discussion.

Of course, Catholics say it is not worship, but their extreme religious honor for Mary disputes that claim. These two things (Mary's part in salvation and prayer) are the vilest in terms of disrespect for God. It was clear that Dr. Hahn spoke as a Catholic as he provided his reasoning in justification of the Catholic honor given to Mary. His arguments, as might be expected, are physical, involving human reason, and thus appealing. In this age of Catholicism, there must be Bible verses, so verses are used, albeit twisted, to make his points. The twisting would be evident to those with some Bible knowledge, but Catholics generally still lack the Bible fundamentals. Dr. Hahn calls Mary, God's greatest creation and then goes to an early church father for support. Dr. Hahn has become one who carelessly handles the scriptures by never addressing the issues that vehemently oppose this idea of Mariology. The thinking part of this Mariology doctrine should be questioning the purpose of this special honor for Mary **relative to God's purpose**. God's purpose has been completed, and people now have a relationship with God. That relationship came about without Mary being honored. She played a part, as did so many, and it was essential as were so many others. The truth is Catholicism gets everything wrong, and there is no road to success within Catholicism. Like Catholicism, Mariology is a distraction from the truth, being an attractive element in maintaining Catholics' faithfulness. It is faithfulness in the Catholic Church, not in God. Dr. Hahn is a disappointment in his speech on this occasion by saying much but nothing of value. He was enhancing what all the cradle Catholics already knew regarding devotion to Mary. However, Dr. Hahn provides reasons to heighten their devotion to Mary. Those people hearing Dr. Hahn need the gospel message, but that is not in Catholic doctrine. So they sit and listen to something that has no connection to God's purpose but is perfectly consistent with their indoctrination.

We have the same problem throughout all Catholic doctrine, and it is a disrespect for the word of God. God's word is perfect in achieving His purpose. As God completed His communication with humankind, there was, as always, a focus on His purpose. God left nothing out that was needed, that is, that would help a person to succeed. The honor for Mary did not come from God but was just another invention in support of the Catholic Church. Although Dr. Hahn tries to justify the exceedingly high honor for Mary as Co-Redemptrix, Mediatrix, and

Advocate using the Old Testament, it amounts to his conjecture and certainly not doctrine. Thus throughout his talk, there are references to the early church fathers, the popes, and the Catholic Magisterium to support this honor for Mary. God is perfect in leaving humankind with what they need to succeed, and Mary plays no part in a person's success. Dr. Hahn is consistent in Catholic methodology in bringing another mystery when God has indicated there are no more mysteries. The irony of Catholicism is in its distractions (such as Mariology) that allow Catholicism to thrive while disguising the things every person needs. In our case (Dr. Hahn's video on Mariology), there is an auditorium full of people listening to Dr. Hahn talk about the "Marian doctrine" when every person in the room needs forgiveness of sins.

Chapter 12
Early church fathers, tradition, and the Magisterium

The early church fathers are discussed throughout this book, and some important conclusions were disclosed. Those conclusions will be further solidified in this chapter. Who are the early church fathers? What is the early church? The early church refers to the church that Christ started in the first century after His death, burial, and resurrection and its progression through about the early seventh century. This period following the inspired period of the first century would unofficially be the early church. The teachings of these early church fathers (really church leaders who did considerable writing) developed a varied mix of the truth and error representative of those churches in different localities. I sometimes refer to these early church fathers as "so-called early church fathers" because, without the so-called preface, it might seem that they have some authority. They had zero authority, and knew they were not inspired. Thus all their writings are not of any value unless they were consistent with the word of God. It is extreme disrespect to God to consider these persons in any special way, in any way capable of bringing the truth different than the scriptures. Nonetheless, I will drop the "so-called" for convenience. Another thing about these early church fathers is that they produced different conclusions in their writings as would be expected since they were not inspired. Their particular individual prominence in more modern times was affected by a favoring of specific things they wrote.

12.1 Writings of the early church fathers reveals confusion

First, there is a tremendous amount of material written by the early church fathers, and there are many different opinions. You can find about anything and frequently quite the opposite on the same issues. In a very brief analysis, three early church fathers indicated baptism was required for salvation, and three said it was unnecessary. One of the early church fathers (Origen 185-254) who supported baptism for salvation went on to claim, "The Church received from the Apostles the tradition of giving Baptism even to infants." This is undoubtedly one of the most oppositional teachings to God's word and reveals the apparent reason why these writings cannot be trusted. Why would anyone ever consider thinking there was any authority in the writings of these early church fathers? Let's take this **statement from Origen** and show how wrong it is, "The Church received from the Apostles the tradition of giving Baptism even to infants." Here is what the scriptures teach and would have been what the apostles knew to be true. Namely, look at the conversions of the New Testament and realize not only were there no infants but that infants would not qualify.

https://heavencoach.com/conversions-of-the-new-testament/

Look at the site below to understand infants have no sin as well as not qualifying as fit subjects for baptism. This document also easily rejects the Catholic invention of original sin.

https://catholicsquestion.com/the-fall-of-catholicism-and-protestantism-in-one-simple-lesson/

It is so easy for someone, in this case, Origen, to say the church (meaning the early church) received from the apostles the tradition of baptizing infants. The term Origen uses here is tradition instead of referring to something taught in the scriptures. The apostles were not passing down tradition but the word of God. Even when there was a favorable use of the word tradition, we have seen it was connected with something from inspiration – it would eventually become scripture. These early church fathers were just men with their ideas, with their private interpretations, and not to be compared with God's means of delivering the truth, namely, "holy men of God spoke as the Holy Spirit moved them." Of course, Origin and other early church fathers are honored (by Catholicism) in their writings because they form the basis for Catholic doctrine. Thus you can expect them to be defended even in the case of this downright lie regarding the apostle's support for infant baptism. God is perfect in His insistence about not changing His word as humankind will not get it right. They will tamper with the word of God and, in effect, damage God's purpose.

There was an amazing amount of scripture in these early times, but different "pieces of scripture" were held by different groups. The one obvious thing they were lacking was the Bible, the group of books we have today. That would have assisted their understanding. Today, we have the Bible, and Catholicism still looks back to the first few centuries of extreme confusion to validate their doctrines. One wonders how the Catholic Church ended up with their teachings, and **it is clear that instead of having a basis in the scriptures, they took a significant part of their doctrine from the early church fathers**. As suggested throughout this book, the early church fathers were not the early fathers of the church Christ started but became the early church fathers of the falling away. Catholicism has been able to sell the idea that the early church father's writings are authoritative even though the scriptures indicate only God's word is authoritative. One should want to know which of the early church father's writings are authoritative. How can doctrines originating from them be validated with all the variation and the various persons who might be considered early church fathers? That is easy. The Catholic Church determines valid doctrine. There is so much at stake, namely your soul. There is certainty in the scriptures because God desiring your success, sends the Holy Spirit to assure you have the truth.

Some of what the early church fathers wrote was correct as long as it was consistent with the scriptures, but often they went further with their ideas, maybe things they thought were needed. Origen was mentioned above in writing that the church received from the apostles the tradition of baptizing babies. This idea violates every aspect of scripture as delivered by the Holy Spirit, and no apostle led by the Holy Spirit would ever indicate such a thing. Indeed the scriptures indicate such an idea opposes the will of God. So, where did Origen get such an idea? Who knows? Fortunately, those who love the truth do not follow the traditions of men, the thoughts of humankind but God's word.

12.2 The evolution of Catholic doctrine

God does not allow changing His word since the truth will disappear. In place of the truth will be something very human and thus could be appealing. These early writings of the church fathers became the basis of Catholicism instead of the scriptures. **Catholicism has no scriptural validity for what would become their core values. Thus they must rely on the early church father's writings. After all, it turns out those were where their values, where Catholic teachings originated.** The early church fathers delivered a mix of scriptures and what they believed. We might say things evolved **out of control** as things like the earthly rule for the church was in some of the early church fathers writings as was some interspersing of the "Real Presence," as was the idea of purgatory and honor for Mary, and Catholicism was just around the corner. Then in Rome, Christianity, or what was thought to be Christianity, was allowed the freedom to practice their beliefs. This ended up bringing more practices of the world into the church. Constantine seeking to clarify what seemed to be the confusion of Christianity, called the first church council. This, of course, would be something very alien to the scriptures, to the organization authorized by God. We were moving from God being the authority to councils of men making the rules. It is a movement from the spiritual to the physical, and in that (physical) condition, there is no value, there is no salvation. The fact that the local bishops accepted and participated in the first church council means the word of God had seriously deteriorated, and one has to wonder if any were Christians, especially in the area of Rome. Catholics like to tie their origins back to the first-century church authorized by the apostles through the Holy Spirit. Catholicism "in doctrine" had appeared to some extent by the fourth century, and sometime before that, the church belonging to Christ had been declining especially in the area of Rome. The church Jesus was building remained in existence although significantly reduced, mainly due to persecution and collaboration with paganism. Yet, some churches established by Paul likely continued to be faithful at this time in certain parts of the world. The argument can also be made that Catholicism without the name was present as early as the doctrine of Christ was being abandoned in the late first century. The point of disassociation would be when the gospel message was changed such that the Lord could no longer add any to His spiritual body, the church. Catholicism in name officially came into being with their first pope, likely pope Boniface III, in 607 AD.

*Note: We need to pause and consider what happened to cause the gradual transition of the church of the first century from good to evil. There was a particular attractiveness of the early church father's writings because they provided the possibility of power, of authority to certain persons. In contrast, the church being built by Jesus provided no earthly benefit to the leadership. "Pre-Catholicism" would latch onto the early church father's writings, and they would be the basis of Catholicism – of what would become the Roman Catholic Church. How do I know they did this? I could say I do not know, but **what happened** is compelling evidence. The Lord's church, with all its virtue, humility, unselfishness, turning of the other cheek, giving up its* *individuality to live for Christ and the gospel was indeed as God designed. The Catholic Church appearance would be the opposite of those things. Catholicism would be the scripture-rejecting force that sought to destroy anyone who opposed them, and that would mean discrediting, torturing, murdering, and doing whatever was necessary. They had to do this because there was no scriptural support for their existence. This power-based paranoid religion was a physical religion and in no way solved the spiritual problem that the church Jesus was building came to resolve.*

"Pre-Catholicism" refers to whatever was brewing in the background in the early centuries that accepted certain selected writings of the early church fathers and was supported by various individuals looking for some earthly value in the church. Some such persons were the bishops of Rome before the seventh century that claimed authority over all the church. They referred to themselves with titles like Vicar of Christ, Vicar of God, Ruler of the church of God, universal bishop. Their intentions were to rule, have authority, and thus something very different from the leadership of the church designed by the Lord. It is this lust for power that was a significant reason the church transitioned from good to evil.

Catholicism in their councils, **sanctions** all the illegitimate means used to establish their authority

Those essential characteristics of Catholicism were a pope (universal bishop over all Christians), the associated apostolic succession, and of course, the associated rule-making. Thus over the early centuries, there were church councils and an abundance of rules. Eventually, their councils would validate the methods they were using. Such a case would be the Second Vatican Council (1962-1965), where the scriptures were placed on par with traditions of the early church fathers and their teaching Magisterium. The bright light, which was the word of God, has dimmed. People would think of Christianity as Catholicism. There would be no salvation. There were still people who knew the scriptures doing the right things, and that included salvation. They were few.

We knew there would be a falling away, and we can see its beginning in the writings of these early church fathers. The thing that characterizes the falling away is differences in the **meaning** of God's word – private interpretations. It requires a great deal of care to always be consistent with the word of God. These early churches had some accurate oral content (conversations) carried down into their times and all or most all of the inspired writings. Undoubtedly, each church did not have all the New Testament, but there was a considerable amount of scripture in the time of these early churches. They were not all gathered into one book until about the fifth century. Considering God's oversight, they had a great deal of the scripture and had a great deal of oral transfer from person to person. Unfortunately, the oral transfer cannot be correctly sustained. It is reasonable to think there were errors in both oral and non-inspired written transmission, but more things were correct than incorrect in the earliest years. The verbal instructions that came down can only be confirmed if they were eventually found in the inspired written documentation. These early church fathers were not infallible but had a certain amount of influence, and their non-inspired writings contained truth (from the scriptures). Again, the error is always defined by things inconsistent with the word of God. As time passed, some of the early church father's writings, personal interpretations took on prominence as various persons desired their teachings to be considered "valuable."

Catholics use the scripts of the early church fathers such as Justin Martyr, Tertullian, Clement of Rome, Ignatius, Polycarp, Hermas, Barnabas, Papias, Ambrose, Augustine, Jerome, and many more to validate Catholic teachings. Although the first two centuries get the most emphasis, the writings of these early church fathers are used extensively for various Catholic evidence through about the fifth century. They do this by claiming that the apostle's authority was passed on to others by the apostles. They might point out that the early church fathers had or may have had direct contact with some of the apostles and passed along other truths. They use the writing of these early church fathers to justify the transfer of apostolic authority through the ages. Specifically, the authority is transferred from one pope to the next. Such doctrines as the Real Presence of Christ in the taking of the bread and the fruit of the vine appear in some of their writings. The word Eucharist is also seen in some of their writings. The "idea of purgatory" is in usage by some of these early writers. The critical element for Catholics is validating their authority over all Christians and specifically via their pope. They could be correct if these early church father's writing were inspired, but they were not and were often in opposition to the scriptures.

The many problems with valuing the writings of the early church fathers

Jesus took great care in announcing the church very gradually from the beginning of His ministry as initially being referred to as the kingdom and specifying its character in various ways such as **not being of this world**, and by a variety of parables such as the parable of the Sower. **The seed of the kingdom is the word of God.** These two qualities define the fundamental nature of the church as being **spiritual** and having its basis in the **word of God**. Of course, everything is being done with God's purpose in mind, namely the salvation of souls, the forgiveness of sins. The kingdom would be spiritual. That is, the church would be spiritual, and those in the kingdom would be spiritual. There would be one rule book, and it would be the word of God, and people were to enter the kingdom in response to the word of God being planted in their hearts. It would be planted there by preaching as the scriptures indicate in 1 Corinthians 1:18-24, "it pleased God through the foolishness of the message preached to save those who believe." The faith that God requires to be pleased (Hebrews 11:6) comes only from the word of God. Jesus was with the apostles before and after His death, burial, and resurrection, speaking of the kingdom. Late in His ministry, as the time for Him to fulfill His mission nears, He introduces the church and promises the Holy Spirit to guide the apostles into all truth. Everything happens as God plans as those with good hearts receive and obey the gospel message, and the reconciliation designed since Genesis 3:15 has been achieved. The local church is gradually and wholly revealed, and God completes His communication with humankind, and thus the work of the Holy Spirit is completed. What is missing? Absolutely nothing is missing, but there needs to be more to satisfy humankind, and the early church fathers bring additions and subtractions to what God has completed.

Since creation, everything that God has done has fit perfectly together as would be expected from God. Realize God's perfection in everything. There is perfection and simplicity, but in humankind, there is pride, there is a better way, and it began in Galatians by changing the gospel message and continues in the early church with many "great ideas." It is inconceivable to look at what God has done carefully, accurately in bringing the message of reconciliation via His Spirit and then throw it "out the window" by accepting the writings of uninspired men who frequently disagree. The church belonging to the Lord is not what humankind wants, very much like the Jews wanted a different Messiah, a very physical Messiah, a ruler, a powerful earthly king. However, in this case, humankind will make the changes they need to have a temporal rule. It might start innocently enough by adding a little here, modifying this or that from the word of

God but always headed towards something more favorable to humankind's thinking – something seeable, touchable – something like signs, wonders. The seriousness of God's word is underestimated. When people think the directions from God are trivial, when they think, "God is love," means He will look past certain sins and allow certain excuses they do not understand God! Here is how God views His love; first, it is on the cross of Christ, and second it is if you love God, you will keep His commandments. The things that are important in the message of Christ relate to the soul, and that message is destroyed when people reject God's word by changing it, by being careless in handling it. These early church fathers with absolutely no authority began to create their views of God's message, and some may have believed they were helping but "down the road," there would be those who would use what they wrote and make it authoritative. The Catholic church doctrine is based on the men looking at other men's writings, picking and choosing words that support their beliefs, and claiming it to be from God.

At a high level, you can get a good idea of what occurred. Below is a chart of the early history of Christianity, **and in its simplicity, it is devastatingly accurate** in describing what happened. It also reveals something that would be expected when the seriousness of God's word is ignored. The church Jesus is building will not exist in the form that allows its purpose to be fulfilled - **if the word of God is changed**. That is, if the doctrine of Christ is altered or very specifically if the gospel message is changed. Obviously, whenever humankind becomes involved in making the rules for God, the truth will be lost, and there will be disagreement. It did not take long for humankind to butcher the truth that God so carefully delivered. Thus it should be no wonder, after all this time, the truth is exceedingly distant from the religions of the world.

The early history of the Christian church

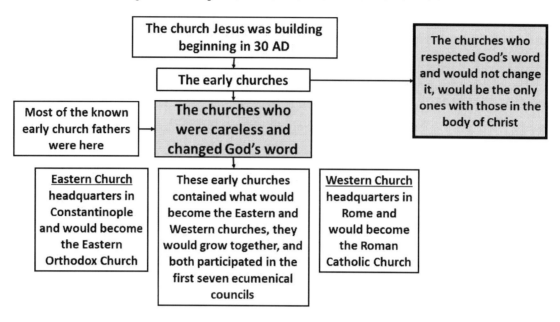

The church Jesus was building beginning in 30 AD

The early churches

The churches who respected God's word and would not change it, would be the only ones with those in the body of Christ

Most of the known early church fathers were here

The churches who were careless and changed God's word

Eastern Church headquarters in Constantinople and would become the Eastern Orthodox Church

These early churches contained what would become the Eastern and Western churches, they would grow together, and both participated in the first seven ecumenical councils

Western Church headquarters in Rome and would become the Roman Catholic Church

Both Eastern and Western churches were developing differently, and the early church councils were a place to attempt to resolve issues. This should indicate the inconsistency of the early church fathers in relation to doctrine. That is, their writings varied from the scriptures and in different ways. God's concern for getting the truth to people is validated by the carelessness in handling His word. The Eastern and Western churches used the writings of the early church fathers in their development. Yet they both believed very differently. Any movement away from the scriptures would result in something very different than God's intention. It would not be long before there was no resemblance with the church Jesus was building. The scriptures are the one valid source of truth and God warns they must not be changed.

The bottom line is that the scriptures exhibit perfect credibility. The early church fathers were not credible, and this may not have been obvious in their earliest writings since they were just beginning to move away from the truth. Any movement from the truth is serious, albeit perhaps not noticed. However, we have the advantage of seeing forward in history and realize these two factions of Christianity would evolve to the Eastern Orthodox Church and the Roman

Catholic Church. It seemed they lived **early on without many disputes** as they were, after all, just the very early churches. There were inevitable disagreements. The place for resolving these was the church councils. If asked which of these two ended up closer to the truth than the other, the answer would be, "close does not matter." There is truth, and there is error, and both had much error, thus both fail. However, against my better judgment and because there is some value in demonstrating their extreme differences and their consequences, there is a noteworthy distinction. Again, both possessed a considerable amount of scripture, and we might say they were both working from essentially the same playbook. As time passes, it seems the Eastern Orthodox church is closer to the truth, and with some study, it appears it has to do with the character of individuals. These differences grow to be more significant, but authority over the church is the most important conflict. Much further in the future, the Eastern Orthodox and Roman Catholic Churches grow markedly farther apart on doctrine and eventually totally sever connections on July 16, 1054 AD. This event is called the Great Schism. On that day, the Patriarch of Constantinople was excommunicated from the Catholic Church by Rome.

There were three causes of the great schism:
- Dispute over the use of images in the church.
- The addition of the Latin word Filioque to the Nicene Creed.
  - This Filioque dispute has to do with whether the Holy Spirit proceeds from the Father - (Orthodox) or from the Father **and** the Son (Roman Catholic).
- Dispute about leadership in the church regarding who should lead and even if there should be a single leader.

Although there are three issues involved, there was only one, and it had been there for the longest time, namely the church's leadership. It is all about church authority.

The Orthodox church was a **fellowship of independent churches** with the ecumenical patriarch of Constantinople holding the formal title or honorary primacy. The Roman church was always seeking to have a universal bishop over all of Christianity. Eventually, as we know, Rome would have their universal bishop, their pope.

I began this ill-advised "journey" to indicate which of these two churches was closer to the truth. The Eastern Orthodox Church recognized from the scriptures that the New Testament churches were **independent with local governance**. They also saw that there was no single earthly head over the church. Many bad things can happen if there is a single head and no one knows this better than God.

12.3 God's wisdom in the design of the local church

There is something that seems obvious and very insightful to me, and it is how God in His wisdom designed His local church to be independent, with no central rule for the churches. There would be no earthly head over the church, just those qualified elders and deacons but always in the role of servants and, of course, the only rule being the scriptures. Indeed, perfect God means perfect method. With a bit of thought, one might realize this independence of the local churches was also a means to guarantee separation of church and state. **The local church would never have any jurisdiction over any other local church.** Indeed the local church would only be local. This seems brilliant. God is consistent and perfect in defining the local church, and as He requires in everything, the details of His directives must be honored. The Eastern Orthodox Churches could see this pattern in the scriptures. Thus they have no ruling head of the church and have independent churches around the world. I do not know the extent they have always maintained it, but it was in their comprehension of the scriptures. The character of Catholicism was very different, with the bishops of Rome always seeking control over all of Christendom. This ruling mania is bad enough if you consider these people making the rules, but as is so often the problem with power, it becomes a never-ending quest for more and more power. Thus, in addition to ruling over Christians, there was a desire to have nations fall under the popes' control. They accomplished much of their desire to dominate the world, and in the process, nothing was to be held back, including torture, murder, and every evil thing. The amount of evil from the Eastern Orthodox Church is essentially negligible in comparison. The Roman Catholic Church had the intense ambition to rule, and an organization that included all their churches worldwide would provide the means to carry out their various agendas. Theirs was not the local organization demanded by the scriptures, nor were their leaders the character of those "in Christ." The New Testament pattern of the local church without a central head was in the mind of the Eastern Orthodox Church. If we seek root cause for the Roman Catholic way, it would be envisioning an earthly leadership for the church Jesus built, an error beginning with privately interpreting Matthew 16:18.

12.4 Early church fathers and Peter as the rock

We have shown that Peter was not the rock in Chapters 6 and 9 and provided the correct meaning consistent with God's purpose and all scripture. Nonetheless, what was the belief of the early church fathers in this regard? It is fair to say that some of them did see Peter as the rock, and indeed at **"first glance of Matthew 16:18,"** this seems a remote possibility. It is an abhorrently flawed conclusion if you understand God's purpose. At a high level, this means that all God has done in creation, in bringing Christ to be the perfect sacrifice opening the door to reconciliation, was to have Peter in some way have the church built on him. Chapters 6 and 9 destroy such an idea. Those who reached such a conclusion were not thinking, which shows why God did not leave the truth in the hands of any person. The one thing God continually warns against is changing His word. In this regard, He is severe, and here are a few verses in Proverbs that point out the seriousness of following God's directions, of heeding His advice, and His **no-mercy attitude** to those who reject Him. Making Peter the rock is truly rejecting God, and one can expect God to be displeased. Proverbs 1:24-29 is a warning to those who reject God's Council.

Proverbs 1:24-29

24 Because I have called and you refused,

I have stretched out my hand and no one regarded,

25 Because you disdained all my counsel,

And would have none of my rebuke,

26 I also will laugh at your calamity;

I will mock when your terror comes,

27 When your terror comes like a storm,

And your destruction comes like a whirlwind,

When distress and anguish come upon you.

28 "Then they will call on me, but I will not answer;

They will seek me diligently, but they will not find me.

29 Because they hated knowledge

And did not choose the fear of the LORD,

God wants a person to take Him seriously. There is nothing more disrespectful than to change the meaning of God's word. It is not carelessness; it is not even difficult to understand God's meaning of Matthew 16:18 because it is the consistent message of all scripture. In the presence of the Jews and all of Jesus' miracles, the Jewish leaders got it all wrong, and it was not carelessness, but it was what **they wanted** from the Messiah that Jesus did not bring. I do not know how some of the early church fathers determined that Peter was the head of the church and that there would be successors to Peter. Of course, one can create a vaguely reasonable-sounding story in that regard from carelessly handling the scriptures. Indeed, in some way, this is what happened and remains convincing to this day within Catholicism. However, Jesus is the head of the church and the rock on which the reconciliation is based. This is the correct meaning when the word of God is properly handled.

The writings of a few early church fathers and the desire of some seeking power in ruling over Christianity has destroyed so many souls

Someone envisioned Matthew 16 could be used to gain control over Christianity. Namely by placing a man, namely Peter, in a place of authority over the church and then the subsequent succession of that position. Sadly, much time is needed to refute the silliness of the private interpretation of these verses. In this book, primarily Chapters six and eight and other places are devoted to ending the nonsense. These verses form the basis of Catholicism but are also the core of God's planned reconciliation. God has fit everything perfectly together to resolve the problem of sin, and the means of doing that are revealed in Matthew 16:15-19. It had been 4000 years leading to the announcement of Jesus as the solution.

Despite the clear understanding of these verses, there will be those who will not accept the truth due to Catholic Church loyalty. Thus we continue with discussing these verses to help. A casual observer of Matthew 16:18 (and surrounding verses) might question the wording, "And I also say to you that you are Peter, and on this rock, I will build My church." It might seem that

Jesus does not need to say, "**you are Peter, and on this rock**." Why doesn't He just say, "**And I also say to you I will build my church**." That is because the rock is a specific component of Jesus, namely the **acknowledgment** of Jesus as the Son of God. This is what men must acknowledge and once acknowledged, follow the directions of Jesus to be saved. It is what Peter preached on the first day of the church, "let all the house of Israel know assuredly that God has made this Jesus, whom you crucified, both Lord and Christ."

Acts 2:36-38

36 "Therefore let all the house of Israel know assuredly that God has made this Jesus, whom you crucified, both Lord and Christ."

37 Now when they heard this, they were cut to the heart, and said to Peter and the rest of the apostles, "Men and brethren, what shall we do?"

38 Then Peter said to them, "Repent, and let every one of you be baptized in the name of Jesus Christ for the remission of sins; and you shall receive the gift of the Holy Spirit.

Peter was not the rock and never assumed such a position. Jesus as the Son of God was the **"rock to be acknowledged."** Indeed, this is what happened in every conversion. Then upon a person's obedience, Jesus added them to His spiritual body, the church.

Note: One more thing on Matthew 16:18 that ought to make a person think.

Matthew 16:18

18 And I also say to you that you are Peter, and on this rock I will build My church."

The verse **could have read**, "you are Peter, and on you, I will build my church." That is not what was said, and that was not what was meant. Realize that on these few words in Matthew 16:16-19, we have a pope, earthly authority in the pope, and the Catholic Church. We have over fifty-plus years of inspiration, and Peter is never mentioned with such authority. There is no discussion of a succession of the apostles, and there is no earthly head of the church. What the apostles did know was that the Holy Spirit led them into all truth. They knew that Jesus was the head of the church. Catholics try to make the case that Peter was the head of the apostles, but that never happens. God blessed him to be intimately involved in bringing the gospel message first to the Jews and then first to the Gentiles. Other of the apostles also were blessed in various ways. To imagine a man standing in place of God, in place of God's Son. It is the exact definition of idolatry.

The good work of the early church fathers

(Amid hard-hitting criticism of the early church fathers, there is this good characterization)

The value of the work of the early church fathers was in their collection and copying of the new testament writings. The writings of these early church fathers from the late first century through about the fifth century contain the vast majority, perhaps all of the New Testament. Much of the scriptures may not be from copying entire letters or gospels but just quotes from those documents. Clement, Ignatius, and Polycarp quoted from every book in the New Testament except Jude and 2 John in the period between 95 to 110 AD. This was the nature of the activity that continued throughout the early centuries.

The early church fathers did not consider their writings inspired or in any way from God. Their writings were historical, and yet Catholicism would use their scripts to justify many of their doctrines. They wrote things inconsistent with the scriptures, often their private interpretations. Perhaps they believed there were better ways of doing things. Catholics claim these early church fathers provided tradition that was valid for the church, as correct as the scriptures. Of course, they have to go to the scriptures to justify this, and they might use passages like 2 Thessalonians 2:15 and 2 Thessalonians 3:6.

2 Thessalonians 2:15

15 Therefore, brethren, stand fast and hold the traditions which you were taught, whether by word or our epistle.

2 Thessalonians 3:6

6 But we command you, brethren, in the name of our Lord Jesus Christ, that you withdraw from every brother who walks disorderly and not according to the tradition which he received from us.

There is a discussion of these verses used by Catholicism to support the tradition of the early church father's writings as authoritative. Please read, Chapter 6 under the fourth verse Marcus Grodi did not correctly understand. That discussion is thorough and scriptural and shows that these verses above cannot validate early church traditions.

12.5 Catholicism must validate themselves outside the scriptures

There is nothing more critical to Catholicism than being able to **make the rules**. They claim apostolic succession is God's way and primarily in the form of their pope. They assert from these early church writings that there is a continual living direction via apostolic succession. There are endless problems with this thinking, and many are discussed in this book. The root problem is, as usual, that the fundamentals are wrong. You cannot build doctrine on a bad foundation, as those new doctrines can be no better than the foundation. In the second century, some in the church were discussing the Real Presence version of the Lord's Supper or speaking of the idea of purgatory as doctrine or accepting the idea of a hierarchy that was over all the Christian churches. It does not mean they were right, but the error that Christ predicted and the error Paul spoke of in changing the gospel message had indeed infiltrated what some people considered Christianity. The missing basics would be the correct understanding of Matthew 16:16-19, John 6:32-55, and Mark 14:22-25, to mention a few.

The ten key aspects destroying this ongoing (post scripture) revelation theory would be:

- In Galatians 1:6-9, Paul declared there were those changing the gospel. This is important because Catholics use the proximity of the late first and second centuries to say the apostles and these early church fathers represented a continuum of the church from the time of inspiration. However, they were not inspired, and the early proximity is meaningless since the perverted doctrines that Paul referred to were contemporary with his inspired writings. **Early in no way means they are right. Right means inspired.**
- The meaning of valid tradition (see Chapter 6 – fourth verse not seen by Marcus Grodi) is different from how Catholicism randomly validates early church father's writings by calling them legitimate tradition. Paul mentioned some tradition as legitimate because he

had previously spoken it (but it was not yet written). These valid statements (now referenced as tradition) were things delivered to him by the Holy Spirit.

- The **apostles never originated doctrine** but received the truth from the Holy Spirit and taught it, and some recorded it – scripture. Nothing can be added to what was recorded throughout the time the Holy Spirit guided them, as, during that time, God also completed His revelation to humankind.

- Catholic created doctrine is the exact opposite of very specific inspired teachings. There is a consistent pattern of Catholic teachings that goes directly against the word of God. Throughout this book, those things are revealed.

- The most fundamental of all of God's rules is not to change the word of God. There must be no additions to or subtractions from the word of God.

- The insinuation that Peter was the rock of Matthew 16:18 is more than terribly wrong, but it destroys the entirety of God's purpose and would not allow God to keep His promises. That is why there is absolutely no truth in such a conclusion. Moreover, God is clear that the rock was the acknowledgment of Jesus as God's Son. There is nothing of greater clarity from God than this essential understanding. Jesus is the awaited Messiah, soon to be the solution and then the head of the church.

- Peter confirms that we have "all things pertaining to life and godliness." It is not hard to understand the meaning of "that which is perfect" from 1 Corinthians 13:8-10 if you love the truth. The correct understanding of "that which is perfect" is that God's word is completed. God has successfully achieved His purpose, and persons have been reconciled to Him – sins have been forgiven. **There is no longer the need for signs, miracles but in the fullness of time, everything that God wished to pass along to humankind has been revealed, and it is much more powerful than any other means to continue to fulfill His purpose.** We have had over 1900 years with God's completed word, and some have aligned with the truth. Catholicism has been the opposition, but the good news is that the word of God can easily show anyone with a good heart, with a love of the truth, the way of righteousness.

- The promised binding and loosening were achieved after the Holy Spirit in Acts 2 delivered to the apostles the gospel message that they were to teach. Thus the initial binding and loosening done by the apostles occurred on that day as the gospel was obeyed (or rejected).

- God is perfect, and He includes all that is needed to succeed in His authorized revelation. Any thought that there needs to be more doctrine or more clarity minimizes God's perfection.

- The correct understanding of Jesus when He referenced His body and blood in both John 6:53-54 and Matthew 26:26-28 was a metaphor. There is a sense that in a person's obedience to the gospel, a person realizes that Jesus did suffer the ravaging of His actual body and blood. Likewise, in the Lord's Supper, the remembrance brings back the memory of the actual sacrifice. The concept of Catholicism's "Real Presence" has no purpose and is nonsensical. Once again, it is fair to say that everything God has done in some way is related to fulfilling His purpose. As discussed in this book (Chapter 9), the Lord's Supper provides the purpose for the remembrance consistent with God's purpose to share in His Divine Nature.

The good and the bad of the early church fathers

The unbiased view of the early church fathers is that they attempted to provide some leadership and care for the inspired word, but they were not always correct. Certainly, they were not consistent, believing the same, writing the same about the early church. Numerous errors were entering the church. The exception is where the early church fathers were helpful. Specifically, they helped bring through these early centuries the word of God. A vast majority, perhaps all of the New Testament, is contained in the writings of the early church fathers. Old Testament scribes over their history copied the Torah and the other books of the Old Testament and were amazingly dedicated and skilled. Their process was comprehensive, involving their attitudes, special notations, materials, and even their quality of work. The persons known as the early church fathers were knowledgeable persons and, from what we know, dedicated to copying and overseeing the copy process. Unfortunately, this does not mean they would, independent of their copy-work, privately interpret the scriptures. They wrote what they believed, and of course, knew it was not scripture. They may have favored their writings, but likely never thought they would be taken as scripture. This is because they did have high regard for the sacred writings (accurately copying them) but not the seriousness of going beyond them in certain ways – they may have believed there could be improvements. Even to this day, people fail to appreciate perfection. That is, there is no way to improve perfection. God is responsible for His word accurately coming down through history, and one of those means was using these early copy-capable persons associated with the churches.

We have God's promise that heaven and earth will pass away but not His words. God's oversight is involved in assuring the written word would come down through the ages. The scribes of old and these early church fathers were the vehicles for God to ensure His word would be delivered correctly. We see how God intervened to assure the promises of Genesis 3:15 and Genesis 12:1-3 were fulfilled in the fullness of time. That interference was outward and often quite dramatic. Although those outward manifestations were essential to those fulfillments, God does not act in those ways since "that which is perfect has come." God planned to have "that which is perfect" delivered at this time. These final scriptures completed in the latter part of the first century would accurately be carried through the remaining history. I do not know **the HOW of creation or the HOW of Matthew 24:35** ("Heaven and earth will pass away, but My words will by no means pass away"). I know that God makes no mistakes, and He assured humankind would have the truth. We have the completed word of God, and it is accurate. On the one hand, we have God in perfection, assuring we have the truth, and on the other hand, we have men looking for something to validate what **they created** as doctrine. It is quite a contrast, and one can expect confusion and lots of explanation and consequently the resulting mess called Catholicism.

12.6 Early church father's writings are NOT inspired

Only the scriptures can be used in matters of faith in matters of truth. If you read the writings of these early church fathers, you are reading history, and even though some things may be true or false, **it is not the word of God**. Once the Holy Spirit completes His work, there can be **no valid additional or different teachings** – the word of God is the only basis of truth. The falling away would begin during the first century, even when the message was being delivered as predicted by Jesus and noted occurring by Paul, i.e., Galatians the first chapter. This leads to a single conclusion consistent with God's requirement that His word must not be changed. **God's word is the one solid thing**. Regardless, if in the first century or the fifth century, the things being taught as doctrine, the things being done by the early church were not correct unless they were consistent with the word of God. There were differences in the writings of early church fathers over many issues – that would be expected as they were not inspired. In addition to the possibility of private interpretations of scripture, we now have various early church father's opinions, perhaps things they believed that might help, improvements that can be made. These writings of the early church fathers were **occasionally** similar, but that only means they were making similar mistakes. They often lacked a full understanding, perhaps like the apostles did with certain things Jesus said BEFORE the Holy Spirit guided them into all truth. They were careless in handling the word of God in a way that far down the road would be similar to how Martin Luther and John Calvin, and many others privately interpreted the scriptures. Once there is a desire for a different meaning of the scriptures, there are all kinds of possibilities. A person could gather similar writings from various early church writers to support their views and disregard opposing things. This may or may not have happened, but it is the kind of thing men do to get what they want. The point is God knows there is no chance of men getting it right. Truth comes from the Holy Spirit's inspiration, and in this last age, that included putting an end to revelation. It makes sense to end God's communication with humankind as the reconciliation has occurred and now will continue to occur in the same successful manner until the end of time.

There are several ways to claim something different than the scriptures for authority. The ones used by Catholicism are early church father's tradition, apostolic succession, and their Magisterium. They also use the scriptures but privately interpret them as needed to support their teachings. This is a mess, and God condemns such with severe warnings for changing His word. **God is wiser than humankind and had the Holy Spirit deliver the truth, confirm the word, and indicate that His word was complete.** That which God sought to avoid in His consistent declaration of not changing His word is precisely what Catholicism embraces. If you go beyond what is perfect (God's completed word), you move away from God. When humankind is involved, you can expect confusion, very different ideas, and various significant divisions of thought. One should be thankful to God for the simplicity of the truth. You do not have to study the voluminous writings of the early church fathers and all their varied teachings or their sometimes similar private interpretations. Read the link below for a short and straightforward, common-sense analysis of the early church fathers.

It is interesting to question why certain doctrines are essential to Catholicism, and there is a very revealing answer. You have the answer if one can conclude that these early church fathers represent the predicted falling away. **The Catholic Church was built to a large extent on the private interpretations of the early church fathers.** I keep ending up with this conclusion. The Catholic Church wants to say they are the continuation of the church that Jesus was building. That is, the church we read of in the scriptures, and they are almost correct. The Catholic Church, in a sense, goes back to the early falling away, not in name, but the momentum towards what will become Catholicism grows from the earliest of errors. Catholics incorporate the things found in the writings of the early church fathers as doctrine. Of all the twists of scripture used to create Catholicism, one is not a twist but the **elimination** of the crucial thing that allows God's purpose to be completed. It is the thing Paul saw being changed in Galatians. I do not know when this essential ingredient of Christianity disappeared, but it was "leaving" somewhere in the early church, and the seriousness of its loss was not comprehended. Once it is gone, or in the process of being lessened, the church is gone. How can that be? Because there are no longer any new Christians, no longer is the Lord adding the obedient to His spiritual body. The simplicity of salvation's requirements, **the gospel message has been corrupted, has been lost!** What has replaced the gospel message? Replacing God's message are disputes, arguments, debates over various private interpretations, and there is a long list of **things not important to God fulfilling His purpose**. We say the message has disappeared, changed, but the message did not die. There would be a small number of saints but not necessarily "historically notable." God's word would remain, albeit under duress from the world. It should not be surprising, regardless if it were Israel often in captivity, or even Jesus going to the cross or His apostles in peril carrying the message or the early saints suffering torture and death, there is opposition to the truth. Now, for a period, the gospel message **seems** to be missing.

If we try to answer why people will choose the teachings of men over God's word, the answer is because they can. They can choose **what they like,** and God will not interfere. God, particularly in **this last age**, does not interfere in any way. Humankind has the completed word of God, and that is all that is needed for those seeking the truth. God's test is perfect in revealing those **not suitable** for sharing in the Divine Nature and at the same time perfect in conversion.

The Catholic Church provides distortion and distraction in its invention of something very different from the scriptures.

Pause for a staggering observation regarding evil

Evil and its associated deceit aggressively show up every time God's goodness and truth appear. People have mentioned life as a battle between good and evil. In Genesis, the tree in the midst of the garden was known as the tree of the knowledge of good and evil. The ability to discern good and evil is highly prized (Hebrews 5:12-14).

One must avoid speculation when discussing the matters of God, yet there is an observation that strikes me as worthy of note. This matter fits the subject of Catholic audacity despite an adverse desire for it to remain concealed. Above, it was mentioned how the good things of God are attacked at every turn. There seems to be a never-ending ordeal as God's way is moving forward to its goal. Even before Jesus, this was apparent. Then Jesus brings the good message of the kingdom, sprinkled with miracles, which results in His murder. Next, with the coming of the truth via the apostles, there are struggles for the apostles and their converts. In the early centuries, there is opposition to the scriptures, the changing of meanings, and even the apparent disappearance of the gospel message. In their carelessness, the early church fathers play a part in losing the message. Indeed, this evil came from within, as Christianity gradually evolved to Catholicism. Catholicism goes forward in history without experiencing the typical devastation related to the things of God. It does, however, extinguish any opposition to its teachings, particularly any scripture-based remnants of Christianity. After all, those well-known mass persecutions, often attempts at genocide against such scripture-believing groups as the Anabaptists, Huguenots, Waldensians, and Albigenses were paranoid reactions to the very apparent threats to Catholic teachings. Catholicism continues ("without harm") and asserts its unique association with God, but it cannot provide eternal successes despite its claims. This replacement for Christianity (Catholicism) becomes a permanent obstacle to the truth. These observations are not without merit. Many thoughts are possible from this analysis, but evil and deceit rise up when goodness and truth appear. Conversely, "good people" seem ineffective in opposition to evil when it emerges. The reason may be that evil, deceit is threatening, and goodness and truth are docile. In the days of Noah, evil grew without opposition to overcome the world at that time, and later the cities of Sodom and Gomorrah were overcome with evil. In both cases, God intervened and ended the dominant evil. It is not and cannot be the character of humankind possessing goodness and truth to act aggressively against such evil, but in these times bring God's message as did Noah in his time. God, as He has promised, will bring a final judgment on evil at the end of time. Evil will be the eventual loser as justice is perfectly administered, and goodness and truth will, albeit in suffering, succeed in their obedience. These observations may have value but carrying this further can become quite speculative – so we leave this contemplation for the reader.

The early church fathers were in no way special

All those in the body of Christ are special because they are spiritual, having been reconciled to God. These early church "persons" later designated as early church fathers were the more highly educated of the period since they could write and had some historical knowledge. The people God uses in fulfilling His purpose are specifically identified, such as the prophets and apostles. After God meticulously **delivers the truth using His Spirit**, some people claim this random group of early church fathers has brought the truth. However, it is considerably different than what God delivered. This is irrational. Everything God has done to accomplish His purpose is perfect, including perfectly rational. Everything about God's character is noble and demonstrated in His love for His creation. When you see chaos in the things religion brings, you are not seeing God, and it is easy to observe confusion and inconsistency in the things written by the early church fathers.

The truth God delivers allows humankind to succeed. It is simple, but it is unknowable unless God reveals it. The simplicity in what God requires of humanity is designed to allow clarity, understanding, and assurance in the actions taken. Behind the simplicity is God's wisdom, which means His purpose, His nature, His perfection in everything. Everything God has done concerning humankind fits perfectly together from creation until the end of time. Do you think humanity could independently know the mind of God? When some person promotes the idea of the Real Presence, of Mariology, of New Testament priests, do these things fit together perfectly as part of God's plan. Unless God very specifically designates these things, they are the inventions of humankind and specifically the early church fathers and those men following them. Who could create such things? There seems to be a huge missing component, and it is the awareness we are dealing with God.

These early church fathers were undoubtedly struggling with their understanding of all that happened during the time of Christ and then during the time of the apostles being led by God's Holy Spirit. The early church fathers were mere men, although some of the brightest of the time as seen in their writings. They were undoubtedly excited about what God had done and left as scripture. At some point, perhaps quite early as suggested, many were not Christians. Once the gospel message has been corrupted, this would be the consequence. That message should be seen as a focus in their writing, but it is not, and without it, all sorts of different things can be imagined, which is what we see, i.e., confusion. One thing consistent with the loss of the gospel message would be the careless handling of the scriptures. Even though the apostles themselves were never originators of doctrine, these early church fathers at times wrote, giving the **appearance** of authority. Catholicism would evolve out of some of the ideas of these early church fathers, and to this day, certain select of these men are read and afforded respect. Fortunately, you do not have to study the voluminous writings of the early church fathers, but all you need is the scriptures inspired by the Holy Spirit as He guided the apostles into all truth. God is very logical and perfectly understands humankind and knew if His instructions were not clear, concise, there would be problems. There is an emphasis in the scriptures to understand God, and He has carefully revealed Himself. Those who respect His word know of His desire for all to be saved. Also, they understand He is not the God of confusion. One more thing, I know of many people in local churches who only use the scriptures, and they believe the same without any central authority. They are in the body of Christ due to strictly following God's directions. Every group that has gone beyond the scriptures does not have the truth. One bewildering thing for those who go beyond the scriptures is how the essential thing, namely, how to have sins forgiven, is not correctly taught.

12.7 This short paragraph is more valuable than all of Catholicism

It ought to strike people that God's message is simple regarding what people need to do to be reconciled to Him and how they are to continue to live. A person does not need to be a scientist and understand black holes, dating the age of things, be an evolutionary biologist, be an astrophysicist, be a theologian studying the history of the early church fathers or hundreds of other "religious technologies." One needs to have **a good heart and love the truth**. Such a person can rightly divide the word of God. It is not necessary to embrace the word of God **AND** the thousands of man-made doctrines. God needs you to **obey the gospel**, remain faithful, grow in the grace and knowledge of God, and bring the gospel message to the world. This last item can keep you busy throughout your lifetime.

12.8 Summary of the early church fathers

There is one more undeniable thing, and it is the conclusion reached throughout this book regarding the early church fathers. One thing missing in the writings of the early church fathers is the conversion methodology of the inspired writings. This ought to be emphasized throughout their writings and consistent in everything they write. Let's look at Paul's statement in Galatians 1:6-9 and know it is true, and it is inspired.

Galatians 1:6-9

6 I marvel that you are turning away so soon from Him who called you in the grace of Christ, to a different gospel,

7 which is not another; but there are some who trouble you and want to pervert the gospel of Christ.

8 But even if we, or an angel from heaven, preach any other gospel to you than what we have preached to you, let him be accursed.

9 As we have said before, so now I say again, if anyone preaches any other gospel to you than what you have received, let him be accursed.

Paul is warning in no uncertain terms that at the time he is writing the letter to the Galatians, some have perverted the gospel. This would mean "that perverted gospel" would produce no Christians. It is no wonder Paul is so aggressive (verses 8 and 9) in describing the seriousness of changing the gospel message.

It is possible that many of the early church fathers were not Christian. They never obeyed the gospel. Yet, they had the scriptures (not all in one place), but the pattern for the forgiveness of sins was provided throughout the New Testament. Catholics like to claim their origin goes back to the first century. However, there is no **secular historical record** of popes from the first century until about the seventh century – this is discussed in Chapters 2, 5 and 9. Indeed there is no earthly head over the church Jesus built, but Jesus is the head. Interestingly, these vaunted early church fathers do not support a line of popes or such an office, although some refer to a single earthly head of the church as desirable. The Catholic Church claims a continuous line of popes from the time of inspiration. Perhaps if we date the falling away from the time Paul was writing Galatians, this tangent in doctrine (this perverted gospel) could have a very early start. The remainder of the first century and continuing through the early centuries would establish the falling away.

The early church father's writings gather momentum throughout the early centuries. The Edict of Tolerance and the Edict of Milan allowed for the acceptance of Christianity but really may have been allowing tolerance for something much different than the church Jesus built. More time passes, and finally, with the official historical designation of a pope in the seventh century, we have a very distinct non-Christian entity called Catholicism. Thus we can connect the Catholic Church with the first century in a negative way. Unfortunately, it is not the church Jesus was building but the gradual growth of the falling away ending in a sophisticated entity called the Catholic Church. Is this what happened? I do not know, but it appears to be so. I do know that there is no association between the Catholic Church and God. The thing missing "early on" is the gospel message. The single thing that should have been emphasized is the gospel message that allows the reconciliation with God. When did it disappear? We know it changed for some in Galatians 1:6-9. We also know that for many, it did not change. Those following the apostle's direction did indeed become Christians. However, many of those in the first century and forward claimed association with "Christianity" but may not have been Christian. That is, never added to the body of Christ by the Lord. We cannot give the date of the falling away for the early churches. We can say it occurred when they moved away from the doctrine of Christ. Paul seemingly, by his declaration, quenched the changing of the gospel message in the churches of Galatia, but who would end similar distortions of the gospel message in the early churches.

Indeed, by the time we get to the fourth century, the Christians in Rome (if they were Christians) were incorporating pagan practices. This would get worse with the Edict of Milan in 313 AD. At this time, the character of Christianity began to take on a ceremonial quality with their hierarchy receiving the honor. There was still no pope, but Constantine treated the church as just another component of the Roman Empire and shortly would call the first church council at Nicaea. It is easy to believe that, particularly in Rome, the doctrine of Christ had slipped away long before the time of the Edict – it would just get worse.

If you look today at the pomp and ceremony of the Catholic Church and the honor paid to Catholic leaders, it evolved from the early centuries and particularly in the association with Rome. In some cases, the bishops of Rome sought to be the universal bishop. This would finally happen formally, as mentioned in the early seventh century. We have the church in Jerusalem that contained the apostles and where Peter was an elder. Then we have various locations for the early church, including the churches Paul started on his missionary journeys. Now beyond the time of inspiration, the church in some locations was changing in ways it no longer qualified to be the church started by Jesus. People either have the doctrine of Christ, or they do not, and not having it means they have neither the Father nor the Son. The church consisting of those "in Christ" designed by God was local and independent of all other local churches. However, with a single head over all the churches, the "local character of the church" would become rare. Maybe a few local churches survived the force of this new ungodly order.

There were many "Christians" in Rome by the fourth century, and some bishops like Innocent I (402-417) in the early fifth century would refer to himself as the "Ruler of the Church of God." As previously mentioned, in 604 AD, the emperor Phocas tried to give the title of the universal bishop to Gregory I, but he refused it. However, a successor, Boniface III, accepted the title in 607 AD. It is incredibly interesting that Catholicism claims popes back to the first century, but throughout history, none of the Roman emperors knew of a universal bishop. Also, some of the early church fathers allude favorably to the concept of a universal bishop, but that points to not having such a person in existence. This problem of the Catholic Church naming their popes back to the time of Peter has been referred to as a lie, just a self-serving need to justify their apostolic succession. The lies needed to cover the initial lie are a characteristic of Catholicism and pointed out for the single reason that there is no salvation in the Catholic Church because there is no truth.

Apparently some of the early church fathers concluded that Peter was the rock of Matthew 16:18. We have shown this to be the worst of conclusions from the scriptures. It is a conclusion with zero merit and directly opposes God's plan. Indeed, many of the eventual doctrines that would comprise the Catholic Church can be attributed to things written by the early church fathers and in this case Peter having a role of authority in the church. One thing of concern in talking about the writings of the early church fathers is that the written documents of those men are mainly under the control of the Catholic Church. We have already seen the audacity of the Catholic Church in naming their popes back to Peter. We have seen the careless handling of God's word, including minimizing God's word, even making it of the same value as the tradition of the early church fathers and creating an "infallible" teaching arm, their Magisterium. Documents they use to support their positions are largely under their control. They are an organization that uses treachery whenever there is any opposition. One would have to be "asleep" not to realize there would also be a great deal of selectivity in promoting certain church fathers and their writings coming down through history. Even though such writings have no validity (not inspired) in terms of doctrine there is an effort to promote their authenticity. I do not know the extent of this effort, but Catholicism has a record of extreme dishonesty. Of course, the beliefs, conclusions of the early church fathers have no credibility. The fact that the Catholic Church looks outside God's designated means of authority immediately validates them in the role of the predicted falling away.

Note: See Chapter 4.2 for the definition of the Catholic Magisterium and a short discussion.

12.9 Something important is missing from the early church

There is one overwhelmingly significant thing, and understanding it reveals the truth about Catholicism and Protestantism, and it is the only important thing. It was confused in Galatians 1:6-9 (written about 50 AD) and then throughout the early centuries by the early church fathers and ultimately lost by Catholicism. This one crucial thing is the gospel message. The message saves and thus allows God to fulfill His purpose. The gospel message was in the making since Genesis 3:15. It is central to the perfection that allows the reconciliation. Everything else is "not all that important." Yet, what do some of those early fathers of the church emphasize? They emphasize everything else. Things like an earthly leader for the church, the Real Presence, infant baptism, Mariology, purgatory, and New Testament priests that are not found in the scriptures. They are distractions from the gospel message. The thing that was largely missing in these early times and throughout much of history is the gospel message. The terminology that I often use is that **life is about the soul and absolutely about nothing else**. The scriptures carry this idea, and one place is Jesus' statement in Mark.

Mark 8:35-36

35 For whoever desires to save his life will lose it, but whoever loses his life for My sake and the gospel's will save it.

36 For what will it profit a man if he gains the whole world, and loses his own soul?

There was one thing to get right, and except those who love the truth everyone else has missed the mark, missed receiving forgiveness of sins, and failed in life, and who is to blame? The blame falls to each person for their poor choices and to religion for false teaching. Indeed, what God made easy, humankind in disrespect for the word of God has made complicated.

When I read the writings of the early church fathers, I was amazed at all they wrote and wondered why all this writing. It is like they are analysts of the scriptures they possess. They get involved in mentioning what others are writing or claiming, and it is never-ending. It reminds me of the warning in Corinthians.

1Corinthians 1:18-19

18 For the message of the cross is foolishness to those who are perishing, but to us who are being saved it is the power of God.

19 For it is written: "I will destroy the wisdom of the wise,

And bring to nothing the understanding of the prudent."

These early church fathers are becoming the first theologians of Christianity and doing a most harmful thing, complicating the scriptures. They do such a good job that even they are confused. They confuse each other and think they are doing some good in bringing clarity. It is a terrible thing because the message from God is simple. When I see the work of Catholicism in trying to validate their religion, it comes to me as a terror since it helps no one and confuses otherwise sincere persons. It also makes me question, "what is the value of a theologian." If you have the truth, preach it. How much do you have to know to obey the gospel and live faithfully? Is there some sort of sin associated with knowing to do good as a Christian and not doing it? There most certainly is, and as usual, God makes this clear in James 4:17, "Therefore, to him who knows to do good and does not do *it,* to him it is sin." I would suggest that instead of critiquing the scriptures, they (of the "so-called Christian churches") should be obeying them.

Chapter 13
The origin of the Catholic Church

13.1 Catholic Church equals the falling away

A summary of the falling away will bring some clarity and help define the origin of the Catholic Church. In determining the **origin** of the Catholic Church, we have to examine "Christianity" over time. Thus the history previously discussed in this book will be helpful. The one consistent thing is the character of Catholicism as being one of deceit, and it is deceit that must be continually inventive to meet whatever the current problem. Imagine lies built on lies for over 1900 years, associated with the falling away – about 1400 years since it was fully established as the Catholic Church.

We had mentioned the falling away throughout this book and have concluded that it was gradual and began when the scriptures were being written and several times indicated how the gospel message was being changed, as mentioned by Paul in Galatians 1:6-9. Jesus warned of this in Matthew 7:15 as the coming of false prophets, and Paul writing to Timothy in 1 Timothy 4:1, said some would depart the faith. Paul also warned the Colossians of being cheated by the tradition of men in Colossians 2:8 and then in 2 Thessalonians 2:3-4, those "in Christ" receive a very descriptive warning.

2 Thessalonians 2:3-4

3 Let no one deceive you by any means; for that Day will not come unless the falling away comes first, and the man of sin is revealed, the son of perdition,
4 who opposes and exalts himself above all that is called God or that is worshiped, so that he sits as God in the temple of God, showing himself that he is God.

God's concern is always for souls, and now maintaining those who have obeyed the gospel is important and thus the warning. Earlier it was mentioned (Chapter 2) that many have considered 1 Timothy 4:1-4 to be a description of the Catholic Church.

1 Timothy 4:1-4

1 Now the Spirit expressly says that in latter times some will depart from the faith, giving heed to deceiving spirits and doctrines of demons,

2 speaking lies in hypocrisy, having their own conscience seared with a hot iron,

3 forbidding to marry, and commanding to abstain from foods which God created to be received with thanksgiving by those who believe and know the truth.

4 For every creature of God is good, and nothing is to be refused if it is received with thanksgiving;

Although the description fits, it also fits others, and thus declaring it uniquely as a reference to the Catholic Church is seen as not particularly unflawed albeit likely. However, 2 Thessalonians 2:3-4 is very specific in pointing out an idolatry-type characteristic of the falling away. Namely, having an association with one who exalts himself above all that is called God and even showing himself that he is God. These things fit most of the early bishops of Rome, such as Leo I (440-461), who convinced the Roman Emperor, Valentinian III, to issue an edict declaring the Roman See as the supreme court of appeal for all bishops. Innocent I (402-417) called himself "Ruler of the church of God." Innocent III (1198–1216) claimed to be the "Vicar of Christ," the "Vicar of God," the "supreme Sovereign over the church and the world." Pius IX (1846–1878) said, "Christ has dictated every dogma of the Roman Catholic Church through His Viceregents on earth." Throughout the history of early "Christianity," many bishops, particularly of Rome and then the popes, sought to take the place of God on earth. They would sit in the position of God, claiming titles of Holy Father, the Vicar of Christ, and so on, and claim to speak for God. The Catholic councils (from the ninth council forward) are used to justify their authority, and their encyclical letters from the councils document this effort. Certainly, in Catholicism, we can see the fulfillment of 2 Thessalonians 2:3-4. The man of sin would not be the fulfillment in a single individual but include those that fit the predicted characteristics, which means all the popes. The early popes in their evil conduct (inquisitions, crusades, heretic savagery among many other terrors) "fit the bill" of these verses. Still, all popes carrying the title of Holy Father and Vicar of Christ qualify as the man of sin in their audacity. They take the place of God, even usurping God by justifying their rulemaking authority by their councils. God's focus remains on souls, and He begins (2 Thessalonians 2:3-4) by saying, "Let no one deceive you by any means." Paul is writing to those "in Christ" in this letter to the Thessalonian church. It will have an application to all the churches belonging to Christ until the end of time. It is a warning that relates to souls because it is a deception that must be avoided. He provides some detail of the danger because it is a deception that comes with the appearance of righteousness and the claim of an association with God. It is devastatingly surprising to learn the source will be those who "exalt themselves above all that is called God or that is worshiped, so that he sits as God in the temple of God, showing himself that he is God." The terror to souls will come from what appears to be within the church, and now we know it grew from men within the church, for instance, some of the early bishops in Rome and eventually in fruition the Catholic popes.

Of course, those under the authority of the man of sin (Catholics) could benefit from these verses by **recognizing** such persons from God's description and the evil brought by their deception. One of the weaknesses of this scenario is that the man of sin, being the individual pope in each period, never sits in the temple of God, but we might say he sits in the temple of apostasy. However, for a very long period to this day, it would **appear** to the world that the popes sit in the temple of God. Nations considered Roman Catholicism to be the center of Christianity, the church belonging to God. 2 Thessalonians 2:3-4 is predicting something to be avoided, namely, being deceived and such a person characteristically exalts himself above all that is called God. Certainly, something is compelling if one appears as God, acting like God – indeed very powerful and **dangerous to the truth**, to God achieving His purpose. These verses are about the **appearance given by this man of sin,** and part of that appearance is the perception that he is sitting in place of God – although not really. This description of the man of sin allows a person to recognize the powerful nature of this deception. This warning indeed amazes the reader concerning the extent and quality of deception, and it also simultaneously shows the magnitude of idolatry. Immediately, one thinks of God's anger for such audacity, and part of that anger must be the outright rejection of God's Son – that is, specifically the rejection of the doctrine of Christ. Only God's **truth** carries the ability to reconcile a person to share in the Divine Nature.

13.2 Deceit everywhere never ending always malicious

Note: In Chapter 2, we established the deceit of Catholicism as they named popes backward to Peter, their first pope. Then as we go through this book, we demonstrate that the Catholic interpretation of Matthew 16:18, which claims Peter is the rock, cannot be true and is inconsistent with God's plan and a malicious fabrication. It is the worst of lies and the foundation for Catholicism. A review of Catholic documents indicates the literature they controlled was always given a Catholic slant, and so we have a history of lies supported by deceitful patronage.

The link below represents the frustration of many persons who realize the futility of opposing Catholic teaching. Catholicism and its doctrines are nonsensical, but how do you defeat their unabashed lies and trickery, indoctrination, and propaganda. How do you defeat their numbers and blind loyalty? The article's author displays some of the methods Catholicism uses to defend its never-ending problems, and the following paragraphs use some of that material to discuss those observations.

https://victorspen.wordpress.com/2015/06/02/the-early-church-catholic/

If a Catholic, for example, attempts to prove that the Assumption of Mary was taught from the early days of the church, they would take this doctrine (as defined in 1950) and associate it with certain isolated words or phrases from the early church fathers. Or, if possible, they might try to associate it with some unrelated scripture. Anything can serve as evidence in justifying the fabrications of Catholicism. **THE TRUTH** from God does not have people searching for justification because God's truth is straightforward, simple, associated with God's purpose, and everything fits perfectly together.

Until the 17th century, the Roman Catholic church **taught that all her doctrines and practices came from the apostles and have never changed from that time.** This was so ridiculous that modern scholars had to conceive of something more reasonable, and they did with Newman's "development theory." This theory supports the understanding and concept of Catholic doctrines changing over time. This "excuse" was devised to explain the massive disconnect between the beliefs of the early church and modern Roman Catholicism. The intellectual argument of Newman is appreciated by Catholic apologists who need such a theory to explain all the problems. Once again, God is not the author of confusion, and like all of Catholicism, they miss the point – the point of simplicity provided by God. Catholicism must portray itself as necessary in providing the truth. Of course, it takes something like Newman's "development theory" to explain Catholicism. The reality is it takes no help to understand the truth, but it takes a love of the truth, a humble attitude that results in your obedience. All that stuff of Catholicism only confuses but with Newman's development theory, it can be explained (but not understood) and supposedly justify why Catholicism has changed. Thus the claim that the doctrines and practices of Catholicism came from the apostles and have never changed was not true. Now Catholics can say, **here is WHY they changed**. Of course, the doctrines and practices of the Catholic Church never came from the apostles, but as shown throughout this book, the Catholic doctrines and practices were typically the opposite of the truth. Moreover, the **Roman Catholic Church is the predicted falling away** and labeled correctly when they give the impression of sitting in place of God as Catholic audacity.

Catholicism and Protestantism continue to damage Christianity

Catholicism should have been effectively exposed centuries ago. Finally, the wounds are so apparent that many have left. Unfortunately, **Christianity has suffered** due to a supposed association with Catholicism. Christianity also has an association with Protestantism and thus suffers a double blow in the world's eyes. The solution used in this book is to **preach the word,** that is, provide the truth. It is also believed that indicating when and why men began changing God's message that evolved to Catholicism will be helpful.

The motivation for this work is to help people to succeed in life. It only requires effort; a love of the truth and the matter can be settled. Unfortunately, the world has become lazy in seeking the deeper meaning of life and many, even seemingly religious persons, believe existence ends at death. Religion has inadvertently created this numbness due to their histories, diversity of beliefs, superstitions, careless handling of God's word, and complicated messages. The "world" has taken advantage of religion's casual and compromising nature to oppose God effectively. Especially to oppose what is seen as Christianity. This opposition is promoted in institutions of higher learning and a media that wants to eliminate God. Thus for many people, God and religion are not acceptable subjects, and it seems "Christianity" is a word of laughable connotations. We have a world of people manipulated to despise the one thing in life they need.

Continuing to expose Catholicism

In Chapter 2, we have shown how Catholicism named popes back to Peter to solidify their connection to Peter and demonstrate the concept of apostolic succession. During the early centuries, no person or group, whether the early church fathers, or any in the local churches, or any of the emperors, knew of these popes. The concept of a single earthly head for the church was something favored by the Roman emperors and some of the early church fathers. Over the early centuries, they promoted this, which proves popes did not exist during those times.

In the 8th and 9th centuries, Catholicism had particular problems in maintaining its control over nations. They took one of their more aggressive actions. If there is one thing that never bothers Catholicism, it is lying for a good cause, and that good cause is the maintenance of Catholicism. After all, Catholicism is built on lies. Everything is a lie; thus, lies are covered by other lies. One well-known lie is called "The *Donation of Constantine."* The ***Donation of Constantine*** (Latin: *Donatio Constantini*) is a **forged** Roman imperial decree.

The 4th-century emperor Constantine the Great, supposedly transferred authority over Rome and the western part of the Roman Empire to the pope. This document was composed probably in the 8th century. It was used, especially in the 13th century, in **support of claims of political authority by the papacy**. For centuries, the "Donation of Constantine" was accepted, giving the popes significant political clout. However, in the 15th century, Nicholas of Cusa, a German cardinal and scholar, proved it was a forgery. It had been forged during the Frankish Empire in the 8th century. In that period, the papacy was constantly struggling for control with the powerful Carolingian rulers (such as the Holy Roman Emperor Charlemagne). Seeing its power threatened, the Church at Rome devised the idea and produced the document that came to be known as "The Donation." Earlier (Chapter 2), we indicated Constantine (and emperors following) knew nothing of a single head of the Christian church, and thus he took a leadership role calling the first church council. There were no popes at that time. Catholicism is willing to take risks in telling lies, creating documents that support their ambition. In times of poor communication, a lie like "the Donation of Constantine" was effective for about 700 years.

13.3 Controlling the message and its distribution

In their control of documents, the Catholic Church never misses an opportunity to promote itself as the one true church dating back to the first century. It has been mentioned that after the eighth council, the councils were called by the Catholic Church. However, the earlier councils were called by the Roman emperors beginning with Constantine in 325 AD. When you look at the Catholic description of the first and subsequent church councils, they read, "First Ecumenical Council of the **Catholic Church**, held in 325 AD" and similarly through the 21st and final council. Catholic, meaning the Roman Catholic Church was not the terminology used at the Nicene council of 325. There was no Roman Catholic Church and, of course, no pope at that time. The infrequent usage of the name catholic (small c) was not pointing to the Roman Catholic Church but, as suggested (further down this page), as a differentiator for those true believers in the church universal.

These earliest church councils (first eight) councils were **not known** by the name Catholic and involved both the Eastern (Orthodox) as well as the Western (Roman) churches. Interestingly, the first church council (325 AD) needed to show they had accomplished something of value and decided to create a creed known to this day as the Nicene Creed. Of course, it has been modified somewhat over the years (especially at the second council) and is still used as an overview of beliefs by the "Christian" churches. The Nicene Creed is used today by the Eastern Churches, whereas the Catholic Church uses the Apostles Creed. The Apostles Creed is believed to be a faithful summary of the apostle's beliefs and was created in the mid-fifth century. Here is what is meaningful to know, none of these creeds are of any value but are blasphemous to God. Once again, it is men speaking for God.

Of course, nothing in the creeds is right because it is not the message from God. You cannot take bits and pieces from scripture and think you have the correct meaning. The councils consisted of a bunch of men trying to agree but promoting their private views. These views are what each had determined from their scripture study, obviously their private interpretations. At the first council, there were about 318 bishops. Do you think having groups of men determine the meaning of the word of God was the intention? God provided the Holy Spirit to deliver the truth. These 318 men finally agreed and published the Nicene Creed. People will believe in the Nicene Creed that they are getting God's message. These creeds are not from God but end up being misleading as they say some true things. A person might think if they believe in the creed, they are in some way benefitted. The doctrines developed by the groups that use these creeds will be

328

hampered in coming to the truth. The Nicene and Apostles creeds are very similar but neither represent the beliefs of the apostles, and we know this because they never created such a document. **What does it take to understand God's word is authoritative and nothing else?** In human reasoning, the creeds are to help the people understand the Christian beliefs. If someone asks you what you believe, you can refer to one of these creeds or even quote the creed you espouse from memory. Do the people following these creeds understand what they are saying? A basic unsaid tenant of the world's religious leaderships is to simplify their truly complicated teachings (i.e., use creeds) to eliminate the questions of authenticity. These creeds are not the message from God but mislead those who seriously need to be seeking God and truth.

It should be evident that **any materials controlled by the Catholic Church have been tampered to their favor.** This would include their church council documents, the writings of the early church fathers, and basically all documents (and as we have seen even paintings) under Catholic control. The Catholic Church claims that they delivered the written Bible text to humankind when God ACTUALLY oversaw the inspired writings. Indeed this is, *"sitting as God in the temple of God, showing himself that he is God."* Fortunately, the word of God was the one thing Catholicism could not change or was very limited in what it could change. God had a providential oversight associated with His commitment that His words would not pass away. All the early texts were not under Catholic control. The various versions were fundamentally the same. Catholicism sought to keep the scriptures under their control by various means and did whatever was necessary to keep the "Bible" from the people. **It should also be evident that the Catholic Church was willing to torture and murder all that opposed its rule and would have little trouble changing, creating any literary documents to their benefit.** Although pathetic, the treachery of Catholic deceit in their tampering of various records to support their beliefs is unfortunate but ultimately not important in today's world. **We have the truth, and it is simple and all we need to succeed**. As God says, "Let no one deceive you by any means." The most deceptive means seem to come from those who say they represent God.

The conclusion from a careful study of non-Catholic produced History points to the Catholic Church growing out of the misuse of scripture. As indicated, practically speaking, the Catholic Church could not change the scripture text but could privately interpret the verses, which they have done to support Catholic doctrine.

13.4 Nicaea Council and Creed - an abomination

Thinking is such a marvelous thing, but it requires some energy. What purpose do the church councils and the Nicene Creed serve? The answer is they provide no value in terms of God's purpose and thus are of no importance to those who seek the truth. The councils build up the prestige of those who attend and **create the appearance of meaningful earthly leadership**. The Nicene Creed and all the other cannons of this first council have no value except to confuse and distract. Does anyone attending these councils realize the church that belongs to Christ is spiritual and has a local (not universal, physical) component? Do they understand the penalty for changing the word of God? Do they know what the scriptures teach concerning having one's sins forgiven? Do they know the mission of those "in Christ?" There are all kinds of very vital things that might be in a more helpful creed. The things included in the Nicene Creed are disjointed because they represent mostly true things but can be viewed in various ways without the context given by God. It is no wonder they finally agreed on the creed as "published" since they are very obvious aspects of God's word. In the depths of all the meaningless statements coming out of the compromise of 318 bishops, we have **three problematic things in this process**.

First, there should be no church councils (see Chapter 2).

Second, the subject matter of the councils is several layers deep in error, and many things are very "physical," as can be seen in the Cannons developed by the council. Here are a couple of examples of the **error propagated** and the **humanlike concerns** dominating their councils. In less than 250 years, "Christianity so-called" is knee-deep in hundreds of things that all look like very human concerns, and doctrinal error abounds. After overviewing all the twenty Nicene Canons from the 325 AD council, I, fortunately, found a **summary of those canons,** and it is provided in the following link:

http://christianapologeticsalliance.com/2013/10/23/council-of-nicea-325-ad/)

The Canons of the Nicene Council deal with one who has been castrated, leadership, the appointment of bishops, how to deal with the excommunicated, early development of the "Pentarchy" (Alexandria, Rome, Antioch, and Jerusalem are named), the Novatians, the character of bishops/presbyters, repentance and restoration of the fallen and public discipline, communion to the dying/sick, regarding use of treasures or wealth in the church by its leaders, the practice of the Eucharist and ranks, Paulianism and rebaptism of heretics (as previously articulated at the Synod of Arles, 314AD), and prayer. The Council also dealt with the calculation of Easter by aligning the celebration of Easter with the Sunday after the full moon following the Spring equinox. The following two sections depict some of the errors and then the human-like concerns from the council documents.

Errors observed in the Nicene Council Canon of 325 A.D.

Essentially everything in the Canon is meaningless. For instance, they discuss the appointment of bishops, but God has already described their qualifications. They establish a certain time for Easter to align with the Sunday after the full moon following the Spring equinox. However, there is no such day of celebration authorized by the scriptures, much less assigning a specific time. It is what is called being layers deep in error. Then they discuss something they call the re-baptism of heretics showing this is another aspect of baptism they do not understand. They discuss something they refer to as repentance and restoration of the fallen and public discipline – where did that come from? The church perfectly defined in the scriptures is being run by men in the early churches, and rulemaking is dominating. These early persons of the church must have thought this to be their job, sort of like managers overseeing a business.

Nonsensical, non-spiritual results in the Canon of 325

Canon number one discusses dealing with one who has been castrated. "If physicians have subjected anyone in sickness to a surgical operation, or if barbarians have castrated him, let him remain among the clergy." The third Canon reads, "The great Synod has stringently forbidden any bishop, presbyter, deacon, or any one of the clergy whatever, to have a subintroducta dwelling with him, except only a mother, or sister, or aunt, or such persons only as are beyond all suspicion." The sixth Canon reads, "Let the ancient customs in Egypt, Libya and Pentapolis prevail, that the Bishop of Alexandria have jurisdiction in all these since the like is customary for the Bishop of Rome also." The fourteenth Canon reads, "Concerning catechumens who have lapsed, the holy and great Synod has decreed that, after they have passed three years only as hearers, they shall pray with the catechumens." Canon 20 reads, "Forasmuch as there are certain persons who kneel on the Lord's Day and in the days of Pentecost, therefore, to the intent that all things may be uniformly observed everywhere (in every parish), it seems good to the holy Synod that prayer be made to God standing."

The **third** problem in this process of church councils is the impossibility of devising a creed that could be correct. There are meaningful connections within the scriptures that allow for the proper understanding. "Separating" pieces of scripture may be costly to reaching the correct meaning. As seen in the many Bible examples, God requires dedicated adherence to His word, including the details. Eventually, these 318 bishops do reach a consensus on the Nicene Creed (and on the twenty Canons) and, in their view, have created something helpful, but it is no more than their private interpretations of God's message. God is serious about what He says, and a person's response to the will of God defines them as loving Him or not. God makes this clear when He says, " If you love Me keep My commands." The seriousness is seen in Peter's statement that, "If anyone speaks, let him speak as the oracles of God." How much variance from God's word is a person allowed? Let us just say that a person needs to take God's word very seriously as though their soul depends on it – because it does.

Someone might say this is just the first council. The church councils may get better. You cannot build on a flawed concept (these councils and their proclamations) and get anything but deeper in error. Of course, that is what happens as men try to make the rules for God. As time passes, the councils will downplay the value of the scriptures by lifting the importance of the early church fathers, the apostolic succession, and their Magisterium – see the outcome of the last council (Vatican II, 1962-1965) in Chapter 6. The result of what is essential, namely souls, is so butchered that all those associated with Catholicism will fail in life. For reference, below is repeated from Chapter 6 and shows how the Catholic Church used Vatican II to validate themselves.

"Hence there exists a close connection and communication between sacred tradition and Sacred Scripture. For both of them, flowing from the same divine wellspring, in a certain way merge into a unity and tend toward the same end. For Sacred Scripture is the word of God inasmuch as it is consigned to writing under the inspiration of the divine Spirit, while sacred tradition takes the word of God entrusted by Christ the Lord and the Holy Spirit to the Apostles, and hands it on to their successors in its full purity, so that led by the light of the Spirit of truth, they may in proclaiming it preserve this word of God faithfully, explain it, and make it more widely known.

Consequently it is not from Sacred Scripture alone that the Church draws her certainty about everything which has been revealed. Therefore both sacred tradition and Sacred Scripture are to be accepted and venerated with the same sense of loyalty and reverence."

13.5 Fourth century Christianity is obviously not Christianity

What is demonstrated here is what happens when the perfect message from God is ignored or changed. This first council is very revealing in its strangeness, somewhat like the strange fire of Nadab and Abihu that brought the wrath of God. Those who reject God's way that He designed for the church should not expect anything different. God's purpose and focus are always on souls. It is not hard to predict the future of what would become the Catholic Church. That organization is correctly called the universal physical church. In the background, the thing missing is that God is perfect, and it is impossible to improve on His pattern for the church. The overriding principle from God in essentially everything is obedience. Worship must be in obedience (spirit and **truth**), salvation must be according to obedience, the pattern of the church (organization, purpose, and so on) must be obeyed. God is holy, serious, and everything He does is related to His purpose and can be seen as spiritual with a bit of effort. The early church certainly by the time of the first church council (we suggest much earlier), had left the word of God, which is the same as leaving the faith.

All this nonsense of the councils does not matter but is shown to help you differentiate between the church built by Jesus and what was happening in the early centuries that ended up being the Catholic Church. God's simplicity in everything avoids the very thing that has happened to the church. It would get worse when Catholicism and their pope were in place. We say that was in the early seventh century – and that also does not matter. There is one defining distinction beginning in this time, and it is how Catholicism begins to grow worldwide. Simultaneously with the appearance of the Catholic Church and its pope, there are very paranoid actions to expand and maintain their authority. Even in this first church council in the fourth century at Nicaea, there is a documented expansion of jurisdiction well beyond the things that should involve the church. That is, there was an incorporation of many worldly things into the church. The falling away was gradual but readily evident by the fourth century.

We are talking about the origin of the Catholic Church in this chapter, and we associate it with the falling away. The Catholic Church is in its maturity the falling away. It is the one place in history where the church started by Christ is distorted as predicted, having the deception referred to and the exaltation of individuals that oppose God and even are called God (Holy Father or Pope). The deception qualifies as the falling away inasmuch as they are rule-makers that thwart God's purpose by changing the message from God, eliminating any possibility for people to receive the benefit planned by God. Indeed the verses in Thessalonians begin as a warning to "let no one deceive you by any means" and then explain what is coming.

This significant distinction defines the Catholic origin and is the coming into existence of the universal physical church. It is the opposite of the spiritual body of Christ. One thing that might be expected from the universal physical church would be the inability to build on error and make it continuously seem reasonable. Every person with a love of the truth can see this. Another thing expected would be an inability to keep God's focus in a worldly physical church. The consequence of this is devastating to every Catholic. In Catholicism, there is no forgiveness of sins, and thus none will share in the Divine Nature.

The name Catholic

The falling away would not be in the **name Catholic**, but it was just the Christian church in the early centuries. This falling away began as early as the first century. It continued with the writings of the early church fathers over the next six centuries culminating in the early seventh century with the first pope. The name Catholic would **now** become prominent.

Note: It turns out that in the early centuries, various groups were seeking to be the ones who would come to a leadership position over Christianity. It would be the Catholic Church, but as suggested, recognition would be around the time of the first pope in the early seventh century.

Catholics like to say it was Ignatius (bishop of Antioch) who first used the word Catholic in the early second century.

The Catholic encyclopedia contains the following first reference to the word catholic concerning the church. The combination "the Catholic Church" (he katholike ekklesia) is found for the first time in the letter of St. Ignatius to the Smyrnaeans, written about the year 110 AD. The words run: "Wheresoever the bishop shall appear, there let the people be, even as where Jesus may be, there is the universal [katholike] Church."

*I am not sure what this means, except Catholics are told it is evidence of an association between Jesus and the Catholic Church. Of course, there was no Catholic church in 110 AD. As you read on, you will see that the word catholic was used to differentiate true believers. However, the Catholic Church claims whenever the word catholic is found it is a reference to the Catholic Church. Of course, Ignatius is not an inspired writer, and again any writing under Catholic control will be slanted to their advantage. Regardless, if it is **naming popes back to Peter**, the **Donation of Constantine, or using the title of the Catholic Church in reference to the first seven church councils,** the **selective use of favorable things written by the early fathers**, or the **numerous lies and threats used to convince nations to do their work against heretics** or against various religious groups and endless other acts of deceit, it is to support their doctrines that have no scriptural basis. After a while, the deceit becomes ridiculous and, in this case, shows their desperation to justify their existence. The scriptures oppose everything Catholic in name and principle. The will of God as delivered by the Spirit of God is the one place where you can have a confident relationship with God. To accept this uninspired man's statement (if he even made it) requires that a person reject all that the Holy Spirit delivered to the apostles by inspiration.*

*Catholic was a new word since it was not used in the scriptures and not found religiously until 110 AD. It was the beginning of this word (catholic) concerning the church but mainly used by some regarding the desire for a universal bishop. In the early church writings, the word universal (likely in the case of Ignatius above) was using the word 'catholic' (spelled in lower case except in modern Catholic literature) from the Greek word catholikos. It means 'universal' and was used to differentiate between true believers who made up the universal church from those who were outside. **This is different from the term 'Catholic Church,'** which includes the idea of papal authority, purgatory, indulgences, etc. The deceit never ends as the Catholic*

Church sees the word universal in the early writings and immediately tags it the "Roman Catholic Church." Most certainly, despite their best efforts, the early church was not "Roman Catholic."

The concept of a universal church and universal bishop are blatantly opposed to the scriptures. The God-defined structure is independent local churches made up of those in the spiritual church. **The spiritual church is the core of God's plan** that allows God to achieve His purpose, with the local church providing support for the ongoing building of His spiritual church. Catholicism does indeed build their universal church with their universal bishop, and both are an abomination. This is because their church is the **universal PHYSICAL church** featuring an earthly head and earthly rulemaking body. It is the perfect opposite of what God specified.

The origin of the Catholic Church has always been a mystery. Unlike other religions, it could not be associated with some person or persons. As we suggest with ample evidence, it gradually evolved from a culmination of errors as early as the first century. It then continued to be developed with various doctrines supported by the writings of select early church fathers. Essentially the Catholic Church was born out of the falling away that was predicted in the word of God.

Chapter 14
Why Catholics remain Catholic

14.1 Religious statistics

Note: Christianity in the United States has fallen about 12% over the last decade. The fall in religious identification and activity has affected both Protestant and Roman Catholic Churches. According to Pew, 43% of adults identify with Protestantism, down from 51% in 2009. And 20% identify as Catholic, down from 23% in 2009.

https://www.theguardian.com/world/2019/oct/17/americans-less-christian-religion-survey-pew

Catholics frequently leave Catholicism, and there are many reasons, but it has been the sex abuse scandals in recent times. A more significant number have not left but consider leaving because they feel the Catholic Church has let them down because of the scandals and how they were handled. Catholicism may even grow in certain areas like Mexico, South America, and Africa. In traditional strongholds of Catholicism, there is a significantly increased ratio of those leaving to those coming to Catholicism. In any case, the reasons Catholics leave are typically not doctrinal, and many have been able to deal with the social issues, and maybe more importantly, many do not know where else to go. Catholics claim 1.37 billion members worldwide, but that is based mainly on some history of baptisms. A better gauge might be their **regular attendance,** and those numbers would be substantially less. Catholics who stop attending are left on the roll. Baptisms are also way down (34%), and considering everything, Catholicism could collapse in the United States unless something changes. The topic is why do Catholics remain Catholic? Whatever percentage of Catholics remain Catholic, there must be a reason. My sample size is terribly small, but since most of the responses are the "same," it is reasonable to believe the rationales given are pretty widespread and representative of the population. The reason I get most often is that it is easy to be Catholic and/or Catholicism is as good as other religions. These are not necessarily the words used, but it is the essence of their answer. The background of such thinking is that they have a poor understanding of Catholicism: the history of its doctrines, the history of Catholicism's development, nonetheless they **think** they understand Catholicism. They believe what they have been taught and have not been very investigative. This casual attitude would be acceptable in many matters but not for the most crucial thing in their existence. Namely, life is about the soul.

85% of those "born" into Catholicism remain Catholic, but this number is highly exaggerated if regular attendance is the criteria. One reason that more do not leave is that people like being Catholic – not very scientific. Someone once wrote religion is experience, image, and story, and this is sadly the case. This seems to point to religion consisting of a very physical set of things that people would use to describe their religion. The only difference between the descriptions of religion would be their experiences, often as viewed in their images and stories in which they have been involved or have been told. This is the very reason we have all these religions, and I think why people become so attached. Indeed, it is the indoctrination and propaganda, which emphasize experience and image and the story. Catholicism provides great experiences, images, and stories. This description is more of an observation of religion by looking in and seeing people going through the motions. Religion can be cold and inflexible with mindless people wandering about, with some being certain and some uncertain in their beliefs. The point of this chapter is to indicate that those are the wrong reasons to associate with and remain in a belief, and in our case, to remain Catholic. However, the formula of experience, image, and the story does work very well with most of the world's institutions (not just religion, i.e., business). The quality of the "allegiance of association" depends on whether the experience, image, and story are a net positive or negative. Conversely, the measure of the religion of God, the God of the Bible, is one where the **quality of a person's association is due to it being the truth**.

14.2 Catholics numb to anything different than Catholicism

Religion if it is the truth, is dealing with God and yes, God is quite different than the "world of religion" imagines. Once again, you can only understand God correctly if He reveals Himself. The real reason to associate and maintain association with God involves the truth. Life can only be successful when it consists of the truth. Why should Catholics leave Catholicism? They should leave because Catholicism is NOT the truth. Many Catholics are stuck in positive experiences, images, and stories, and thus there is not much reason to leave. We are talking about people who remain Catholic despite the scandals, despite the rules that seemingly should not be religious, despite the human-devised authoritarian rule, despite the terrible history of cruelty, and this list of problems can be quite long.

Nonetheless, there is a significant number that remains Catholic. The one thing that can move a person away from Catholicism is the truth, which is sadly not on their list – they believe they already have the truth. Although I dislike this description of religion (experiences, images, and stories), it explains why people stick with their beliefs and their religion. It can be challenging to talk to someone about truth and encourage "understanding what they believe" if understanding has never been in the conversation of their religious life. It might have been in the background at the beginning of their association with Catholicism but has long ago been replaced by positive experiences, images, and stories.

There is quite a contrast between one living as a Catholic and one who is "in Christ." A Catholic can go through the required motions defined by Catholicism and do that without disturbing their lives. It is a crime that Catholics do not have sufficient knowledge to understand their life needs to be **seriously devoted to God** if they are to succeed. Those "in Christ" have an awareness of the seriousness of living how God requires, and it fills their waking hours.

14.3 Many pathetic reasons for remaining Catholic

One oxymoronic reason Catholics remain Catholic is that their teachings are consistently unreasonable, confusing, and changing, and in that condition, there is something mysterious, and this must be God's way. This points to a typical weakness with Catholics: an exceedingly poor understanding of God and God's word.

In contrast, those who know scriptures can see how everything fits together perfectly in providing the truth. Catholicism fits their deceit together in a way that may appear logical and can effectively convince people. An example might be inventing the doctrine of original sin (an "at birth" condition), then needing to baptize babies, then needing something other than baptism to forgive committed sins. They invent the confessional and the need for priests, then realize they need to have Mary (mother of Jesus) free from all sin. They create a doctrine teaching she was born without original sin (Immaculate Conception). Then because of her purity, they need to have her bypass death and ascend to heaven and be with her Son. Indeed, all this cannot be false. **Yes, it is**, beginning with the non-scriptural invention of original sin! Nonetheless, all this and so much more can be overwhelming to the point of acceptance. So once again, Catholics must clean up a complicated, fictitious doctrine and all of its associated fallout by creating a new group of deceitful doctrines.

In all religions, there are emotional aspects. They can be powerful and shut the door to "anything different" due to those **moving experiences and vibrant thoughts**. Emotion can be a confining "jail cell" that shuts out the truth because someone has been overwhelmed. The origin of most religious beliefs has been experienced in conjunction with a great deal of emotion. The emotion may be related to family history with Catholicism, it may be related to a miracle that is associated with Catholicism, it may be related to the Real Presence, it may be related to a devotion to Mary or a hundred other things that are in a person's background as a Catholic. There can also be an economic aspect that shuts the door to accepting anything that opposes Catholicism. This might be an exceedingly powerful factor to continue the lie, especially among clergy on the payroll. The livelihood of individuals drives all sorts of unethical decisions in business. In the clergy, it may be worse since there may be little or no other opportunities to earn a living. It is a terrible reason for remaining Catholic, but it can be a powerful influence blocking the truth for some persons.

Evidence of error in Catholicism, no matter how powerful, falls on deaf ears. Many Catholics believe it is wrong to entertain/consider anything different in religion than Catholicism. I refer to this as the "perfect storm" for any religion. They have shut the door to anything different, and of course, it has its heritage in pride. It is pride in what they believe and how they arrived at that belief – they are so sure. It is challenging for a person to accept they have been manipulated, as suggested in this book.

14.4 Nothing is challenging about being a Catholic

There is another reason Catholics remain Catholics and Protestants remain Protestants, and it has to do with their comfortable religious lifestyle. Leaving Catholicism and going into the truth can be difficult because you need to live your life for Christ and the gospel. Most importantly, that means not living it for themselves. Catholics may respond, "I already live my life for Christ," and begin naming various Catholic rites/duties they perform. In truth, they are living their life for the Catholic Church, which they believe is equivalent to living it for Christ.

However, there is an infinite difference between living your life for Christ versus living it for the Catholic Church. Your life "in Christ" becomes one wherein everything is not what I want, but what God wants of me. Every decision must now consider God's point of view. Some decisions will be tough, very challenging, and perhaps might become difficult for those I love. This is why people seeking the truth concerning their souls have many questions regarding things that may be challenging in their new belief. It is like the case of the young rich ruler who wanted to follow Jesus, but when he learned what was required, he walked away from the thing he sought – being a disciple of Christ. Why does God make it difficult for a person to live as a disciple? God wants to achieve His purpose of having all come to repentance, be obedient. Yet He can only accept those who are worthy. We might say dedicated to God's will, in order to share in the Divine Nature. God is sorting out such persons, and for example, a timid person concerning doing God's will, may not please Him. God has high expectations for those "in Christ" in consideration of living for Him and the gospel. If you ponder all scripture, certain characteristics please God. They are things like being unselfish, humble, courageous, kind, placing others above self, having a love of the truth, and being devoted to doing the will of God. These are more than words, more than attitudes but are demonstrated in the choices you make every day. This is the kind of person you need to be, and if you are not, you need to become such a person. Some can do that when they realize they are "in contact" with God. It begins in repentance and your ongoing commitment to living without sin. Catholicism does not bother you with "such difficulties." You can be a Catholic and live pretty much as you please, maybe not perfect, perhaps not always pleasing but good enough to get you into purgatory.

*Note: It is **not** difficult to know **what to do, but living your life for Christ can be challenging**.*

14.5 Another thought on Catholics remaining Catholic

The evidence against everything Catholic is overwhelming, but who will listen. I learned something from typical, everyday Catholics who were average to above average in their Catholic participation. I was seeking their true thoughts about Catholicism, and it revealed something which should have been expected from their training. Yet, it answers my question as to why

Catholics remain Catholic. Catholics do not have a reasonable understanding of God, but they have a good grasp of the Catholic method. Good knowledge of God would have them respecting God's word as the highest form of reverence by honoring it in obedience and not the Catholic Church. That would mean taking seriously the word of God and nothing else! They would see that only God was perfect. The Catholic Church has been shown to be wrong in everything, and the first thing is thinking Peter is the rock, and then it goes downhill from there.

In Catholicism, there is the freedom to think of God pretty much any way they wish. If they want to think of God as "God is love," that would be fine, or if they're going to think of God as one who works in mysterious ways, that would also be acceptable. In the framework of how they define those two concepts, anything would be satisfactory. Like Protestantism, there is no objection to a personal relationship with God. Protestantism and Catholicism support personal communication with God as possible. A Catholic variation on communication would involve Mary or one of their saints being the mediator with God. Typically they mean a mediator with the One who is the mediator with the Father, namely Jesus. Of course, God desires a personal relationship with each person **through His Son**. It is a spiritual relationship that is **ONLY established** in obedience to the gospel. Being told you have a personal relationship with God or believing you have one does **not** mean the relationship is real. God has a defined way to have a relationship with Him. God is not how you want to make Him.

A better understanding of God will help you leave Catholicism. The most basic discernment of God is understanding His purpose, which is YOU, and He will be successful when YOU obey the gospel and remain faithful until death resulting in sharing in the Divine Nature. Understand that God wants none to fail (2 Peter 3:9, 1 Timothy 2:4), but He also reveals most will fail (Matthew 7:13-14). Again, if you understand God, that makes perfect sense; otherwise, it will seem problematic. Although you are right to think God is love, you need to understand what that means, and that can begin by understanding what it does not mean. It does not mean that there can be any compromises with His word. Since God cannot lie (Titus 1:2), dying in sin means you will suffer eternal loss – no excuses. This in no way means God is not loving, but it points to God also being perfect in distributing justice, and as explained in this book, God is the perfect absence of evil and thus cannot share eternity with evil. These are basic understandings of God, like the understanding God has left humankind with no mysteries – all man needs is easily understood and revealed. Peter is exact in proclaiming that we have all things that pertain to life and godliness. What is missing? What is mysterious? Nothing!

Religion likes to be involved in defining what is sinful, what is acceptable, but why? God has defined sin such that those associated with sinful things will not inherit the kingdom of God. There is nothing to be discussed, nothing that can be modified, and one should understand that there is no flexibility with God. Everything becomes very simple for those who understand the seriousness of the scriptures. Certainly, there must be some circumstances, some considerations that change how sin might be viewed. There is not, but respect what God has declared, and if you have some valid extenuating circumstances, some special considerations realize God can and will perfectly manage them. However, it would be misleading to think your personal difficulties will allow you to escape living in opposition to the clear directives from God. Do not focus on possible excuses, extenuating circumstances to provide you eternal relief. In fact, such things are telling you that something is wrong. Why are you counting on excuses? Make the needed changes such that your route to heaven is conventional, God's way. Live with a dedication to the truth.

As a Catholic, what is your awareness of the seriousness of lying? It should be as follows in Revelation.

Revelation 21:8

*8 But the cowardly, unbelieving, abominable, murderers, sexually immoral, sorcerers, idolaters, and **all liars** shall have their part in the lake which burns with fire and brimstone, which is the second death."*

Humankind likes to minimize lying but not God. Religions like to categorize sin, and there is a world of classification for sin. If you understand God, you can see all the discussion around sin is foolish – believe God! He warns humankind not to die in sin, any sin. That, for many people, might seem cruel, but God in love provides a remedy for sin, and that is where your focus needs to be. Understand God when He declares the fear of the Lord is the beginning of knowledge. Many people might think this is wrong, but in God's perfection, He knows fearing Him is wise since it is exceedingly better than failing in life. All these "understandings of God" have a single reason that He might fulfill His purpose in as many as possible. God's love saturates the world in the only way it can, namely by His way, because that way can result in eternal success for people.

Catholics see God differently because the Catholic Church portrays God differently than the scriptures, whereas those "in Christ" see God as He has defined Himself. Since all those "in Christ" have only one guide, namely the word of God, they all see God (in their devotion not to change His meaning) the same. You need to understand God and His character as He has revealed Himself. Catholicism has not allowed Catholics that option, but they see many different versions of God and His directives. Typically, those teachings are changing, being argued, being debated, and it will never end. Unless you can see your way, away from Catholicism, you are headed for the worst of possible ends.

14.6 A more convenient time and the end of time

Regardless of your religious belief (if any), the matter of your soul is most important. It would be careless of me if I did not encourage you to move away from Catholicism or Protestantism or any other belief that is not the truth. Also, to make that change with some urgency.

Paul spoke to Felix, the governor of the region, in Acts 24. He spoke of faith in Jesus, and after hearing him, Felix was fearful of the consequences since Paul mentioned the judgment. In a quandary, Felix tells Paul he will call for him at a more convenient time.

Acts 24:25
25 Now as he reasoned about righteousness, self-control, and the judgment to come, Felix was afraid and answered, "Go away for now; when I have a convenient time I will call for you."

This sad account of Felix "rings true" and is understandable, representing the procrastination of perhaps most people. It is doubtful Felix lacked any evidence but may have seen some unfavorable consequences if he responded as Paul suggested. The idea of waiting for a more convenient time sounds very modern, as excuses go. Thus a short section follows on the subject of the end of time and the urgency it represents.

The timing for the end of the world – the fascination of it

We are talking about the soul, about salvation, about getting into a relationship with the savior, about the gospel message. The **urgency** of doing what is necessary to succeed in life needs to be on each person's mind. When Jesus returns, we will have died, or we may be alive. In either case, what follows is the destruction of all things physical and the final judgment.

One of the most solid things that can be understood from God is that **no one knows the timing for the end of the world**. The scriptures indicate not even the Son. We also know there will be no signs of Jesus' return. In a bit of discernment, I often say that "no signs" is the sign. One needs to be most respectful of God in this matter. Yet, people generally lack this understanding that the end of time is unknowable. They deeply desire to know when, and there is great speculation and many theories. I will tell you something that is not a sign, but it might provide something to consider. Few had an awareness of one subject discussed throughout this book but now may have accepted the meaning of, "that which is perfect." It refers to the **completed word of God,** which signaled the end of supernatural interactions and ended the revelations from God to humankind. It was over nineteen hundred years ago when "that which was perfect" came. These changes in God's operation will continue until the end of time. It seems these changes signal a winding down of what God began with creation. All that remains is determining how many will be added to the body of Christ before the end. The end could be ten thousand plus years from now, or it could be today. The unknown time for the end is in no way suggested by this thought except to say things appear ready inasmuch as there are no more revelations from God, no more supernatural events, and the end has been defined, for example, in 1 Thessalonians 4 and 2 Peter.

1 Thessalonians 4:15-17

15 For this we say to you by the word of the Lord, that we who are alive and remain until the coming of the Lord will by no means precede those who are asleep.

16 For the Lord Himself will descend from heaven with a shout, with the voice of an archangel, and with the trumpet of God. And the dead in Christ will rise first.

17 Then we who are alive and remain shall be caught up together with them in the clouds to meet the Lord in the air. And thus we shall always be with the Lord.

2 Peter 3:10-12

10 But the day of the Lord will come as a thief in the night, in which the heavens will pass away with a great noise, and the elements will melt with fervent heat; both the earth and the works that are in it will be burned up.

11 Therefore, since all these things will be dissolved, what manner of persons ought you to be in holy conduct and godliness,

12 looking for and hastening the coming of the day of God, because of which the heavens will be dissolved, being on fire, and the elements will melt with fervent heat?

The point is one should, in this most important of life's matters, be prepared. Live as though the end is close instead of thinking it is in the very distant future. The advice from the scriptures is, "now is the day of salvation."

2 Corinthians 6:2

2.......... Behold, now is the accepted time; behold, now is the day of salvation.

It always comes back to how badly do you want heaven, badly enough to live your life for Christ and the gospel? The world of Catholicism and Protestantism do not offer you a good end, and being trapped therein will require a diligent effort to escape.

Chapter 15

The substantial scriptural mistakes of Catholicism

15.1 Disrespecting the scriptures has resulted in Catholicism

The following is more than a list as it includes some brief information on each mistake. Some things are missed or misunderstood by both "Christian" giants (Catholicism and Protestantism). These are **some categories** that are typically not questioned but just accepted in how they have been presented.

- Regarding the rock of Matthew 16
- Saints
- Sin
- The forgiveness of sin
- The church
- The leadership of the church
- The directive of God to not change His word
- The afterlife
- That which is perfect
- The Scriptures are the only authorized revelation from God
- Worship must be in Spirit and Truth
- Many more, however, this is sufficient to understand the futility of Catholicism and Protestantism

The "why of Catholicism's existence" is always the **disregard of God's word.** The associated characteristics of people that allow such disrespect are pride, selfishness, hatred, cowardice, ego, greed, envy, and immorality, to mention a few.

If you are a person who has conquered the damages of religious deceit by seeking God and then obeying the gospel AND you live for Christ and the gospel, you are on the road to heaven.

You have left behind all those things unacceptable to God. You are "in Christ." You are in His spiritual body, the church. It is the church Jesus is building, and it is not the Catholic Church. You can be referred to as a saint and holy since you have been set aside for God. In coming to the truth, you learned God's only means to communicate with humankind was through the scriptures and that God has finished His revelation. You would see the church leadership is local in terms of elders, and they are servants, helping. They receive no honor. The rule is only the scriptures. You know the consequences of success and failure in life and how to work with Christ as your advocate in prayer, and how to seek forgiveness of any future sins. You understand the seriousness of your commitment to avoid sin.

You have a reasonable understanding of the tragic history of what people thought was Christianity but was Catholicism. You also know that "humankind's Christianity" has always resulted from people changing God's meaning. "Thus, you get it," and continue to grow in the grace and knowledge of God and do the prime work of bringing the gospel message to the world. Your life is lived for Christ and the gospel. Now, we will very briefly cover the huge misses of Catholicism (and Protestantism). These are things as a child of God you now understand, and as you better understand them, you can be more effective in the work of evangelism. Revealing the truth in each matter is the best way to understand the mistakes of Catholicism.

- **Regarding the rock of Matthew 16**

    This fundamental error belongs to Catholicism. The end of Catholicism for every Catholic can be as simple as understanding the rock of Matthew 16:18. The rock is the declaration of Jesus as the Son of God and certainly it is not Peter.

- **Saints**

    Saints are those in the church, "in Christ." Catholicism creates a special class of honor for its saints, simply an invention. Catholicism gives the appearance they control all things spiritual. Indeed they act as though in every way they are God on earth. The Catholic hierarchy has brazenly placed themselves over everything related to God, even selecting those for special honor as saints. The truth is all those "in Christ" have been set aside for God and thus the title of saints.

- **Sin**

    The critical element in God's test is God-defined sin. Sin is universal – all have sinned. God cannot share His Divine Nature with evil (sin), and thus there needs to be a means to have sin forgiven. Essentially, everything God has done from Genesis is related to the sin problem, and of course, Jesus is the solution. Despite God's clarity defining sin, Catholics and Protestants are liberal in their interpretations and rules concerning sin and provide zero relief (forgiveness) for the most significant of humankind's problems.

- **The forgiveness of sin**

    Forgiveness of sins is the same as salvation. Sin must be forgiven to have a relationship with God. The means of doing this is defined with clarity. Examples of conversion are provided. God creates a significant and unique way to have sins forgiven associated with the death, burial, and resurrection of Jesus. Neither Catholicism nor Protestantism gets this right, and consequently, there is no value in an association with either. Forgiveness of sins is realized in obedience to the gospel.

- **The church**

    Perhaps the most straightforward thing God provides to humankind is the church that Jesus said He would build. Catholicism and Protestantism are religions of extreme complexity and very distant from the truth. The church Jesus started is simply a **spiritual body** that a person gains affiliation in the obedience to the gospel message. The Lord Himself adds that obedient person to His church. This is what Jesus meant in Matthew 16 when He said He would build His church. The Lord knows the heart of each person and thus their sincerity, i.e., in repentance. He is the only one that can qualify a person for His spiritual body, the church. Also, in the first century, the Holy Spirit would gradually reveal the character of a local church consisting of those who were spiritual via their obedience. The local church consisting of those in His spiritual body would be God's vehicle to carry forward the gospel message until the end of time.

- **The leadership of the church**

The local church is the place for those "in Christ. " The local church consists of elders, deacons, and members. The church organization has qualifications for the elders and deacons. Of course, the only rulebook is the word of God. God builds in several important characteristics to the local church. First is their independence from all other local churches of the saints. This keeps the church free from many of the world's issues and promotes focus on its only mission, evangelism. In the elder qualifications, there is wisdom, humility, and an attitude of service. The elders oversee those "in Christ" to assure their edification while being dedicated to holding fast the faithful word. Catholicism and Protestantism are distant from the truth, very worldly and seldom have persons with the qualifications God requires for elders. The elder in the scriptures must be a plurality of elders. The elders have oversight over the local church and do not lord over the members – but are servants, shepherds, guides. The local church makes no rules concerning spiritual matters but relies only on the word of God. They safeguard God's meaning – no changes. The qualifications of elders are the opposite of the leaders of the "churches of the world." God did not create an earthly head for the church. He created a helper for His local church, one with oversight and dedication to the word. Those in the body of Christ understand the mission of each individual "in Christ" and the entire local body. Peter was an elder in the church at Jerusalem and would do as Jesus indicated in that role, namely shepherd His flock. The defined worship of the local church follows further down in this chapter.

- **The directive of God to not change His word**

God has consistently revealed throughout His word the unyielding, indisputable direction never to change His word. Since we only receive things about the truth of life from God, anything different involving religion or spirituality would be incorrect. Catholicism does not accept this, but they create doctrine and craft various ways to justify their teachings. Protestantism also has its different organizations for rulemaking. When humankind makes "religious" rules, they will always conflict with God's way.

- **The afterlife**

    The afterlife is no mystery, and since God defines success concerning salvation (forgiveness of sins), there should be no confusion. Basically, in each person's lifetime, they either succeed or fail. The judgment follows physical death, and although there is a reasonable understanding of the afterlife, Catholicism creates the very human idea of purgatory. The basic understanding of life has to do with God's purpose to share His Divine Nature, and that end is only for those "in Christ."

- **That which is perfect**

    Truly one of the big misses of Catholicism and Protestantism is the failure to understand that God has completed His revelation to humankind. Simultaneously with having that which is perfect, God is no longer involved as in the past with such things as signs, as miracles. His communication with humankind has ended in completing the divine message, and correspondingly there is no other external means (signs, miracles). Here is an excellent distinction if you can make it. Realize the power of God's word and how, in its completion, everything has been revealed. You can go into God's word and know everything of importance, that is, EVERYTHING of importance. Remember, life is about the soul and really about nothing else. That in itself is a powerful distinction. God's word is so encompassing that nothing else is needed. Nothing can aid more in a person's conversion, not signs, not miracles, not talking with someone from beyond the realm of humankind. One should not underestimate the power of the scriptures. Take seriously what Peter says, "as His divine power has given to us all things that pertain to life and godliness." Believe that we need nothing else. We have all things required to succeed. We know what to do, how to live, how to help others, and how to communicate with God. What would be the value of, for instance, a miracle? Would you be more confident? The correct answer is you would not be more confident because, in the completed word of God, you know God, you know the truth. The history of miracles has never made a lasting impression on people, as was the case of the Israelites escaping Egypt or those fed by Jesus with loaves and fishes. However, the truth, the completed word of God has sustainability.

o Coming to grips that God has completed His communication with humankind sometime in the latter part of the first century means there will be no future doctrines, no future messages, no need for any further directions to humanity. This destroys the idea of Catholicism concerning the early church fathers offering some additional teaching. In Protestantism (as well as Catholicism), there have always been people claiming some communication with God and at times, even miracles. God has completed His revelation to humankind. The thing to understand is that nothing else is needed for God to accomplish his purpose. If you understand that, then you would have the highest respect for that which is perfect – God's completed word. Yet what do we have but people looking for other sources of truth and in the Catholic case declaring their traditions, their apostolic succession, and their Magisterium to be equivalent in doctrine. Catholicism is "sitting in the place of God" and is masterful in destroying souls.

Note: For clarity, there will be no further communication from God to humankind since God has provided all needed for success. However, for those "in Christ" God has provided a means **to contact Him** *in prayer through their advocate, His Son.*

- **Scripture is the only authorized revelation from God**

    Interestingly, the one thing that Protestantism got right was the first thing dropped as some Protestants moved to Catholicism. This is, of course, Sola Scriptura or the recognition that truth only comes from the scriptures. There is only one valid communication from God, and it is the one He authorizes, and in consideration of His purpose, God completes His part **perfectly**. God does not leave the truth to chance, and he continuously warns about changing what has been delivered. Just as He assured everything in creation worked perfectly, i.e., the spin of all the heavenly bodies, He also ensures that what matters most was achieved. Namely, He assured that the truth has come down from Him accurately throughout time.

- **Worship must be in spirit and truth**

Humankind makes a mess of this critical issue of worshipping God. Even in the earliest times, with a great deal of ignorance, "remote people" attempted to worship God. They did not know God or how to worship Him. They could not succeed because God had not revealed the essential elements of worship. Their intentions were likely good, although not qualifying as worship. The Athenians received some information from Paul regarding their worship inasmuch as how it was **not acceptable** to God, the true God. The things said in Acts 17 represent how **not** to worship. In some ways, those things represent how many in "Christianity" worship today.

Acts 17:24-27

24 "God, who made the world and everything in it, since He is Lord of heaven and earth, does not dwell in temples made with hands.

25 Nor is He worshiped with men's hands, as though He needed anything, since He gives to all life, breath, and all things.

26 And He has made from one blood every nation of men to dwell on all the face of the earth, and has determined their preappointed times and the boundaries of their dwellings,

27 so that they should seek the Lord, in the hope that they might grope for Him and find Him, though He is not far from each one of us;

God **in this last age** has specified how He is to be worshipped. First, not just anyone can worship God. This might be surprising to many, but realize we only know the things of God if He reveals them. As you understand God, you may recognize from a study of God as He has revealed himself that He is the perfect absence of evil. Indeed, He seeks those who are sinners and can face up to their sins. Yet He cannot be approached by sinners other than seeking Him and truth. You might say those on a path of getting "into Christ" are on a course to have their sins forgiven. Worship comes only from those who can approach God as worshippers. Worshippers are those who please God, and they can in no way worship God unless they are first without evil, without sin. Then such a person is in a condition to approach God. Jesus makes this very clear in John.

353

John 4:24

24 "God is Spirit, and those who worship Him must worship in spirit and truth."

There is an important conclusion from God's word. You must be in the body of Christ to meet the requirement of worshipping in spirit. The fact that a person or group of people desire to worship God does not mean they can. This can be shocking to the world of religion, but it is God's way to qualify a person for worship. You are eligible by obeying the gospel. You cannot put the cart in front of the horse and expect to go anywhere. If you are sincere in your quest for truth, this realization can allow you to see the depth of error in Catholic and Protestant churches. We consistently declare they have nothing right. The recognition neither of these organizations has ever worshipped God might take your breath away.

The truth part of worshipping in "spirit and **truth**" is doing as God directs. The world of religion worships God by developing things that **they believe will please Him,** when what God requires for worship is obedience. Paul admonished the Athenians, "God does not dwell in temples made with hands, nor is He worshipped with men's hands." The idea of "men's hands" is being worshipped by the way men devise.

Worship is always an honor to God **in obedience** as opposed to being worshipped by "men's hands." We can see the ways to worship God are contained in the manner of worship by the local church. We can say that remembering God's Son on the first day of the week as directed would be worship. We can say that speaking to one another in psalms and hymns and spiritual songs making melody in our hearts would be worship. We can say that supporting the local church's work as purposed in our hearts would be worship. We can say that being devoted to growing in the grace and knowledge of God was worship. Dedication to and bringing the gospel message to the world would be worship. All these things are "obedience things" done by those in the body of Christ, and you might also note they are spiritual things done by those who are spiritual.

15.2 The consequence of not taking God seriously

So how close are Catholicism and Protestantism to the truth? We might say that neither is in any way close. God is serious, truthful and these religions are neither. There is just one thing you can associate with both, namely failure. People believe Christianity is what they want to make of it when God has precisely defined Christianity. Therein lies the humility God requires – doing things God's way. What a mess humankind's religions have made of the truth. Since so many have it wrong, it might seem an excuse, but it is not. It is best to go back to "square one" and seek God, seek truth, and live the way God directs. That will begin with obeying the gospel. God's way is quite simple, and the various complicated religious organizations of humankind are only distractions.

Chapter 16
Summary and more conclusions on Catholic audacity

16.1 Catholicism misleads, but this book's true interest is souls

The subject emphasized in this book is the Catholic Church's disregard for the scriptures. They claim the highest respect for the scriptures, but they miss the critical aspect of respect. The respect for God is the respect for God's word, and you cannot do that if you are changing His word in any way, which means not adding to it or taking away from it, or making any substitutions. Paul warned about changing the gospel message, and Catholicism has massacred the gospel message. This is a strong rebuke of what they have done, and as its seriousness "sinks in," you realize Catholicism does not provide a means for sins to be forgiven. Life is about the soul and absolutely about nothing else, and there is no success outside the body of Christ.

This summary should be relatively short, but it has grown somewhat to clarify further the points made in the book. The truth was preached in the first century as the Holy Spirit guided the apostles. The truth is all a person needs. There was no Catholic Church in the first century, yet people were saved and added to the body of Christ, which is added to the church Jesus is building. The church Jesus was and continues to build is, as He indicated, not of this world being His **spiritual** body. The audacity of Catholicism is the changing of God's word, and the outcome is a very physical church that cannot address the problem Jesus came to solve – a spiritual problem, namely sin. The gospel message is perfect and accomplishes God's purpose in all those who are obedient. In Chapter 5, the tables show God's means for achieving salvation, and it is quite simple and representative of the conversions of the New Testament. Also shown is the apparent means of attaining salvation in Catholicism. **There are no conversions even remotely like the Catholic means of salvation in the New Testament.** Every aspect of Catholic conversion is alien to the scriptures in teaching and principle. Catholic conversion represents the opposite of how God saves. Salvation in Catholicism is built on original sin, which is non-existent. I say "built on original sin" because many other things were needed to "protect" that invention. Once they appeared, those things essentially replaced God's means to achieve salvation. Catholicism would claim Catholic salvation was built on Christ, but they do not have the doctrine of Christ. They are not the church Christ continues to build, and the invention of original sin leads to creating a non-scriptural path that **does not forgive sins**. The obvious realization is that Catholic doctrine conflicts with the word of God in all its teachings.

Protestant conversions to Catholicism have brought apologetics that is more Bible-based. However, those Protestants must accept the early church father's writings and agree with the idea of apostolic succession. The huge stumbling block for all of Catholicism is Matthew 16:15-19. The use of these verses in support of the Catholic Church is the ultimate blasphemy to God. God's purpose is spiritual and about the quality (of individuals). In contrast, Catholicism is a physical church that focuses on quantity to build a robust and worldly rulemaking institution.

16.2 Here is what is important

You are alive, and irrespective of your involvement in Catholicism or Protestantism or anything else, you are still, regardless of your "sin state," capable of winning your very personal battle with sin. It is a true and worthy statement that **it is not how long you are in the kingdom of God (His spiritual church) but what you do with the time you are there**. The truth is overwhelming, and even if you are the pope of the Catholic Church or the two mentioned as Catholic converts from Protestantism, you need the gospel message. You now know the truth, and it makes sense and needs no defense. There is certainty in God's way, and that provides you with the perfect assurance you are doing the right thing.

16.3 Many nails in the coffin of Catholicism

You might think that the consequence of **Peter not being the rock** would mean there is no Catholic Church. That would be correct. However, that FACT by itself is of a very minor consequence. The truly heavyweight, massive consequence is the loss of souls, perhaps your soul in following the teachings of Catholicism. Consequently, as a Catholic, the gospel message is never taught. Thus it cannot be obeyed, and there is a failed life. Therefore, believing Peter is the rock ultimately leads to your failure in life, and in that sense, the consequence is the most crucial

357

thing in the life of every Catholic. It is quite easy to understand that Peter is not the rock. Since Catholicism fails with their understanding of Matthew 16, it is easy to reject Catholicism altogether. Rejecting Catholicism is like a silver lining behind the cloud because it cracks open the door to the truth and the potential for sharing in the Divine Nature.

There is an apparent thought for many readers, and it follows. Catholicism is the religion of deception, and if you love the truth, you might have noticed this. Yet, how can this be? There are many thousands of Catholic teachers, and the two discussed in this book are outstanding in terms of knowledge and thoughtful presentations. It must seem inconceivable that Catholicism is so far from the truth. The consequences of its teachings are the opposite of what people are looking for in terms of an eternal destination. Here is the answer to this quandary. First, it is fair to realize that it is not only Catholics. There are lots of Muslims, lots of Protestants, and lots of people of other religions. These substantial "religions of the world" each have a massive number of members, an enormous number of supporting documents, and a vast number of apparently knowledgeable leaders, yet there is no truth. They teach many different doctrines but are not close to the truth. A honest and straightforward answer to why so many have so much wrong is **that people do what they want, believe what they want, and do not have a love of the truth**.

Why is Catholicism so far from the truth? **Why is essentially everything wrong**. How can everything be wrong? Everything wrong means all the doctrine, the whole concept of the Catholic Church, the inability to differentiate between the spiritual and physical, religious honor for persons, and everything in their catechism, all their councils. The "everything wrong" is really in itself the answer to the how and why of this disaster called Catholicism. The best way to understand this is to point out something mentioned throughout this book: the Catholic fundamentals are wrong. The most fundamental error is the creation of an earthly head for the church – their pope. Everything built on such a structure fails. There are many sub-errors, like failing to see the things that are metaphors and in other cases failing to see the things that are literal. There is no excuse for failing to see the metaphors because while the literal might seem reasonable, there is evidence in God's perfection that eliminates the literal conclusion.

An example of this was how the Real Presence is a metaphor and how God's complete revelation on the subject shows it is not literal (see Chapter 9). Another key sub-error is the invention of original sin and all the subsequent creations needed to support original sin. The leadership of the rulemaking Catholic Church is in the hands of men, and they cannot fit anything together in their doctrines, whereas the truth perfectly fits everything together.

Something notable that seems not to be noted

I will pick a point in time. Let us say 1950 and say before this there was little use of the Bible by Catholics. There were references, but the more common book was the Catholic Missal. The Missal contained the prayers, important chants, and necessary instructions for celebrating the mass (Latin: missa) in the Roman Catholic Church throughout the year. This would be the book carried by Catholics, including the children of a certain age. It was as a child what I considered to be the book of Catholicism. My non-Catholic friends carried their Bibles, and Catholics carried their Missals. You would never understand God or the word of God using the Catholic Missal.

There was a recent albeit gradual shift in the capability of Catholic debaters to defend Catholicism. I was amazed until I realized that these more effective debaters were Protestants who had become Catholics. They were unlike the priests of their time since they had solid scripture knowledge and experience. Time has passed, and Catholics use the Bible, and those more recently brought through the priestly regimen have a much better understanding of the scriptures. During these non-bible Catholic times, Catholics seldom questioned what they were taught. Catholicism had done an excellent job of keeping the scriptures away from Catholics. Their Missals were an acceptable means of knowledge, and the Bible was not needed. As time passed, the Bible became more available, and in this intervening time, Catholic apologists had created reasonable defenses.

Now with the Bible in the hands of Catholics, there was a significant weakening of Catholicism. Nonetheless, Catholicism continues to promote Bible use. Of course, they tout the Bible along with the teachings of the early church fathers, the apostolic succession, and their Magisterium as the "complete package" for Catholicism. They stand on a hill and say Catholicism provided the Bible to the world, that only Catholics have the Eucharist, and frequently teach only Catholics are going to heaven. That is where Catholicism is today.

As discussed in this book, one might ask why these two Protestant ministers knowledgeable in the scriptures became Catholic? It seems the same reasons that resulted in their rejection of Protestantism would have them also rejecting Catholicism. The shock of identifying the error of Protestantism opened their minds to the possibility of Catholicism. There was a difficult road ahead to accept Catholicism since Protestants were raised with strong warnings against Catholicism. As Protestant ministers, they knew of the Catholic problems, and some would vigorously teach against Catholicism. Nonetheless, once they accepted the fundamental teachings that justify Catholic authority, many other Catholic doctrines could be rationalized. I could not help but think that after discovering the errors of Protestantism, they must have thought, "what other choice did they have." Catholics who question their beliefs are typically aware of fundamental problems with Protestantism. Protestants who realize problems with their doctrines still see the many difficulties of Catholicism. Thus there may seem to be no good solution for the problems of those who question. Neither Dr. Hahn nor Marcus Grodi nor these questioning Protestants or Catholics realizes Catholicism and Protestantism are both terribly wrong. They both have incorrectly narrowed the Christian field to be either Catholic or Protestant.

So what is notable that is not noted? It is a movement to the scriptures by the Catholic Church in terms of sanctioning their members in its use. Catholicism now believes they have sufficient apologetics to respond to the many problems Catholics will find in the scriptures. Although Catholic apologists have developed responses to the many difficulties that may satisfy some Catholics, they will never satisfy one who loves the truth.

16.4 The pathetic and ineffectual cover-ups of Catholicism

Oh, how easy it is to justify all the past horrors of Catholicism and the Catholic hierarchy who committed them. When Catholics are asked about bad popes, their immorality, their cruelty, and murders, they say – yes, this was terrible, but they all kept to their primary duty of upholding the "faith." That faith is in the Catholic Church – INCREDIBLE.

In this and other books (and webpages) by this author, it is pointed out in a detailed and evidential study that "God is the perfect absence of evil." God will never share His Divine Nature with evil, and His test of humanity sorts good from evil. God could never be associated with an evil organization such as Catholicism. God is aligned with the church His Son continues to build, and it is pure, without sin. The gospel message provides forgiveness of sins, and those obedient to that message are added to the spiritual body of Christ by the Lord Himself – His spiritual church. God requires people to seek Him with their whole being, "And you will seek Me and find Me when you search for Me with all your heart" Jeremiah 29:13. God has done His part by providing the means for the reconciliation of each person. If you look at the characteristics God requires of those "in Christ," there is no evil there. To get "into Christ," there needs to be a certain attitude, and the primary element is humility. The characteristics of the leaders of Catholicism have been very much the opposite of what God requires. Peter describes the character God requires.

2 Peter 1:3-8

3 as His divine power has given to us all things that pertain to life and godliness, through the knowledge of Him who called us by glory and virtue,

4 by which have been given to us exceedingly great and precious promises, that through these you may be partakers of the divine nature, having escaped the corruption that is in the world through lust.

5 But also for this very reason, giving all diligence, add to your faith virtue, to virtue knowledge,

6 to knowledge self-control, to self-control perseverance, to perseverance godliness,

7 to godliness brotherly kindness, and to brotherly kindness love.

8 For if these things are yours and abound, you will be neither barren nor unfruitful in the knowledge of our Lord Jesus Christ.

However, there is nothing as disturbing as the rulemaking Catholicism has claimed for its leadership. It is the worst of offenses to think that Peter was the rock of Matthew 16:18. God's plan from Genesis 3:15 included many things over the next 4000 years to bring Christ. Then Jesus suffers and dies in obedience to the Father, which opens the door to the gospel message— followed by the completion of the communication with humankind. Before the end of the first century, there was a movement away from the scriptures. The significance of even seemingly minor deviations in God's word would be devastating. There is no such thing as minor deviations from God's truth. Who could judge the true magnitude of any deviation? If we "fast forward" a bit, the outcome of these many, at times seemingly innocent variations results in the Catholic

361

Church and their pope by the early seventh century. In the name of God, Catholicism will carry out all sorts of evil.

Sometimes the word inquisition is used because it conveys the horror that is associated uniquely with Catholicism. Indeed, the Catholic church is the **church of the inquisition,** and it would be hard to be eviler than that. Yet, there were thousands of evil actions taken in the name of God and always in protective paranoia. Worse than this title (church of the inquisition), they are the church that deceives to the loss of souls of all who follow Catholicism.

God, as mentioned, does not interfere in this last age (last days, Hebrews 1.1,2) with humankind even in the most severe cases of deceit – such as Catholicism. We have that which is perfect for guiding us, and it easily allows a person with a love of the truth to differentiate truth from error. How easy is it to see that the rock of Matthew 16:18 is not Peter? How easy is it to see the historical evidence of evil in Catholicism and how it continues to this day in very subtle ways as well as outwardly? How easy is it to see the characteristics of Catholic leaders and their followers compared to how Peter describes they must be? They are very far from the model God requires, and that model would disallow the actions that characterized their history.

The leadership of Catholicism will suffer the most severe retribution of God as they stole the name of God. Those who follow the Catholic Church will fail in the only thing that matters – the salvation of their souls. Many think God allows this terrible religion, but He allows choices, and Catholicism is the worst possible choice. A love of the truth can easily let a Catholic know there is no connection between Catholicism and God. Also, righteousness is evident in the gospel message, and each person can choose to align with the truth.

16.5 Coming to grips with Catholicism

The **Catholic Church opposes the purpose of God** by teaching error and thus negates the possibility of a successful life, heaven. The extreme immorality of the Catholic hierarchy over history is seen in their actions that exhibit profoundly evil persons. It should be apparent that these same people in the early centuries created the doctrines of Roman Catholicism. One would expect to find in Catholicism something exceedingly far from the doctrine of Christ, and you would not be disappointed.

*Note: You would be correct to say there are many fine people in the Catholic Church, and I know many such as family, friends, and even Catholic priests. The world would say these are good people. **Goodness as seen by God such that the person is a candidate for heaven is defined by God as those without sin.** Thus God's measure is very objective. If you want to succeed in life, you must reach the "level of performance" God requires. Unlike the teachings of Catholicism, what God requires makes perfect sense and is easily understood. However, it can be challenging to commit to such a life unless there is a love of the truth and an unselfish attitude. You will be on solid ground with a good start if you understand your **subjective definition of goodness** is quite different than God's objective criteria. Yet, those you see as good may be the best candidates for sharing in the Divine Nature. As it turns out, even those at the other end of **your goodness scale** might also be good candidates. The gospel message is quite powerful as one comes to understand God's purpose and His nature.*

16.6 Individuals are missing in the collective Catholic Church

The Catholic Church has many interesting characteristics that reveal its true nature. One thing that might bring some clarity is how Catholicism is very collective in its dealing with people. On the other hand, God's truth and mode of operation have a singular quality emphasizing individuals. The ongoing spiritual war is each person versus sin – very singular. This is something that needs to be highlighted. The idea of "collective" is Catholicism's dealing with people as a group and, as previously mentioned emphasizing quantity versus quality. The quantity aspect of Catholicism is not so apparent but nonetheless a critical observation of their character. That aspect is displayed in the corporate nature of the Catholic Church, which overwhelms the individual. The collective nature of Catholicism is somewhat hidden but can be seen in its lack of emphasis on souls. They would deny this, but how often are souls discussed, how often is salvation mentioned and in their place are many Catholic processes like the Catholic mass, like a multitude of liturgies, like much discussion of social issues, like the emphasis on their sacraments, like their various involvement in worldly activities, like their charities. This list of things is quite long. Catholics learn how to view/honor their pope, their saints, their priests, and Mary. Then there are the ever-changing rules for their mass, for confession, for sins, and the

Real Presence. Catholics define for their members how specific sins are to be viewed. They announce to all Catholics the results of their councils, and they are binding on the "Catholic family." It is all just another aspect of the complication of the Catholic Church. Indeed, Catholics never realize **what is missing** as they participate in the various Catholic activities/practices. Namely, where is the emphasis on their soul, salvation, and the singular mission for the church that relates to the soul and salvation? Those subjects are neatly fit in some corner to say the soul is important, but their actions speak louder than their claims.

God is interested in **individual responses** to the gospel message. The distinction here is God's concern for each individual and how they need to realize there is a war, which is very personal between each person and sin. There must be an individual response that includes a commitment to God's way, that will continue the remainder of their lives. Each person acting in obedience to the gospel message is **added individually to the body of Christ**, a spiritual "organization." They each must live apart from sin based on their repentance and fulfill God's directive of how to live (for instance, Galatians 5. 22-25). They each become capable teachers of the truth and are devoted to bringing the gospel message to a lost and dying world. Their worship is spiritual, and every individual memorializes the Son on the first day of the week. Each part of authorized worship involves an individual commitment, which means a devotion to worship as God specifies.

Amid all these things Catholics do, where is the individual. The individual can be lost in all the ever-changing teachings of Catholicism, in all the Catholic processes, rites, and rules. Catholicism may not even know how they arrived at this corporate culture, but it is a by-product of changing the gospel message. Catholics are to have faith in the Catholic Church. The gospel message has individuals responding in obedience to receive forgiveness of sins. They individually believe what God the Father revealed to Peter. They repent of their sins (a turning from sin in their life) and go into the watery grave, dying to their sins and rising out of the water into a new life – sin is gone. The Lord, Himself, adds the obedient individual to His spiritual church. There is a very personal one-on-one with God. It is difficult to understand how a relationship with God is achieved in Catholicism, how sins are forgiven.

The truth has a person having **faith in God**, very singular. Catholics would say that is what they mean, but it is not what they always say and never what they do – they teach faith in the Catholic Church. God's means of reconciliation is very singular – just one way. Catholicism is very confused, and Protestantism, in their acceptance of "somethings Catholic," has been corrupted. Less obvious is how Catholicism has corrupted the non-Christian religions of the world. This latter outcome is the result of **making Christianity appear as something much different** and something to be avoided. Christianity, as in the church Jesus is building, and Catholicism (and Protestantism) are extreme opposites in every way, but unfortunately, this is not well understood.

Being raised a Catholic with all the indoctrination, all the propaganda is overwhelming and produces a particular Catholic dedication. However, every Catholic eventually sees problems that, if pursued, can lead a person away from Catholicism. Some may go as far away as atheism; others stay close enough that they can quickly return. Then some get beyond Peter being the rock to the real meaning. The truth will not have you ever leaving it as it is compelling, providing the highest confidence of an incredibly marvelous end. The truth is easy to understand but can be challenging to live as you live for Christ and the gospel and not for yourself. With a bit of effort, you can recognize that Catholicism is a human-devised organization having no association with God. Indeed, Catholicism appears in its grandeur to be the place of God on earth. It is the single most significant deception in the history of the world because it negatively impacts the eternity of so many people.

16.7 God will get those He wants
(If you can think for yourself - the truth will be pretty obvious)

As I often mention, thinking is more than having thoughts; but it is a creative process, a logical process, and a process of contemplation. Do Catholics and Catholic hierarchy understand what they believe. They think they do, but the issue of truth is likely seldom considered. Catholicism is more of a given, and the subject of truth was resolved a very long time ago, and Catholicism withstood the test. The door for anything different was shut long ago for most Catholics. Presenting the truth as this book does will only interest a few Catholics, and those will be the ones that love the truth more than what they currently believe. We point out the seriousness of eternal outcomes and the reasonableness of what God has done and is doing to achieve His purpose through His word. The one thing that is so apparent and destroys the whole concept of Catholicism is Peter being a pope, anyone being a pope. This is so against God, God's character, plan, and purpose, that it is much more than just a lie but the most devastating and blatant lie in the history of the world. It is not some "theological close call" that could be or could not be. The devastation resulting in human suffering and eventually impacting all Catholic people in terms of eternal loss is catastrophic. Placing a person in the position of God and rejecting God's Son as the answer for humankind (the rock) is the very reason God says, "it is a fearful thing to fall into the hands of the living God." **God's Son is rejected when the doctrine of Christ is rejected,** and the most apparent element is changing the gospel message. Changing the gospel message keeps God from fulfilling His purpose. The belief that Peter is the rock of Matthew 16:18 produces a trickle-down of hundreds of doctrines ending with the Catholic system that cannot forgive a single sin.

Catholics need to consider the big picture and a few of those things are:

- Sinners forgive sinners as opposed to the sinless One admitting the obedient ones to His spiritual body. Jesus adds those obedient to the gospel message to His spiritual body, the church. BUT here is the Catholic Church saying Jesus does not need to do that since they forgive sins using their priests. They also baptize babies to wipe away their imaginary original sin. If you read the post below, you can easily see Catholic's original sin as a fabrication.

  (https://catholicsquestion.com/the-fall-of-catholicism-and-protestantism-in-one-simple-lesson/)

- To think that God started a worldly physical church with a human head and then never indicates such a pattern is ridiculous. Peter could have acknowledged such a plan – but he did not. In the process of guiding the apostles into all truth, the Holy Spirit could have indicated such a system – but He did not. God is meticulous in bringing the truth, including every detail from Genesis 3:15 and somehow never discloses the concept of a pope and an earthly rulemaking body. However, the Lord via the Holy Spirit defined His church as spiritual, the essence of salvation, and the local body consisting of those He added to the spiritual body, His spiritual church.

- It has been suggested that Catholicism is the opposite of the truth in everything, absolutely no truth. Yet, a Catholic voice says they believe in Jesus, which is the most important thing. Unfortunately, the scriptures teach that unless you have the doctrine of Christ, you have neither the Father nor the Son. Jesus also makes it clear that "Not everyone who says to Me, 'Lord, Lord,' shall enter the kingdom of heaven, but he who does the will of My Father in heaven." There is a simple path to have a valid relationship with God. Catholicism and Protestantism teach something different than what people need. People need THE TRUTH to be successful. 2 Thessalonians 2:10 is clear in this regard, "and with all unrighteous deception among those who perish because they did not receive the **love of the truth**, that they might be saved."

- There is something extraordinary about the truth, and it is how everything from God fits perfectly together. There is assurance, and there is the knowledge that God shares with you. There is a real connection that has Christ living in you continuously. There is a way to share in the Divine Nature that only exists for those "in Christ," and you can manage life's difficulties within the truth.

- God's design of His test assures the people He wants will succeed since their characters are sufficiently humble and unselfish to accept God's ways. Initially, they accept the gospel message and then continue to live for God's Son and the gospel. The Catholic Church never provides the basics to its followers. Thus they do not understand God's test and the importance of their character in initial and continuing obedience. They never grasp the seriousness of God's word since it has been minimized by Catholic-derived equivalent forms of authority.

16.8 Religion has no value unless

The purpose of religion is to help people be eternally successful; otherwise, what is the value. There is nothing more sinister than the "religions of the world." This is because they provide false hope. The truth is precious and highly desired, but an individual's effort to find it often falls short. The scriptures emphasize the essential unyielding nature of the effort required to be successful in life. A person needs to have an attitude of uncompromising fervency that is, will not accept anything less than the truth. The good news is that the truth is easily understood and makes perfect sense given God's nature and His purpose. The scriptures point to simplicity (such as seen in the gospel message) as a characteristic of the truth, and thus, those bringing complexity will be far from the truth.

As this book is ending, there is a thought that is quite simple and can be helpful. **The key to the truth is understanding God as He has revealed Himself and His purpose.** Getting these things right can make your journey to the truth relatively easy. God wants His creation to succeed as this is His purpose. Thus He has made it easy to succeed within the framework of His essential requirement that He cannot share His Divine Nature with evil, with sin. He devised a test to sort people into either good or evil. He did this so each person will decide their eternal fate by how they live, particularly how they live in relation to God-defined sin. Also, God knowing every person will fail (sin), provides a solution. His Son is the solution, and in the process of obedience, the Lord Himself places each person in a unique spiritual location called the church. It is **His spiritual church**, His spiritual kingdom. At the center of assuring the truth is provided accurately to humankind, God provides the Holy Spirit. The truth is written down by certain persons in the process of inspiration. It is all very straightforward, and in fact, thousands of people responded to the truth in the early days after the gospel is preached the first time. Congruent with the initial conversions in Acts 2, the reconciliation pattern in its simplicity is repeated in each New Testament conversion.

Where did all the complexity in religion originate? Well, obviously from humankind. God's means of salvation was provided, and people responded, and for the first time since the sin of Adam and Eve, there was reconciliation with the Creator. God continues to provide help through the remainder of His revelation in terms of encouragement, how to remain faithful, and how to access Him. He guards the truth by indicating His inspired word must not change. The gospel message must not change. We are provided with a sufficient number of examples of how people are saved from their past sins, and there is no other pattern for salvation. The other things contained in this final message from God remain associated with God achieving His purpose. Yes, His purpose has been achieved in some but now, going forward, how many will be included in sharing the Divine Nature?

16.9 Important to the continual fulfillment of God's purpose

The following is a list of things God reveals over the fifty-plus years the Holy Spirit works with the apostles. The list is relatively short and critically important to God completing His purpose. The events of Acts 2 began the reconciliation and now the message is carried to others and with a good response through the remainder of the inspired period. We now know the gospel message, but what else does God want to reveal in His last message to humankind? These are the things specifically for those "in Christ" to understand that God reveals **after** the gospel message is preached the first time in Acts 2. Although the gospel message will never change, there will be something different, so clarity is always important. The "something different" will be humankind's possession of the completed word of God and the disappearance of things no longer used that previously declared God. Those things are no longer needed because the word of God is complete, perfect in every way, and that means perfect in conversion. Humankind always wanted and still wants signs and miracles, but those who love God accept His way, embrace His truth, and know what He has done is exceedingly better. Signs and miracles are in the past, but their function might be considered to exist in a spiritual sense through God's completed word.

Note: Since God no longer communicates with humankind by miraculously displaying Himself as God in the process of providing evidence of Himself, of His Son, it is just another simplification. One way remains for humanity to know the truth, to know what is truth. Only God's word provides what humankind needs, and in its completed state (all revealed), it is perfect.

*Another note: As simple as God's message, it has been butchered by the Catholic Church. The confusion will continue, and since they lack awareness of God's ending of miracles, signs, and personal directives from beyond our realm, they will participate in various of these things claiming such outward "manifestations." We are familiar with how God had acted miraculously in the past to demonstrate who He was, such as to Abraham, Moses, and Pharoah. We have many examples of Jesus performing miracles and the Holy Spirit using miracles, signs when working with the apostles to confirm the word of God. God's intent is clear in ending these things. God's **completed word** has replaced these things because it is better. These previous means were seldom lasting in the minds of those who benefitted, such as the Israelites escaping Egyptian bondage. However, God is still involved with humankind. Any aspect of God's involvement is always supernatural. However, it is no longer about demonstrating His existence,*

369

who He is, who Jesus is, and things that encourage a person's conversion. Here are some examples of God's activity in this last age, and they are all in the category of unseen things.

- *God is in the background of everything, or it does not exist.*
- *Jesus adds the obedient to His spiritual body following their obedience.*
- *Jesus is the mediator with God the Father in prayers from those "in Christ."*
  - *Prayers answered are unseen things involving the one praying and not an outward sign in any way related to conversion.*
- *Jesus is the advocate with God the Father in consideration of the prayers of those "in Christ" related to their repenting and asking God that their sins might be forgiven.*
  - *A person's obedience to the gospel involved repenting, that is, committing to sin no more. On that basis, their past sins were forgiven. Unfortunately, many people fall back into sin, and God in His wisdom provides an Advocate and a means for those future sins to be forgiven.*

There remains one last openly outward miraculous thing, and it is the last thing that will occur and ends what was begun in creation. Jesus will return in the air and take those "in Christ" with Him to be forever with the Lord. Then the end of all things physical and the final judgment.

16.10 Faith can be so powerful in this last age

We have indicated that saying you have faith in God properly understood is having faith in God's word – the true and only source of faith. Now we have the completed word of God – all that God will be providing to humankind and all that is needed. How many people can realize that God's word is far superior to signs, miracles, even personal directives from God? I do not know how many, but those who succeed will be following the inspired word of God and not some group of men making the rules concerning their salvation. Some persons may say they heard from God or that you can trust them because there were miracles or signs involved, which will provide you with some assurance. God did not leave humankind in the hands of persons who can claim just about anything to convince you of whatever they teach. It is valuable to realize that people's claims concerning signs, miracles, and declared communications with God confidently indicate, even warn, that you are dealing with deceit. Indeed, Romans 10:17 is clear, "So then faith comes by hearing, and hearing by the word of God." Now God's word is complete, and thus how strong your belief can be in the One you cannot see? The Creator intended to leave humankind with His most powerful weapon, and so much can be accomplished in this realization.

16.11 God fits everything perfectly together

The following is a short list of some random but essential things for your understanding of God and His plan. Those "in Christ" understand these things, but the thought here is to consider how God fits everything perfectly together. Keeping this conversation going concerning **understanding God** will be powerful in your growth. Indeed continued growth is critical for the success of those "in Christ." The list is related to God, His purpose, how He will achieve it, the church, the Lord's Supper, worship, and the gospel message. Even in this short random list, one can see how everything fits together with a focus on accomplishing God's purpose. Jesus comes after 4000 years with a message, and it is preached as the kingdom. The solution God was bringing would gradually be revealed, and everything in "God's time." The event allowing the reconciliation would be costly to Jesus but would be what God the Father required. In their time with Jesus, the apostles were being prepared for their role, and at the right time, the specifics of their work would be revealed. God did various things to support the message, and one of those things would be "recruiting" the unlikely Saul (Paul) in service to the gospel. One can examine the scriptures and notice a plan from the beginning and how everything fits perfectly together. You can see how everything is going in one direction to accomplish God's purpose. The list is not in any particular order but amounts to pieces that can be seen as fitting together in achieving God's purpose. The list consists of individual events or declarations, or processes that each play a part in promoting God's purpose. They stand alone doing their part, such as the first one below, where Jesus emphasizes the apostles preaching the gospel message. Then the second one where Paul is selected to bring the message (and we learn primarily to the Gentiles) or the third where sin's consequence is emphasized. Next, the role of the Holy Spirit and the gradual revelation of the local church followed by some important things for acceptable living "in Christ," some help and warnings, and finally, the end of communications between God and humankind. Each of these things and many more contribute to achieving God's purpose. They all fit perfectly together, along with everything going back to Genesis 3:15. Jesus' arrival, preaching, His death, burial and resurrection, His ascension, His kingdom initiated, and then the description of the end, and all play parts in support of God's purpose. Regardless of whether they look back to what has happened or to the present regarding how they are to live and their responsibilities or to the future, it is information for the potential child of God. It is the truth about life and what could be their life and really how **they can fulfill God's purpose** in their obedience. Again we can say that all God is doing is in support of realizing His purpose, namely your success.

The Catholic Church or the many invented "Christian" religions of humankind do not support God's purpose but may claim to do such. They support the furtherance of their respective religions. Each of these religions seems to realize that they need to have some continuity, some synergy in the various doctrines they promote but examine them and ask if the things of these religions support God's purpose.

Those in the body of Christ realize all things in the "word of truth of the gospel" support God in achieving His purpose. Specifically, they are integral to the salvation of souls, and when God's word is rejected, what is the consequence for souls.

- One important thing for our understanding is something Jesus told the apostles regarding bringing the gospel to the world. Matthew 28:18-20 and Mark 16:15,16 are directions given to the apostles critical for God's purpose. The apostles will, of course, die, but those converted, those "in Christ" will carry on the work of the Lord in seeking and saving that which was lost.

  o Matthew 28:18-20

    18 And Jesus came and spoke to them, saying, "All authority has been given to Me in heaven and on earth.
    19 Go therefore and make disciples of all the nations, baptizing them in the name of the Father and of the Son and of the Holy Spirit,
    20 teaching them to observe all things that I have commanded you; and lo, I am with you always, even to the end of the age." Amen.

- o Mark 16:15-16

    15 And He said to them, "Go into all the world and preach the gospel to every creature.

    16 He who believes and is baptized will be saved; but he who does not believe will be condemned.

- Paul is recruited directly by the Lord, and he becomes the most prolific person in bringing the message, particularly to the Gentile world. As is mentioned throughout this book, God the Father's part is done as is the Son's, and when this event occurs, the Holy Spirit is still active in bringing the truth to the apostles. Although we say Jesus' part in terms of His sacrifice is complete, there is one thing remaining to have God fulfill His purpose, and it is occurring as the apostles bring the gospel message to the world. This must be ongoing until the end of time to fulfill God's purpose to share in the Divine Nature. Jesus will take an important step in promoting that process. Specifically, Jesus makes an "appearance" from heaven to Paul. From Paul's account, "a great light from heaven shone around me." Paul inquires who is speaking, "Who are You, Lord? And He said to me, "I am Jesus of Nazareth, whom you are persecuting." The striking thing is how important this event is in terms of God's purpose being fulfilled. It reminds me of how God the Father revealed to Peter who Jesus was, and that event was central to all that God planned and so unique that God the Father would Himself deliver this to Peter. Now Jesus from the right hand of God would communicate with Paul. God does everything in support of His purpose, and in these two cases, God the Father and the Son bring powerful emphasis to the importance of these events. Amazing!

- God defines sin in great detail. There should be no misunderstanding, and God associates sin with those **who will NOT inherit the kingdom of God**. Instead of people objecting to what God defines as sin, think in terms of the seriousness of what He declares.

- Also, going back to before Jesus' death, burial, and resurrection, we have Jesus telling the apostles that they would have a way of remembering Him represented by the elements associated with His sacrifice. Now we see the fulfillment in the Lord's Supper during this period when the Holy Spirit works with the apostles to bring all truth.

- God is gradually revealing more information about the church. The apostles immediately recognize the significance of the church Jesus said He would build, and they know it is spiritual. Now He has the Holy Spirit reveal additional aspects of the church. As always, God is perfect in defining things for humankind. I will summarize the characteristics of the church per the revelation.
    - The church consists of those in the spiritual body of Christ added by the Lord upon their obedience. Thus the church is spiritual, and this is the **prime understanding** and where a person must be in relation to salvation.
    - God defined a place for those who were spiritual such that His purpose could be fulfilled by those "in Christ" **working together**. He defined an organization and appropriately referred to it as the church since all its members were in the spiritual body of Christ – His church. The Lord's local church has no central organization or head but was local with elders (plurality), deacons, and others (members). The oversight was in the hands of elders who must meet very specific requirements. There was no rulemaking but a leading of the flock to assist their ultimate success while fulfilling the church's mission.
    - The local church has a single rulebook, the word of God.
    - The church has a single mission – evangelism, which is commensurate with each person's mission (each person "in Christ") and was precisely the mission of Jesus – seeking and saving that which was lost.
    - All aspects of the local church worship are spiritual since they are done in spirit and truth.
- God defines certain qualities expected, really required for those "in Christ."
- God provides certain warnings to those "in Christ."
- God tells humankind this (what we know as the New Testament) is His final communication with them. In this last age, with the completed word of God, there will no longer be any need for signs, miracles, or other direct communication to individuals from God. God's plan has been completely revealed, and nothing more is needed to convince people of who He or His Son is, or is there any need for such things in terms of supporting conversions. Humankind has now lived over 1900 years with God's completed word, and there have been no "supernatural events." This turns out to be an

excellent way to differentiate truth from error, as many people and organizations have claimed such events.

- God defines a way for His children (those "in Christ") to have future sins forgiven.
- God defines a means for those "in Christ" to communicate with Him through His Son.

There is nothing else to be known because the reconciliation has taken place, and God, in effect, has laid the foundation for the remaining time. God has a laser focus on achieving His purpose, and thus in His wisdom, everything about life has been revealed. No additional communication is needed. There is so much value in the purity, in the fullness of God's message, and all in support of your success, namely that you can share in the Divine Nature. You can be sure that, as always, the things revealed have an association with God fulfilling His purpose.

When the simplicity of the requirements of God is mentioned, we are talking about understanding what God requires, and it is not difficult. A person chooses to obey the gospel and commits to abandon sin and living for Christ instead of self. They have made the right choice. Catholics never understand these choices, and thus they cannot make them. The person **obedient to the gospel** has their past sins forgiven. Otherwise, there can be no forgiveness. The obedient person who lives a faithful life will receive the crown of life – heaven – share in the Divine Nature. Indeed, the Christian life is not easy to live, but it is the only life worth living because of its end. There is a certainty in that end, which also can bring peace during earthly existence.

16.12 Nothing in Catholicism fits together

(How could it? It was devised by humankind.)

The complexity of religion, specifically Catholicism, "in its complexity" allows their adherents to believe they are doing the right thing. Let's look at the complexity of Catholicism and how it misleads Catholics to think heaven might be in their future. First, we can list the inventions of Catholicism that are central to their religion and without any scriptural authority. There are many hundreds of these Catholic devised aberrations from the truth. The most significant ones will have many sub-deviations, and the following are just a few of the prime abnormalities:

- A pope and the associated hierarchy

- The teaching body of Catholicism – Magisterium

- The doctrine of infant baptism

- Priests in the new testament

- Confessing sins to a priest

- The Real Presence

- Honor for persons other than God

- Mariology

- Baptism by sprinkling

- Church councils

- Worship that in no way qualifies as worship (not in spirit and truth)

- Prayer that in no way qualifies as prayer

- All sorts of special feasts and ceremonies

- And the list seems never-ending

What is the purpose of all this "stuff?" God focuses on souls, on achieving His purpose, and none of these things address your success. The gospel message addresses the soul's salvation by an individual's obedience, and then that person continually demonstrates their love for God by keeping His commands. Worship is straightforward and pleasing to God in your obedience. The truth from God when obeyed has you living your life for Christ and the gospel and not living it for the Catholic Church.

When we talk about Catholicism not fitting everything together versus the scriptures fitting everything perfectly together, we mean EVERYTHING. That is everything from Genesis 1:1 to Revelation 22:21. Everything fits with God's purpose. Everything fits with God's test. Everything fits with God being the perfect absence of evil. Everything fits with the fact that God cannot lie. Absolutely NOTHING in Catholicism fits together. So when they create a doctrine such as original sin and then fit it together with baptizing babies and the need for priests to forgive committed sins and the Immaculate Conception of Mary and the Assumption of Mary, they have fit together a string of errors. None of these things is fitted to God's purpose. Catholicism is infinitely distant from fitting together the things of God – it is well beyond being obvious.

16.13 The true horror – no forgiveness of sins

In all that Catholicism has created, there is no forgiveness of sins. What is the purpose of "this Catholicism?" How could God accomplish His purpose in anything Catholic? Every item of Catholicism violates God's mandate to respect His word by not changing it. The irony is that the changes eliminate any possibility for success, beginning with those involved in creating the aberrations and then affecting all those who would be Catholic.

There are many interesting aspects to figuring out the consequences of error involved with Catholicism. Here is one that might help your understanding. There is no indication of a need for Bible SCHOLARSHIP to be successful in life. The message is simple, obedience is simple, and what is required going forward is simple to understand but challenging for the proud, selfish person to live. The world of religion is filled with **theologians.** It seems all religions have their theologians, their men, and women with expertise in their beliefs. Theologian defined: A theologian studies the nature of God, religion, and religious beliefs. Interestingly, most religions use the term theologian in describing their experts, although some may use the term philosopher.

Each of the world's religions has its theologians or philosophers, and they support the organization of their beliefs. The common usage of the word theologian is one devoted to the study of God, religion, and religious beliefs, typically as a "full-time job." That is why people involved with religion, such as in Catholicism as a priest, bishop, archbishop, cardinal, or the pope, **may** say, "I am no theologian." They indicate they are not into the deeper study of religious matters and thus do not have the detailed expertise of a theologian. Their statement is a fallback when there is a religious conversation where they are uncomfortable, maybe a problematic question. One might think that if theologians are needed, God's message is not simple, which would be logical. Why would it be necessary to have people devoting their entire life to studying God, God's nature, and religion? Of course, it is needed if we look at the world's religions and all their complexity. However, the truth from God is provided in the word of truth of the gospel and requires no such expertise. In Acts 2, people were converted, and there was no more than the brief explanation by Peter, and then that same message was taught throughout the first century by the apostles. The subsequent lives of those people were guided by simple instructions on how to live to remain faithful. In the Lord's church, there is no category like that of a theologian. Once again, understanding God and His purpose help us to see that God would not do anything to complicate what people need to do, how people need to live. Such complication would work against His purpose to share the Divine Nature with as many as possible. Admittedly, humankind has made it difficult with their religions since they have nothing to do with God, and consequently, the complication. The most complicated with all their hierarchy, with all their rules, is Catholicism.

The world has come to see all religions as complicated and wonders if any have the truth. Due to that complexity, people depend on religious persons to lead them, to help them be eternally successful. The more religious credentials they have, the better. This may be logical, but it is not the truth. The thing most logical is that the truth only comes from God, and that is because how else can we know things outside our realm. Also, in God's wisdom, He carefully had His Holy Spirit deliver the truth and thus effectively took humankind out of the "truth business." There is one source of truth, namely, as with faith, "faith comes by hearing and hearing by the word of God." Likewise, the only source of truth is the word of God.

How different is the truth

God's plan, the church of His Son, has no theologians because they are not needed since the scriptures are clear, and just like people succeeded in Acts 2 by obeying the gospel message, it will continue in simplicity until the end of time. Complication and confusion came as men changed the message and then needed to begin justifying what they did. Of course, once humankind became involved with creating doctrine, there would be hundreds of different beliefs, and each would develop its own theologians.

The religion of God is not complicated. Seek the truth, find it, obey it, and live it. Part of living the truth is bringing the gospel message to others. God's expectation for each of those in the Lord's church is to bring the gospel message to the world. The closest thing to a theologian in the Lord's church is one who is "in Christ," using the scriptures only and being careful not to change the meaning. Those "in Christ" must grow to be teachers.

Hebrews 5:12-14

12 For though by this time you ought to be teachers, you need someone to teach you again the first principles of the oracles of God; and you have come to need milk and not solid food.

13 For everyone who partakes only of milk is unskilled in the word of righteousness, for he is a babe.

14 But solid food belongs to those who are of full age, that is, those who by reason of use have their senses exercised to discern both good and evil.

God's expectations are high for those "in Christ." There is no other class or title for those who bring the truth. Why are those "in Christ" different than theologians or the other titles of religious persons? First, they are "in Christ" via their obedience, and that addition to the spiritual body of Christ is only made by the Lord Himself. Second, they respect God's word and will not change it. Thus there is no need to filter the scriptures but take the meaning provided by God. Lastly, they are focused on bringing the gospel message to the world.

Signs that Christianity is not present

Here are a few easily observable indicators Christianity is not present in a church:

- Complexity versus simplicity in the doctrine, especially salvation related
- An organization that includes rulemaking, a hierarchy
- A dedication to many different tasks, versus only evangelism
- The character traits of the leaders compared to what God requires
- A history of immorality, greed, and evil
- A misalignment of everything with the word of God
- A significant theological/apologist organization
- There are many more distinguishing characteristics of Christianity's absence

Those "in Christ" are not searching for meaning. They already know the meaning. This has been mentioned before but maybe not with the adaptation as here. There is something very noticeable in the Catholic mode of operation. Catholicism spends much of their time defending their teachings, which should be realized by those doing the apologetics. It should bother them. If you know the truth, you will need to do "little to no work" defending the truth. As the scriptures say, "preach the word." Catholicism in defending their doctrines can become even more complicated and require all sorts of defenses, all sorts of human reasoning. The salvation that comes from God is the gospel message, and it is preached, obeyed, and lived. No defense or special defenders are required for the truth.

16.14 The most important thing in your life

How can anyone overcome the Catholic Church? Despite all the evidence, all the logic, Catholics will remain Catholic. Otherwise, reasonable people who generally perceive right from wrong and make good decisions are in Catholicism's swamp of deceit. It is not the brilliance of the Catholic Church but something that happened in the "midst of Catholicism" that makes it difficult to leave and even challenging to question. It is the net sum of a hundred different things, and you cannot escape.

Something observable in Catholicism from 10,000 feet can be compared to **the Lord's church** and provide the confidence needed to leave Catholicism. Consider the **topics of interest** to the Catholic Church and their hierarchy and even the focus of their members. There will be a hundred different things, but where is the concern for souls? It may not make their list. Generally, it would be included in the Protestant list, although perhaps not prominently. The church belonging to the Lord would have souls as the priority, and possibly there would be no other items. This book has a single reason for its creation, and it is souls. Again, life is about the soul and ultimately about nothing else. All the things you see as **so important** are not of any importance, and with the wisdom from above, you can treat them as not all that important during your lifetime. All these things fill our lives and demand our attention and yet the one thing that matters most, namely our soul may not get any attention. In the day-to-day world, the soul is the only thing in life that should be our focus. Otherwise, it will be a shock at the end when you find out that life was truly only about the soul. Before us is God's purpose, and the scriptures indicate how God will achieve that purpose. There is an emphasis on souls and Jesus states the reason for His presence on earth was to seek and save that which was lost. All these things from God always point to the reconciliation, and it culminates in the gospel message that is possible because of Jesus' death, burial, and resurrection. At the other end of the spectrum is the Catholic Church that emphasizes faith in the Catholic Church. When the Catholic Church is at the center of your beliefs, then the Catholic Church's things are what is important – all those man-made teachings. On the other hand, if you are in the church belonging to Jesus as we read about in the

New Testament, then the emphasis is on the soul, the soul's salvation and the **means** to continually build the Lord's church, that is, by the gospel message.

Catholicism has been pretty well dismantled in this book. Piece by piece removed with great clarity. Yet, can it move a person to change the direction of their life? One thing is so overwhelming that even the most devout Catholic cannot remain Catholic unless they sear their conscience. Catholicism knows that everything crumbles under the weight of this one thing. All the cover-up done by Catholicism over many centuries, all the suffering, torture, and murders used to protect the lies and maintain their sovereignty, yet one of their inventions cannot be protected. It happens to be their most treasured deceit, their basis for everything Catholic. It is just one of the hundreds of things that eliminate Catholicism from having any relationship with God. Yet this one thing is so powerfully problematic that all the other problems seem insignificant. **It is that Peter is NOT the rock of Matthew 16:18.** That has been demonstrated throughout this book. If Peter is the rock, then nothing makes any sense, Christianity makes no sense, Genesis 3:15 makes no sense, God's purpose could never be accomplished if Peter is the rock. This is Catholicism's Waterloo, and it is a fortunate thing for all Catholics who love the truth – they have a solid reason to escape from what will be a failed life.

Along with the recognition of Catholicism's fall, there are consequences. Consider that **everything** the Catholic Church has ever done, has ever taught is wrong. It is overwhelming, but we can simplify the situation by pointing to each Catholic. Life is about the soul, and thus the one thing necessary is that you hear the gospel message and respond to it. You can move from the complexity of Catholicism to the simplicity of being in the body of Christ – His spiritual church. Then for the first time, you will be on the road to heaven.

Made in the USA
Middletown, DE
13 January 2022

58552855R00210